Politics and Violence in Central America and the Caribbean

Hannes Warnecke-Berger

Politics and Violence in Central America and the Caribbean

palgrave
macmillan

Hannes Warnecke-Berger
University of Leipzig
Leipzig, Sachsen, Germany

ISBN 978-3-319-89781-3   ISBN 978-3-319-89782-0   (eBook)
https://doi.org/10.1007/978-3-319-89782-0

Library of Congress Control Number: 2018942510

© The Editor(s) (if applicable) and The Author(s) 2019
This work is subject to copyright. All rights are solely and exclusively licensed by the Publisher, whether the whole or part of the material is concerned, specifically the rights of translation, reprinting, reuse of illustrations, recitation, broadcasting, reproduction on microfilms or in any other physical way, and transmission or information storage and retrieval, electronic adaptation, computer software, or by similar or dissimilar methodology now known or hereafter developed.
The use of general descriptive names, registered names, trademarks, service marks, etc. in this publication does not imply, even in the absence of a specific statement, that such names are exempt from the relevant protective laws and regulations and therefore free for general use.
The publisher, the authors, and the editors are safe to assume that the advice and information in this book are believed to be true and accurate at the date of publication. Neither the publisher nor the authors or the editors give a warranty, express or implied, with respect to the material contained herein or for any errors or omissions that may have been made. The publisher remains neutral with regard to jurisdictional claims in published maps and institutional affiliations.

Cover illustration: blickwinkel / Alamy Stock Photo
Cover design by: Akihiro Nakayama

Printed on acid-free paper

This Palgrave Macmillan imprint is published by the registered company Springer International Publishing AG part of Springer Nature.
The registered company address is: Gewerbestrasse 11, 6330 Cham, Switzerland

Acknowledgments

This book would not have been completed without the support, the help, and the advice of so many people and interview partners. I want to express my gratitude to all of them. I wish to thank Heidrun Zinecker that she introduced me to the topic of violence and that she offered me her insights into the history and the politics of El Salvador. I want to express my sincere thanks for her guidance, for her advice, and for the inspiring conversations we have had and hopefully will continue to have. Furthermore, I want to thank James Dunkerley for his helpful comments and for appreciating the research I am conducting.

Without any doubts, this research would look different without sharing a wonderful time with Hartmut Elsenhans. His comments have been a strong stimulus for this project, his advice always kept me to rethink my ideas, and finally, he was the person who brought me to political economy. At University of Leipzig, Michael Riekenberg moreover taught me to keep my mind open to the very empirics. He brought me to culture and for this I thank him.

Thomas Plötze's critiques and honest commentaries have been an important pillar for my work. Sebastian Huhn furthermore supported me with his advice. Without the helpful conversations with both of them, I would not have been able to conduct this research. Kristin Seffer, Stefanie Dreiack, Sebastian Hoppe, and the colloquium at the chair of international relations supported me with their input. Many thanks for this!

Jeanette Aguilar and the team of the Instituto Universitario de Opinión Pública (IUDOP) provided me a welcoming and productive environment in El Salvador. The Jacaranda in San Salvador and all its members supported me: Clara, Daniela, Conor, Max, and finally Nelson; I want to thank all of you! I would not have been able to do this research without the conversations and the support of Mari. She is an amazing friend! Tim in Kingston and Martha in Belmopan made this research possible. Special thanks to Neil Wilcock for his extensive help in improving the manuscript.

My warmest thanks are reserved for my family. Thank you Matthias for mapping the gang turfs. Thank you very much Gudrun for always encouraging me to continue. Your support has always been the greatest help of all. Thanks you very much Frieda and Henriette that you enrich us every day.

Finally, this book is especially dedicated to my parents.

CONTENTS

LIST OF ABBREVIATIONS

ARENA	Alianza Republicana Nacionalista (Nationalist Republican Alliance), El Salvador
BEC	Belize Estate and Produce Company, Belize
BPD	Belizean Police Department, Belize
FMLN	Frente Farabundo Martí para la Liberación Nacional (Farabundo Martí National Liberation Front), El Salvador
FUSADES	Fundación Salvadoreña para el Desarrollo Económico y Social (Salvadoran Foundation of Social and Economic Development), El Salvador
GSU	Gang Suppression Unit, Belize
IMF	International Monetary Fund
IML	Instituto Medicina Legal (National Forensic Institute), El Salvador
JCF	Jamaica Constabulary Force, Jamaica
JLP	Jamaican Labor Party, Jamaica
MNC	Multinational Corporations
MP	Member of Parliament
ORDEN	Organización Democrática Nacionalista (Democratic Nationalist Organization), El Salvador
PCS	Partido Comunista Salvadoreño (Salvadoran Communist Party), El Salvador
PNC	Policía Nacional Civil (National Civil Police), El Salvador
PNP	People's National Party, Jamaica
PUP	People's United Party, Belize
SAP	Structural Adjustment Programs
UDP	United Democratic Party, Belize

LIST OF FIGURES

CHAPTER 1

Introduction

Despite their many differences, El Salvador, Belize, and Jamaica have in common that they lead international statistics on crime and violence. These three societies even surpass countries that are plagued by wars and civil wars. Today's violence in Central America and the Caribbean seems to be "diffuse" (Call, 2003, p. 843), "anomic" (Zinecker, 2001, p. 166), and emerging out of the struggle of ordinary people against each other (Pereira & Davis, 2000). In contrast to former times of civil war when violence was perceived as political in nature, peacetime violence is said to serve criminal and more economic ends. Today, it is violence in peace (Zinecker, 2014).

With regard to violence, El Salvador, Belize, and Jamaica have three similarities. Firstly, violence is predominantly an urban phenomenon. Secondly, public discussion and academic discourse both express a certain bias towards scapegoating youth gangs, highlighting the nexus between drugs, youth gangs, and politics. Finally, politics opt to combat violence with repression. Even though the social and geographic context of assaults and the most visible actors of violence are known, violence *itself*—the modus operandi of violence or as the study will call it here, the forms of violence actors are exerting—is still of minor interest.

Violence in Central America and the Caribbean reflects a deep frustration that easily morphs into blind rage. It is a diffuse, disruptive, and destructive violence; violence seems to follow individual passions rather than political aspirations. It seems as if violence has lost its purpose. For

© The Author(s) 2019
H. Warnecke-Berger, *Politics and Violence in Central America and the Caribbean*, https://doi.org/10.1007/978-3-319-89782-0_1

the majority of society, these events are reason for indignant headshaking. People disgustedly turn away from this "new" brutal and frightening violence. At the same time, the number of clicks of brutal videos on YouTube are higher than ever. People seem to have a "perverse fascination" with violence (Avruch, 2001, p. 624). Newspapers are filled with bloody stories; TV programs claim to be on the ground when it happens. Violence is on the return—a resurgent social evil in our meanwhile "civilized" world.

Violence appears unevenly in the world, however. The great bulk of current deadly violence takes place in the Global South, and more than 70 percent of all violent deaths in the world occur in non-conflict settings, settings that are not categorized as interstate or civil wars (Geneva Declaration Secretariat [GDS], 2015, p. 57). Seen from this perspective, the study of violence requires links to the analysis of development processes to be able to explain this emerging social cleavage.

For some time now, the contemporary world system has become increasingly fragmented (Elsenhans, 2015). Today's violence is one expression of this fragmentation. Historically, violence followed at least three waves after the end of World War II. With every wave, the topography, the predominant actors, but most notably, the structure of violence changed (Warnecke-Berger & Huhn, 2017). First, the forming social movements for national liberation after the Great Depression of the 1930s had been successful in organizing violence. Even though World War II overshadowed the struggle for independence of many liberation movements, the success of the Cuban revolution provoked a proliferation of guerrillas, and with them, violence occurred as a predominantly rural phenomenon. Violence at this time was either the vehicle to form a revolutionary subject (Fanon, [1961] 2010) or a repressive means for colonial or state authorities to brutally repress the claim for autonomy and liberation. In this context, violence was an expression of power and domination. It arose out of societal tensions between social classes, that is, between the subaltern and the ruling class. Violence in this setting is vertical, exposing a disparity of power differentials. Either it challenges authority and domination in times of revolution or rebellion, or it ensures security and "peace" through overt repression or hidden, quiet, and symbolic violence. While assuming power and aiming at producing development, both the state-classes that were born out of the anticolonial movements and the landholding oligarchies failed politically and their promises did not materialize (Elsenhans, 1991). The result was rising national debt, and by the end of the Cold War, almost every society in the Global South had to accept structural adjustment policies.

As a second wave of violence with a vanishing role of ideology and dissolving larger political objectives after 1989, ethnic violence came to the fore. The wars on the Balkans and in West Africa as well as the genocide in Rwanda are examples for that: Segments of remaining state-classes made use of ethnic motives instead of ideology to organize followers, thereby producing an immense output of violence. Violence thus shifted from being class-led to being identity-led.

As a third wave of violence, finally, the world system entered an "age of insecurity" (Davis, 2006) with the rise of neoliberalism. In many places the retreat of the state and resulting "governance voids" (Koonings & Kruijt, 2004) contributed to further fragmentations of violence. Furthermore, the topography of violence changed with violence occurring increasingly in urban encounters. Religious terrorism, warlords, gangs, and everyday ordinary "criminal" violence are expressions of this fragmentation. These different phenomena have in common that the scale of social organization of violence is not as high as during the first two waves. The objective of this violence is not to organize masses of people or to mobilize an entire social class. Quite the contrary, it is anomic and diffuse violence that does not occur at particular places, does not know clear enemies, and that is not politically motivated. This violence is not directed against the state or intended to challenge the social fabric. In short, it is "horizontal violence" (see for the concept Warnecke-Berger, 2017 and Chap. 2 in this study). Typically, horizontal violence involves equally powerful rivals. No rival is able to overpower the opponent and to establish structural domination. Violence then is inscribed in a horizontal relation between equally powerful actors.

The advent of horizontal violence illustrates that capitalist growth has been too weak to create a homogeneous world economy. Economic rent, defined as a form of economic surplus, which is appropriated by political means, eventually overpowers capitalist profit, which is ultimately based on rising mass incomes translated into net investment (Elsenhans, 2015; Kalecki, 1971). This has two implications: firstly, the contrast and polarity between the West and the Global South increases further. Secondly, this transformation leads to the reconfiguration of traditional class contradictions. One expression of this arising class constellation is the need of smaller social groups within the same social class to struggle for access to economic surplus. It is a struggle about social recognition and about bare survival. Increasingly, horizontal violence is nested within these conflicts.

THE EMPIRICAL PUZZLE: VIOLENCE IN CENTRAL AMERICA AND THE CARIBBEAN

In present discussions on violence in Central America and the Caribbean, authors focusing on the recent change of violence predominate. With only few exceptions, the argumentation provided by these authors draws on new causes of contemporary violence. This narrative highlights that globalization and/or neoliberalism produced new patterns of exclusion and marginalization, which finally led to frustration and violent outbreaks. The reformation of labor markets and the specialization on new comparative advantages left particularly young people without proper job opportunities. At the same time, the state retreated from society. As a result, the rise of youth gangs, growing underground economies, and the emergence of ungoverned spaces go hand in hand. Although this body of literature mentions different triggers of violence, it focuses on general schemes of violence rather than on the question of why certain actors exert particular forms of violence (see for a detailed discussion of the literature, e.g. Warnecke-Berger & Huhn, 2017).

A second argumentation follows a historical strand and focuses on continuities of violence. This narrative explains today's high levels of violence through the recourse on the causes and developments of former violent eruptions throughout the 1970s and 1980s (e.g. Kurtenbach, 2007; Steenkamp, 2005). While this body of literature intends to explain the continuity of certain forms of violence, it runs the risk of logical fallacies (violence produces more violence). Alternative explanations are sparse and unfortunately exclusively concerned with historical events rather than the historical processes in the *longue durée* (but see for an analysis of historical processes e.g. Holden, 2004; Pearce, 2010; Sives, 2010).

While the first line of argumentation tends to exclude history from analysis, the second line focuses on violent clashes in the 1980s. It has to be acknowledged, however, that violence already was a social problem in times well before the 1970s and 1980s. The detailed analysis of these periods in Central America and the Caribbean, however, is still in its infancy.

Figure 1.1 shows the homicide rates in El Salvador, Jamaica, and Belize over a longer period beginning in the 1930s. In El Salvador, starting with the massacres of 1932 where almost 40,000 people were killed, the homicide rate has always remained relatively high. The graph shows a peak in 1980 when the civil war broke out. The rate peaks again in 1989 during the guerrilla's final offensive and increases after the Peace Accords of 1992

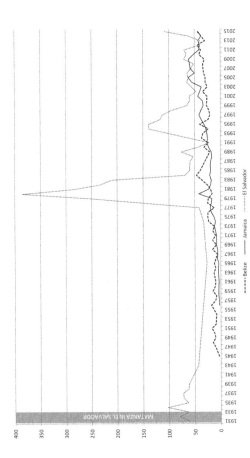

Fig. 1.1 Homicides per 100,000 inhabitants in El Salvador, Jamaica, and Belize, 1930–2015. (Sources on **El Salvador** for the 1930s are found in *Boletín Oficial de la Policía Nacional, Órgano Mensual de la Dirección General del Cuerpo, AGN El Salvador*; for the civil war period, see Naciones Unidas (1993), for the 1960s, see Pan American Health Organization [PAHO] (1978, 1982), Seligson and McElhinny (1996); for the post-war period, see United Nations Office on Drugs and Crime [UNODC] (2007a), Programa de las Naciones Unidas para el Desarrollo [PNUD] (2009), and own collection of police statistics emitted by *Policía Nacional Civil* and *Instituto Medicina Legal*. The sharp increase in homicides after 1992 may be a statistically produced fact since relevant state institutions experienced serious challenges in compiling the data. Data on **Belize** is derived from colonial and post-colonial police reports, and as of the 1990s from the statistical institute as well as PNUD (2009) and the UNODC online database. Own data is collected from Annual Report of the British Honduras Police Force, Various Issues, Belize Archives & Records Service, Anr Box 23, #171 and the Statistical Institute of Belize: Abstract of Statistics, Various Issues. One of the main difficulties was the estimation of the population size. The only data available comes from the Statistical Institute of Belize, however, the 2010 census uncovered serious problems with population estimates after 1980. The data used here is calculated based on 2010 census data, from which the data was also inferred for the time between 1991 and 2000. Data on **Jamaica**, finally, derives from Harriott (2000), UNODC (2007b, 2011), and data emitted by the Jamaica Constabulary Force)

until 1996 to then decrease and oscillate around 55 homicides per 100,000 inhabitants. Since the 1930s, the lowest level documented in El Salvador was around 24 homicides in 1965. In Jamaica, the homicide rate steadily increases as of the 1950s. It peaks in 1980, in 1997, and in the mid-2000s. Recently, deadly violence decreased considerably; however, it remains at a high level.

Regarding Belize, the figure again shows that violence is not a new phenomenon. At first glance, incremental changes in the rate attract attention. Since the Belizean population is very small, minor changes in the absolute number of homicides largely affect the overall homicide rate. Second, the level of violence already fluctuated well above 20 homicides per 100,000 inhabitants in the 1950s. The rate peaks in 1983 and then continues on a high level with immense variation, decreases after 1996 before finally it increases again in the years that follow.

Both argumentations mentioned above need to be redefined in the light of Fig. 1.1. First, this figure informs the hypothesis that violence is structurally embedded in all three societies. Although quantitative data on Belize and Jamaica during the 1920s and 1930s is sparse or does not exist, literature suggests the Great Depression of the 1930s as a major critical juncture of violence. While this time was the initial period of decolonization, which paved the way to independence in Jamaica and Belize (Bolland, 2001), it was the period of a major outburst of genocidal violence in El Salvador (Dunkerley, 1982). The Central American crisis, the Salvadoran Civil War, a near state of civil war in Jamaica, and the post-independence peak of violence in Belize then mark a second critical juncture. In recent times, finally, the homicide rate of all three societies has converged at an overall high level.

Today's literature on violence in Central America and the Caribbean in large part makes use of quantitative methods and mainly deals with homicides (see e.g. UNODC, 2007a, 2007b). However, these statistics reveal nothing about perpetrators of violence and their modus operandi. In discussions on violent actors in the region, the focus clearly lies on youth gangs and organized crime (Shifter, 2012; e.g. UNODC, 2012). Yet, the debate often fails to acknowledge that the presence of gangs or organized crime does not necessarily translate into violence. While both groups of violent actors are serious challenges for security, it is more than doubtful whether these are the only existing violent actors. The knowledge about *all existing* violent actors, about the forms of violence these actors employ in particular social contexts, and about the violent relations among each other is still limited.

In **El Salvador**, this regional perspective on gangs and organized crime translates into a bias towards youth gangs or *maras*. *Maras* are long-lasting, robust, hierarchically organized, transnational, and particularly violent youth gangs (Zinecker, 2014, p. 230). High-ranking politicians such as the former minister of justice and public security, David Mungia Payés, cited in a newspaper interview (*La Prensa Gráfica,* 2012), associate 90 percent of all homicides with *maras*. The police, however, attribute 30 percent to *maras*, and the national forensic institute, which produces the most credible statistics, attributes only 10 percent to *maras* (Instituto Universitario de Opinión Pública [IUDOP], 2014). Research on *maras* focuses on their historical origins in the United States (Ward, 2013) and in Central America (Argueta Rosales, Caminos Alemán, Mancía Peraza, & los Angeles Salgado Pacheco, 1992; Levenson, 1989), on (transnational) gang structures (Cruz, 2010; Zilberg, 2004), the embeddedness of youth gangs in their social environment (ERIC, IDESO, IDIES, & IUDOP, 2001), on identity and gang culture (Nateras Domínguez, 2010), and on civil society and state reactions (Hume, 2007; Wolf, 2017). Although authors steadily assert that youth gangs are predominant violent actors throughout Central America, "the research panorama remains relatively sparse, with new research occurring only very sporadically, although there is a proliferation of articles based on secondary literature as the topic becomes very much in vogue" (Rodgers & Jones, 2009, p. 4). Mara *violence*, however, is seldom taken under closer examination.

Other violent actors enjoy less attention than *maras*. This is surprising since research has indicated the diversity of violent actors in the region (Winton, 2011). Authors and experts acknowledge that apart from youth gangs, at least the following violent actors are present in El Salvador: the police, actors engaged in social cleansings and death squads, and unknown actors exerting criminal violence; the latter group being recognized as the largest part of overall violence. Available data thus suggest that actors other than youth gangs are (still) present in El Salvador. Research on these actors and in particular on the forms of violence these actors deploy, however, is rare or still lacking.

The discussion on violence in **Jamaica** runs along certain lines, such as the link between violence and politics (Stone, 1980), between violence and drugs (Clarke, 2006), between violence and organized crime (Harriott, 2008), and finally between violence and local communities (Levy, 2009). A detailed analysis of violence itself and of different forms of violence, however, still lacks. The discussion is likewise biased towards gangs as predominant violent actors. Government officials attribute 90 percent of all homicides to gangs (Leslie, 2010, p. 3). Official statistics, in contrast, show that 53 percent of murders in 2009 were gang related. While violence was already high in the 1980s, gang violence has increased considerably in the last two decades. Studies focus on the historical development of gangs (Gray, 2004), gang structure (Leslie, 2010), state-gang relations (Jaffe, 2013; Sives, 2002), gangs as organized crime and their involvement in the drug economy (Brana-Shute, 2002; Clarke, 2006), perceptions of gangs (Moser & Holland, 1997), the embeddedness of gangs in community life (Jaffe, 2012), and gang-combating policies (Harriott, 2003). These contributions show that gangs evolved outside of politics, became attached to politics, and lately emancipated from politics. While this latter argument seems most plausible, a detailed analysis of the dynamics of forms of violence exerted by these gangs still lacks. As in El Salvador, gang violence, hence the violent modus operandi itself, is not a major research task. Other violent actors are analyzed to a lesser extent, although data recognizes at least the following violent actors: the police and violence on a community level; on the one hand, internally among community residents and on the other hand, externally among communities. Again, research on these actors and on the forms of violence these actors deploy is rare.

Since academic interest only recently shifted towards violence in **Belize**, empirical data on the phenomenon is still weak. While certain studies suggest that the general patterns of violence in terms of age distribution, gender, and weapons used are similar to those in Jamaica and El Salvador, an in-depth analysis lacks (an excellent exception is Gayle & Mortis, 2010). So far, studies remain on a very general level and focus on the link between violence, drug trade, and organized crime in Belize (Bunck & Fowler, 2012; López, 2013; Peirce & Veyrat-Pontet, 2013) or collect basic data on citizen security. Similar to the other two cases, government officials steadily asses that the vast majority of violence in Belize is related to gangs (Sistema de Integración de Centroamérica, Secretaria de la Integración Social [SISCA], United Nations Population Fund [UNFPA], & Interpeace, 2012). Apart from some preliminary studies on gangs in Belize, there is no comprehensive analysis to date. Public media speculates about *maras* being in Belize, even though police intelligence negates their presence. Not only gangs but also human rights activists often criticize the police force for brutalizing communities and prisoners. However, a study on human rights violations has not yet been conducted. In the case of Belize, therefore, this present study has to break new ground.

To sum up, studies on violence in Central America and in the Caribbean uncovered the general causes for high levels of violence as well as their consequences for economic and political developments. The literature is biased towards (youth) gangs and/or organized crime. Other violent actors, although accounting for a large part of violence, are either excluded from analysis due to lacking sources or simply ignored. There are excellent studies on violent actors, however, empirical research fails to examine their modus operandi. The discussion still does not consider forms of violence a proper research object.

THE THEORETICAL PUZZLE: EXPLAINING FORMS OF VIOLENCE

In the light of the rise of this diffuse violence in not only Central America and the Caribbean, but also on a global scale, social sciences react with a multiplication of terms and concepts. Terms like "citizen-on-citizen" (Pereira & Davis, 2000, p. 4) or "diffuse violence" (Call, 2003, p. 843) in our "age of insecurity" (Davis, 2006) and in times of the "globalization of violence" (Appadurai, 2006) express a deep uncertainty and the quest to regain a sober academic view. It is said to be a "new violence" (Briceño-León & Zubillaga, 2002; Koonings, 2012) that erupts in spaces in which the state is absent, in so-called governance voids (Koonings & Kruijt, 2004). Attributions to violence are abundant, and academic debates struggle with the "immense diversity of forms of violence" (Arias & Goldstein, 2010, p. 20).

Yet, the concept of forms of violence is meant to close this gap, to overcome this uncertainty, and to develop the analytical language to capture these phenomena. However, what this concept intends to analytically describe remains more than unclear. Indeed, the concept of forms of violence still seems to be an empty formula by means of which everything is categorized that escapes common classification.

Although authors recently stated the problem of a "lacking typology of violence" (Lorenz, 2004, p. 12), those typologies do exist. Distinguishing and subdividing different types and forms of violence, however, comes with huge challenges and close restrictions that often render typologies useless. Some authors include perpetrators (e.g. youth gangs), resource-based violence (e.g. drug affiliated violence), and victims (e.g. femicide) in the same taxonomies and typologies and mix up different levels of analysis.

Moreover, typologies are often located on different explanatory levels: they classify macro-level processes but integrate micro-level phenomena, and vice versa. Typologies of forms of violence "vary along a number of dimensions" (Jackson, Zahn, & Brownstein, 2004, p. 255) and inconsistently distinguish or link up (1) the level of action; (2) the nature and the degree of force employed; (3) the outcome of the force; (4) the injury; (5) the target; and finally, (6) the intentional motivation.

Partly, this inconsistency is rooted in the disciplinary division of labor in social sciences. While political science predominantly researches political violence, sociology and criminology research deviant behavior and crime. The different analytical views on violence are thus an expression of each disciplinary self-image. Furthermore, some authors try to distinguish structural violence from physical violence by calling both a form of violence (Galtung, 1969). Others refer to different aggregate levels of violence as forms of violence by distinguishing individual, collective, and state-led (Imbusch, 2002b). A third group of authors distinguishes different forms of violence according to the motivation such as political, economic, criminal, and social violence (Moser, 2004, p. 4). Apparently, just like the term "violence," the concept of "forms of violence" itself is highly disputed and a clear definition has not been offered yet. To make matters worse, a discussion on the concept of forms of violence is still missing. Instead, the term often functions as a demarcation line for research on causes of violence: research does not go beyond this line since what the term seeks to grasp withstands scientific analysis. Since the recent meta-theoretical *turns* have been impacting social science analyses, the search for causes has lost importance. Two positions are arguing against each other: rationalists against constructivists; that is to say, "old" against "new" researchers, or in other words, it is about whether to ask the question "Why" or rather "How" violence occurs (see for an overview, e.g. Aijmer & Abbink, 2000; Imbusch, 2002a; Schmidt & Schröder, 2001; Whitehead, 2004). The latter group of authors criticizes that research on violence focuses on the structural reasons of violence. In the same breath, they advocate for an analysis of violence *itself*. Von Trotha (1997, p. 20), for instance, euphorically states, "the key to violence is to be found in the forms of violence itself. This is the first and most important principle of a genuine analysis of violence." Indeed, this is understood as a "microscopical analysis of violence" (ibid.), in which the detailed analysis of practices of violence should enjoy major attention. Thick descriptions of violent interactions and the turn towards discourses on violence replaced the search for causes of violence. In this regard, research on violence follows a much broader trend: the rise of post-modernist thought. This trend led to a deep divide between ontological and epistemological discussions, between structuralists and post-structuralists, or between rationalists and constructivists.

Unfortunately, this divide did contribute very little to elucidate violence. Yet it is surprising that even this recent and "new" sociology of violence has not been able to formulate what forms of violence actually are and how they have to be explained so far. Researchers recently mentioned that "(…) the question of why such violence might take particular cultural forms – such as specific kinds of mutilation, 'ethnic cleansing', or other modes of community terror – has not been adequately integrated" (Whitehead, 2007, p. 44). The claim to research violence in its forms was almost never met (but see Auyero, De Lara, Agustín Burbano, & Berti, 2014).

This divide further translates into a particular new division of labor in research on violence beyond disciplines. While the faction of political economy focuses on the structural background and produces rich insights on the causes of violence (see e.g. Cramer, 2006; Zinecker, 2011 for an overview), it excludes the detailed analysis of violence itself, of the very acts of violence. The other faction in turn conducts a detailed analysis on these practices of violence, the very doing of violence, particularly through a strong reliance on cultural theory (Das, Kleinman, Ramphele, & Reynolds, 2000; Scheper-Hughes & Bourgois, 2007). It however misses to explain the structural background against which violence evolves.

If we think of violence as a river, then the two different riversides are those two different approaches. However, not only do they have different perspectives onto the river, they also have different research objects on which they focus. While one body of literature researches the flow of the river—its contours, its beginning and its end—the other body researches the smallest units of which the river consists—the very drops of water, their vibrancies, and movements. While the political economy approach to violence, particularly when focusing on the contexts of developing societies, is primarily concerned with the flow of violence, it misses to zoom into the very acts of violence, the single drops of water. Culturalist approaches to violence, in turn, accentuate acts and practices of violence and provide thick descriptions of their sequences. In doing so, however, these latter approaches fail to relate the single drops of water to the entire flow.

Starting from these observations, a rather complex conceptual puzzle unfolds. Firstly, it is completely unclear, what forms of violence are, how they should analytically be handled, what they comprise, and how they are related to each other. Secondly, and since the concept of forms of violence is rather vague, it remains unclear how to explain forms of violence.

Towards a Relational Concept of Forms of Violence

Reacting on these empirical and theoretical challenges, this study raises two questions. On the one hand, it asks what forms of violence are. On the other hand, it asks what the causes of forms of violence are. Thus, this study demarcates a still obscure explanandum and has to find a theoretical as well as a methodological route towards an explanation of this explanandum. By raising these two questions, this study situates itself in the overlay of two analytical levels, the explanations of causes of violence and the understanding of violence. It sets in where and when violence already happened. The study intends to understand and to explain the forms of violence, their emergence and their dynamics, rather than explaining violence per se.

In a first conceptual step, this book develops a relational understanding of violence. The book distinguishes between vertical and horizontal violence. Vertical violence is defined as violence between actors whose relations are characterized by inequality and asymmetries of power. Either elites use vertical violence against subalterns to maintain the status quo, or subalterns exert violence to struggle against the status quo. In contrast to vertical violence, horizontal violence establishes reciprocal relationships among the actors. Horizontal violence is violence between equals in which more powerful and higher-ranking authorities are not able or do not want to intervene. This relational understanding of violence concentrates on the social interactions that violent actors build through exerting violence. The focus point of either vertical or horizontal violence is not the motive of individual violent actors, but the structure of the relation between different social actors. This distinction has far-reaching effects for the following argumentation. The exclusive focus on vertical violence would lean on central categories of political science. However, these categories fail to understand and to explain horizontal violence.

Following this relational concept of violence, this book defines the term form of violence in the following chapter as a set of violent practices that a social actor routinely uses to make claims on other social actors. This definition highlights that forms of violence cannot be reduced to violent actors themselves. A single violent actor can employ different forms of violence, or the actor can specialize in a single form of violence. This means, that for instance, youth gangs are not forms of violence, but they can employ one or multiple forms of violence. This book understands a single form of violence as a particular repertoire of violent practices.

In a second conceptual step, this book develops a theoretical approach to explain forms of violence, which involves the two alleged contradictory approaches to violence—political economy and culturalist theories. The present book claims to construct a theoretical bridge, eventually linking both riversides. By starting from the riverside of political economy, the study gradually incorporates culturalist approaches finally spanning the river.

The study shows that resources abundance and rents do not cause violence directly. It demonstrates that economic rents are socially embedded in a conflictive social environment. Neither resource scarcity nor resource abundance is able to explain violence and the forms violence takes. This study argues that resource insecurity is more likely to explain violence. The study shows that rents tend to verticalize social relations and ultimately lead to social closure. Both processes are likely to produce violence. This understanding of the social embeddedness of rents requires a historical perspective. Resource insecurity becomes only visible if temporally preceding social structures are likewise scrutinized. Political economy is able to show the general circumstances under which violence becomes opportune and to derive social spaces structurally enabling violence. However, at this point, the explanatory power of political economy ends. It remains outside the political economy approach to show what specific form of violence is employed by social actors recurring to violence within these spaces.

Here, cultural theory comes in. Recent praxeological approaches show that social practices follow rules, which are inscribed in cultural scripts. The book translates this idea to the study of violence. In executing violence, social actors activate and use these cultural scripts. Cultural scripts that practices of violence follow emerged historically and change over time. Again, historical analysis of the dynamics of the scripts becomes important.

Finally, there is the question of how cultural scripts are activated in social spaces that structurally enable violence. The book argues that within these spaces, violence needs to be socially organized. The concept of social organization of violence illustrates the crucial role of strategic agency. It is this concept that eventually links the political economy part and the cultural theory part of the bridge. By mobilizing and organizing violence, social actors activate cultural scripts of violence through strategic action and link practices of violence to each other: forms of violence emerge.

This study intends to consider the socioeconomic context of violence, the flow of the river in its entirety, as well as to come close enough to violent practices, to the single drops of water. On this center position on the bridge, it is possible to distinguish the waves, their movements, their directions, and their composition from the flow of the river.

THE METHOD

This theoretical bridge comes with huge methodological challenges. In the words of Marcel Mauss (1990 [1924]), violence is a total social fact. It is a basic pillar of society. Writing about violence means therefore and perhaps necessarily to write a *histoire totale*, a total history. If we look into libraries and bookshops, however, such a total history does not exist and will probably never be written. Violence is subject to almost every social science sub-discipline and even beyond. However, a proper discipline researching violence has not emerged, nor did a canonical method of studying violence evolve. Research on violence faces a fundamental methodical dilemma regarding the ontological and epistemological dimension of violence. Unlike research on other subjects in social science research, research on violence faces particular methodical challenges in the identification of its research object. It is almost impossible to observe violence directly. Researchers cannot "look at" violence as they would look at other research objects. Except for some rare and exceptional cases, violence remains inaccessible. Since researchers try to systematize diffuse and threatening events and to make meaning of these experiences, violence escapes from codifications that are too narrow. In this sense, violence is a blurry phenomenon (Nordstrom & Robben, 1995). It is able to destroy language and discourse, and at the same time, it generates rumors and gossip, thus producing discourse. Violence is embedded in cultural modes of action and at the same time, it transgresses traditional ways of experiencing and acting. It is inscribed in somatic experiences and produces subjectivities. At the same time, violence harms, humiliates, mutilates, or even destroys the body.

The ontological perspective on violence never escaped the bipolarity between order and disorder.[1] This dimension intensively determines where to search for violence and how to study it. In a nutshell, if humans are good, someone or something has to force them to be violent. If people are bad, they will be violent if nobody hinders them to do so. In addition to this ontological dilemma, likewise epistemological and even ethical issues have to be considered. In writing about violence, researchers, at least implicitly, portray their own understanding of violence. Thinking, speaking, and writing about violence always uncovers the moral beliefs and convictions of researchers concerning their research object. Studying violence perhaps necessarily means to destroy the distance between researchers and their object. In an interview, Michael Taussig highlights this dimension in a provocative way. Asked about his personal experiences in his life as an anthropologist of violence, he stated in an interview with the *New York Times* (2001) that "the facts were so bad, so stark, and yet I wanted to see more (...) I started becoming a kind of violence junkie. I wanted the material to get wilder and more violent, and I started wondering about that: What is it in me? Am I a bad person?" With regard to the methodical dilemmas, his questions reveal the difficulty to distinguish the ontics from the epistemology of violence. Consequently, it is hard to separate the lived experience of violence from the ways of studying and reflecting violence.

These issues and the proposed theoretical bridge thus impose far-reaching challenges for the research design. To describe it from a positivistic standpoint, the independent variables derived from the political economy approach can be integrated in a historical comparative research design. However, to be able to control for the second research dimension, culture and cultural scripts, this method needs to be complemented with praxeological arguments. In the intersecting dimension between both riversides, a micro-macro problem evolves.

First, this book solves this problem by changing focus points. It initially focuses on the structural social setting in which actors have to move and then zooms into the situation where and when social action takes place. The first methodological step is a historical comparative analysis to focus on spaces in which violence becomes possible. Then, the book zooms into these spaces to reconstruct practices of violence. Following the analysis of sequences of these practices, this study elaborates on cultural scripts of violence. Finally, both methodological dimensions are connected with the analysis of strategic action. The book shows that both riversides can be linked up with the proposed theoretical bridge.

Second, in order to research causal relationships and to cope with the possibilities of diffusion because of cultural transfers at the same time, this book draws on the ideas of *Universalgeschichte* once developed by Karl Lamprecht (1988) at the end of the nineteenth century. Taken together, the present study shows that it is possible to control for processes of diffusion and cultural transfer, if diffusion and cultural transfer are made accessible for empirical research, or if it will be theorized by integrating diffusion into a redefined world system analysis. Both possibilities necessarily merge into a historically inspired, most different systems design. In order to research causal relationships of forms of violence, the research design needs to include cases that show similar forms of violence in diverging political, economic, and cultural settings. The comparison of El Salvador, Jamaica, and Belize meets these requirements. These cases show extraordinarily high levels of violence and, at the same time, similar forms of violence. This cross-regional and cross-cultural comparison is completely new within international research of violence.

Finally, this book demonstrates the advantage of qualitative methods in researching violence, particularly of qualitative interviews, focus group discussions, and participatory observations. The book relies on extensive field research experience in Central America and the Caribbean. It is based on 143 interviews with perpetrators and victims of violence, academic experts, and members of civil society organizations, police officers, and politicians. Additionally, focus groups discussions and participatory observations were conducted during several months of field research.

A NOTE ON CHALLENGES

This study elaborates an analytical concept of forms of violence and develops a theoretical as well as methodological route towards an explanation of forms of violence. It interprets the current divide in research on violence and perhaps in the entire theoretical landscape of social sciences as a challenge and a possibility to benefit from both poles.

Preceding this claim, the book is based on several convictions, which are both personal and theoretical in nature. As a young scholar trained in political economy, the author recognized that researching violence not only requires to look at the larger social processes that eventually lead to violent eruptions, such as revolutions, but likewise to focus on the very act of violence. Yet, this latter focus is not central to political economy. Political economy therefore is both limited in its explanatory power and limiting, as it does not allow for a holistic treatment of the research subject. Wanting to find an approach as comprehensive as possible, the study increasingly turned towards more culturalist approaches to violence. However, it is still driven by the political economy imperative to look at the big picture. Even if it only indirectly addresses the question of why violence evolves and how entire developments of society are thereto related, they constitute the starting point of the thoughts on violence set out in this book. The more the study focused on culture and on culturalist theories, the more mistrust arose against the very nature of developing terms and concepts in political economy. It is more rooted in the tendency of political economy to impose terms and concepts on empirical phenomena, in its tendency to try to frame empirical reality by means of an external, or in a certain sense, superior language. One of the finest examples to explain this mistrust is the heavy weight of the concept of statehood in academic debates on violence. It is not about the highly interesting relationship between violence and statehood, but about the constant reference to statehood. In this perspective, violence evolves where (and as soon as) the state does not function. It is a talk about deficiencies, fueled by normative statements on how the world should properly develop. Social order then equals statehood, and violence is the root of chaos. This mistrust led this study to reject the a priori focus on statehood and therefore to abandon the traditional academic path of political science. Culturalist approaches, in contrast, claim to focus on violence "from within" and therefore to come across violence "in distance to the state" (Riekenberg, 2014). This distance is important because it invites to reflect on the very nature of violence without considering external conditions, without creating an artificial language to bracket violence. Only this finally lays the very micro order of violence open.

However, there seems to be a contradiction: How can somebody come close enough to violence, trying to understand violence somehow from within, and simultaneously see the "big picture?" Or to put it in other words, how can somebody connect political economy with—on the first view diametrically opposed—theoretical traditions, such as culturalist theories, in order to attain a proper definition and explanation of forms of violence?

This contradiction, which initially evolved out of a certain personal "feeling" of how to look at violence, runs like a thread through this entire study. It relates to the epistemological position in thinking and writing about violence, it affects the analytical vocabulary in analyzing violence, it concerns the relationship between micro- and macro-levels of analysis, and finally, it impacts the methodological way to access violence.

Notes

1. From the early beginnings of social sciences, the analysis of violence in European history of ideas was built on the assumption that the human being is fundamentally negative. Exemplarily, those ideas are expressed in the Hobbesian view regarding the state of nature: If there is no superior authority forcing human beings to control their means of violence, they cannot solve conflicts peacefully. Violence is associated with the danger of falling back into the state of nature, and therefore produce chaos and evil. Consequently, violence is either linked to the failure of social order or even directly equated with disorder. Apparently, basic thoughts on how society is constituted cannot escape the idea of something known as a general rupture that leads to the possibility of civilization. Although largely different in their background—and only to mention the most known— Freud's (1924) theory on the constitution of culture through the patricide, Girard's (1972) theory of the sacrifice, and even Foucault's (2001) thoughts on the origins of discourse (where he relies on Nietzsche's interpretation of the state of nature, although with some contradictions; see Warnecke, 2012), all rely on the idea of an initial rupture. Once established, social order condemns violence, either through moral values or through the physical control of the means of violence. Explaining violence thus means to identify those ruptures in the social order leading to violence. Following the Hobbesian idea of social order, processes of institutionalization of the means of violence are emphasized. If human beings are prone to be bad, violence and its domestication is constitutive for social order. In this vein, the state emerges as the final institution to control violence. However, a careful look into the literature on the relationship between states and violence clarifies that the state not only plays a central role as a structural force for violence, but—and this seems to be quite often neglected—as a perpetrator as well. Thus, the relationship between state and violence, either as a unidirectional or as a reciprocal, is difficult and still to be understood.

   If human beings are intrinsically peaceful, an outside force (e.g. the society, the state, neighbor countries) has to cause people to exert violence. This tradition inspired by Rousseau can be found, although largely different in other theoretical aspects, in the work of Norbert Elias and his theory of the civilizing process. Although violence may be conceptualized as a means of which all humans dispose having bodies, it becomes possible to integrate the act of violence into a larger process of conflict. Violence then has to be treated as a stage of a conflict. Consequently, this second concept of analyzing violence leads to a completely different research design focusing on actors, perpetrators, and their interrelations.

REFERENCES

Aijmer, G., & Abbink, J. (Eds.). (2000). *Meanings of Violence: A Cross Cultural Perspective.* Oxford, UK: Berg.

Appadurai, A. (2006). *Fear of Small Numbers: An Essay on the Geography of Anger.* Durham, NC: Duke University Press.

Argueta Rosales, S. G., Caminos Alemán, G. S., Mancía Peraza, M. R., & los Angeles Salgado Pacheco, M. de. (1992). Diagnostico sobre los grupos llamados "maras" en San Salvador. Factores psicosociales que prevalecen en los jóvenes que los integran. *Revista de Psicología de El Salvador, 11*(43), 53–84.

Arias, E. D., & Goldstein, D. M. (2010). Violent Pluralism: Understanding the New Democracies of Latin America. In E. D. Arias & D. M. Goldstein (Eds.), *Violent Democracies in Latin America* (pp. 1–34). Durham, NC/London: Duke University Press.

Auyero, J., De Lara, A. B., & Berti, M. F. (2014). Uses and Forms of Violence Among the Urban Poor. *Journal of Latin American Studies, 46*(3), 443–469.

Avruch, K. (2001). Notes Toward Ethnographies of Conflict and Violence. *Journal of Contemporary Ethnography, 30*(5), 637–648.

Bolland, N. O. (2001). *The Politics of Labour in the British Caribbean: The Social Origins of Authoritarianism and Democracy in the Labour Movement.* Kingston, Jamaica: Ian Randle.

Brana-Shute, G. (2002). Narco-criminality in the Caribbean. In I. L. Griffith (Ed.), *The Political Economy of Drugs in the Caribbean* (pp. 97–112). Basingstoke, Hampshire: Palgrave Macmillan.

Briceño-León, R., & Zubillaga, V. (2002). Violence and Globalization in Latin America. *Current Sociology, 50*(1), 19–37.

Bunck, J. M., & Fowler, M. R. (2012). *Bribes, Bullets, and Intimidation: Drug Trafficking and the Law in Central America.* University Park, PA: Pennsylvania State University Press.

Call, C. T. (2003). Democratisation, War and State-Building: Constructing the Rule of Law in El Salvador. *Journal of Latin American Studies, 35*(04), 827–862.

Clarke, C. (2006). Politics, Violence and Drugs in Kingston, Jamaica. *Bulletin of Latin American Research, 25*(3), 420–440.

Cramer, C. (2006). *Civil War Is Not a Stupid Thing: Accounting for Violence in Developing Countries.* London: Hurst.

Cruz, J. M. (2010). Central American Maras: From Youth Street Gangs to Transnational Protection Rackets. *Global Crime, 11*(4), 379–398.

Das, V., Kleinman, A., Ramphele, M., & Reynolds, P. (Eds.). (2000). *Violence and Subjectivity.* Berkeley, CA/Los Angeles: University of California Press.

Davis, D. E. (2006). The Age of Insecurity: Violence and Social Disorder in the New Latin America. *Latin American Research Review, 41*(1), 178–197.

Dunkerley, J. (1982). *The Long War: Dictatorship and Revolution in El Salvador*. London/New York: Verso.

Elsenhans, H. (1991). The Great Depression of the 1930s and the Third World. *International Studies, 28*(3), 273–290.

Elsenhans, H. (2015). *Saving Capitalism from the Capitalists: World Capitalism and Global History*. New Delhi, India: Sage.

ERIC, IDESO, IDIES, & Instituto Universitario de Opinión Pública (IUDOP). (2001). *Maras y pandillas en Centroamérica: Volumen I*. Managua, Nicaragua: UCA Editores.

Fanon, F. (1961/2010). *Les damnés de la terre*. Paris: La Découverte.

Foucault, M. (2001). Die Wahrheit und die juristischen Formen. In D. Defert & F. Ewald (Eds.), *Schriften in vier Bänden: Dits et ecrits* (Vol. 2, pp. 669–792). Frankfurt a.M, Germany: Suhrkamp.

Freud, S. (1924). *Totem und Tabu: Arbeiten zur Anwendung der Psychoanalyse*. Leipzig, Germany: Internationaler Psychoanalytischer Verlag.

Galtung, J. (1969). Violence, Peace, and Peace Research. *Journal of Peace Research, 6*(3), 167–191.

Gayle, H., & Mortis, N. (2010). *Male Social Participation and Violence in Urban Belize: An Examination of Their Experience with Goals, Guns, Gangs, Gender, God, and Governance*. Belize City, Belize: RESTORE Belize.

Geneva Declaration Secretariat (GDS). (2015). *Global Burden of Armed Violence 2015: Every Body Counts*. Cambridge, UK: Cambridge University Press.

Girard, R. (1972). *La Violence et le Sacré*. Paris: Grasset.

Gray, O. (2004). *Demeaned But Empowered: The Social Power of the Urban Poor in Jamaica*. Kingston, Jamaica: University of the West Indies Press.

Harriott, A. (2000). *Police and Crime Control in Jamaica: Problems of Reforming Ex-Colonial Constabularies*. Kingston, Jamaica: University of the West Indies Press.

Harriott, A. (2003). Policing and Citizenship: The Tolerance of Police Violence in Jamaica. *West Indian Law Journal, 28*(1), 51–73.

Harriott, A. (2008). *Organized Crime and Politics in Jamaica: Breaking the Nexus*. Kingston, Jamaica: Canoe Press.

Holden, R. H. (2004). *Armies Without Nations: Public Violence and State Formation in Central America, 1821–1960*. Oxford, UK: Oxford University Press.

Hume, M. (2007). Mano Dura: El Salvador Responds to Gangs. *Development in Practice, 17*(6), 739–751.

Imbusch, P. (2002a). "Mainstreamer" versus "Innovateure" der Gewaltforschung: Eine kuriose Debatte. In W. Heitmeyer & J. Hagan (Eds.), *Internationales Handbuch der Gewaltforschung* (pp. 124–155). Wiesbaden, Germany: Westdeutscher Verlag.

Imbusch, P. (2002b). Der Gewaltbegriff. In W. Heitmeyer & J. Hagan (Eds.), *Internationales Handbuch der Gewaltforschung* (pp. 24–55). Wiesbaden, Germany: Westdeutscher Verlag.

Instituto Universitario de Opinión Pública (IUDOP). (2014). *La situación de la seguridad y la justicia 2009–2014: Entre expectativas de cambio, mano dura militar y treguas pandilleras.* San Salvador, El Salvador: IUDOP.

Jackson, S. L., Zahn, M. A., & Brownstein, H. H. (2004). The Need for a Theory of Violence. In M. A. Zahn, H. H. Brownstein, & S. L. Jackson (Eds.), *Violence: From Theory to Research* (pp. 251–261). Burlington, MA: Elsevier.

Jaffe, R. (2012). Crime and Insurgent Citizenship: Extra-state Rule and Belonging in Urban Jamaica. *Development, 55*(2), 219–223.

Jaffe, R. (2013). The Hybrid State: Crime and Citizenship in Urban Jamaica. *American Ethnologist, 40*(4), 734–748.

Kalecki, M. (1971). *Selected Essays on the Dynamics of the Capitalist Economy 1933–1970.* Cambridge, UK: Cambridge University Press.

Koonings, K. (2012). New Violence, Insecurity, and the State: Comparative Reflections on Latin America and Mexico. In W. G. Pansters (Ed.), *Violence, Coercion, and State-Making in Twentieth-Century Mexico: The Other Half of the Centaur* (pp. 255–278). Palo Alto, CA: Stanford University Press.

Koonings, K., & Kruijt, D. (Eds.). (2004). *Armed Actors: Organized Violence and State Failure in Latin America.* London/New York: Zed Books.

Kurtenbach, S. (2007). *Why Is Liberal Peace-building So Difficult? Some Lessons from Central America* (GIGA Working Papers). Hamburg, Germany: German Institute of Global and Area Studies.

Lamprecht, K. (1988). *Alternative zu Ranke. Schriften der Geschichtstheorie* (Hans Schleier, Ed.). Leipzig, Germany: Reclam.

La Prensa Gráfica. (2012, January 6). ¿Quién comete los homicidios en el país?

Leslie, G. (2010). *Confronting the Don: The Political Economy of Gang Violence in Jamaica.* Geneva, Switzerland: Small Arms Survey.

Levenson, D. (1989). Las "maras": Violencia juvenil de masas. *Polemica, 7*, 2–12.

Levy, H. (2009). *Inner City Killing Streets: Community Revival.* Kingston, Jamaica: Arawak Publications.

López, J. (2013). *Organized Crime and Insecurity in Belize.* Washington, DC: Inter-American Dialogue.

Lorenz, M. (2004). Physische Gewalt – ewig gleich? Historische Körperkontexte contra absolute Theorien. *Wiener Zeitschrift zur Geschichte der Neuzeit, 4*(2), 9–24.

Mauss, M. (1990 [1924]). *Die Gabe. Form und Funktion des Austauschs in archaischen Gesellschaften.* Frankfurt a.M, Germany: Suhrkamp.

Moser, C. (2004). Urban Violence and Insecurity: An Introductory Roadmap. *Environment and Urbanization, 16*(2), 3–16.

Moser, C. O. N., & Holland, J. (1997). *Urban Poverty and Violence in Jamaica.* Washington, DC: World Bank.

Naciones Unidas. (1993). *De la Locura a la esperanza: La guerra de 12 años en El Salvador: Informe de la Comision de la Verdad para El Salvador.* San Salvador, El Salvador/New York: United Nations Publications.

Nateras Domínguez, A. (2010). Etnografías de violencia y muerte: la Mara Salvatrucha y el Barrio 18. *Iztapalapa Revista de Ciencias Sociales y Humanidades, 31*(69), 87–108.

New York Times. (2001, April 21). Anthropology's Alternative Radical. *New York Times.*

Nordstrom, C., & Robben, A. C. G. M. (Eds.). (1995). *Fieldwork Under Fire: Contemporary Studies of Violence and Survival.* Berkeley, CA/Los Angeles: University of California Press.

Pan American Health Organization (PAHO). (1978). *Health Conditions in the Americas, 1973–1976.* Washington, DC: Pan American Health Organization.

Pan American Health Organization (PAHO). (1982). *Health Conditions in the Americas, 1977–1980.* Washington, DC: Pan American Health Organization.

Pearce, J. (2010). Perverse State Formation and Securitized Democracy in Latin America. *Democratization, 17*(2), 286–306.

Peirce, J., & Veyrat-Pontet, A. (2013). *Citizen Security in Belize* (IDB Technical Note: Vol. 572). Washington, DC: Inter-American Development Bank.

Pereira, A. W., & Davis, D. E. (2000). New Patterns of Militarized Violence and Coercion in the Americas. *Latin American Perspectives, 27*(3), 3–17.

Programa de las Naciones Unidas para el Desarrollo (PNUD). (2009). *Informe sobre Desarrollo Humano para América Central, 2009–2010: Abrir espacios para la seguridad ciudadana y el desarrollo humano.* San Salvador, El Salvador: PNUD.

Riekenberg, M. (2014). *Staatsferne Gewalt: Eine Geschichte Lateinamerikas (1500–1930).* Frankfurt a.M, Germany: Campus.

Rodgers, D., & Jones, G. A. (2009). Youth Violence in Latin America: An Overview and Agenda for Research. In G. A. Jones & D. Rodgers (Eds.), *Youth Violence in Latin America: Gangs and Juvenile Justice in Perspective* (pp. 1–24). New York/Basingstoke, UK: Palgrave Macmillan.

Scheper-Hughes, N., & Bourgois, P. (Eds.). (2007). *Violence in War and Peace: An Anthology.* Malden, MA/Oxford, UK/Carlton, Victoria: Blackwell.

Schmidt, B. E., & Schröder, I. W. (Eds.). (2001). *Anthropology of Violence and Conflict.* London: Routledge.

Seligson, M. A., & McElhinny, V. (1996). Low-Intensity Warfare, High-Intensity Death: The Demographic Impact of the Wars in El Salvador and Nicaragua. *Canadian Journal of Latin America and Caribbean Studies, 21*(42), 211–241.

Shifter, M. (2012). *Countering Criminal Violence in Central America* (Council Special Report: Vol. 64). New York: Council on Foreign Relations.

Sistema de Integración de Centroamérica, Secretaria de la Integración Social (SISCA), United Nations Population Fund (UNFPA), & Interpeace. (2012). *National Public Policy Proposal: Prevention of Youth-Involved Violence in Belize 2012–2022*. Belize City, Belize.

Sives, A. (2002). Changing Patrons, from Politician to Drug Don: Clientelism in Downtown Kingston, Jamaica. *Latin American Perspectives, 29*(5), 66–89.

Sives, A. (2010). *Elections, Violence, and the Democratic Process in Jamaica, 1944–2007*. Kingston, Jamaica: Ian Randle.

Steenkamp, C. (2005). The Legacy of War: Conceptualizing a 'Culture of Violence' to Explain Violence After Peace Accords. *The Round Table: The Commonwealth Journal of International Affairs, 94*(379), 253–267.

Stone, C. (1980). *Democracy and Clientelism in Jamaica*. New Brunswick, NJ: Transaction Publishers.

von Trotha, T. (1997). Zur Soziologie der Gewalt. In T. von Trotha (Ed.), *KZfSS Sonderheft: Vol. 37. Soziologie der Gewalt* (Vol. 37, pp. 9–56). Opladen, Germany: Westdeutscher Verlag.

United Nations Office on Drugs and Crime (UNODC). (2007a). *Crime and Development in Central America. Caught in the Crossfire*. Wien: United Nations Publications.

United Nations Office on Drugs and Crime (UNODC). (2007b). *Crime, Violence, and Development: Trends, Costs, and Policy Options in the Caribbean*. Wien: United Nations Publications.

United Nations Office on Drugs and Crime (UNODC). (2011). *Global Study on Homicide, 2011: Trends, Contexts, Data*. Wien: United Nations Office on Drugs and Crime.

United Nations Office on Drugs and Crime (UNODC). (2012). *Transnational Organized Crime in Central America and the Caribbean: A Threat Assessment*. Wien: United Nations Office on Drugs and Crime.

Ward, T. W. (2013). *Gangsters Without Borders: An Ethnography of a Salvadoran Street Gang*. Oxford, UK/New York: Oxford University Press.

Warnecke, H. (2012). Gewalt und Diskurs: Die "Gewalttheorien" von Georges Batailles und Michel Foucault im Vergleich. In M. Riekenberg (Ed.), *Zur Gewaltsoziologie von Georges Bataille* (pp. 177–195). Leipzig, Germany: Leipziger Universitätsverlag.

Warnecke-Berger, H. (2017). Forms of Violence in Past and Present: El Salvador and Belize in Comparative Perspective. In S. Huhn & H. Warnecke-Berger (Eds.), *Politics and History of Violence and Crime in Central America* (pp. 241–279). New York: Palgrave Macmillan.

Warnecke-Berger, H., & Huhn, S. (2017). The Enigma of Violent Realities in Central America: Towards a Historical Perspective. In S. Huhn & H. Warnecke-Berger (Eds.), *Politics and History of Violence and Crime in Central America* (pp. 1–22). New York: Palgrave Macmillan.

Whitehead, N. L. (Ed.). (2004). *Violence*. Santa Fe, NM: School of American Research Press.

Whitehead, N. L. (2007). Violence & the Cultural Order. *Daedalus, 136*(1), 40–50.

Winton, A. (2011). Grupos violentos en Centroamérica: La institucionalización de la violencia. *Desacatos, 37*, 111–124.

Wolf, S. (2017). *Mano Dura: The Politics of Gang Control in El Salvador*. Austin, TX: University of Texas Press.

Zilberg, E. (2004). Fools Banished from the Kingdom: Remapping Geographies of Gang Violence Between the Americas (Los Angeles and San Salvador). *American Quarterly, 56*(3), 759–779.

Zinecker, H. (2001). Gewalt als Legat: Überlegungen zur Präfiguration unvollendeter Transformationen in Kolumbien und El Salvador. In W. Höpken & M. Riekenberg (Eds.), *Politische und ethnische Gewalt in Südosteuropa und Lateinamerika* (pp. 149–171). Köln, Germany/Weimar, Germany/Wien: Böhlau.

Zinecker, H. (2011). Gewalt- und Friedensforschung – funktioniert der entwicklungstheoretische Kompass? In P. Schlotter & S. Wisotzki (Eds.), *Friedens- und Konfliktforschung* (pp. 139–182). Baden-Baden, Germany: Nomos.

Zinecker, H. (2014). *Gewalt im Frieden: Formen und Ursachen der Gewaltkriminalität in Zentralamerika*. Baden-Baden, Germany: Nomos.

CHAPTER 2

Political Economy and/or Culture? Theorizing Forms of Violence

In the theoretical landscape of research on violence, there are two disciplines that are mostly concerned with the phenomenon: political economy and cultural theory. While both disciplines conduct research on violence and have developed a significant body of literature, their perspectives on violence differ fundamentally. Political economy approaches to violence employ a macro perspective and are able to describe structural determinants for violence. However, they miss to consider singular events, acts, and sequences of violent practices, and the resulting dynamics. Culturalist approaches to violence, in turn, focus on the micro level and fail to relate the single incidents to the structural conditions. If we think of violence as a river and the disciplines as riversides with an interest in the river, the politico-economic body of literature is most concerned with the flow of the river while the culturalist body of literature focuses on single drops of water, on their vibrancies, and on their movements.

Building a bridge to cross the river and to link both riversides thus not only contributes to an ongoing theoretical discussion on violence and to the elaboration of a middle position between the two largest research traditions, but also encourages to consider forms of violence. This book has a focus on certain formations inside the flow of the river, on its waves and swirls, on the patterns and forms that result when single drops of water come together. Although this may raise deep-reaching ontological and epistemological questions, the following chapter proposes a theoretical approach to conceptualize forms of violence.

© The Author(s) 2019
H. Warnecke-Berger, *Politics and Violence in Central America and the Caribbean*, https://doi.org/10.1007/978-3-319-89782-0_2

The study takes position between both riversides in order to benefit from both approaches. To reach this position, this chapter focuses on building a bridge to link the riversides. Starting from the riverside of political economy, the study gradually incorporates culturalist approaches and thereby introduces struts to finally span the truss that crosses the river.

An explanation of forms of violence equally requires focusing on the political economy of rent, particularly on the social embeddedness of rents, and examining practices of violence. Linking both approaches helps to understand the social organization of violence and strategic action. In mobilizing and organizing violence, social actors strategically rely on resources and on cultural scripts. Forms of violence emerge out of processes in which both resources drawn from political economy and cultural scripts drawn from theory of social practice are interlinked and activated. Figure 2.1 illustrates this argumentation.

To start building this bridge, this chapter first develops a preliminary definition for the central term of this study—forms of violence. Second, it argues for a relational concept of violence. Third, and this is the main contribution of this chapter, it provides an initial starting point for the development of a theory to explain forms of violence based on the metaphor of the bridge.

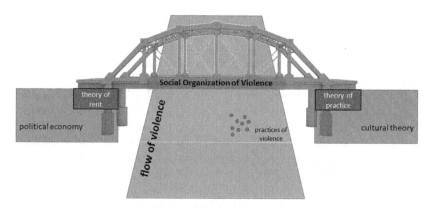

Fig. 2.1 The social organization of violence between political economy and culture. (Source: own elaboration)

Defining Forms of Violence

In order to define forms of violence, the category needs to be distinguished from two neighboring phenomena. First, forms of violence differ from the violent actors. Youth gangs, death squads, or militias are violent actors but they are not forms of violence. Violent actors, even though they might resort to violence, can never fully be reduced to particular violent acts. Violent actors are essentially social actors. Additional features such as, for instance, membership or hierarchy need to be considered for their classification (Schlichte, 2009a). Second, forms of violence have to be distinguished from violent acts and practices of violence. An act or a practice is a singular event in the course of a larger history. Form and formation, in contrast, refer to something more durable than a single event (Feldman, 2008). Violent actors, individuals or collectives, might use several forms of violence. It is also possible, however, that violent actors specialize in a single form of violence, or even in the exertion of a single act of violence, and constantly reproduce it (Tilly, 2003, pp. 35–36).

Charles Tilly's (2003, 2006, 2008) and his colleagues' (McAdam, Tarrow, & Tilly, 2001) work on contentious politics and his term "repertoire" as well as elaborations on the concept of "repertoire of violence" (Wood, 2008, p. 541) offer further useful insights for the identification of an intermediate level between social actors and social practices. Tilly's approach highlights effects of repertoires on politics of contention. He defines repertoire as a "clustered, learned, yet improvisational character of people's interactions as they make and receive each other's claims" (Tilly, 2006, p. 35). In his idea, contentious politics is not about the singular social practice, even though the researcher needs to look at this practice. Repertoires are clusters and sets of quite different although not infinite social practices. Transferring Tilly's idea to the study of violence, the question of why certain forms of violence emerge and practices of violence become linked to each other in such forms gains importance.

Accordingly, this study defines form of violence as a specific set of violent practices that a social actor routinely uses to make claims on other social actors. Form of violence in this understanding as a repertoire merges an ideational as well as a material component. Repertoires are material in the sense that they exist due to acts of violence that actually occurred. Repertoires are at the same time ideational in the sense of meaning systems and therefore repertoires link knowledge on acts of violence to topographies of violent practices and cultural scripts.

This concept of forms of violence shows that violence is predominantly socially embedded. As Elwert (2002, p. 342) argues, it is not the very act of violence that attracts primary attention but "the forms of its channeling, synchronization, and classification in strategic relations have to be explained. Violence is always channeled. Certain targets, victims, weapons, battlefields, and even times can be defined. Insofar, violence is always – in every society – constrained."

Forms of violence may include different practices of violence. The knowledge about these different practices and their relation to each other, however, is part of a meaning system. These meaning systems, which guide and inform the practical execution of violence, can be weak, strong, and even rigid (Tilly, 2008, pp. 15–16). While in some situations specific practices of violence are mandatory (e.g. in the case of *rites de passage* where practices of violence appear to be normatively required), in other situations practices appear to be more contingent.

This definition allows to concretize the concept of forms of violence and to distinguish between the categories brought into discussion at the beginning of this chapter. Firstly, forms of violence comprise acts or practices of violence. They link both different and similar acts of violence with each other through rules that govern the exertion of violence. Secondly, violent actors employ forms of violence by exerting sets of violent practices. Moreover, violent actors are able to employ different forms of violence. Therefore, forms of violence are not directly related to specific violent actors. While some violent actors may specialize in one well-defined form of violence,[1] others might apply several forms of violence. Finally, a particular form of violence is not the essence of a violent actor. Thus, forms of violence are not fixed. They change over time.

TYPOLOGIZING FORMS OF VIOLENCE

Contemporary discussions on violence—academic and public alike—are guided by certain shared a priori ontological assumptions. The distinction between political and criminal violence, for instance, seems to be fundamental for policy-makers. When something becomes political, the entire policy machine is mobilized and needs to produce quick answers to "resolve" violence. However, when violence remains criminal, it "only" needs to be processed by the criminal justice system.

In contrast to these a priori assumptions on a certain ontology of violence, this chapter argues for a relational understanding of violence. This understanding does not exclusively highlight the violent actors' motivations but instead focuses on social relationships that violent actors establish with other social actors by waging violence. The social relation in which forms of violence are embedded is the pivotal interest of this study.

Vertical Violence

Research on violence has a longstanding structuralist tradition. This tradition conceives of violence as an expression of power, authority, and domination, and considers it tightly related to social stratification, durable inequalities, and ultimately statehood. Accordingly, violence emerges from societal tensions between individuals, groups, or social classes because of perceived differences in power relations. Additionally, violence is usually assumed to occur between actors of different social positions, that is, between "them above" and "them down there" (Dahrendorf, 1958; Rössel, 2002). Violence is an instrument in the struggle between the subaltern and the ruling class.[2] The structuralist tradition thus perceives violence as being vertical, exposing a disparity of power differentials. Violence either challenges authority and domination in times of political turmoil, rebellion or revolution, or violence ensures security and "peace" through overt repression or hidden, quiet, and symbolic forms (Bourdieu, 1990, pp. 122–135).

Authors concerned with vertical violence often recognize that in cases of potential vertical violence, violence is only rarely exerted, as it is assumed that dominant groups, or the ruling class, dispose of means to integrate the subaltern class. Those means are entangled with authority and hegemony, clientelism or even participation in violence (Graziano, 1976; Kerkvliet & Scott, 1977). Instead, "relative decreasing differentials of power" (Elias, 1977, p. 130) between individuals or groups are more likely to be accompanied by open violence when traditional forms of managing social conflicts inscribed in authority and hegemony fail to reach their goals.[3] However, if violence takes less instrumental or less challenging forms, the structuralist tradition tends to ignore it.

Horizontal Violence

Lately, a type of violence that does not (or at least only indirectly) challenge statehood or the social fabric has attracted the attention of researchers. Writing about this violence and without referring in the first place to concepts such as statehood or *Herrschaft* leans towards an ethnological and anthropological perspective. These disciplines inherited a much more nuanced perspective on situations described as regulated anarchy than political science and sociology have (Sigrist, 1979). Violence in this tradition is considered horizontal by nature as it emerges in situations in which equally powerful rivals are in opposition to each other and none of them has the means to overpower the rival permanently (e.g. Coser, 1964 concentrated his work on intergroup conflicts that resemble this horizontal type). In contrast to the disparity of power differentials highlighted by the political science perspective, these approaches focus on social context in which none of the involved actors can durably trust that the rival acts peacefully in the future.

Without external interference, horizontal violence tends to lead to a violent equilibrium between opponents and uncertainty becomes immanent.[4] In such an equilibrium, violence is constantly reproduced because peaceful and non-violent strategies are perceived by all involved actors as too risky (Helbling, 2006). Violence turns into "the only credible social script for public performance" (Whitehead, 2004a, p. 18). Horizontal violence contains a strong sense of reciprocity,[5] since violence is followed by violence, and actors exert violence in reaction to violence previously exerted by their rivals (Tyrell, 1999, p. 275).

Without the direct intervention of superior authorities able to control the means of violence, rituals manage the escalation of violence (Blok, 2000, pp. 24–25). Additionally, structuring emotions such as those resulting from the violation of honor, for instance, become crucial for the mobilization and control of violence. In a certain sense, these emotions serve to "cultivate" violent conflicts (Dubiel, 1998). Emotions cultivate violence in the absence of other institutional resources. They provoke and at the same time control horizontal violence in this equilibrium. Examples for the cultivation of violence are vendettas, feuds, and cycles of revenge (Black, 1990; Boehm, 1984; Elster, 1990; Spittler, 1980; Turner & Schlee, 2008).

Conceptualizing Violence as Horizontal and Vertical

Both perspectives are not mutually exclusive. They simply make different assumptions on the social relationship in which violence is embedded. However, a clear distinction between both types of relationships, horizontal and vertical, allows for the elaboration of a typology, which is fundamental for the further discussion. Figure 2.2 illustrates this typology.

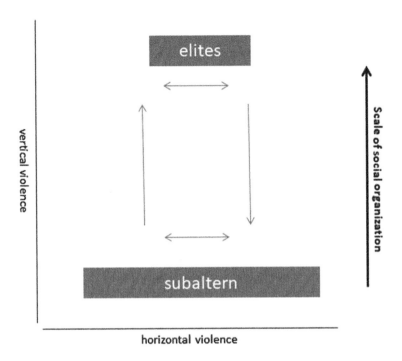

Fig. 2.2 Typology of forms of violence. (Source: own elaboration)

The figure distinguishes between vertical and horizontal violence on the respective axis. While horizontal violence is defined as violence between equally powerful rivals, vertical violence develops in situations in which disparities of power exist, and in its extreme form, between the elite and the subaltern class. The right arrow displays the scale of social organization of violence, which indicates the number of individuals involved in violence exertion.

In the case of the vertical violence, a range spans from violence at the highest organizational scale exerted directly by the state (state-sponsored violence) through official institutions (police or military) to indirect repression by paramilitary or extra-state forces (Stohl, 1986; Stohl & Lopez, 1984). According to this logic, vigilantism is a form of vertical violence.[6] In the case of para-militarism and death squads, violence is directly connected to state authority and is therefore located on a very high organizational scale. In the case of grassroots vigilantism (Huggins, 1991; Kalyvas &

Arjona, 2005), the organizational scale only seldom transcends the community. In the reverse case, the scope reaches from "everyday forms of resistance" (Scott, 1985), peasant rebellions (Kurtz, 2000), working-class strikes or revolts (Thompson, 1971) to revolutions (Goldstone, 2001).

In the case of the horizontal violence, the most organized form is horizontal violence between factions and/or segments of the elite. Segmentary violence in civil wars among different power blocks are examples of horizontal violence. The other side of the spectrum of horizontal violence shows the reciprocal use of violence between subaltern people or groups, or, as it is called today, "citizen-on-citizen violence" (Pereira & Davis, 2000, p. 4).

When applying this relational perspective, the ontological distinction between criminal and political violence as a definitional precondition of violence research and as the disciplinary border between political science approaches to (political) violence and criminological approaches to (criminal) violence, becomes blurred and meaningless. In the relational approach elaborated here, these differences remain secondary. In turn, the distinction between horizontal and vertical violence permits to grasp the grey area between "political" and "criminal" violence instead of creating residual categories such as social violence. This distinction allows for the study of the relationship between different (violent) actors in which different forms of violence are embedded and therefore for a focus on the "relationship between a violent actor or actors and at least one other actor who may or may not engage in violence" (Hanagan, 2003, p. 121). Through the perspective that considers violent actors in relation to other (violent and rivalling) actors, violence becomes a relational concept.

EXPLAINING FORMS OF VIOLENCE

Studying forms of violence implies two challenges. The first challenge relates to the dimension of agency. Forms of violence express social actions. The second challenge relates to the term form or formation. Forms of violence are a set and thus a more or less stable conglomerate of either the same or different violent practices. In this sense, it requires a certain level of stability. Analytically, form of violence embraces both concepts, agency as well as structure.

Consequently, explaining forms of violence requires both levels of analysis: the macro level to examine social structures and the micro level to explore acts of violence. This study employs a political economy perspective.

However, it will include culturalist theory into the theoretical framework, which allows for the analysis of micro dynamics of violence and hence of acts of violence.

In order to specify this idea, the metaphor of a bridge crossing a river to link distinct and initially disconnected riversides provides a useful illustration. A bridge consists of at least two bridge pillars that carry the superstructure of the bridge. On both riversides, the construction of the bridge begins by elaborating the pillars, then continuing towards the truss. In this study of forms of violence, one riverside is the political economy approach; the other riverside is the one of culturalist theory. The political economy perspective being the starting point, the first pillar on part of the political economy riverside consists in the theory of rent. The second pillar is constructed based on culturalist practice theory. Finally, the superstructure of the bridge, the truss, that rests on both pillars and connects them, represents the focus on the mobilization and organization of forms of violence.

Political economy as one riverside explains in which general circumstances violence emerges. It primarily focuses on why violence becomes opportune and on how social actors operate in a structured and yet conflictive social setting. By focusing on how the access to economic surplus affects the development of social classes, class alliances, and the terms of trade between social classes, political economy is able to show how congealed structures eventually encourage the emergence of violence.

It will be argued that political economy approaches are able to exemplify how changes in the politico-economic context shape dynamics of social conflicts and their escalation into violence if they focus on the appropriation of economic surplus and therefore on the difficult interplay of economic and political spheres. Economic rent as a form of economic surplus serves as a useful concept as it allows to understand economic surplus extraction and to link politics with economics. A detailed study of the genesis, appropriation, and realization of rents helps explain the distribution of resources among different social actors. By using a political economy approach, it will, firstly, be possible to study the *longue durée* in order to strengthen explanations of contemporary problems of violence through historical contextualization, and secondly to pay attention to issues of (under)development in the study of violence. Taken together, political economy details and emphasizes the structural processes through which violence becomes opportune. It focuses on social situations generally prone to violence.

The trigger for violent escalations, however, remains outside the scope of political economy (Zinecker, 2011, p. 174). Moreover, political economy takes forms of violence for granted and shows minor interest in approaching micro dynamics of violence. On a theoretical level, political economy limits itself by not giving scope to action theory and agency. From a political economy standpoint, this chapter argues that opportunities, spaces, and situations prone to violence only become violent if they are recognized and understood by relevant actors and if they are grasped and included into a meaningful background of social action. This argument suggests the integration of the second pillar of the bridge: a culturalist approach.

Social action and its meaning, commonly defined as culture, is central to recent approaches of practice theory, which perfectly fit into the argument. Praxeological approaches are able to show why violence has specific expressions at the micro level. Praxeology accentuates implicit and rule-based social behavior and thus processes that (re)produce social practices (see e.g. Bourdieu, 1990; Giddens, 1984; Reckwitz, 2002; Schatzki, Knorr-Cetina, & Savigny, 2001; Shove, Pantzar, & Watson, 2012). Praxeological approaches not only concentrate on motivations that tend to instruct violence. They also study violence as performative acts in which communication about and through violence becomes important (Schröder & Schmidt, 2001, pp. 9–12). Practice theory shows how social practice is deeply influenced by cultural knowledge (Hillebrandt, 2014). Through practice theory, rules and routines of how to behave in the process of doing become evident. These rules and routines come together in cultural scripts.

The term practice of violence or violent acts describes the smallest analytical entity of violence in this study (e.g. slapping, fist fighting, stabbing, gun shooting, etc.). Practices of violence "no less than any other kind of behavioural expression, are deeply infused with cultural meaning and are the moment for individual agency within historically embedded patterns of behaviour" (Whitehead, 2004a, p. 9). Furthermore, this study argues that practices of violence are not applied arbitrarily. Instead, certain rules influence or even govern the conduct and behavior of actors involved in the violent game. Thus, practices can only be understood if they are studied in relation to the historical processes out of which they develop.

Due to their orientation towards constructivism and the focus on the study of material artefacts and its cultural construction (hence products of social practice), praxeological approaches fail to address the importance of resources in the conduct of social practice. The term resources[7] points to the theoretical bridge pursued in this chapter. In the following, this study integrates resources into the study of social practice at the micro level and thus intend to create a theoretical connecting factor between political economy and praxeology. The next theoretical step therefore consists in linking different practices of violence to forms of violence. Even though both pillars are necessary for the construction of the bridge, there is still a certain theoretical disconnection since they are located on different explanatory levels. Linking both levels consequently requires focusing on the superstructure of the truss bridge.

This superstructure consists in the concept of social organization of violence.[8] In processes of social organization of violence, cultural scripts encounter resources, which allow for the execution of practices of violence. Resources as well as cultural scripts are closely related to strategic action and social actors become "enabling actors" of violence (Bourdieu, 1990, p. 61).

The organization of violence involves power. Power, in this sense, is the transformative capacity of strategic action "to refer to agents' capabilities of reaching (...) outcomes" (Giddens, 1979, p. 88). Following Bourdieu, "it is the source of these strings of 'moves' which are objectively organized as strategies without being the product of a genuine strategic intention which would presuppose at least that they be apprehended as one among other possible strategies" (Bourdieu, 1990, p. 62). Strategic action thus is one possible mode of social action and not the only one (Willems, 2012, pp. 457–458). Furthermore, strategic action becomes possible if resources are available for it. Resources, however, only become accessible if they are perceived as useful for the exertion of particular repertoires. The social organization of violence merges the availability of resources with cultural scripts. In essence, both the availability of resources and cultural scripts are the driving forces for the reproduction of violent acts over time and space, hence, for forms of violence.

Linking both pillars of the bridge (political economy and practice theory) with its superstructure (organization of violence) therefore explains the causes of forms of violence. While the political economy of violence identifies structurally congealed situations in which violence becomes opportune, the study of micro dynamics of violence takes these situations as starting points to understand the micro processes of escalation and de-escalation and their entrenchment with violence. Each is relevant in the concept of social organization of violence. In essence, the metaphor of the bridge represents the development of a theory of forms of violence. This theory intends to respond to recent desiderata in research of violence, namely, "theory building as sense making" (King, 2004, p. 453) of violence.

The First Pillar: Political Economy of Violence

The underlying political economy argument is that the mode of sociation (Simmel, 1992/[1908]; Tönnies, 1922) in societies in the Global South is not dominated by market structures but by non-market structures ultimately based on economic rents. The debate on rent and rent economies generally relates the presence and/or dominance of certain economic rents to a specific type of political behavior (Auty, 2001; Beblawi & Luciani, 1987; Burchardt & Dietz, 2014; Gudynas, 2009; Omeje, 2010; Ross, 2001). However, this is a rather limited approach, as it tends to disconnect the political from the economic realm and thus leads away from the study of violence.

Rent economies, or the mere existence of a particular type of rent, do not inevitably generate violence. Violence does not necessarily originate from rent economies, but can originate from specific types of rent economies under particular political conditions (Zinecker, 2014, pp. 49–50). The analysis of violence by means of theories on rent economies does not depend on the recognition of the existence of rents per se, but on the embeddedness of rents in a social climate, which is shaped by the conflict about the access to economic surplus.

In economic terms, the existence of surplus that cannot be absorbed based on net investment (as it would be the case in capitalist societies)[9] creates the opportunity to appropriate this surplus in the form of rent (Elsenhans, 2015). Rent is defined as a revenue, which evolves because of market restrictions, monopolies, or political power (Elsenhans, 1997). Therefore, rent-based modes of production are characterized by the centralized access to economic surplus, and the control and redistribution of surplus is highly interwoven with political power.

The concept of rent thus links the economic with the political realm. In order to grasp this complexity, the source of rents need to be distinguished from the mode of its appropriation. Source of rent describe the material (e.g. oil, copper, bauxite in the case of mineral products; remittances and foreign wage in the case of migration; coffee and other agricultural products in the case of agrarian production) and the technical basis on which rent arises (e.g. ground rent, differential rent (Marx, 1972 [1894], pp. 653–697), neoclassical consumer and producer rents, and innovation rents (see Khan, 2000 for an overview on this type of Schumpeter rent). The existence of economic rents signals that surplus is available. The mode of its appropriation describes the political access to rents and therefore its original realization in physical or monetary terms. For its realization, it has to be appropriated through (non-economic) political means. The distinction between these two subcategories illustrates that in presence of economic rents, politics can hardly be separated from economics. Both realms are virtually interwoven.

This terminological differentiation ensures a more nuanced analysis of the appearance of economic rents and, at the same time, it turns the attention to its societal effects. Regarding violence, two tendencies are especially important: Rents tend to verticalize political relations and they promote social closure. These tendencies of rents are likely to encourage social actors to resort to violence.

The first tendency, the verticalization of political processes, results from the political effects of rent appropriation and allows to draw conclusions about the particular distribution of resources in a society (Elsenhans, 1996). The social setting through which economic surplus is appropriated is highly relevant for the class alliances behind those settings (e.g. the state).[10] Two different forms of appropriation can be distinguished. Firstly, when state positions guarantee the access to surplus, the elite is defined as a state class. The "bureaucracy" in this sense constitutes a centralized class, which collectively appropriates the available economic surplus and secures a part of it for its own reproduction as an apparatus and as a class (Elsenhans, 1996). To maintain its power and its access to the surplus, it is "caught between self-privileging and the compulsion to legitimize" (Elsenhans, 1996, p. 200). Therefore, the state class is dependent on both: on consumption and the presentation of its own luxury to gain prestige and on distributional mechanisms to allow for the inclusion of the subaltern class. As a result, the state class is segmented and trapped in an "unending rivalry between the individual members of the state class for influence, prestige, and money" (Elsenhans, 1996, p. 221).

Secondly, when economic power secures access to surplus, the elite is defined as an oligarchy. Oligarchy then means the control of the economic surplus due to the control over factors of production, mostly over land and labor (Zinecker, 2007, pp. 205–210). This implies that an oligarchy organizes the defense of its wealth on its own without necessarily making use of the state (Winters, 2011, p. 32). Contrary to state classes, oligarchies are more exclusive as they do not depend on the systematic clientelist inclusion of the subaltern class. Instead, for their own reproduction, oligarchies have to exclude the subaltern class from the access to surplus as well as maintain economic and political stability what sometimes appears mutually exclusive.

In the case of state classes, factions of the ruling class form segments through which the subaltern class gets included, as the subaltern class itself is excluded from the direct access to surplus (Gramsci, 1971, pp. 52–55). Although perverse due to their clientelist nature, these class alliances are vertical. State classes are characterized by an immanent struggle over rents. This struggle takes place inside existing institutional settings of rent (re)distribution. As the inclusion of the subaltern class usually involves funds, which trickle down through various channels, conflicts are expected to appear at each stage of (re)distribution.

In the case of an oligarchic monopolization of the economic surplus, however, and as long as the ruling class refuses to integrate the subaltern class, the struggle about the access to this surplus is not channeled through existing institutions. From this point of view, oligarchies are much more exposed to threats from outside their own institutional setting. The most important question then is how the subaltern class is mobilized, organized, and integrated into an institutional setting that is able to maintain the power of the elite.

Verticalization does not only secure the powerful position of elites. The elite in control of available surplus maintains its control based on political, non-economic means and the exclusion of the majority of the population from the access to the surplus. In fact, violence as a political strategy either to get access to rents or to prevent others to do so appears rational for both the elite as well as the subaltern class. In this sense, in verticalized social settings, opportunities for violence arise. This, however, is not the only politico-economic factor that encourages violence.

The second tendency of rents is that they are likely to promote social closure.[11] Since social and political loyalty has to be generated in order to appropriate rents, the access to rents also relies on symbolical categories, social distinction, and specific modes of communication. Through social closure, thus, rents can be translated into symbolical resources and group membership. What initially evolves as a conflict over divisible issues such as material and often monetary resources (since rents are yet to be realized), steadily bears the risk of shifting towards conflict over non-divisible issues (Dubiel, 1998; Hirschman, 1994).[12] The tendency for social closure and the capacity to transform divisible in non-divisible conflicts are given due to the peculiarity of class alliances. The class antagonism under the dominance of rent is often mitigated by clientelism and patronage due to marginality. Indeed, clientelism and the reciprocal confirmation of moral bonds between elites and factions of the subaltern class are decisive factors for the stability of societies. At the same time, clientelism is a strategy for survival of the subaltern class as long as other opportunities are absent. In this context, changes in the structure of surplus will challenge the social fabric's maintenance. In situations of economic change, aggravated social conflicts are likely. On the subaltern level, income decreases and livelihoods become precarious. On the elite level, the struggle over rent intensifies when the elite maintains its social role and power.

In both tendencies, the ambivalence of rent comes to the fore. While rent is most likely to stabilize social structures, changes in the predominance of rent, and hence in the structure of economic surplus, have a catalyzing effect. Changes in this structure require actors to redefine their objectives and to (re)negotiate their room for maneuver vis-à-vis rival actors. Thus, economic changes affect the terms of trade between the elite and the subaltern class. It also has consequences for the horizontal relationships between different factions of the elite as well as between factions of the subaltern class. In the wake of such changes, the struggle over rent intensifies and challenges established forms of rent appropriation. Together, these two tendencies are likely to encourage the use of violence either to further maintain or to challenge and in consequence to overcome the realization and appropriation of rents.

In theoretical terms, spaces in which violence becomes possible but not necessary evolve during critical junctures and periods of significant change. Once entered into this enabling space, violence becomes a potential mode of action for social actors (see for the concept of enabling spaces of violence, e.g. Baberowski, 2012). The political economy approach shows under which circumstances these spaces evolve. At the same time, the approach allows to formulate assumptions about the distribution of material and symbolical resources social actors dispose of in these social spaces. As the access to these resources becomes precarious within these spaces, actors are not able to make use of situational information in order to calculate future actions. Contingency becomes evident in these moments of rapid change. Usually, actors resort to experiences and knowledge they have gained previously. In this sense, history extends into the present and influences the actors' choices and behavior.

These spaces only signal the propensity towards violence. Through the study of these spaces, the analytical examination of the processes through which agency is entangled with violence becomes sharpened. At this point, the explanatory capacity of political economy meets its limits. While political economy theory is able to show under which circumstances spaces of violence evolve, it is not able to explain what forms of violence are exerted within these spaces. Answering the question what particular form of violence eventually evolves has to be complemented with a closer examination of micro dynamics of violence, and therefore requires the opposite riverside's perspective.

The Second Pillar: Micro Dynamics of Violence

The second pillar of the theoretical bridge proposed in this chapter offers an approach to access the dynamics of violent interactions at the micro level. Culturalist practice theory provides the toolkit to zoom analytically into spaces of violence derived by the political economy approach above. At the micro level of analysis, the study of micro dynamics of violence complements the first pillar of the bridge as it describes the precise mechanisms because of which actors resort to particular violent practices (Riches, 1986; Stewart & Strathern, 2002).

This pillar builds on the initial assumption that forms of violence are cultural phenomena. Apart from the consideration of the political economy of violence, an explanation of forms of violence requires an understanding of the social order of violent acts at the micro level. In this light, practice theory presents a suitable complementary approach to acts of violence. Practice theory highlights that human action is rule-based; social practices follow certain rules, and social actors first have to learn these rules in order to activate social practices. Transferred to violence, it points out how processes of escalation and de-escalation provide actors with tacit knowledge on how and when to resort to particular violent acts.

Social actors exerting violence have to resort to certain ideas of how and when to conduct violent acts. Those ideas, as social theory has recently shown (Bongaerts, 2007), do not have to be explicit for social actors. Different to the disruptive effects of violence in violent situations these ideas and meanings outlast the single moment. Hence, the larger historical process has to be taken into consideration to understand the mechanisms through which violence is caused and how the meaning of violent acts is produced (Blok, 2000). Even those acts of violence that seem unthinkable and appear senseless for outsiders can later be seen as the "macabre forms of cultural design and violent predictability" (Appadurai, 1998, p. 229; Inhetveen, 2005, p. 36). In essence, "the universe of violent acts is thus constituted by the historical and cultural knowledge of violent actors, and the performative felicity of a given violent act is itself part of the wider meaning of violent acts, just as interpretation of the culture and history of violent actors is needed if nonparticipant observers are to understand the meanings of their violence. How violence is inflicted, on whom and when, has to be joined to a consideration of why violence occurs in that specific context" (Whitehead, 2004b, p. 63).

Violence is deeply interwoven with cultural meaning systems. However, those meaning systems, discourses, and culture do not exist independently. In a certain sense, these terms are analytical tools to uncover continuities, routines, and procedures. They are analytical terms to understand what is possible in a certain situation and what is completely outside the spectrum of possible social action in other situations. In terms of violence, they tell us a lot about which acts are perceived as legitimate and which are not or which acts are understood in a certain way. These similarities leave marks in the cultural memory of societies and therefore become accessible for research. This mark can be defined as a cultural script of violence. It is a "set of accepted social rules governing how the violent game is played: who is a legitimate target; the level of violence that can be meted out, from destruction of property to murder; and what counts as a sufficient condition for escalating from one level to the next" (King, 2004, p. 440). By uncovering this set of social rules, practice theory allows to determine which particular forms violent expressions may take once they evolve. This study of micro dynamics of violence thus combines the political economy of violence with a detailed approach to practices of violence.

In order to approach the rules governing the conduct of violence, the cultural scripts of violence, the study of micro dynamics of violence has to take a step back. Historical similarities, certain patterns of action, or social rules are not directly observable. They come into being due to the researcher's imagination and due to the work with their objects. In the case of violence and especially in the sense of micro dynamics of violence, the most revealing object is the act of exerting violence. This is essentially based on the theory of practice as it stresses the pivotal role of social practices—acts of doing and exerting—and their relation to practical knowledge. Practice theory thus "enables us to chart a course in between a number of more oversimplified approaches" (Stewart & Strathern, 2002, p. 154).

Practice theory criticizes both utilitarian action theory, which postulates utility maximizing human beings (*homo oeconomicus*) as well as norm-oriented action theory, which regards the realization of social norms as an action trigger mechanism (*homo sociologicus*). Implicit or "tacit knowledge" (Polanyi, 1966) cannot be processed actively and willfully because it has to be understood as practical knowledge, which is entangled with embodied practices. Practical knowledge withdraws from language and communication. Routines perfectly express this state: routinized "behavior" is done without questioning it. Practice theory emphasizes at least six issues of social practice arguing against conventional action theory (Page & Mercer, 2012): social practice is contextual; it changes slowly; it is transferable and passes to other people; it is embodied; it is a result of tacit knowledge; and it is characterized by strategic (inter)action and not only by the actor's aims to conduct the practice. Some inspiring exceptions apart, research on violence never took notice of practice theory (but see, e.g. Krämer, 2007; Liell, 2004).

To benefit from practice theory for research on violence, it is crucial to understand the role of knowledge in the multiple processes of creating, doing, exerting, and (re)producing social practice. This role becomes evident in its definition: social practices are defined as knowledge-based activities; as "a routinized way in which bodies are moved, objects are handled, subjects are treated, things are described and the world is understood" (Reckwitz, 2002, p. 250). Therefore, knowledge is bound with practice through routines of object handling (e.g. using a knife; fighting with a knife; pulling the trigger of a gun). Those routines are expressions of implicit and tacit knowledge accumulated into habitualizations (e.g. knife thrower; gunman; etc.) (Bourdieu, 1990; Elias, 1994). Violent practices are activities that make practical use of knowledge finally inflicting physical damage on other people.

Social practice theory thus turns to the dynamics of violence. Additionally, it leads to the study of those "social processes that generate them, not (...) of the motives and emotions carried by damage-doing people" (Tilly, 2003, p. 16). Social practice "is related to the (re)production of meaning through those actors entangled in practice" (Hillebrandt, 2009, p. 36). Implicit and local knowledge links social practice to collective spheres of experience (Reckwitz, 2002). Even though social practice is contingent in the sense that it is hardly possible to reproduce exactly the same practice repeatedly, it is not arbitrary.

Studying violent acts exemplifies "how violent processes fit into the culturally available orientations for the people's social action and how they are perceived, interpreted and assembled to an entity of meaningful social practice in their everyday lives" (Riekenberg, 2003, pp. 16–17). In the course of exerting violence (e.g. a knife fight), actors resort to implicit knowledge on how to conduct social practice (e.g. how to brandish the knife) and on particular resources (e.g. the physical force to use the knife and the knife as an object itself). Moreover, exerting a particular act draws on the actor's motivations and on the whole ensemble of social factors involved.

Following this understanding, social practice contains a cognitive element in the sense of tacit knowledge and cultural scripts as well as a material element in the sense of resources that enable actors to "do" the particular practice. While tacit knowledge and cultural scripts are the principal focus of practice theory, the analysis of resources of which actors have to dispose in doing social practice remains under-theorized (Saar, 2008, p. 206).

Related to the cognitive element of social practice, cultural scripts are defined as prototypically simplified ideas of the world. These scripts are entangled in networks, consequently organizing social and cultural meanings (Wimmer, 2005, p. 33). They reduce insecurity through the stabilization of meaning; without these symbolical and cognitive elements, radical and totally contingent situations of decision-making would evolve (Mezirow, 1991, p. 5). Cultural scripts are activated selectively in everyday patterns of thinking, acting, and perceiving and therefore instruct social practice (Wimmer, 2005). Thus, by using practice theory and its particular focus on practical knowledge it is possible to explain why specific practices are exerted and others not.

Cultural scripts are not automatically activated and therefore do not per se lead to action.[13] In order to get activated by social actors they have to be learned and mobilized through strategic action.[14] During the process of exerting a specific social practice, actors resort to cultural scripts, which are understood as a "toolkit" (Swidler, 1986). Cultural scripts provide action with meaning and produce subjective rationality.

How are violent acts and cultural scripts linked? First, violent acts are the fundamental expressions of violence at the micro level. Cultural scripts guide the (violent) actor in how to exert violence. They are the rules and tacit knowledge "behind" these practices. Once mobilized by strategic action, these landscapes of knowledge that entangle particular modes to exert violence get activated and lead to the act. In other words, routines can be built upon the entanglement of practices of violence and related tacit knowledge.

How the use of resources and the activation of cultural scripts are linked with each other cannot be explained by practice theory. Although the study of micro dynamics of violence highlights the relevance of specific situations in which violence has already occurred, this focus on the violent act ignores the processes in which these micro dynamics are embedded. Therefore, the second pillar of the theoretical bridge ends at this point. Practice theory shows that violent acts are deeply influenced by culture. The conduct of violence relies on tacit and practical knowledge that is condensed in cultural scripts. These scripts are learned. At the same time, practice theory shows that the conduct of violent acts is based on strategic action and hence on the selective activation of cultural scripts. How these scripts are activated and why social actors resort to violence is not addressed by practice theory. In this central issue, practice theory benefits from explanations proposed by political economy. This finally brings me to the superstructure of the bridge that intends to link both political economy and practice theory.

Bridging the River: The Social Organization of Violence

Forms of violence emerge because violent actors resort through strategic action to particular resources and cultural scripts that enable them to (re) produce certain sets of violent acts. These sets of violent acts are defined as a form of violence. This study defines the process of (re)producing sets of violent acts as the social organization of violence. Forms of violence are based on the utilization and exploitation of resources in their material and symbolical sense. From this perspective, the emergence of forms of violence is related to power: the "organisation of violence is a particular source of social power" (Shaw, 2009, p. 98) because violence once organized "can be socially productive" (Bates, Greif, & Singh, 2002, p. 599). However, forms of violence are also influenced by culture: The conduct of violent acts is inscribed in meaning systems and cultural scripts.

The (re)production of violent acts by violent actors is based on the selective activation of cultural scripts in which the execution of violent acts is inscribed. The activation of cultural scripts depends on resources of which the actor dispose and on which strategic action it is based.

The concept of social organization of violence highlights that violence needs to be mobilized in order to be executed. It describes how "mutually sustaining cultural schemas and sets of resources (…) empower and constrain social action and tend to be reproduced by that action" (Sewell, 1992, p. 22). Mobilization of violence depends on strategic action and involves processes such as manipulating, bargaining, convincing of other actors to join the violent game, and sometimes even force. In the individual case, actors have to resort at least to emotional forces (sometimes even overcoming internal barriers) to exert violence (Collins, 2008). In the collective case, these individual patterns have to be exploited to synchronize the behavior of a group of people. The synchronization of cultural meaning through strategic agency appears to be a pivotal expression of power. Those who are able to give meaning to violent acts then become particularly powerful. In this sense, certain violent acts are enculturated by manipulation, new cultural scripts are created and existing scripts are even modified (Collins, 1990; Inhetveen, 2005).

Mobilizing violence, synchronizing violent acts along cultural scripts and finally organizing practices of violence as forms of violence, requires the investment of resources such as time, physical force, and remuneration, but in some cases, money as well as objects and artefacts such as weapons.

The next central question after having explored why certain violent actors resort to particular forms of violence thus is how violent actors are enabled to reproduce a particular set of violent practices repeatedly. A key principle in this context is that "action and social organization are entirely related to and dependent on each other, produce and reshape, make and re-make each other in a process of permanent co-production" (Halbmayer, 2000, p. 39).

This principle issue also implies the possibilities for the (re)production of violent acts by violent actors. As "violence is not a timeless expression of frustration endowed with the same meanings and significance across time and space" (Adelman, 2010, p. 395), the driving force behind violence is its strategic mobilization that eventually leads to its social organization. The concept of social organization of violence explains how acts of violence are reproduced over space and time, how acts of violence obtain a coherent form, and how violent actors are enabled to reproduce this form by exerting particular violent acts. The analysis of social organization of violence therefore requires a focus on "how the duality of structure operates in social life: of how continuity of form is achieved in the day-to-day conduct of social activity" (Giddens, 1979, p. 216).

Conclusion

This theoretical chapter initially developed a definition of forms of violence. Forms of violence are a specific subset of violent practices that a social actor routinely uses in making claims on others. Following this definition, forms of violence link the very doing and exerting of violence with the violent actor who is doing and exerting violence. Actors employ one or more forms of violence, but they cannot be reduced to these forms. In turn, forms of violence consist of violent practices. Secondly, this chapter developed a relational approach to violence. The distinction of vertical from horizontal violence allows to highlight that violence is socially embedded. The very nature of violence then does not depend on the actors' motivation, as the concept of political and criminal violence would suggest, but on the actors' interaction when making claims on each other.

The subsequent step advocates a bridge between the two metaphoric riversides, namely between political economy approaches and culturalist theories. This bridge seeks to cross the river and thereby to encourage researchers to position themselves on the bridge between the two pillars to get a closer look on the waves and swirls, on forms of violence. Starting from the riverside of political economy, the chapter elaborated on the political economy of economic rents and the capacity of rents to shape social relations and gradually approached culturalist theories. Subsequently, the chapter looked at forms of violence from the other riverside, through the lens of culturalist theories, and introduced the concept of social practice, emphasizing the role of practices of violence. These practices, as theory of social practice suggests, follow rules and routines that were termed as cultural scripts of violence instructing social action by delivering the implicit knowledge how to conduct violent practices.

Notes

1. However, this seems to be an exception. As an example, research on torture produced rich insights regarding this issue. In this light, it was even possible to distinguish different social habitus of torturers who specialize in

a certain way of torturing their victims (Agger & Jensen, 1992; Huggins, Haritos-Fatouros, & Zimbardo, 2002; Inhetveen, 2011; Mackert, 2011).

2. Drawing on the work of (Gramsci, 1971, p. 51) who distinguished the ruling class from the subaltern class, as "the historical unity of the ruling classes is realized in the State, and their history is essentially the history of States and of groups of States. But it would be wrong to think that this unity is simply juridical and political (though such forms of unity do have their importance too, and not in a purely formal sense), the fundamental historical unity, concretely, results from the organic relations between State or political society and civil society (…)". In contrast, the subaltern classes "(…) by definition, are not unified and cannot unite until they are able to become a "State": their history, therefore, is intertwined with that of civil society, and thereby with the history of States and groups of States."

3. In the broader field of conflict studies, especially two positions address how these patterns transform into violence. First, neorealism in international relations, initially developed by (Waltz, 1979), describes the international system as an anarchic structure due to lacking superior authorities that would theoretically be able to function as mediators. Hence, every single state has to ensure its security by reducing the risk for being attacked (Jervis, 1978). In a stylized situation, the security dilemma describes the unlikelihood of security coalitions arguing that the most rational option in the perception of involved actors leads to a defect of the coalition. Every task undertaken by involved states changes the nature of the security dilemma, possibly leading to its intensification and hence to escalations. War, in this sense, is the rational outcome of the intensified search for security. War becomes opportune if former modes of security production fail (e.g. alliance building and therefore balancing against rising superpowers) and peaceful actions are perceived as too risky. Recently, a similar approach was used to study the behavior of armed groups and terrorists (Vinci, 2009) as well as the violence of rebel groups against other rebel groups (Fjelde & Nilsson, 2012). Second, anthropology of warfare focuses on similar issues. (Helbling, 2006) argues that violence becomes possible because peaceful strategies are perceived as far too risky by involved conflict actors. Anthropology further concretizes how these structurally given situations lead to violent outbreaks.

4. For instance, in dyadic conflicts, violent actors are not able to resort to mediation and settlement of violent conflicts since no third party exists that might be able to intervene. Horizontal violence then became opportune because "exit" was unavailable or implied high costs while "voice" equaled violence (Converse, 1968; Hirschman, 1970; Koch, 1976).

5. The literature on reciprocity did not consider violence. However, the concept of horizontal violence implies reciprocity. See for an overview on reciprocity, e.g. (Adloff & Mau, 2005; Gouldner, 1984; Stegbauer, 2002).
6. Vigilantism is a very vague and indefinite concept. Following (Johnston, 1996), vigilantism consists of six factors: (1) at least minimal planning on behalf of the agitators; (2) it has to be undertaken by private agents (police officers may participate as private persons; police officers commit acts that are illegitimate; officer follows a force policy that constitutes a form of violence or illegitimate coercion; (3) voluntary activity of active citizens; (4) violence as a necessary element; (5) the objective to control, either in the political, in the criminological, or in the social sense; and (6) as a reaction to a perceived (subjective) or objective collapse of the social order. Regarding the motivations for direct vigilante violence, vigilantism can be further subcategorized depending on its social scale either as crime-control vigilantism, as social-groups vigilantism, or as regime-control vigilantism (Rosenbaum & Sederberg, 1976). In the case of death squads, vigilantism is highly entangled with state authority and therefore located on a very high organizational scale. Concerning the relationship between vigilantism and state authority, it "presumes the existence of the state" (Abrahams, 1998, p. 9) although it has to be clarified that "some forms of violence that challenge the state's monopoly come into being due to decisions of state agencies" (Schlichte, 2009b, p. 311) themselves.
7. On a very basic level, resources are defined as "the media whereby transformative capacity is employed as power in the routine course of social interaction" (Giddens, 1979, p. 92). Resources therefore are "anything that can serve as a source of power in social interactions" (Sewell, 1992, p. 9). Two types of resources can be distinguished (Giddens, 1979, 100): Authoritative resources as "capabilities which generate command over persons" and allocative resources as "capabilities which generate command over objects or other material phenomena," which will be defined in this study as material or economic resources and symbolical resources. Resources therefore are twofold: human and nonhuman. Nonhuman resources are "objects, animate or inanimate, naturally occurring or manufactured, that can be used to enhance or maintain power; human resources are physical strength, dexterity, knowledge, and emotional commitments that can be used to enhance or maintain power, including knowledge of the means of gaining, retaining, controlling, and propagating either human or nonhuman resources" (Sewell, 1992, p. 9). In this sense, the term resources combines elements on which political economy focuses, namely economic resources and forms of economic surplus as well as resources that practice theory approaches, namely symbolical resources in the sense of "actual or potential resources which are linked to possession of a durable

network of more or less institutionalized relationships of mutual acquaintance and recognition – or in other words, to membership in a group" (Bourdieu, 1986, p. 50).

8. Social organization is commonly referred to as the antipode of violence. Brought into discussion from the Chicago School, social organization was associated with the control of violence (Janowitz & Burk, 1991), and eruptions of violence were precisely attributed to social disorganization (Shaw & McCay, 1942). In a certain sense, the Chicago School treated violence as something external to social organization. In contrast to the Chicago School and following the praxeological approach, violence is indeed entangled with social organization (Jackman, 2002, p. 407).

9. Surplus can take either the form of rent or the form of profit. Capitalist profit, however, depends on specific market structures, which do not develop automatically. Kalecki (1971) shows that profit depends on net investment, which is ultimately based on rising mass incomes due to strong bargaining power of labor (Elsenhans, 1983).

10. The state is one possible solution as it provides the administrative structure to organize the access to rents and at the same time centralizes and redistributes the economic surplus.

11. Social closure was developed early on by (Weber, 1968, p. 43); the concept, however, did not enjoy primary attention in the reading of Weber. It describes the process of marginalization and exclusion of non-belonging, of distancing and disposing strangers, and finally the construction of we-groups. (Wimmer, 2013) relates social closure to ethnic boundary making processes.

12. Conflicts vary in the quality of their object. They can either be classified as conflicts over divisible resources such as power, money, and territory or as conflicts about non-divisible issues such as norms and values, recognition, truth, ideology, or the arrangement of the future. In the former case, divisible conflicts are about more/less, in the latter case, they are about either/ or and create a "winner-takes- all" mentality. The literature shows how initially perceived divisible conflicts shift towards non-divisible conflicts through mobilization, manipulation, and agency (e.g. in the case of ethnicity by ethnic entrepreneurs). In this process, divisible conflicts are reframed as non-divisible conflicts as a precondition for further mobilizations along ethnic lines.

13. How practical knowledge arranged in cultural scripts is experienced, processed, and used individually as well as collectively remains traditionally outside the conventional research scope of social sciences. This is exactly the starting point where cognitive science comes into play. In recent years, authors of cognitive anthropology (Casson, 1983; D'Andrade & Strauss, 1997), social psychology (Schneider, 1991), and cultural sociology

(Cerulo, 2002) have been doing ground-breaking and pioneering work explaining "how cultural processes enter into individual lives and how such processes enter into some kinds of collective behavior" (DiMaggio, 2002, p. 275). Results show that human beings dispose of much larger stocks of knowledge as they can translate into action. This stock of knowledge is divided into cultural scripts. In this line, a cultural script is defined in cognitive science as a "building block of culture," and as "chunked networks of loose procedures and understandings which enable us to deal with standard and recurring situations" (Bloch, 1991, p. 185). Scripts are arranged hierarchically. These scripts are learned through practical experience and are subsequently (re)arranged into new cognitive networks, or they support and join yet existing ones. "There is (…) considerable evidence that learning is not just a matter of storing received knowledge, as most anthropologists implicitly assume when they equate cultural and individual representations, but that it is a matter of constructing apparatuses for the efficient handling and packing of specific domains of knowledge and practice" (Bloch, 1991, p. 189).

14. Learning therefore functions as a path-dependent sequence of meaning production. Results in cognitive science point out that information that is already entangled with existing scripts or information that disturbs those scripts is noticed and processed more likely rather than information orthogonal to existing scripts (DiMaggio, 1997).

References

Abrahams, R. (1998). *Vigilant Citizens: Vigilantism and the State.* Cambridge, UK: Polity Press.

Adelman, J. (2010). The Rites of Statehood: Violence and Sovereignty in Spanish America, 1789–1821. *Hispanic American Historical Review, 90*(3), 391–422.

Adloff, F., & Mau, S. (2005). Zur Theorie der Gabe und Reziprozität. In F. Adloff & S. Mau (Eds.), *Vom Geben und Nehmen: Zur Soziologie der Reziprozität* (pp. 9–57). Frankfurt a.M., Germany/New York: Campus.

Agger, I., & Jensen, S. B. (1992). Die gedemütigte Potenz: Sexuelle Folter an politischen Gefangenen männlichen Geschlechts: Strategien zur Zerstörung der Potenz. In H. Riquelme (Ed.), *Zeitlandschaft im Nebel: Menschenrechte, Staatsterrorismus und psychosoziale Gesundheit in Südamerika* (pp. 48–75). Frankfurt a.M.: Vervuert.

Appadurai, A. (1998). Dead Certainty: Ethnic Violence in the Era of Globalization. *Public Culture, 10*(2), 225–247.

Auty, R. M. (2001). The Political Economy of Resource-Driven Growth. *European Economic Review, 45*(4/6), 839–846.

Baberowski, J. (2012). Räume der Gewalt. *Forensische Psychiatrie, Psychologie, Kriminologie, 6*(3), 149–157.

Bates, R., Greif, A., & Singh, S. (2002). Organizing Violence. *Journal of Conflict Resolution, 46*(5), 599–628.

Beblawi, H., & Luciani, G. (Eds.). (1987). *The Rentier State.* London: Croom Helm.

Black, D. (1990). The Elementary Forms of Conflict Management. In School of Justice Studies (Ed.), *New Directions in the Study of Justice, Law, and Social Control* (pp. 43–69). New York: Plenum Press.

Bloch, M. (1991). Language, Anthropology and Cognitive Science. *Man, 26*(2), 183–198.

Blok, A. (2000). The Enigma of Senseless Violence. In G. Aijmer & J. Abbink (Eds.), *Meanings of Violence: A Cross Cultural Perspective* (pp. 23–38). Oxford, UK: Berg.

Boehm, C. (1984). *Blood Revenge: The Anthropology of Feuding in Montenegro and Other Tribal Societies.* Philadelphia, PA: University of Pennsylvania Press.

Bongaerts, G. (2007). Soziale Praxis und Verhalten – Überlegungen zum Practice Turn in Social Theory. *Zeitschrift für Soziologie, 36*(4), 246–260.

Bourdieu, P. (1986). The Forms of Capital. In J. G. Richardson (Ed.), *Handbook of Theory and Research for the Sociology of Education* (pp. 46–58). New York: Greenwood Press.

Bourdieu, P. (1990). *The Logic of Practice.* Stanford, CA: Stanford University Press.

Burchardt, H.-J., & Dietz, K. (2014). (Neo-)Extractivism: A New Challenge for Development Theory from Latin America. *Third World Quarterly, 35*(3), 468–486.

Casson, R. W. (1983). Schemata in Cognitive Anthropology. *Annual Review of Anthropology, 12*(1), 429–462.

Cerulo, K. A. (Ed.). (2002). *Culture in Mind: Toward a Sociology of Culture and Cognition.* New York: Routledge.

Collins, R. (1990). Violent Conflict and Social Organization: Some Theoretical Implications of the Sociology of War. *Amsterdams Sociologisch Tijdschrift, 16*(4), 63–87.

Collins, R. (2008). *Violence: A Micro-Sociological Theory.* Princeton, NJ: Princeton University Press.

Converse, E. (1968). The War of All Against All: A Review of the Journal of Conflict Resolution, 1957–1968. *Journal of Conflict Resolution, 12*(4), 471–532.

Coser, L. A. (1964). *The Functions of Social Conflict.* New York: Free Press.

D'Andrade, R. G., & Strauss, C. (Eds.). (1997). *Human Motives and Cultural Models.* Cambridge, UK: Cambridge University Press.

Dahrendorf, R. (1958). Toward a Theory of Social Conflict. *The Journal of Conflict Resolution, 2*(2), 170–183.

DiMaggio, P. (1997). Culture and Cognition. *Annual Review of Sociology, 23*(1), 263–287.

DiMaggio, P. (2002). Why Cognitive (and Cultural) Sociology Needs Cognitive Psychology. In K. A. Cerulo (Ed.), *Culture in Mind: Toward a Sociology of Culture and Cognition* (pp. 274–281). New York: Routledge.

Dubiel, H. (1998). Cultivated Conflicts. *Political Theory, 26*(2), 209–220.

Elias, N. (1977). Zur Grundlegung einer Theorie sozialer Prozesse. *Zeitschrift für Soziologie, 6*(2), 127–149.

Elias, N. (1994). *Die Gesellschaft der Individuen*. Frankfurt a.M., Germany: Suhrkamp.

Elsenhans, H. (1983). Rising Mass Incomes as a Condition of Capitalist Growth: Implications for the World Economy. *International Organization, 37*(1), 1–39.

Elsenhans, H. (1996). *State, Class and Development*. New Delhi, India: Radiant Publishers.

Elsenhans, H. (1997). Rente. In U. Albrecht & H. Vogler (Eds.), *Lexikon der Internationalen Politik* (pp. 439–447). München, Germany: Oldenbourg.

Elsenhans, H. (2015). *Saving Capitalism from the Capitalists: World Capitalism and Global History*. New Delhi, India: Sage.

Elster, J. (1990). Norms of Revenge. *Ethics, 100*(4), 862–885.

Elwert, G. (2002). Sozialanthropologisch erklärte Gewalt. In W. Heitmeyer & J. Hagan (Eds.), *Internationales Handbuch der Gewaltforschung* (pp. 330–367). Wiesbaden, Germany: Westdeutscher Verlag.

Feldman, A. (2008). *Formations of Violence: Narrative of the Body and Political Terror in Northern Ireland*. Chicago: University of Chicago Press.

Fjelde, H., & Nilsson, D. (2012). Rebels Against Rebels: Explaining Violence Between Rebel Groups. *Journal of Conflict Resolution, 56*(4), 604–628.

Giddens, A. (1979). *Central Problems in Social Theory: Action, Structure and Contradiction in Social Analysis*. London: Macmillan.

Giddens, A. (1984). *The Constitution of Society: Outline of the Theory of Structuration*. Cambridge, UK: Polity Press.

Goldstone, J. A. (2001). Toward a Fourth Generation of Revolutionary Theory. *Annual Review of Political Science, 4*(1), 139–187.

Gouldner, A. W. (1984). *Reziprozität und Autonomie. Ausgewählte Aufsätze*. Frankfurt a.M., Germany: Suhrkamp.

Gramsci, A. (1971). *Selections from the Prison Notebooks of Antonio Gramsci*. New York: International Publishers.

Graziano, L. (1976). A Conceptual Framework for the Study of Clientelistic Behavior. *European Journal of Political Research, 4*(2), 149–174.

Gudynas, E. (2009). Diez tesis urgentes sobre el nuevo extractivismo: Contextos y demandas bajo el progresismo sudamericano actual. In J. Schuldt, A. Acosta,

A. Barandiará, A. Bebbington, M. Folchi, A. Alayza, & E. Gudynas (Eds.), *Extractivismo, política y sociedad* (pp. 187–225). Quito, Ecuador: CAAP/ CLAES.

Halbmayer, E. (2000). Socio-cosmological Contexts and Forms of Violence: War, Vendetta, Duels and Suicide Among the Yukpa of North-Western Venezuela. *Sociologus, 50*(1), 37–63.

Hanagan, M. (2003). Violence and the Rise of the State. In W. Heitmeyer & J. Hagan (Eds.), *International Handbook of Violence Research* (pp. 121–137). Dordrecht, The Netherlands/Boston: Kluwer Academic Publishers.

Helbling, J. (2006). *Tribale Kriege: Konflikte in Gesellschaften ohne Zentralgewalt.* Frankfurt a.M., Germany: Campus.

Hillebrandt, F. (2009). *Praktiken des Tauschens: Zur Soziologie symbolischer Formen der Reziprozität.* Wiesbaden, Germany: VS Verlag für Sozialwissenschaften.

Hillebrandt, F. (2014). *Soziologische Praxistheorien: Eine problembezogene Einführung.* Wiesbaden, Germany: VS Verlag für Sozialwissenschaften.

Hirschman, A. O. (1970). *Exit, Voice and Loyalty.* Cambridge, MA: Harvard University Press.

Hirschman, A. O. (1994). Social Conflicts as Pillars of Democratic Market Society. *Political Theory, 22*(2), 203–218.

Huggins, M. K. (Ed.). (1991). *Vigilantism and the State in Modern Latin America: Essays on Extralegal Violence.* New York: Praeger.

Huggins, M. K., Haritos-Fatouros, M., & Zimbardo, P. G. (2002). *Violence Workers: Police Torturers and Murderers Reconstruct Brazilian Atrocities.* Berkeley, CA/Los Angeles: University of California Press.

Inhetveen, K. (2005). Gewalt in ihren Deutungen: Anmerkungen zu Kulturalität und Kulturalisierung. *Österreichische Zeitschrift für Soziologie, 30*(3), 28–50.

Inhetveen, K. (2011). Towards a Body Sociology of Torture. In T. von Trotha, J. Rösel, & R. Geißler (Eds.), *On Cruelty – Sur la cruauté – Über Grausamkeit* (pp. 377–387). Köln, Germany: Köppe.

Jackman, M. R. (2002). Violence in Social Life. *Annual Review of Sociology, 28*(1), 387–415.

Janowitz, M., & Burk, J. (1991). *On Social Organization and Social Control.* Chicago: University of Chicago Press.

Jervis, R. (1978). Cooperation Under the Security Dilemma. *World Politics, 30*(2), 167–214.

Johnston, L. (1996). What Is Vigilantism? *British Journal of Criminology, 36*(2), 220–236.

Kalecki, M. (1971). *Selected Essays on the Dynamics of the Capitalist Economy 1933–1970.* Cambridge, UK: Cambridge University Press.

Kalyvas, S. N., & Arjona, A. (2005). Paramilitarismo: una perspectiva teórica. In A. Rangel Suárez (Ed.), *El poder paramilitar* (pp. 25–45). Bogotá, CO: Fundación Seguridad & Democracia.

Kerkvliet, B., & Scott, J. C. (1977). How Traditional Rural Patrons Lose Legitimacy: A Theory with Special Reference to Southeast Asia. In S. W. Schmidt, J. C. Scott, C. Landé, & L. Guasti (Eds.), *Friends, Followers, and Factions: A Reader in Political Clientelism* (pp. 439–458). Berkeley, CA/Los Angeles: University of California Press.

Khan, M. H. (2000). Rents, Efficiency and Growth. In M. H. Khan & K. S. Jomo (Eds.), *Rents, Rent-Seeking and Economic Development: Theory and Evidence in Asia* (pp. 21–69). Cambridge, UK: Cambridge University Press.

King, C. (2004). The Micropolitics of Social Violence. *World Politics, 56*(3), 431–455.

Koch, K.-F. (1976). Konfliktmanagement und Rechtsethnologie: Ein Modell und seine Anwendung in einer ethnologischen Vergleichsanalyse. *Sociologus, 26*(2), 96–129.

Krämer, M. (2007). *Violence as Routine: Transformations of Local-Level Politics in KwaZulu-Natal (South Africa)*. Köln, Germany: Köppe.

Kurtz, M. J. (2000). Understanding Peasant Revolution: From Concept to Theory and Case. *Theory and Society, 29*(1), 93–124.

Liell, C. (Ed.). (2004). *Kultivierungen von Gewalt: Beiträge zur Soziologie von Gewalt und Ordnung*. Würzburg, Germany: Ergon.

Mackert, J. (2011). Im Auftrag des Staates: Die geheime Gesellschaft der Folterer. *Berliner Journal für Soziologie, 21*(3), 431–459.

Marx, K. (1972 [1894]). *Das Kapital. Kritik der politischen Ökonomie: Dritter Band: Der Gesamtprozeß der kapitalistischen Produktion* (MEW: Vol. 25). Berlin, Germany: Dietz Verlag.

McAdam, D., Tarrow, S. G., & Tilly, C. (2001). *Dynamics of Contention*. Cambridge, UK: Cambridge University Press.

Mezirow, J. (1991). *Transformative Dimensions of Adult Learning*. San Francisco, CA: Jossey-Bass.

Omeje, K. C. (Ed.). (2010). *Extractive Economies and Conflicts in the Global South: Multi-Regional Perspectives on Rentier Politics*. Aldershot, UK: Ashgate.

Page, B., & Mercer, C. (2012). Why Do People Do Stuff? Reconceptualizing Remittance Behaviour in Diaspora-Development Research and Policy. *Progress in Development Studies, 12*(1), 1–18.

Pereira, A. W., & Davis, D. E. (2000). New Patterns of Militarized Violence and Coercion in the Americas. *Latin American Perspectives, 27*(3), 3–17.

Polanyi, M. (1966). *The Tacit Dimension*. Garden City/New York: Doubleday.

Reckwitz, A. (2002). Toward a Theory of Social Practices: A Development in Culturalist Theorizing. *European Journal of Social Theory, 5*(2), 243–263.

Riches, D. (1986). The Phenomenon of Violence. In D. Riches (Ed.), *The Anthropology of Violence* (pp. 1–27). Oxford, UK: Blackwell.

Riekenberg, M. (2003). *Gewaltsegmente: Über einen Ausschnitt der Gewalt in Lateinamerika*. Leipzig, Germany: Leipziger Universitätsverlag.

Rosenbaum, H. J., & Sederberg, P. C. (1976). Vigilantism: An Analysis of Establishment Violence. In H. J. Rosenbaum & P. C. Sederberg (Eds.), *Vigilante Politics* (pp. 3–29). Philadelphia, PA: University of Pennsylvania Press.

Ross, M. L. (2001). Does Oil Hinder Democracy? *World Politics, 53*(3), 325–361.

Rössel, J. (2002). Die klassische Konflikttheorie auf dem Prüfstand: Determinanten der Intensität und Gewaltsamkeit von sozialen Konflikten. *Schweizerische. Zeitschrift für Soziologie, 28*(1), 47–67.

Saar, M. (2008). Klasse/Ungleichheit: Von den Schichten der Einheit zu den Achsen der Differenz. In S. Moebius & A. Reckwitz (Eds.), *Poststrukturalistische Sozialwissenschaften* (pp. 194–207). Frankfurt a.M., Germany: Suhrkamp.

Schatzki, T. R., Knorr-Cetina, K., & Savigny, E. v. (Eds.). (2001). *The Practice Turn in Contemporary Theory.* London/New York: Routledge.

Schlichte, K. (2009a). *In the Shadow of Violence: The Politics of Armed Groups.* Frankfurt a.M., Germany/New York: Campus.

Schlichte, K. (2009b). Na krilima patriotisma: On the Wings of Patriotism: Delegated and Spin-Off Violence in Serbia. *Armed Forces & Society, 36*(2), 310–326.

Schneider, D. J. (1991). Social Cognition. *Annual Review of Psychology, 42*(1), 527–561.

Schröder, I. W., & Schmidt, B. E. (2001). Introduction: Violent Imaginaries and Violent Practices. In B. E. Schmidt & I. W. Schröder (Eds.), *Anthropology of Violence and Conflict* (pp. 1–24). London: Routledge.

Scott, J. C. (1985). *Weapons of the Weak: Everyday Forms of Peasant Resistance.* New Haven, CT: Yale University Press.

Sewell, W. H. (1992). A Theory of Structure: Duality, Agency, and Transformation. *American Journal of Sociology, 98*(1), 1–29.

Shaw, C. R., & McCay, H. D. (1942). *Juvenile Delinquency and Urban Areas: A Study of Rates of Delinquency in Relation to Differential Characteristics of Local Communities in American Cities.* Chicago: University of Chicago Press.

Shaw, M. (2009). Conceptual and Theoretical Frameworks for Organised Violence. *International Journal of Conflict and Violence, 3*(1), 97–106.

Shove, E., Pantzar, M., & Watson, M. (2012). *The Dynamics of Social Practice: Everyday Life and How it Changes.* Los Angeles: Sage.

Sigrist, C. (1979). *Regulierte Anarchie: Untersuchungen zum Fehlen und zur Entstehung politischer Herrschaft in segmentären Gesellschaften Afrikas.* Frankfurt a.M., Germany: Syndikat.

Simmel, G. (1992/[1908]). Untersuchungen über die Formen der Vergesellschaftung. In *Soziologie. Gesamtausgabe* (Vol. 11). Frankfurt a.M., Germany: Suhrkamp.

Spittler, G. (1980). Konfliktaustragung in akephalen Gesellschaften: Selbsthilfe und Verhandlung. In E. Blankenburg, E. Klausa, & H. Rottleuthner (Eds.),

Alternative Rechtsformen und Alternativen zum Recht (Jahrbuch für Rechtssoziologie und Rechtstheorie, Vol. 6, pp. 142–164). Opladen, Germany: Westdeutscher Verlag.

Stegbauer, C. (2002). *Reziprozität: Einführung in soziale Formen der Gegenseitigkeit.* Wiesbaden, Germany: Westdeutscher Verlag.

Stewart, P. J., & Strathern, A. (2002). *Violence: Theory and Ethnography.* London: Continuum.

Stohl, M. (Ed.). (1986). *Government Violence and Repression: An Agenda for Research.* New York: Greenwood Press.

Stohl, M., & Lopez, G. A. (Eds.). (1984). *The State as Terrorist: The Dynamics of Governmental Violence and Repression.* Westport, CT: Greenwood Press.

Swidler, A. (1986). Culture in Action: Symbols and Strategies. *American Sociological Review, 51*(2), 273–286.

Thompson, E. P. (1971). The Moral Economy of the English Crowd in the Eighteenth Century. *Past & Present, 50,* 76–136.

Tilly, C. (2003). *The Politics of Collective Violence.* Cambridge, UK: Cambridge University Press.

Tilly, C. (2006). *Regimes and Repertoires.* Chicago: University of Chicago Press.

Tilly, C. (2008). *Contentious Performances.* Cambridge, UK/New York: Cambridge University Press.

Tönnies, F. (1922). *Gemeinschaft und Gesellschaft: Grundbegriffe der reinen Soziologie.* Berlin, Germany: Karl Curtius.

Turner, B., & Schlee, G. (Eds.). (2008). *Vergeltung. Eine interdisziplinäre Betrachtung der Rechtfertigung und Regulation von Gewalt.* Frankfurt a.M., Germany/New York: Campus.

Tyrell, H. (1999). Physische Gewalt, gewaltsamer Konflikt und 'der Staat' – Überlegungen zu neuerer Literatur. *Berliner Journal für Soziologie, 9*(2), 269–288.

Vinci, A. (2009). *Armed Groups and the Balance of Power: The International Relations of Terrorists, Warlords and Insurgents.* London/New York: Routledge.

Waltz, K. N. (1979). *Theory of International Politics.* New York: McGraw-Hill.

Weber, M. (1968). *Economy and Society: An Outline of Interpretive Sociology* (G. Roth & C. Wittich, Ed.). Berkeley/Los Angeles: University of California Press.

Whitehead, N. L. (2004a). Introduction: Cultures, Conflicts, and the Poetics of Violent Practice. In N. L. Whitehead (Ed.), *Violence* (pp. 3–24). Santa Fe, NM: School of American Research Press.

Whitehead, N. L. (2004b). On the Poetics of Violence. In N. L. Whitehead (Ed.), *Violence* (pp. 55–77). Santa Fe, NM: School of American Research Press.

Willems, H. (2012). *Synthetische Soziologie: Idee, Entwurf und Programm.* Wiesbaden, Germany: VS Verlag für Sozialwissenschaften.

Wimmer, A. (2005). *Kultur als Prozess: Zur Dynamik des Aushandelns von Bedeutungen.* Wiesbaden, Germany: VS Verlag für Sozialwissenschaften.

Wimmer, A. (2013). *Ethnic Boundary Making: Institutions, Power, Networks.* Oxford, UK: Oxford University Press.

Winters, J. A. (2011). *Oligarchy.* Cambridge, UK/New York: Cambridge University Press.

Wood, E. J. (2008). The Social Processes of Civil War: The Wartime Transformation of Social Networks. *Annual Review of Political Science, 11*(1), 539–561.

Zinecker, H. (2007). *Kolumbien und El Salvador im longitudinalen Vergleich: Ein kritischer Beitrag zur Transitionsforschung.* Baden-Baden, Germany: Nomos.

Zinecker, H. (2011). Gewalt- und Friedensforschung – funktioniert der entwicklungstheoretische Kompass? In P. Schlotter & S. Wisotzki (Eds.), *Friedens- und Konfliktforschung* (pp. 139–182). Baden-Baden, Germany: Nomos.

Zinecker, H. (2014). *Gewalt im Frieden: Formen und Ursachen der Gewaltkriminalität in Zentralamerika.* Baden-Baden, Germany: Nomos.

CHAPTER 3

The Roots of Current Violence: Historical Comparative Perspectives on El Salvador, Jamaica, and Belize, 1500–1980

The initial focus on larger periods, on the *longue durée*, allows integrating the three cases under study into a larger picture usually described as globalization. Surely, this "big picture" leans on a grand narrative exposing the significance of particular events and ignoring the significance of others. Elsenhans (2015) provides such a grand narrative. He argues that capitalism initially emerges out of a specific class antagonism only to be found in Western Europe in the eighteenth century. Concentrating on these internal dynamics, he shows that the subaltern class was able to raise and strengthen its bargaining power vis-à-vis the elite. In this process, internal demand for industrial products developed, which ultimately led to the emergence of capitalist profit. Accordingly, capitalism is a weak and unstable mode of production that depends on the bargaining power of the working class. Only in capitalism can politics become separated from economics. Although capitalism emerged endogenously, it tends to be expansive. According to Elsenhans, capitalism is nonetheless too weak to transform non-capitalist modes of production into a self-sustaining capitalist system in which profit dominates. In the periphery, capitalism has merely produced waves of *incomplete* penetration causing unequal economic developments on a global scale. These inequalities render it necessary to talk about areas in the sense of different regional patterns of development and their integration into the world system. This approach follows Bayly's (2004) distinction between archaic and modern globalization. Archaic globalization refers to the expansion of agrarian

© The Author(s) 2019   59
H. Warnecke-Berger, *Politics and Violence in Central America and the Caribbean*, https://doi.org/10.1007/978-3-319-89782-0_3

empires of the *ancien régime*. Due to comparative advantages and through long-distance trade, empires or city-states or both came into contact with each other and intensified economic relations.

THE LEGACIES

Latin America and the Caribbean were integrated into the emerging world system by force, initially to satisfy the demand for precious metal due to negative balances of payments of European monarchs with the Far East. The search for gold and silver was the driving force behind this archaic globalization and finally led to the creation of a hierarchical world order. While archaic globalization and the first wave of Europe's expansion towards the New World sought to sustain the *ancient régime*, this motivation changed with a second wave of expansion. Once established, capitalism transformed social relations and integrated those relations functionally into an expansive system of social (re)production. With increasing capitalist economic interactions on a global scale, globalization entered a modern stage and these patterns altered dramatically. Thus, globalization entered a qualitative new stage in the mid-nineteenth century. With the emergence of the "global condition" (Bright & Geyer, 2012), core capitalist societies initially experienced steady economic growth and processes of democratization. However, the periphery at that time did not equally participate in these processes. With the emergence of the global condition, the worldwide political and economic hierarchy was determined. What happened in the periphery, however, were significant changes, since systems of (re)production were reorganized according to the needs and demands of core capitalist societies.

These global processes shaped the three cases under research differently. The integration of the Caribbean and Latin America temporally varied. While the first wave of integration produced the economic roots of today's political economy of the Caribbean, the independence of Latin America was a first harbinger of the second wave. Central America followed this trend and integrated following the second wave. Apart from this temporal difference, Jamaica, El Salvador, and Belize were shaped immensely by the integration into the emerging world system. By concentrating on the production and appropriation of economic surplus, this section reveals these changes by focusing on legacies of surplus appropriation, its particular political forms, and emerging class configurations. The section parallels these findings by looking at the embeddedness of violence into these social formations.

The Historical Origins of Rent-Led Development

Jamaica was the first of the three societies that attracted the attention of metropolitan great powers. Initially, the island was integrated into the world system by Spain, which then was quickly replaced by Great Britain. The reason for Jamaica's integration was sugar production. El Salvador, which became part of the Spanish colonial empire, initially relied on indigo production.[1] Its integration intensified almost 200 years later with the Liberal Reforms in 1881/82 and the advent of coffee. At this time, sugar production was already in decline in Jamaica. Belize's role was to export logwood[2] and mahogany. Its integration accelerated throughout the eighteenth century. In all three societies, the integration into the world system created incentives to appropriate economic rents. This appropriation was mainly based on the ownership of land although the structure of landownership and the means to appropriate rent differed considerably. In El Salvador, an independent peasantry could develop until the Liberal Reforms, given that landownership, until then, was less exclusive than in Jamaica and in Belize. In Belize and Jamaica, in contrast, the dominance of slavery impeded the lower strata to access their means of subsistence autonomously.

As part of the Captaincy General, El Salvador was initially not attached to larger economic and political networks. Central America in general played a minor role in the Spanish Colonial Empire (MacLeod, 1973). Inside Central America, a small elite settled in Guatemala City where it dominated trade and internal economic activities. During the eighteenth century, El Salvador saw a rise in indigo production. While Guatemalan colonial elites controlled the financing and marketing of the crop, production was organized in both large haciendas as well as in small peasant communities on the Salvadoran territory (Lauria-Santiago, 1999). At the same time, the expanding indigo economy gave rise to neighboring economic sectors, such as cattle farming and food production. Despite being dominated by large landholders, indigo production provoked increasing production by peasants (Lindo-Fuentes, 1995). In contrast to Jamaica, where slavery impeded the development of an independent peasantry, these peasants, either ladino[3] or indigenous, were able to secure independent access to land and to safeguard economic autonomy vis-à-vis the landholding elite. During the post-independence period, El Salvador became "a stronghold of small-scale peasant producers with secure but complex (and often different) access to land" (Lauria-Santiago, 1999, p. 35).

The late step towards integration into the world system came with the Liberal Reforms in 1881 and 1882, which deeply transformed the Salvadorian society. These reforms were responsible for initial processes of state formation, the beginning of oligarchic domination by the famous 14 families, and the development of class antagonism. These changes determined a new development path that was challenged and modified in the following years of the Great Depression. The objective of the Liberal Reforms was the privatization of communal land; subsequently, this altered indigenous and peasant traditions of land use.

These reforms encouraged the cultivation of coffee, which caused, on the one hand, a first wave of land concentration and an increase of wealth of a small elite,[4] and on the other hand, the establishment of wage labor as the dominant labor relation on the coffee fincas. During this period, El Salvador saw the rise of two new subaltern groups: semi-proletarians who worked seasonally on the coffee fincas, and *colonos*, resident labor to whom landlords provided plots to engage in subsistence production (Gould & Lauria-Santiago, 2008).

Although coffee cultivation started well before, the Liberal Reforms virtually made coffee to the sole engine of economic and social developments. Coffee production grew particularly in the western departments of El Salvador on Vulcan slopes where Indian peasant communities were strong. The Liberal Reforms therefore deeply changed the political economy of El Salvador. During the colonial era and in post-independence times, labor was scarce in contrast to land. With the Liberal Reforms this ratio turned. By the end of the nineteenth century, 20 years after the Liberal Reforms, the agrarian frontier was closed and land became scarce (Lauria-Santiago & Gould, 2004, p. 198). With increasing population (population of El Salvador between 1880 and 1930 almost doubled with an annual growth of 2.06 percent, see Cardenal Izquierdo, 2002, p. 21), the pressure of land scarcity even intensified and led to a second wave of land concentration in the 1920s. During this wave, many poor peasants were forced either to abandon their plots and to fully work on the coffee fincas or to migrate to cities (Wilson, 2004, pp. 101–107). From this time on, urban and rural social situations diverged. With increasing coffee production, the export-oriented wing of the oligarchy increased its power relative to coffee producers and established itself as a dominant faction (Lindo-Fuentes, 1990, p. 182; North, 1982, p. 31). Particularly export-oriented oligarchy members invested a minor part of their rent incomes in urban infrastructure and petty industries (Dunkerley, 1982, p. 20).

Consequently, a new group of urban artisans developed based on wage labor (Zamosc, 1989, pp. 60–61).

To sum up, El Salvador was integrated into the world system through its coffee production. Coffee production led to the decomposition of the independent small holding peasantry and at the same time to the formation of a textbook oligarchy (Colindres, 1977). At the same time, urbanization increased and created a distinct social environment in cities. While in rural areas of El Salvador repression and the expulsion of peasant communities dominated, urban centers and particularly San Salvador experienced a process of limited urban democratization.

Jamaica was discovered by Spain and served for long time as a geographical hinterland for buccaneers and pirates. With the arrival of the English and the defeat of Spain in Ocho Rios in 1657, the island became increasingly important for Europe.[5] After some decades of conflict between buccaneers and newly arriving white planters, the latter took over the island and founded large plantations (Dunn, 1972, p. 149). The increasing demand for sugar in the colonial homeland led to Jamaica's specialization in sugar production. With increasing real wages in Europe, this specialization was self-reinforcing since sugar became democratized in Europe and demand for sugar grew (Mintz, 1987). Jamaica therefore was integrated into the world system as a prime producer of sugar, particularly for the European market. Regarding its economic importance and its geopolitical role, Jamaica was the "powerhouse" (Higman, 2008, p. 3) in the Atlantic world for the British Empire. While sugar production at early stages was still modest (Eltis, 2003, p. 63), by the late seventeenth and the beginning of the eighteenth century, transportation technology brought Jamaica into the range of European slave and commodity markets (Eltis, 2000, p. 27) and led to the triangular slave trade (Curtin, 1969; Inikori & Engerman, 1998). After 1655, the slave population in Jamaica increased considerably (Curtin, 1969, p. 56). The production system changed in line with this trend. Until then, plantations and slavery dominated the economic sphere, at least until Emancipation.[6] During this phase, labor scarcity dominated Jamaica's economic situation since the reproduction of labor was not guaranteed and slaves had to be imported continuously.

The Jamaican society at that time was clearly dominated by a white[7] oligarchy of planters, who formed a "racist oligarchic parliamentarism (...), backed by a more or less non-governing colonial office" (Stinchcombe, 1995, p. 13).[8] The large majority of the population therefore was enslaved and subordinated to a small oligarchy of white planters, either residents in

Jamaica or absentee owners. In 1834, the population was as large as 368,600, with only 4.5 percent whites and 84.1 percent slaves. Around 11 percent was either freed colored or freed black people (Heuman, 2003, p. 657). Freed colored people, although economically marginalized, often received preferential treatment and enjoyed higher job opportunities on plantations.

Although the class of white planters remained the most prominent political force in Jamaica, they got under serious pressure. Externally, the planter oligarchy lost influence in the British Parliament that redefined its positions vis-à-vis the Colonial Office (Porter, 1999). This new and problematic role was echoed by serious internal challenges. Even though the oligarchy introduced several laws to constrain the economic freedom of newly freed slaves quickly after Emancipation, the planter class could not impede slaves to transform into "proto-peasants."[9] After Emancipation, small peasant freeholdings increased considerably (Eisner, 1961, pp. 210–235; Holt, 1992, p. 146). While slavery and plantation production should have impeded the development of an independent peasantry, the supply of labor increased with a growth of the population after Emancipation and led to a small peasant economy (Marshall, 1968; Mintz, 1996).

However, this peasantry was never independent in the sense of a precapitalist production unit oriented towards subsistence, since it remained related to and sometimes even dependent on plantations and therefore differed immensely from El Salvadoran peasant communities (Mintz, 2003). Small peasants were not concentrated in the hinterland but in central parishes, where subsistence farming was compatible with occasional work on plantations (Sheller, 2001, p. 50). By 1865 and as a reaction to the Morant Bay rebellion, Jamaica became Crown Colony. The local plantocracy lost direct control, the House of Assembly was closed, and executive powers of the governor of Jamaica increased. This, however, was not the loss of total control of the planter class, since land ownership remained centralized and was never touched by the Crown.[10]

Even before Emancipation, the plantation economy began to deteriorate. Sugar prices as well as income from sugar exports peaked in 1805, subsequently falling almost throughout the whole nineteenth century (Galloway, 1989). In line with decreasing prices, sugar as percentage of total exports began to decrease. Beginning in the 1880s, many plantation owners switched to the production of banana (Bulmer-Thomas, 2012, p. 111). At the same time, banana production created new opportunities for small peasants.[11] The decomposition of sugar plantations led to the emergence of a small but growing brown middle class that had its roots in the administration and management of sugar plantations, and became increasingly engaged in merchandise activities or was able to buy small plots of land (Beckford & Witter, 1980, p. 44). About 50 years later, this "brown" middle class would become an important political force.

In summary, the integration of Jamaica into the world system produced a sharp bifurcation between slaves on the one hand, and a white and wealthy planter class on the other hand. Both colored people and freed slaves were socially and economically excluded. While sugar production served as a vehicle for integration, it became seriously challenged with the end of slavery. At the end of the nineteenth century, banana production served as an initial substitute but did not absorb enough labor. The consequence was intensified urbanization and the formation of squatter settlements around the capital city of Kingston (Clarke, 2006).

Belize developed as a frontier zone between Guatemala and Yucatan (Restall, 2014). From its early beginnings, the economic structure was based on slavery, forestry, and the export of primary products (Bolland, 2003). The beginning of the settlement at the mouth of Belize River dates back to the mid-seventeenth century. At that time, the territory today known as Belize[12] served as an area of retreat for pirates and buccaneers who plundered Spanish trade ships. With the Treaty of Madrid in 1670, Spain had to recognize British naval dominance in the Atlantic world (Davies, 1974). In Belize, this treaty encouraged former pirates to engage in logwood cutting instead of attacking the Spanish trade. Insecure property rights, the small population, and the steady threat from Spain impeded the development of a domestic economy. Initially, Belize therefore developed as a "logwood economy" (Bulmer-Thomas & Bulmer-Thomas, 2012, p. 41). However, at the time when the Treaty of Paris legalized logwood exports in 1763, the logwood economy was already declining in profitability. In the early 1770s, the economy experienced serious pressure. With increasing demand for English luxury furniture, mahogany served as a profitable alternative to logwood. Britain mahogany imports increased considerably, particularly during the nineteenth century. The share of these imports coming from Belize was traditionally high (up to 80 percent) (Bulmer-Thomas & Bulmer-Thomas, 2012, p. 71).

Like in Jamaica, although some 100 years later, slavery became a dominant feature of the Belizean economy with the shift towards mahogany export. In 1783, 75 percent of the population of around 3500 people mainly living in and around Belize Town (what later became Belize City) were slaves (Bolland, 2003, p. 54). Following the Caste War in Yucatán, an increasing number of Maya refugees settled in the northern and southern districts (Reed, 2001). The Maya remained largely untouched and engaged in subsistence production.

Timber extraction differed considerably from plantation work in Jamaica (Bolland, 1981). Firstly, cutting timber required shifting the production unit from location to location instead of producing sugar on a permanent production site. Secondly, cutting logwood did not require large amounts of capital as producing and refining sugar did. While in Jamaica most plantation slaves worked in larger groups, mahogany gangs were smaller groups of 10 up to 12 slaves. However, mahogany trees are large, heavy, and grew in the interior of the country, and in contrast to logwood, more capital, more land, and especially intensive labor was needed.

With the alternation of exports from logwood to mahogany, land ownership became a key factor.[13] As mahogany trees grow sparsely and scattered in the interior of the country, the economic shift from logwood to mahogany encouraged initial cutters to concentrate large amounts of land in their hands. By the end of the eighteenth century, a well-established forestocracy controlled almost the entire country "owning most of the land and people, controlling all of the trade, import and export, wholesale and retail, and also controlling the judicial, legislative, and administrative organs of the settlement, called the Magistracy and the Public Meeting" (Bolland, 1981, p. 601).[14] This "forestocracy" led the overall majority of inhabitants into dependency (Ashcraft, 1969; Ashdown, 1981, 1982).

Unlike most other plantation economies in the Caribbean, the end of slavery in Belize did not lead to a depression or the end of primary (forestry) exports. On the contrary, mahogany exports continued to play the most important role until the late 1950s. What changed, however, were labor relations. After Emancipation, employers used labor laws to control the workforce. The truck system was intended to fulfil these requirements (Bolland, 2003): Wages were paid in advance and the laborer had to purchase his supplies prior to working in the wood-cutting gangs in the interior. The effect was that laborers ruinously spent their money together with their families (in particular during Christmas holidays) and then had to buy their daily supplies on credit during work seasons; indebtedness was the consequence. Comparable to Jamaica but different to El Salvador, restrictive labor laws as well as the monopolization of land impeded the development of an independent peasantry in Belize.

The main families engaged in forestry, services, and export maintained a complex relationship towards the colonial state. From the early beginnings of the settlement, they held public meetings and passed various resolutions. However, Great Britain regularly appointed superintendents who had to report to the governor of Jamaica. This caused the local oligarchy to come in conflict with the Empire. With the arrival of Superintendent George Arthur in 1814, this situation even intensified. The superintendent secured the Crown's authority to all future dispositions of unclaimed land. Even though this land was of inferior quality and of marginal importance for the mahogany producers, the Crown became the single largest landholder with huge possessions south of river Sibun.

By the late 1850s, mahogany exports experienced a sharp decline in quantities and prices, however, recovered two decades later (Bulmer-Thomas, 2012, Appendix, Table A.10). During this period, many of the larger landlords were unable to repay credit loans that they had been granted in London. British merchants used this opportunity and bought huge amounts of lands. This second wave of land concentration in the hand of metropolitan capital increased considerably throughout the nineteenth century with the effect that a single company, the Belize Estate and Produce Co., Ltd., "owned about half of all the freehold land of the colony" (Bolland, 1981, p. 602). By 1862, Belize became Crown Colony. The legal status of Belize changed the relation between the oligarchy and the Colonial Office. On the one hand, the Colonial Office recognized the oligarchy's economic weight although direct participation in political decision-making was unwelcomed. On the other hand, the colonial state provided economic stability by controlling and securing labor relations.

In summary, the integration into the world system in Belize was achieved through logwood and mahogany. Particularly for the extraction of the latter, slavery was introduced. A result of that shift in export goods was the concentration of land in the hands of a small forestocracy and later on, towards the end of the nineteenth century, in those of a single company. Since forest products were the only economic engine, no peasantry apart from the Maya population evolved.

At the turn of the twentieth century, all three societies served for a long time as primary producers and were, in this capacity, integrated into the world system. Although the sources of rent differed (sugar, mahogany, and coffee), rents were mainly appropriated through land ownership.

In Jamaica, the plantocracy formed a racial oligarchy, which monopolized access to land and produced sugar on slave plantations. Also in Belize, a landholding class emerged whose economic importance was rooted in export promotion and slavery. Both countries lacked a considerable and independent peasantry. First signs of a peasantry in Jamaica never led to a full development; in Belize, the oligarchy were even able to prevent this trend completely. In El Salvador, in contrast, independent peasants secured autonomy, at least until the Liberal Reforms. Until then, the forming oligarchy was able to distribute virtually the whole country under their own family members through the exclusion of peasants.

As an effect, labor relations differed considerably between the three cases. The Salvadorian economic roots in colonial times are to be found in subsistence farming and the hacienda system. The advent of coffee production challenged these roots and provoked the sharp social bifurcation between the oligarchy and the impoverished mass. Nevertheless, El Salvador experienced the development of an independent peasantry. Although this class almost entirely dissolved in a long process, at least cultural autonomy could be partially preserved. This is a main contrast to Jamaica and Belize. Slavery on the plantation in Jamaica and in the mahogany camps in Belize formed a legacy and prevented an independent peasantry from developing the internal market. The introduction of all three societies into the world system established oligarchic rule. While these oligarchies differed considerably in terms of the source of rent out of which it originated (coffee vs. sugar vs. mahogany), they were able to monopolize exportation and access to land. In the first decades of the twentieth century, these oligarchies came under serious pressure. In El Salvador, land concentration enforced the creation of two new subaltern groups, and therefore challenged the traditional social structure. In Jamaica, the decline of slavery and subsequent problems in developing an independent peasantry led to urbanization, particularly in Kingston. In Belize, the mahogany trade was unable to create full employment, at least at the beginning of the second decade of the twentieth century, and created increasing unrest, markedly in Belize City.

Emerging Cultural Scripts of Violence

These legacies were by no means static. Particularly in Jamaica and El Salvador, this social configuration has been challenged and disputed in several major occurrences. Apart from all differences, all three societies experienced a sharp bifurcation between a powerful oligarchy and the majority of the population. Violence was a continuing mode of either maintaining or challenging this antagonism. Vertical violence thus was almost ubiquitous in these times.

This view is supported by empirical evidence exemplifying that repression as well as rebellions have been endemic. In El Salvador, ethnic peasant communities continuously rebelled throughout the eighteenth and the nineteenth century (Tilley, 2005). In Jamaica, where dozens of slave riots occurred until 1865,[15] the judicial system served as a pivotal instrument in controlling slaves, and freed slaves and small peasants after Emancipation (Dalby, 2000). In Belize, vertical violence becomes particularly manifest in the case of punishment against slaves and workers (Bolland, 2003, p. 66).

By zooming on some of these violent events, this section generally confirms the importance of vertical violence. Furthermore, it shows that the characteristics of violence were different. In El Salvador, vertical violence mainly associated with the Liberal Reforms of 1881/1882 was accompanied by continuing ordinary horizontal violence. Due to a lack of detailed sources on a particular event in the case of El Salvador, this section supports this hypothesis by reinterpreting available data. Different to El Salvador, Jamaica did not experience horizontal violence. The analysis of the Morant Bay rebellion, one of the most important violent events in Jamaica's history because of its scale both in the insurgency as well as in the government's reaction, exposes that insurgent vertical violence even relied on colonial cultural scripts. Thus, continuing ordinary horizontal violence particularly based on the mobilization and the defense of honor indicates the strength of cultural scripts of violence in distant to superior authorities[16] in El Salvador. In contrast to El Salvador, extreme verticalization in Jamaica due to slavery explains the unavailability of autochthonous cultural scripts. Belize is a hybrid in this regard and this section shows that horizontal violence, even though perhaps not as deeply rooted as in El Salvador, played an important role.

In El Salvador, ordinary horizontal violence seems to have continuously accompanied vertical violence. This parallelism will become clearer in the next section when the interrelations between horizontal and vertical violence can be shown in detail by the example of the insurgency of 1932. This section prepares this argument by providing a collection and reinterpretation of the sparse sources on horizontal violence in the nineteenth century.

In 1847, a press article commented on the state of security in El Salvador. The anonymous author acknowledged that

> you can see a multitude of lazy children in the street, jobless, without going to school, without knowing what their parents are doing, and without that anyone would take care of their behaviour and education (...) All of them wear daggers, knives, and other prohibited weapons under their shirts, all day and night, in the city as well as in the countryside. (Gaceta Del Salvador, 1847, p. 7)[17]

In a statistical overview about crimes committed in the first two months of the year 1848, the *Gaceta Del Salvador* (1848, p. 208) reported that 97 homicides were committed and even more persons were injured. Several decades later, in 1883, the *Diario Oficial* (*Diario Oficial,* 1883) published several statistics on crimes in El Salvador showing that the number of homicides and serious crimes in proportion to the size of the population remained stable. Of course, the figures need to be treated with caution and are not reliable. If we turn to the codification of the crimes, however, it is interesting to note that a considerable share of serious conflicts was classified as not clearly related to politics but to passions (or were at least interpreted in that way). Many of these violent conflicts took the shape of family wars, vendettas and cycles of revenge (Herrera Mena, 2011). In this case, honor and shame as well as the production of rumors and fears served as the regulating force of violence because no other durable institutions existed (Riekenberg, 2014; Taylor, 1979).

This cultural script entangling violence with honor can even be observed in the numerous internal wars of federation all over Central America. During the first half of the nineteenth century, El Salvador was engaged in at least 10 wars with its neighbor countries so that "war became a way of life" (Lindo-Fuentes, 1990, p. 48). It resulted in 2546 dead persons in more than 40 battles, which is consistent with other sources about Central America warfare in the nineteenth century (Euraque, 2000). Homicidal violence in this period seemed contrastingly low compared to warfare outside of Central America. It is surprising that warfare violence did not provoke even larger lethal outcomes. Warfare violence, which was exerted mostly by ordinary people from the countryside or members of local militias, was embedded in the local logic of everyday live. Without direct involvement of superior state authorities, rituals and forms of moral economy regulated everyday interactions and conflicts, particularly inside the peasantry. In this context, honor constituted "a right that had to be defended daily, against many threats, and at very high costs" (Piccato, 2001, p. 81). Conflicts violently escalated because firstly, honor rarely serves as a durable means of organizing violence; secondly, because other means were lacking; and thirdly, because it might not have been possible to continuously mobilize honor in these everyday confrontations.

At the time when the Liberal Reforms were introduced in 1881, violence began to change. On the one hand, repression increased considerably. Violence that was driven by state institutions such as the forming police force as well as militias on behalf of landlords exposes that vertical violence became a dominant feature of everyday life. On the other hand, horizontal violence seems to have continued. The Liberal Reforms were accompanied by the destruction of culturally codified allocation and the redistribution of land use rights. This tradition had been relevant for the peaceful management of conflicts. Inasmuch as this tradition lost its validity, the production of security became a serious issue. Increasingly, honor violence was connoted with newly emergent meanings. With the increasing fragmentation of the peasantry during the Liberal Reforms and the expulsion from their land, violence was linked to robberies in rural areas, the theft of coffee, and conflicts with new landlords about land-use rights. Violence thus occurred in relation to denied access to means of subsistence. The theft of cattle and coffee, particularly in the western part of the country where the concentration of arable land in the hands of the forming oligarchy was more advanced, was perceived by the elite as such an immense problem that, in reaction, a specialized police force was formed (Alvarenga, 2006, pp. 86–90).[18]

This change might suggest that honor violence faded away and was replaced by a new cultural script of violence. However, the change seems more complex and did not lead to the dissolution of honor violence. Instead, this section supports the view that even though *conflicts* switched towards a vertical level, *violence* still remained horizontal. This is a crucial argument because it claims that micro phenomena, such as practices of violence, do not necessarily occur in accordance with the macro level, such as larger conflicts, in which they are embedded. Between both levels exist intersections, but they have to be created by strategic action.

With the intensification of elite struggles over indigenous lands and the clientelistic incorporation of local bosses, local conflicts were co-opted into politics (Ching, 2014). With the emergence of a national, even though still fractionalized, elite, local conflicts about honor and the regulation of everyday life were integrated into larger arenas: municipal elections (Suter, 1996b). Local power holders had to organize their votes to get access to political positions such as *alcaldes* or chiefs of militias. These local bosses were part of even larger networks led by national leaders and the wealthiest oligarchic families, who were struggling for higher positions in the growing state apparatus. Both cultural scripts of violence, honor violence and subsistence violence, now were attached to politics. That is not to say, that violence was per se transformed, but its meaning was altered. Horizontal violence still occurred, however, power brokers construed it for their own political aspirations.

The manipulation of cultural scripts seems to be an important strategy to link superior scales of political action into local-level politics. A showcase of this process is the integration of ordinary people first into militias and later on into networks of social control and vigilance (Alvarenga, 1998). Violence exercised by previously normal citizens was now exercised on behalf of institutions even though the (private) conflicts remained the same. Violence in ordinary conflicts did not completely lose its previous meanings; they were, however, manipulated and linked to new cultural scripts: violence to control. In the process of state formation this was an inexpensive way of centralizing rudimentary state functions in the hands of the elite. Later on, the same principles were used in the formation of large networks of political control in the countryside as it was the case of the *Liga Roja*, a trade union with the objective to co-opt the working class into oligarchic rule. Similar processes can be observed, for instance, in the emerging discourses on the penitentiary system, which were linked to social hygienic ideas of social control (Herrera Mena, 2007). Local meanings of violence as a possible force to regulate conflicts were challenged, however, never disbanded.

Even though vertical violence as repression (the Liberal Reforms were indeed imposed by force) or of rebellion predominated, the discussion suggests that horizontal violence continued as honor violence. Nevertheless, horizontal violence changed, perhaps fragmented, and, as this chapter argues, became co-opted into the rising authoritarian oligarchic rule. This is a provocative hypothesis as it would ultimately mean that the emerging authoritarian oligarchic regime did not manage to control violence, but concentrated on meanings of violence instead of focusing on practices of violence. The validation of this hypotheses, however, is difficult since historical sources are still too sparse to reach a final conclusion.

For Jamaica, horizontal violence seems to be almost entirely absent. With the focus on vertical violence, however, this section shows that even cultural scripts of insurgent vertical violence heavily relied on existent cultural scripts provided or imposed by colonial authorities. A rebellion, which had its roots in conflicts over taxes, wages, and the local judiciary system dominated by a white planter, the famous Morant Bay rebellion, serves as a show case. The central issue particularly for small settlers and peasants at this time was "access to land as a means of resisting the necessity to work on the estates" (Bakan, 1990, p. 88). At the same time, the Morant Bay rebellion was paralleled by longstanding fears of black conspiracies to overthrow the dominant white plantocracy (Heuman, 1994, xiii). Although the rebellion itself was not a spontaneous eruption but planned and organized in various meetings held in Native Baptist chapels, the rebellious crowd itself acted as a mob. Paul Bogle, Baptist deacon and key leader, knew how to charge grievances and feelings of relative deprivation with religious meanings (Heuman, 1995). One observer noted that participants "took the oath, they kissed a large book, the Bible. Paul Bogle gave them a dram and gunpowder which they drank" (Heuman, 1994, p. 6). Bogle organized several hundred black men to march into Morant Bay. While walking into the town, the crowd was singing, "dancing and blowing horns," and carrying a red flag. They were poorly armed: Some had guns, but most of them wore sticks. The mob first attacked the police station and took guns and other weapons. Subsequently, the crowd marched towards the courthouse where the parish vestry held its regular meeting. After some skirmishes with the local militia, the crowd burned down the courthouse and killed several members of the vestry. Taken together, 18 of the vestry and the protecting militia, and seven members of the mob were killed that day (Heuman, 1994, p. 3).

As an immediate response, the governor of Jamaica, John Eyre, feared to lose control of the island since he assumed an island-wide black conspiracy. He ordered government troops to crush the rebellion. Several hundred blacks were killed, often innocent. Through this slaughter, "the government was intent to establishing its authority and on stifling black political expression of any kind" (Heuman, 1994, p. 143). In the aftermath of the rebellion, Jamaica became Crown Colony; and the Jamaica Constabulary Force was created several months after the rebellion. As an effect, the colonial office fortified its position against the white planter class and gained control in Jamaica. Even though the formal system of government transformed into the common system of Crown Colony, "land policy, laws and magistracy were not substantially changed in the nineteenth century" (Craton, 1997, p. 336). Violence was either oriented to challenge these inequalities, as the Morant Bay rebellion shows, or simply redefined as a threat to the plantocracy's domination. The Jamaican path of dealing with violence was repression.

After having described the sequence of events of the Morant Bay rebellion, looking at practices of violence will show that mob violence used by subalterns to challenge elite suppression followed certain moral economies of violence. Three issues will receive attention in the following section as they expose the cultural script of violence. Firstly, the exertion of violence was based on everyday meanings (e.g. moral beliefs about good and bad). Victims were targeted selectively. Persons perceived as good were spared from sanctions; persons perceived as bad were injured or killed. Secondly, the internal organization of the mob calls for examination. Carrying a flag and marching in line resembles military warfare and therefore points to the cultural appropriation of colonial warfare. Dancing, singing, blowing horns, in contrast, may have served to overcome fears and to secure group cohesion. At the same time, these practices were deeply rooted in experiences of slavery and racial subordination and formed part of a cultural resistance against colonial repression (Meeks, 2000). Thirdly and lastly, the mobilizer Paul Bogle was a translator of these scripts. He was able to organize violence by transferring Native Baptist Christian ideas of justice into the material life world of landlessness and injustice. The Morant Bay rebellion best exposes this cultural script. At least since this event, mob violence entangling appropriated and autochthonous practices of violence was a recurrent form of violence in Jamaica.

Belize shared some of the developments with Jamaica and others with El Salvador. Comparable to Jamaica, the forestocracy feared social unrest in the country. As in El Salvador and Jamaica, violence was predominantly vertical, and the riot of 1894 disclosed that Belize was deeply divided along class and racial lines. Contrary to Jamaica and to El Salvador, however, the forestocracy rarely relied on open repression. Thus, the comparatively modest output of violence attracts attention, both violence of the rioters as well as of opposing officials. During the riot of 1894, the rioters, armed with sticks and fences, mainly intended to attack stores and property without, however, exerting overt violence. They demanded higher wages without touching the land issue (Ashdown, 1980). Almost the same happened again in 1919 when Belizean soldiers of the British West Indian

Regiment, who were fighting in World War I, articulated popular discontent (Ashdown, 1978, p. 67). In both cases, forms of violence resemble one another and are best classified as related to bread-and-butter issues. These two events suggest certain similarities with Jamaica, although the reaction of the forestocracy and the colonial state never had the same intensity as in Jamaica.

At the same time, some evidence points towards a similarity between Belize and El Salvador related to the depth of horizontal violence. At the turn of the century, Robert Wyatt (1908), the British Honduran commissioner of police, reported to the Colonial Office in London about the state of security in the Crown Colony. In his report, he stated that "quarrels apparently without any reason commence and a deadly blow is given" and that "all the serious crimes of violence against the person were committed in out-of-the-way places far from a Police Station." Of course, Robert Wyatt speaks as a state official. However, it is remarkable that he recognized that ordinary conflicts quickly escalated into violence "without any reason" and in "out-of-the-way places far from a Police Station" in distance to the state. However, there are still too few reliable sources to get a more detailed view on violence in Belize at this time.

The discussion showed that violence in all three cases was already deeply embedded in each society. While in Jamaica cultural scripts of violence originated as a mixture of appropriated as well as autochthonous scripts and merged into mob violence as it could be seen in the Morant Bay rebellion, El Salvador presents clearly autochthonous cultural scripts rooted in everyday peasant life. These scripts are based on honor as well as the struggle for subsistence. In this regard, Belize resembles more Jamaica than El Salvador. While in all three cases vertical violence surely dominated, a closer look on El Salvador and Belize suggests the importance of horizontal violence. This is even more surprising since the political economy of all three cases points to the immanence of a vertical conflict setting between oligarchies and the subordinated majority.

At the turn of the century, the political economy of Jamaica, El Salvador, and Belize was characterized by the heavy dependence on few export commodities. All three societies virtually developed along these commodities: Not only did the economies rely on exportation of these commodities, but also the entire social fabric. This unbalanced export orientation rendered all three cases particularly prone to external economic shocks. Indeed, exactly this situation turned out to be fatal during the world economic crisis in the 1930s.

CHALLENGING THE LEGACIES: THE GREAT DEPRESSION OF THE 1930s

After a short period of (unbalanced) growth, the global condition got under immense pressure in the third decade of the twentieth century. The Great Depression was the result of this pressure, but it was flanked by two world wars (James, 2001). The Great Depression and the two world wars led to the short twentieth century. Violent eruptions were the most visible historical events during this time (Bolland, 2001; Wolf, 2001). The Great Depression of the 1930s therefore functions as a lens through which rapid social change can be analyzed in detail. During these decades, for the first time for all three cases, quickly accelerating experiences of globalization became compressed and translated into concrete patterns of social action. In the aftermath of the Great Depression, "national" political regimes were established or institutionalized, promises for development were made, and alternative development paths were searched. In terms of political economy, the Great Depression challenged yet established institutional forms of political power, authority, and domination. The first three decades of the twentieth century formed part of the "*Sattelzeit*" (Koselleck, 1972, xvi) of Latin American and Caribbean modern politics. Zinecker (2007, p. 209) develops a useful typology of the political economy of regime change. She distinguishes for Latin American societies three paths in which political forms of rent appropriation changed. Firstly, existing oligarchies were displaced by emerging state-classes through large-scale social movements. Secondly, existing oligarchies did split into a modernized, middle-class oriented and a more traditional wing. Finally, a third path describes the self-transformation of the oligarchy towards a completely new type of oligarchy. Jamaica clearly followed the first path, El Salvador the latter, and Belize the second path, giving rise to a particular hybrid elite. Even though the Great Depression produced similar resonances in each case, the cases varied decisively in their reactions and decisions how to deal with violence. In the light of the *longue durée*, the Great Depression thus reveals a moment of major divergence.

The Great Depression of the 1930s provoked major uprisings in all three cases. Beginning with El Salvador in 1932, Belize in 1934, and followed by Jamaica in 1938, these uprisings challenged the development path that had previously been taken by these societies. In El Salvador, the uprising encouraged an institutional alliance between the oligarchy and the military under subsequent economic and political exclusion of the mass, which was maintained at least for the following 70 years. In Jamaica and Belize (although the question of political independence was prolonged in Belize due to the border conflict with Guatemala), and different to El Salvador, national independence movements arose from these uprisings. In both cases, these movements and their leaders became pivotal mobilizers of violence, although through different means. The differences between Jamaica and Belize are related to the different effects of the Great Depression in both societies. While in Jamaica and Belize rent appropriation continued, the social class that was able to gain access to rents differed. In Belize, the "old" forestocracy diversified and secured their access to rents. In Jamaica, in contrast, a newly emerging middle class was able to partly displace the "old" plantocracy.

Economic Collapse and Worsening Social Conditions in the 1930s

Since all three societies under research relied on few single export commodities as "national" engines of growth and social welfare, their economies nearly collapsed during the Great Depression. All three societies experienced a sharp fall in export earnings and encountered serious difficulties in maintaining their social fabric. The onset and the course of the Great Depression proceeded with similar intensity but differed sharply in its temporality and its outcomes in terms of political economy.

El Salvador, temporally the first of the three societies that had experienced a major uprising, was hit by the depression after almost 50 years of steady growth in coffee production. By the beginning of 1932, erupting social problems as well as long-lasting traditions of violence culminated in the short rebellion and subsequent mass killings of the *matanza*. As land in relation to people was scarce, the world economic crisis of the 1930s accelerated social problems and led to increasing levels of unemployment (Bulmer-Thomas, 1987, pp. 48–67). Under the impression of economic decline, the first free election took place in March 1931, and Arturo Araujo became president. Despite his claims to initiate social reforms, the Great Depression led to shrinking government revenues and forced him to abandon reforms. In the face of worsening economic conditions and fears of social unrest, he made concessions to the military (Paige, 1997, p. 111). Nevertheless, the military revolted in a coup d'état on December 2, 1931 and General Maximiliano Hernández Martínez was proclaimed the new president. Worsening economic conditions were paralleled by political deprivation, and brought urban communists and rural peasant together to revolt against the deplorable social reality.

Jamaica, in contrast to El Salvador, already experienced a secular but slow decline in the sugar industry long before the Great Depression. During the 1930s, however, sugar and banana prices nearly collapsed (Post, 1978, p. 88). In the early 1930s, unemployment rose to levels never seen before—at least 25 percent of the population remained unemployed (Edie, 1991, p. 30). It was an economic trigger, which culminated in 1938 and led to the largest labor uprising the country ever experienced.

The Belizean economic situation, similar to Jamaica, slightly deteriorated even before the crisis of the 1930s. For the first time in history, Belize experienced a serious labor surplus in 1914 (Bulmer-Thomas & Bulmer-Thomas, 2012, pp. 106–110). In 1929, mahogany exports collapsed. In 1931, Great Britain furthermore abandoned the gold standard and thereby significantly increased Belizean export prices. Export volumes sharply declined after 1930. Moreover, the country was hit by a devastating hurricane in 1931, which caused serious damage, particularly in Belize City (Grant, 1976, pp. 61–65). Unemployment was on the rise forcing colonial authorities to provide resources from the Colonial Development Fund. These funds were mainly directed towards the middle class and the forestocracy; the working poor and therefore the great majority only partially benefited from public works programs. In this regard, the economic crisis was underlined by political grievances similar to El Salvador.

Because of these processes, all three cases experienced social unrest. In El Salvador, the government reacted to the uprising of 1932 with a genocide of indigenous peasants. In Belize, the labor uprising of 1934 provoked government concessions, and in Jamaica, the labor uprising of 1938 initiated decolonization.

Cultural Scripts of Violence During the Great Depression

Even though the Great Depression seems to have produced similar effects in each case, a detailed analysis of practices of violence exerted during each uprising underlines that once again harsh changes in the political economy translated into changing cultural scripts of violence. These cultural scripts of violence, even though changing, still fit into already established cultural experiences. Only after the Great Depression, major changes in the evolution of cultural scripts came to the fore.

El Salvador was the first of the cases that experienced turmoil. Violence in El Salvador still remained predominantly rural. Although urban communists were driving forces behind the planning and the organization of the uprising that took place in 1932, urban agency was still modest compared to the explosion of rural unrest in the countryside. Since the regime imposed by Hernández Martínez came under international pressure (Dur, 1998) and faced serious internal tensions, the government was forced to hold communal elections. Beginning with heavy electoral fraud during the communal elections in 1932, the Salvadoran Communist Party (*Partido Comunista Salvadoreño*, PCS) embarked on the preparation of a rebellion. Major mobilizing groups were the PCS under the leadership of Jorge Fernández Anaya and Augustín Farabundo Martí, university students, artisans as well as wageworkers in San Salvador, and certain parts of the military. However, the military government discovered the plans for revolution; the attempted takeover of a military barrack in San Salvador by the revolutionaries on January 16 failed. Two days later, Farabundo Martí was arrested and executed shortly thereafter.

In rural areas of El Salvador and particularly in the western departments, the rebellion took another shape. After some initial riots, people revolted on January 22, 1932. The centers of the uprising were Juayúa, Izalco and Nahuizalco in Sonsonate and Tacuba in Ahuachapán, particularly where oligarchic coffee cultivation quickly increased after the Liberal Reforms. However, none of these towns was held by the uprising mass for more than a couple of days. Shortly after the beginning of the uprising, the military struck back. Military raids in the towns led to mass executions and in the following weeks to the planned genocidal annihilation of indigenous peasants and alleged communists (Suter, 1996a).

Although the uprising as well as the government's reaction was a clear demonstration of vertical violence, horizontal violence continued to play an important role. This becomes evident in practices of violence exerted in the uprising shortly before the mass killings of the *matanza* in 1932. Historical accounts emphasize certain ritualizations of violence (Dunkerley, 1982; Pérez Brignoli, 1995). The insurgents assembled in front of the villages that they wanted to invade, shouting and making noise. Once they got into the villages, they eventually arrested or killed the *alcalde*, plundered the local food shop, and got drunk. At the end, the "defeated" (and often *ladino*) women had to cook and to dance for them on the local market square. All this indicates more the production of spectacles than a clear revolution against "the state" or "the elite" and points to still existing cultural scripts of violence entangled in peasant life (Gould, 2010). Finally, the social figures able to mobilize violence during the uprising call for attention. While in an urban environment, leftist political activists such as Farabundo Martí gained support by means of ideology, in rural milieus *caciques* and members of the traditional *cofradías*, such as José Feliciano Ama, functioned as social commuters since they spoke Spanish and indigenous languages and were therefore able to translate between these two social realities.

Another case in point is the quantitative dimension of violence in the uprising and the following events. According to Anderson (Anderson, 1971, p. 35) the insurgents caused 35 homicides. The government troops killed between 10,000 and 40,000 persons in the aftermath of the uprising. Low levels of lethal violence are particularly consistent with historical research on segmentary violence in Latin America in the nineteenth century (Riekenberg, 2003). With the integration of the rural indigenous communities in larger political networks, the violence during the uprising(s) got a clear political connotation without fully losing local meanings. That is to say, the reciprocity of everyday interactions continued to play an important role. At the same time, reciprocity lost its integrational capacity to manage all practices of violence. Instead, the state's capabilities for repression dramatically increased. The events of 1932 and the mass killings of rural people finally overshadowed the process of clientelistic integration of the subaltern class. However, the mass killing did not simply end this process, but transformed clientelism (Ching, 2004). In addition, violence became embedded into state institutions of repression, such as the army or the *Guardia Nacional*. Violence then played an important role in forcing subordinate groups into networks of clientelism and controlling them as workers on the coffee *fincas* without destroying horizontal violence and the deeper meaning of honor violence as an appropriate resource to regulate conflicts between each other.

Temporally the last of the three societies, Jamaica got into serious turmoil in 1938. Trouble first began in January 1938 at the Serges Island sugar estate in St. Thomas. In May, strikes resumed and increased at Fromes estate in Westmoreland and did set the first phase of the rebellion (Phelps, 1960; Post, 1978; St. Pierre, 1978; Thomas, 2012). What initially began as a riot on the sugar estates quickly became a large-scale strike, subsequently spreading into Kingston and throughout the island. In June, the dock workers in Kingston went on strike as a second phase of the uprising, followed finally by banana workers as a third phase (Post, 1969,

p. 337). By the end of June, it became clear that the colonial administration was not able to handle the situation other than by force. The disturbances only ended when the governor proclaimed a state of emergency and ordered intensive patrols on the streets (Bolland, 2001, p. 332).

During these strikes, eight persons were killed, 32 wounded by gunshots, and 139 had other injuries. No white persons were killed (Bakan, 1990, p. 116). A closer look on practices of violence reveals that yet established cultural scripts still remained untouched. First, as in 1865, the uprising mass selected targets purposefully. Rather than killing people, the mass opted to destroy property. Second, certain practices were used repeatedly. In Kingston, striking workers "barricaded the streets and broke streetlights to prevent police from operating effectively at night. In the rural areas, cane fields were set ablate, roads were blocked to prevent police access and telephone wires were cut to impede communication among the authorities" (Bakan, 1990). Third, there were more violent incidents in rural areas, especially where banana workers lived, than in the cities and particularly than in Kingston. And finally, in Kingston, strikes were not only well planned and organized, they also reveal a certain moral economy of violence. On May 23, for instance, striking workers even patrolled the streets, ensuring that no trains circulated during the strike. When they encountered a street vendor who had been looted by youths "the strikers took up a collection to repay the vendor for the loss" (Bakan, 1990, p. 117). Social scripts thus guided violence and even called for compensations if these cultural rules have been violated.

The low level of overall violence was mainly attributed to the two leaders of the movement, Norman Manley and Alexander Bustamante. It is interesting to note that at least Bustamante often drew on traditional Christian metaphors in his speeches, such as good against evil, messianism and martyrdom, and the rule by divine right. By referring to these imaginaries, he managed once again to merge longstanding traditional cultural meanings with actual political activism. The incidents of 1938 therefore show major similarities with yet existing cultural scripts of violence. Much resembles the mob violence already analyzed above. In contrast to the Morant Bay rebellion, where some hundreds revolted, now, the 1938 labor uprisings constitute a large-scale social movement rooted in the organization of the labor movement. Although the uprising initially began in rural areas—symptomatically for Jamaica's development path on a sugar estate—it quickly moved to urban encounters, mainly to Kingston. Therefore, the uprising not only marks a critical juncture in terms of the scale of organizational capacities brought forward by political leaders (Bustamante and Manley), but likewise a turning point in the topography of violence. From this time on, the primary site of violence shifted towards Kingston.

Even though Belize was equally facing an uprising during the Depression years, it did not take the shape of El Salvador's violent escalations. Firstly, the mobilizers were not peasants struggling for land, but urban workers claiming better working conditions. Secondly, the colonial state did not react with overt repression but with incorporation. However, and in contrast to Jamaica, the Belizean political system was still strong enough to safeguard the class position of ruling elites and to provide opportunities to incorporate dissidents.

In 1934, troubles began with several strikes and riots. On October 1, the leaders were able to close down works on the Belize Estate Company's mill. Then, the mass "marched to the premises of the coconut exporter, Manuel Esquivel, assaulting the owner and stealing some cash while others went to the Public Works Department yard where they smashed the main gate. Having closed the town's main employers, the crowd, armed with sticks, marched off to Queen Street to the Town Board offices where the people's leaders met the police and a fight ensued in which several constables were assaulted. In the fracas, one Absolem Pollard was shot" (Ashdown, 1978, p. 65). In the end, however, the unemployment movement led by Antonio Soberanis Gómez, its founder and leader, faded away without profoundly transforming Belizean society as it happened in Jamaica. Similar to Jamaica and El Salvador, violent incidents during the uprising followed yet established cultural scripts of violence. The particular characteristic of Belize consists in the fact that the colonial state managed to associate itself with these established cultural scripts through social concessions and by means of material co-optation.

Why did the Great Depression produce different effects in these three societies? Why did the Salvadorian state react violently while the Belizean and Jamaican state made concessions? In order to answer these questions, it is important to point to the asynchroncity of each uprising under review. The situation in El Salvador during the Great Depression is characterized by shifting power relations that opened a window of opportunity for violence. The events of 1932 and the mass killings of rural people seriously challenged both the expulsion of subaltern groups, particularly of peasant communities from their land, and the clientelistic co-optation of the subaltern class. During the time before the uprising, El Salvador experienced an atmosphere fueled by enormous tensions. Although power differentials between the subaltern and the ruling class diverged, the insurgents were able to produce an "intensity of fear" (Gould, 2010, p. 89) that was perceived by the elite as credible enough to threaten political stability. Both central groups, semi-proletarians and *colonos*, struggled against the monopolization of land ownership and thereby challenged political authority and domination. Furthermore, the forms of violence employed by the insurgents show that practices of violence still followed cultural scripts that had their origins in moral economies of peasant communities.

In Jamaica, this structural feature did simply not exist. Therefore, it would be more useful to compare the uprising of 1932 in El Salvador with Jamaica's Morant Bay rebellion in 1865. The Morant Bay rebellion in Jamaica developed due to a similar window of opportunity for violence. Power relations between the dominant planters and subordinated freed slaves shifted as in the 1930s in El Salvador. Similar to El Salvador in the 1930s, shifting power relations in Jamaica during the Morant Bay rebellion were accompanied by fear of the loss of the elite's own material and cultural dominance. These fears are likely to explain the military reactions in El Salvador and Jamaica. Contrary to the Morant Bay rebellion, Jamaica's labor movements as well as El Salvador's peasant movements were politically divided during the Great Depression (and in Jamaica additionally because of personal differences between Manley and Bustamante); previous experiences of land expulsion in El Salvador helped to overcome this divide. In Jamaica, the sugar industry had been declining for several decades and peasants as well as wageworkers had already experienced high levels of internal stratification. As in Belize, political unrest and riots claimed higher wages and favorable work conditions. In short, uprisings, while short and more isolated in nature, were based on bread-and-butter strategies without seriously challenging the basis of society and therefore fitted into yet existing cultural scripts of mob violence.

Even though clientelism was and still is a longstanding feature in all three societies, the masses' claims were more severe in El Salvador as they touched on land issues as one fundamental pillar of elite domination. Belizean and Jamaican elites as well as the Colonial State did not face serious difficulties to incorporate moderated claims. Indeed, the Colonial Office quickly reacted with the Colonial Development and Welfare Act in 1940 (Edie, 1991, p. 32). In El Salvador, clientelist political incorporation of subaltern groups began to interact with processes of state formation and finally led to embedding violence into state institutions of repression, such as the army or the *Guardia Nacional*. In Jamaica, both the organizers and mobilizers of violence in Jamaica became major promoters of state formation and later leaders of independence. In Belize, the mobilizers of violence during the Great Depression later never assumed major roles. Furthermore, Belizean, Jamaican as well as British Colonial authorities identified valves, such as social concessions, to release pressure.

Eventually, the violent events of 1932 in El Salvador exposed that processes of state formation were challenged by newly arising subaltern groups. Elites did not possess mechanisms to include these new groups. In Belize, in contrast, yet established social classes, mainly wageworkers suffering from unemployment, organized themselves, and rioted. As the traditional system still offered opportunities for elites to incorporate distrust, the elite reaction was never large-scale violence. In Jamaica, the planter elites were seriously challenged. However, the colonial state incorporated the movement politically while ignoring major economic claims. Finally, horizontal violence still had a strong impact in El Salvador even though the overall incidences were political in nature. In Jamaica and Belize on the other hand, violence was much more directed against superior authorities, constituting targets of both political and economic relevance.

With regard to violence, the uprisings marked a critical juncture in all three cases. In El Salvador, the uprising was answered with a genocide. While the uprising itself reveals the importance of particular cultural scripts, in the aftermath of the uprising an institutional setting was established based on the economic and political exclusion of the subaltern class. Also in Jamaica and Belize, violence was directed against autochthonous elites and the colonial state. In contrast to El Salvador, however, the uprising mass was incorporated into politics in Jamaica by newly emerging political parties. Consequently, political parties emerged as primary mobilizers of violence during the twentieth century in Jamaica. Once again, Belize followed a hybrid path. While subaltern groups were excluded as in El Salvador, political parties managed to integrate the local scale by the mid-1950s and thus to incorporate local-level politics. When co-optation in El Salvador occurred, it was mainly achieved by focusing on cultural meanings of violence instead of channeling economic resources towards the lower strata. Jamaica took the opposite path. In Jamaica, mobilizers of violence were able to resort to economic resources, thereby mobilizing violence through political parties. In Belize, finally, violence was generated as political parties intended to strengthen their local base, thereby changing the distribution of economic resources and providing new cultural scripts to the local level.

In Search for Alternatives

All three societies drew their lessons from the Great Depression and subsequent political turmoil. In economic terms, the third decade of the twentieth century challenged the traditional path of integration into the world system and led to the search for alternatives. In all three societies, diversification of export commodities enjoyed primary attention. Even though coffee production and exportation continued to be the predominant model in El Salvador, the production of sugar and cotton expanded, and regional strategies of economic integration flourished (Bulmer-Thomas, 1987, pp. 150–173). In Jamaica, soon after its recovery, multinational companies (MNC) invested in the extraction of bauxite (Davis, 1985). While sugar and bananas continuously constituted an export share up to 90 percent until the end of the 1950s, bauxite became the prime export commodity in Jamaica in the 1960s (Huber & Stephens, 1986, p. 22; Jefferson, 1972, p. 48). This trend was paralleled by a steady increase in tourism as a source of foreign reserves. In Belize, diversification of exports meant to abandon mahogany as the primary export commodity. And indeed, by the end of the 1950s, non-forestry products such as sugar and citrus replaced mahogany (Bulmer-Thomas & Bulmer-Thomas, 2012, p. 114). While the dominance of rent in general persisted in all three societies, the structure of rent incomes and their mode of appropriation changed after the Great Depression. In Jamaica, the upcoming mineral sector allowed for the appropriation of differential rents and gave rise to a prototype of state-class (Kaufman, 1985; Payne, 1994). El Salvador, in contrast, resisted fundamental changes and oligarchic rule continued while the military served as a political substitute (Guidos Véjar, 1980). Belize formed a hybrid case in which oligarchic segments continued to play an important role while a new state-class-driven segment emerged with increasing state activity (Shoman, 1990).

In this post-World War II period, different dynamics of violence became evident in all three cases. While in Jamaica forms of violence emerged inside the political arena and originated in the distribution of material resources, the forms of violence in El Salvador continued to follow co-optation. In Belize, finally, signs of both dynamics are observable. However, in this latter case, there are too few reliable sources to reach a conclusion.

Institutionalizing the Appropriation of Rents

The emergence of a centralized, rent-driven political regime in Jamaica aided political leaders to channel economic resources in a top-down way. Violence played an important role in resource channeling. The access to resources allowed political leaders to gain national power via elections, but they needed to organize marginalized communities to get their votes. At the same time, violence encouraged urban marginalized communities to strengthen their bargaining position vis-à-vis political leaders. As an effect, urban marginalized communities violently struggled against each other to put their respective politician back into office. At this initial stage, violence was embedded in a positive sum game between political leader and urban marginalized communities as both were able to realize their political and economic aims. In effect, violence in Jamaica predominantly emerged inside the political system, marginal communities became integrated into this system and the institutional setting of this system became important for rent channeling. In El Salvador, on the contrary, oligarchic rule based on the exclusion of the subaltern class. Violence emerged predominantly in distance or even in opposition to the political system. An exception, however, was repression. Authoritarian oligarchic rule opened spaces, in which co-optation could take place by forming state-led organizations of repression. This process shaped violence to a great extent. At the same time, this process provoked that revolutionary violence evolved to alternate this entire system. The case of Belize exposes a mixture of both comparing cases. While rent appropriation via traditional channels continued, political parties struggled to establish links with local communities. Both processes created conflicts at the local scale. Increasingly, however, by managing these conflicts, people resorted to symbols of the state, namely to party identities. This was an open door for political leaders. When they obtained access to economic resources at the state level, they were able to support and proliferate party identities. By channeling rents into these conflicts, political leaders intended to strengthen their power base at the local level. Accordingly, violence originated in distance to the state. Inasmuch politics became influenced by state-class rule, however, violence got co-opted by the state-class faction.

In El Salvador, authoritarianism once installed with the presidency of Hernández Martínez merged with oligarchic rule (Stanley, 1996; Williams & Walter, 1997). Nevertheless, gradual changes occurred between 1948 and 1970 leading some authors to classify the political system as an "*autoritarismo desarrollista*" (Mariscal, 1979), which introduced some social reforms. The economic background of this change was the intensified search for an alternative economic development model. While coffee production and exportation continued to play the most important role, first the diversification of exports and second a moderate import substitution enjoyed additional emphasis (Bulmer-Thomas, 1987). Without challenging the authoritarian oligarchic development path, sugar and cotton production increased by the end of the 1950s. The diversification of export crops, however, did not translate into the fractionalization of the oligarchy since the same families engaged in coffee production and exportation also controlled these new sectors, and new oligarchic families expanded into commerce (Aubey, 1969; Colindres, 1976). Sugar and cotton production expanded particularly to the coastal regions of El Salvador, creating a third wave of land concentration. *Colonos* who formerly had founded their basis of subsistence in these regions during the 1920s were mainly affected by this process. Consequently, the structure of income within the peasantry diversified: A first group of peasants was able to increase their holdings by renting new land. A second group found employment opportunities either on a full-time basis on sugar, basic grain, and coffee plantations or as seasonal wageworkers. The third and largest group, however, was left dispossessed (Downing, 1978, p. 10). Many of this third group were forced to leave their land and to migrate into the cities or to neighboring Honduras. These developments led to growing urbanization and the expansion of squatter settlements, particularly in the north and the southwest of San Salvador (Lungo, 2000; White, 1975).

In Jamaica, the Great Depression led to "constitutional decolonization" (Munroe, 1972), adult suffrage, and self-government in 1944, and in line with Belize, to a Westminster model of government. While British colonialism impeded autochthonous political organizations or even civil society associations to develop during the nineteenth century, evolving political parties, which had their roots in the labor movement of 1938, filled this gap. Two hegemonic parties evolved around their leading figures Norman Manley and Alexander Bustamante.[19] Both political parties bifurcated politics in Jamaica. Subsequently, political controversies of any kind were forced to operate within this party framework being related either to the People's National Party (PNP), or the Jamaican Labor Party (JLP) (Gannon, 1976). Even though the parties' access to state revenues increased during this stage, it was only with formal independence and increasing taxation of bauxite that state revenues grew. Development was heavily inspired by the Jamaican economic author Arthur William Lewis (1950) and his model of industrialization by invitation in which he proposed the attraction of foreign capital to overcome the internal labor surplus. As a result, foreign capital dominated major branches of the economy. Economic planning, however, remained at low levels. At least until the mid-1960s, both parties did not challenge this model of development (Lacey, 1977, p. 19). Even in this early stage of diversification, economic growth was uneven. The leading sectors were mining and tourism. Manufacturing was dependent on the mining sector, and agricultural production steadily declined after the 1930s. In particular, agricultural production for the domestic market dropped (Jefferson, 1972, pp. 75–80). As an effect, the peasantry shrank in relative terms and Jamaica became dependent on food imports (Beckford & Witter, 1980, p. 64). At the same time, population increased from 1.2 million inhabitants in 1943 to more than 1.8 million in 1970 (Basil, 1980, p. 22). From the 1950s until the late 1980s, the population grew faster than GDP, leading to high rates of under- and unemployment. With increasing incentives to appropriate bauxite rents, however, both parties were able to strengthen their multi-class basis and particularly to incorporate the lower strata. Although patronage and clientelism dominated the political regime and indeed was functional for the state-class, the inherent problems of the established development model (industrialization by invitation) unquestioned by both parties led to deteriorating economic conditions and rising unemployment (Huber & Stephens, 1986, p. 56). At the end of the 1960s, Jamaica was dependent on food imports more than ever as well as on a high import share of the local manufacturing sector. Additionally, Jamaica suffered from declining foreign investments in the mining sector.

As a reaction to the crisis of the 1930s, the Colonial Office decided to gradually open up the political system of Belize. Adult suffrage was established in 1954, and the country gained self-government in 1964. Independence, however, was delayed until 1981 because of border issues with Guatemala (Shoman, 2010). During the formation period of national politics of the 1950s, the country was suddenly hit by hurricane Hattie in 1961. The hurricane almost completely destroyed Belize City, caused serious damage in the entire country, and rendered thousands homeless. The hurricane furthermore led to a wave of emigration towards the United States when economic perspectives worsened (Babcock & Conway, 2000, p. 75). Even the police force experienced labor shortages and it was assumed that this problem would persist "so long as men are tempted to leave the service to seek more lucrative employment outside – particularly in the United States of America" (British Honduras Police Force, 1965). In the 1960s, thousands of Belizeans migrated towards the north to find better job opportunities.

With the demise of mahogany production and increasing diversification towards both citrus production in the south as well as sugar production in the north of the country, the United Kingdom seized to be Belize's primary trade partner and the United States took on that role instead. By 1970, sugar alone reached almost 50 percent of domestic exports, and increased up to 80 percent some years later due to rising international sugar prices (Bulmer-Thomas & Bulmer-Thomas, 2012, p. 115). Even though sugar and citrus production remained concentrated in larger land holdings, both new export crops provided substantial opportunities for peasants to engage in small-scale agricultural production for exportation.[20] By the 1970s, the shift towards sugar and citrus not only generated new economic opportunities for formerly dependent rural workers. This process also revealed increasing social stratification, both inside the forming peasantry as well as among long existing local communities.

At the same time, this economic change was paralleled by political incentives to mitigate social stratification. Since the vast majority was integrated into formal politics through the right to vote, a highly competitive two-party system became dominant. By 1948, the Colonial Office established formal political processes at the town level by bringing town boards and councils into existence (Colonial Office, 1948). These reforms were intended to weave the national scale into local-level politics. What initially began as a democratic process, however, led to new political cleavages at the town level. Newly elected politicians and town leaders obtained access to national funds and resources. As a result, factionalism at the town level was fueled by partisan politics. This factionalism is still an outstanding political factor in Belize. "Endemic faction-fighting" (Moberg, 1991, p. 104) within and between both parties persists up until today. At the same time, however, clientelism and patronage are prime guarantors of stability.

In El Salvador, the incomplete implementation of a new development model resulted in the worsening of economic conditions for the entire subaltern class. Livelihoods became increasingly precarious. At the same time, the third wave of land concentration increased social stratification within the lower strata, eventually dissolving the remaining peasantry and leading to urbanization as well as increasing political grievances. Jamaica already experienced both processes before the Great Depression. In Jamaica, the improved access to rent revenues from bauxite exports coupled with the lacking economic opportunities particularly for people living in impoverished urban areas allowed the arising state-class to easily co-opt the lower strata through rent channeling. In contrary to both El Salvador and Jamaica, Belize's peasantry grew during this period in numbers. The internal stratification of the peasantry and the fostering of political linkages between local communities and political parties accompanied this process.

Integrating Established Cultural Scripts into New Social Contexts

In the post-World War II period, not only did the political economy of rent appropriation experience major changes and open new enabling spaces of violence, but it also, challenged established cultural scripts of violence. In Jamaica and to a certain degree in Belize, cultural scripts of violence were fueled by party identities and underpinned by channeling economic resources particularly towards the lower strata according to a trickle-down principle. In El Salvador, rent appropriation in the hands of the oligarchy impeded similar processes. In this latter case, the manipulation and mobilization of cultural scripts, however, regained importance.

In El Salvador, urban and rural encounters began to develop distinctively. That is to say, violence followed distinct cultural scripts in both topographies.

In the countryside, the diversification of peasant income coincides with the reestablishment of repression and the mobilization of violence for control. By the mid-1960s, traditional clientelist networks of early state-formation were increasingly used to integrate the wealthier group of peasants into violent organizations to control neighbors and to form vigilantes (Arnson, 2002; Lauria-Santiago, 2005). These networks could draw on an extensive tradition of repression established during the turn of the century. Repression in El Salvador was initially organized by militias and then in the threefold police force, the *Guardia Nacional*, the *Policía de Hacienda*, and the *Policía Nacional*. In the mid-1960s, General José Alberto "Chele" Medrano founded the *Organización Democrática Nacionalista* (ORDEN), a right-wing para-state organization and an "expansive counterinsurgency intelligence gathering network" (Mazzei, 2009, p. 148). According to Medrano (cited in Nairn, 1984, pp. 21–22), the aim of ORDEN was to "indoctrinate peasants regarding the advantages and the disadvantages of the communist system (...) and to fight the plans and actions of international communism." Out of this intelligence network, ORDEN quickly developed into an umbrella organization of different death squads with the objective to suppress subaltern groups. ORDEN grew into a mass base for repression with almost 100,000 members, transforming wealthier peasants into rank-and-file members (McClintock, 1985, p. 207).

Practices of violence brutalized during this time with the increasing use of torture by ORDEN. Many victims were found with tied hands, destroyed bodies, multiple shots in the back, and with the initials of the particular death squad carved into the chest. Victims were targeted selectively with the aim of bringing them to justice (Dickey, 1983). A broad discourse of justice allowed the right-wing mobilizers to interfere in different sorts of conflicts. Membership of ORDEN increased by means of ideology and due to the successful mobilization of fears of spreading communism, particularly among the first group of better-off peasants. However, membership also grew because of non-political and even personal motivations since ORDEN itself opened individual windows of opportunity for individuals to use violence to settle longstanding conflicts. Lauria-Santiago (2005, p. 95) argues that "sometimes the killing of peasants was tied to conflicts with local landowners; at other times the mere act of organizing activities with a popular ideology of liberation was perceived as a threat and repressed." Oral history accounts further stress that "community members organized through ORDEN to massacre their neighbours (...) transforming criminals into paramilitary murderers" (Silber, 2011, p. 53). In these rural encounters, ORDEN could heavily draw on existing cultural scripts of violence to control and integrate these scripts into a massive apparatus of para-state repression.

In urban encounters, and particularly in San Salvador, violence followed an economic logic. Before the rise of ORDEN, the emergence of left-wing guerrilla organizations and the following civil war are mostly treated as a period of relative tranquility with regard to violence in the literature. A (re)interpretation of available sources, however, points to the centrality of horizontal violence, even at this time.

A particular form of violence, which attracted attention in newspapers during this time, was street fighting between different supporters of school basketball teams, so called *barras estudantiles* (Savenije, 2009). *Barra* violence initially began as small fights between different groups of supporters during or after sport events. Soon, it developed into the "search for opportunities for confronting with its rivals" (Savenije & Beltrán, 2005, p. 21). Violence became detached from sports. These youths met at night and picked up *riñas* (brawls). A newspaper article in 1959 stated that

> there were small quarrels and street fights that ended with the intervention of police officers. Then certain students used giant straps and cinches to hit those from the opposing barra, followed by the use of stones, bricks and cudgels as forceful weapons. The progress of barbarism continued (…). And now, firearms come out, stones continue to be thrown with the consequent destruction, and even priests are beaten. (La Prensa Gráfica, 1959, p. 18)[21]

Practices of violence therefore involved fistfights, slingshots, stones, and sticks. Rarely, knives were used, and hardly ever guns. Although very little is known about particular sequences of violence apart from singular newspaper articles, the descriptions provided by Savenije (2009) signals that honor still was a veritable cultural background against which the actors themselves interpreted "their" violence. Honor violence, however, was translated from rural peasant life into an urban topography. Violence in these circumstances served as a means to establish and to maintain group solidarity and to create identity for youths engaged in *barras*. As well as in Jamaica, early "youth gang" violence came close to hooliganism, as it will be discussed later on. Different to Jamaica, however, hooliganism was disconnected from party politics and mainly oriented towards internal group cohesion.

At the time that honor as a cultural script of violence might have flourished in these social settings and therefore still endured in urban encounters, a new cultural script gained more and more visibility. The author of a continual press review called *"Crónica de El Salvador"*[22] wrote in 1952 that

> The first day of the year – we can take, however, every other day as an example – was a bloody date for El Salvador (…) resulting in 21 killed and 21 serious injured persons. And there was no revolution, and no uprising of any political character (…) Only there have been some spontaneous eruptions of a bad population which is spreading how we can observe it every day in the press. (Estudios Centroamericanos [ECA], 1952, p. 56)[23]

A few years later, a series of articles appeared in the same journal describing an even worsening situation:

the delinquency in El Salvador takes a more and more serious and threatening character ... During the last days, San Salvador lived moments of panic
when in the middle of the day and in the centre of the capital various thieves
have been surrounded by numerous heavily armed police agents for various
hours, inside established commercial shops where they had intended to rob,
and the one and other made use of their firearms, resulting in one murdered
and two injured persons; acts illuminating the very serious situation. (ECA,
1956, p. 304)[24]

By comparing these descriptions, it is interesting to recognize how representations of violence have changed in these years. The notion of honor
in interactions of violence disappeared, perhaps with rising economic and
social modernization and increasing state control. Despite the state's
increasing incentives to modernize its institutions, authors continued to
describe the police in various articles as incapable to combat crime
effectively.

Thus, horizontal violence still played a decisive role in urban areas in
personal conflicts without clear reference to repression or revolution. The
principal motive to conduct violence, however, shifted from the defense of
honor and the claim of social recognition towards economic means, primarily access to economic resources and/or access to the market. While
detailed data on these urban encounters of violence are still lacking, this
increasing awareness of urban violence developed parallel to increasing
urbanization, growing urban squatter settlements, and cultural transformations inside marginalized communities. Expanding market relations to
the countryside without providing bargaining power to the lower strata
not only led to urbanization and urban marginalization but likewise to
problems of social integration. These processes brought about a diffuse
household income structure as household members had to rely on several
forms of often precarious income to sustain their livelihoods. The search
for identity in the conduct of violence on the one hand, and the increasing
economization of violence to obtain access to the means of urban survival
on the other hand, are crucial effects of this period.

Although the emerging state-class in Jamaica established patronage
and clientelism as main social stabilizing features, it was unable to incorporate the entire society into its development model during this whole
period from the early 1940s until the end of the 1960s. Large sections of
the marginal population were not integrated at all. As a consequence,
alternative political ideas and movements developed during the 1960s,

particularly among the marginal population. Simultaneously, Jamaica saw the rise of new problems, such as increasing crime and politicized mob violence (Gray, 1991).

Young male persons between 17 and 25 years of age were mainly affected by this trend (Headley, 1988, p. 72). Many of them found refuge in youth gangs and became engaged in petty crimes. At this time, however, the youth gang phenomenon was still local and did not provoke violence. Until the mid-1960s, "inter gang rivalry was unknown" (Chevannes, 1981, p. 393). Instead, violence was mainly attributed to party conflicts. By linking established cultural scripts of mob violence with party identities, violence came close to hooliganism. However, the level of violence was still low and violence was still sporadic. Party related violence mainly involved the use of sticks and knives and not guns (Sives, 2003, p. 51).

After splitting up into two oppositional party organizations in 1942, both the BITU/JLP and the TUC/PNP struggled to increase their voter basis beyond the working class towards the marginalized urban poor. Violence during this period served as an instrument "to increase support on one hand and protect a position, on the other hand" (Sives, 2010, p. 11). Party clashes triggered the use of violence. The parties reacted by forming groups specialized in protecting party and union meetings, "providing 'strongarm' men for the platform speakers and developing strategies to ensure they could campaign" (Sives, 2010).

In the face of an increasing marginalized urban subaltern class, however, the parties in government faced a dilemma: To win elections, both parties were forced to gain support by the marginalized. But the poor's demands exceeded available resources (Headley, 1996). A simple outlet valve for this dilemma was that parties in power exclusively favored their own affiliates, thereby starting to victimize members of the other party. In line with this process, the patterns of violence began to change when in power both the JLP and later on in the same way the PNP channeled economic rents into housing programs for their corresponding supporters.[25] These programs not only created a strong partisan identity at the communal level, they also increased clientelism as a functional relationship between the lower strata and political leaders inside the two segments of the state-class. In consequence, so-called garrison communities emerged. A garrison community is a "political stronghold, a veritable fortress completely controlled by a party. Any significant social, political, economic or cultural development within the garrison can only take place with the tacit approval of the leadership (whether local or national) of the dominant party" (Figueroa & Sives, 2003, p. 65). Garrisons are an extreme illustration of social closure. This pattern of clientelist politics created strong party identities at the community level. Moreover, the constituencies' Members of Parliament (MP), often termed as "political bosses" (Stone, 1980, p. 97), politically governed these communities and were able to centralize community networks.

Inside garrisons, a strong sense of party identity is maintained by political bosses from the outside and by party militants from within the community. In the Jamaican case, rent-driven social closure generated a "totalitarian social space" (Figueroa & Sives, 2002, p. 85), which not only manipulated, redefined, and absorbed violence but also increasingly produced its own form. Initially, this was a top-down principle. Inasmuch as local communities were needed in political struggles at the national scale, a complex relationship between the garrisons and the MPs evolved. In this process, political bosses became increasingly dependent on party militants who enforced party identity at the local scale and ensured the voters' support during elections. Simultaneously, local communities with party identities were able to "negotiate" their participation in the process of rent distribution with the MP. At the local scale, therefore, party members sought to establish contacts to yet existing youth gangs and the already existing party militias. In exchange for resources and employment on construction sites, these gangs had to ensure "political" security for the MPs.[26]

The political instrumentalization of youth gangs by politicians had serious effects for the gangs themselves as well as for the form of violence they engaged in. Firstly, the internal structure of these gangs altered. Gangs developed internal hierarchies and a leadership with close links to politics. By accessing employment opportunities, the gang leaders were able to materially organize their fellows. Secondly, and because of the financial support provided by powerful politicians, gangs were able to culturally attract new members. For example, they developed distinct outfit styles, were able to organize dance evenings, for example, and therefore gained status and prestige within the community (Gray, 2004, p. 80). Finally, while practices of violence in the 1950s and early 1960s mainly implied the use of sticks and knives, now, guns entered into these conflicts. As a result, the quantitative level of violence increased, particularly during the elections in 1967 which confirmed the JLP in power. In addition, the forms of violence altered. Now, militant party gangs with access to guns increasingly confronted each other and violently battled over political turf.

Political identity inside the communities and particularly inside the garrisons consolidated and led to clearly demarcated enemies as well as friend-and-foe dichotomies. While gangs had earlier perceived each other as rivals, now, they used the terms enemies.[27] Although cultural scripts still resembled their predecessors, they became integrated into politics. Eventually, this type of partisan violence between the two main parties on a horizontal level became functional for the political system itself because violence ensured that people remained within the system. In this framework, increasing gang violence, crime, and partisan political violence is hardly to separate.

Belize experienced similar diverging topographies of violence. Rural and urban encounters of violence likewise followed different paths. In rural areas, particularly in the north and south of the country where the production of new export crops such as sugar and citrus dominated, violence was challenged by traditional although changing modes of conflict management. With the formation of new political arenas at the local scale (town councils), national party politics introduced patronage linkages into local communities, which led to "sporadic personalistic conflicts" (Moberg, 1991, p. 220) over the access to resources that were delivered by clientelist networks. Consequently, many Belizean villages became divided by party identity along partisan factional lines in contrast to class cleavages. Evidence from anthropological research further indicates that "community members define[d] themselves by their affiliation with either the People's United Party (PUP) or the United Democratic Party (UDP), the major political parties active [at this time] at the village and national levels" (Moberg, 1991, p. 219). Similar to Jamaica, party politics were translated into local communities, virtually "affecting every home in the nation" (Sutherland, 1998, p. 63). Belize followed Jamaica in the sense that each party in power stigmatized their rivals and tended to "punish individuals of the opposite political allegiance." In Jamaica, however, this same process became a dominant feature in organizing violence and for the emergence of new forms of violence. In Belize, in contrast, local conflicts about access to party patronage networks and therefore to available resources provided by the parties in power overlaid yet existing conflicts and did not necessarily create them. Already existing conflicts between individuals and whole families led members of village councils of the party in power to "settle political and personal vendettas against village families with whom they are feuding" (Sutherland, 1998, p. 63). Factional disputes quite often erupted into violence and dominated political village life.

Horizontal violence then was reinterpreted and mobilized by political figures and therefore connected to partisan alignment. Moreover, these conflicts were charged by newly available national resources such as the "Aided Self-Help" program or other funds provided by the national government to strengthen the state's role in society (Moberg, 1992b, p. 14). In this light, the state grew not by institutionalizing its core, but by providing resources as well as symbols and meanings able to challenge horizontal violence in order to link itself with the periphery.

In summary, forms of violence in all three societies altered with changing socioeconomic conditions after the Great Depression. While the direct access to resources via the state in Jamaica transformed gangs and linked them to party politics, violence in El Salvador was organized in different structures. Instead of accessing practices of violence as it happened in Jamaica, El Salvador's way of dealing with violence consisted in concentrating on cultural scripts and the meanings of violence. In El Salvador, existing cultural scripts of violence as control and violence as a means to gain access to surplus and/or the market were redefined by strategic action, and the mobilizers used newly emerging institutions to organize violence. In Jamaica, in contrast, cultural scripts had to be imposed and later on merged with party identities. While in Jamaica, the organization of violence was achieved by channeling rents through clientelism into the hands of violent perpetrators, the situation in El Salvador was more complex. Here, longstanding conflicts were exploited by mobilizers to readjust forms of violence and to manipulate them for political utilization. Due to a lack of sources in Belize, a clear interpretation is hardly possible. However, existing evidence points to a mixture of both. While parties tried to co-opt local-level politics as it was the case in Jamaica, they distributed resources to town councils. At the same time, they delivered new cultural scripts of which local actors then disposed in their struggles against competing factions. In that, the Belizean way resembles that of El Salvador.

INCREASING UNREST AND POLITICAL CRISIS IN THE 1980s

During the 1970s and particularly in the 1980s, internal conflicts intensified in all three societies. In Jamaica, Michael Manley gained power in 1972 and subsequently tried to implement a new development path in the framework of democratic socialism (Huber & Stephens, 1986; Kaufman, 1985). As the term itself signals, political conflicts between the two leading parties were fueled by diverging ideologies during Manley's two terms in office. Conflicts in El Salvador were similarly politicized and ideology played a major role. In 1980, a civil war began, which lasted for 12 years. The political economy of El Salvador at that time was heavily influenced by the civil war. Even though the focus on coffee exports remained, the internal fractional division of the oligarchy between a traditional wing and a self-modernizing wing deepened and finally led to the oligarchy's acceptance of the Peace Agreements in 1992 (Zinecker, 2004). Different to both Jamaica and El Salvador, the political economy of Belize further consolidated its development path of sugar and citrus exports. As a result, Belize experienced the loss of food self-sufficiency, slowing economic growth, and the development of an urban marginal class—developments that had affected Jamaica and El Salvador already in the early 1950s. Belize gained political autonomy in 1981 after having followed a peaceful road to independence. However, worsening urban conditions provoked increasing crime rates and accelerating violence.

In Jamaica as well as in El Salvador, the longstanding conflict between the elite and the subaltern class became increasingly interwoven with ideology at the beginning of the late 1960s and headed straight into escalatory spirals of violence. In Belize, the independence claim was the primary political content of political struggle and covered ideological differences about economic policy or development among the political parties. In El Salvador, the exclusive nature of authoritarian oligarchic rule impeded a reformist change from within the political regime and provoked the civil war. The Jamaican state-class in contrast was still strong enough to manage even a very high level of violence internally.

Structural adjustment programs (SAPs) were introduced in Jamaica in 1977 and marked the end of Manley's democratic socialism and its aspirations to challenge the traditional way of rent-led development. In El Salvador, in contrast, SAPs were introduced by the oligarchy itself during the civil war by the end of the 1980s and further consolidated oligarchic economic domination in a new, even non-authoritarian style. Finally, Belize was forced to accept SAPs in 1983 shortly after independence. In all three cases, SAPs resulted in increasing migration to the United States, the forced diversification towards non-traditional export commodities, privatization of state enterprises, and the liberalization of foreign trade.

Challenging the Traditional Way of Rent-Led Development

In El Salvador, the mono agrarian export model based on coffee production and exportation came into deep crisis. The international price for coffee declined and the oil crisis led to increasing costs of production. Consequently, El Salvador suffered from deteriorating terms of trade beginning in 1977 (Segovia, 1996, p. 33), and a serious balance of payments crisis began to crystalize. The worsening economic situation was paralleled by the return of refugees from Honduras in the aftermath of the "Soccer War" in 1969. While formerly available land for subsistence cultivation had already been appropriated by large landlords in the decades before, El Salvador was not able to economically integrate this migrant inflow. The rural landless or near landless population grew considerably and constituted almost 35 percent of the total workforce (Acevedo, 1996, p. 22). While the objective pressures towards land reform increased, the political regime was unable to address that demand. Already frustrated by the economic conditions and increasing repression of labor movements and unions, the subaltern class was further excluded from formal politics by electoral fraud in the 1972 and 1977 national elections. A final step to change this framework peacefully was made by a younger generation of reformist members of the military who revolted in a coup d'état against the traditional authoritarian government in 1979. This radical-reformist alternative eventually failed to transform the Salvadoran society as it became isolated soon after the coup started (Zinecker, 2007, pp. 640–666).

The first guerrilla organization emerged in 1970 and several guerrilla groups followed in the subsequent years. But it took 10 years until the major guerrilla organizations founded the Farabundo Martí National Liberation Front (*Frente Farabundo Martí para la Liberación Nacional*, FMLN) in 1980 (Brockett, 2005; Dunkerley, 1982). The murder of Archbishop Romero in 1980 by members of ORDEN and the failed revolution in January 1981 marked the beginning of the civil war. It continued until the signing of the Peace Agreements in 1992 and claimed more than 75,000 lives.

The civil war imposed a new framework for El Salvador's political economy because it altered the relationship between the military and the oligarchy. Supported by USAID, the government initiated a land reform, nationalized coffee exportation as well as the banking sector. The probably most important processes, however, were the self-modernization of the oligarchy together with the introduction of SAPs. Before, the oligarchy had been composed of two competing factions, one engaged in coffee production and the other in the financing and marketing of coffee. This latter group eventually became dominant (Zinecker, 2004). With the presidency of Alfredo Cristiani, this modernized oligarchic faction finally gained power and implemented SAPs prepared by the think tank Salvadoran Foundation of Social and Economic Development (*Fundación Salvadoreña para el Desarrollo Económico y Social*, FUSADES). The modernized oligarchic faction was able to fulfil SAPs' conditionalities imposed by the International Monetary Fund (IMF) by privatizing state-owned companies. At the same time, this section of the oligarchy made use of the conditionalities in order to expand into new economic branches such as banking, assembly production (*maquila*), wholesale, and other service activities (Albiac, 2007).

While the top end of the Salvadorian society was able to consolidate oligarchic rule by means of modernization, the lower strata experienced deteriorating living conditions due to the implementation of SAPs and the civil war. The civil war forced thousands of Salvadorians to leave their country and to migrate either to their Central American neighboring countries, namely to Belize and to Honduras, to the United States, or from the war-torn departments of Morazán and Chalatenango towards San Salvador. In this latter case, large refugee and squatter settlements evolved, particularly in the surrounding areas of San Salvador, such as Mejicanos and Soyapango. This situation even worsened with the 1986 earthquake, which devastated large parts of San Salvador and had its most damaging effects in those areas where refuges had settled. The outmigration to the United States caused remittances to become a dominant feature of the Salvadorian economy as well as a livelihood strategy for many households (Funkhouser, 1992). Furthermore, the urban informal sector increased while formal employment decreased during SAPs. While both Jamaica and El Salvador started with huge differences, SAPs required the adaptation of a similar development model: the reliance on few export commodities and the compensation of export fluctuations with alternative capital flows such as remittances. The macroeconomic consequences of these changes were similar for both economies. However, the political economy approach showed that although deep changes took place, the initial development path continued to have an effect.

In Jamaica, the alternative path was entered peacefully via elections. Michael Manley came to power in Jamaica with national elections in 1972. He implemented his idea of democratic socialism in a time when the model of industrialization by invitation came into deep crisis causing rising rates of un- and underemployment. According to the democratic socialism idea, national development should be based on the channeling of bauxite rents into productive capacities, thereby following the standard vision of development through state-classes in the post–World War II period. To implement this idea, the PNP under Manley worked on three goals in particular: firstly, to increase government revenues; secondly, to create economic incentives for the development of new economic capacities; thirdly, to establish ideological hegemony to be politically able to achieve the first two goals. Higher taxation of the mining sector was meant to increase the government's room for maneuver (Huber Stephens, 1987). Diversification of bauxite outlets, an augmentation of forward linkages in the processing of bauxite, the reduction of foreign ownership, the nation-alization of key economic branches such as utilities and banking, and first steps towards an agrarian reform should serve to fulfil the second goal. Finally, the emergence of mass political organizations to establish political hegemony and to overcome political patronage and clientelism was intended to reach the third goal. While government revenues increased due to the imposition of the bauxite levy, bauxite production declined after 1973, leading to a serious balance of payments crisis in 1976 (Davis, 1984; Huber & Stephens, 1986, p. 337). Finally, the PNP government was forced to negotiate SAPs with the IMF, which were accepted and implemented in 1977 with the usual and deep-reaching conditionalities (Anderson & Witter, 1994). Although the PNP government restricted the distribution of clientelist housing programs in 1976, it continued patron-age politics (Sives, 2010, p. 96). In the end, Manley's efforts to change the development model of Jamaica "proved unsuccessful because his gov-ernment's policies were undermined by a hostile external environment (political and economic), internal resistance by the Jamaican bourgeoisie and administrative failures" (Bulmer-Thomas, 2012, p. 407). What changed, however, was the income structure of the urban poor. With the implementation of SAPs, formal employment decreased and the number of informal, often precarious jobs increased (Clarke & Howard, 2006). At the same time, marginality increased considerably. Subsequently, outward migration accelerated, particularly towards the United States.[28] Thus, the PNP government in Jamaica challenged the traditional development model without overcoming the state-class centered path, and El Salvador's self-modernizing oligarchy slightly expanded into new branches without abandoning the mono agro export model.

Belize in contrast resisted fundamental changes and continued to focus on sugar and citrus exports, slightly expanding into banana and shrimp production. Low investments and the poor state of infrastructure impeded the Belizean economy to diversify beyond the shift from mono forestry exports to mono agricultural exports. The only valve was the developing tourist sector, however, with only minimal marginal effects since it was focused on cruise ship tourism (Everitt & Ramsey, 2008).

World economic changes affected Belize during its independence period following 1981 and forced the country to accept SAPs. In Belize, the ultimate trigger was the Mexican foreign exchange crisis in the mid-1980s, which led to declining imports and re-exports, causing serious domestic economic problems (Barnett, 1985). At the same time and perhaps even worse, world sugar prices slumped after 1981 and seriously hit Belize's foreign exchange reserves, which were heavily dependent on sugar exports (Alvarez, 1988).

With accepting SAPs, the government had to engage in two important issues: privatization of state-owned property[29] and liberalization of the agricultural price regime (Shoman, 2011, p. 343). The latter issue was particularly important. As an effect of liberalizing the price regime of agricultural products for export as well as for the internal market, SAPs produced significant stratification within the peasantry at the community level. Some peasants retreated from staple food production and engaged in subsistence production while others intensified their export orientation (Moberg, 1992a, p. 2). This stratification caused enormous tensions at the local scale (Moberg, 1996, p. 322). In urban areas, unemployment was on the rise during the 1980s (Everitt, 1986, p. 110). Even though Belize City was rebuilt after hurricane Hattie in 1961 and the political capital moved to Belmopan, the city has been facing overpopulation and housing shortages, in particular for the lower strata (Ashcraft, 1973, p. 162).

First Signs of Dissolution: Losing Control of Cultural Scripts of Violence

Regarding violence, the already established development path showed first signs of rupture. Co-optation either via the mobilization of particular cultural scripts in El Salvador, or via resource channeling in Jamaica and the creation of new cultural scripts of violence still persisted. However, in both societies forms of violence began to change and to escape from their previous embeddedness, while in Belize new forms of violence emerged.

In El Salvador, vertical violence dominated the decades preceding the civil war, and it increased with the revolution and the civil war. The level of violence already peaked before the outbreak of the civil war. With the military coup of 1979, multiple centers of power arose and led to escalating spirals of violence. Complementary to the confrontation between different guerrilla organizations and the authoritarian oligarchic government, the struggles among different factions inside the military elite as well as the oligarchy caused violence to escalate. The guerrilla gained organizational strength by forming both horizontal alliances between the five different guerrilla groups as well as vertical alliances between revolutionary military wings, political parties, and mass organizations (Dunkerley, 1982, pp. 87–102; Zinecker, 2007, pp. 308–298). Thus, different organizational pyramids evolved and encountered each other on a horizontal level, which may be useful to explain escalating war-related violence. Eventually, the guerrilla and the military found themselves in a mutual stalemate, in which the guerrilla showed that it was even able to invade the oligarchy's resident areas of San Salvador in its Final Offensive in 1989. However, the guerrilla was not able to overthrow the authoritarian oligarchic government.

The military force together with the different police forces were heavily engaged in repression, but they were complemented by large-scale death squad violence exerted by ORDEN.[30] Essentially, ORDEN managed to organize violence with an ultra-right wing ideology. The mobilization of violence through ideology was moreover coupled with the continuing co-optation of ordinary horizontal violence. Longstanding family and community conflicts then encouraged "community members organized through ORDEN to massacre their neighbors." Moreover, "the antagonism and feuding between neighbors and kin, had ignited violence during the war" (Silber, 2011, p. 53). In the same vein, recent quantitative studies on the civil war suggest that forms of violence, in particular those employed by state organizations, "diversified" (Hoover Green, 2011, p. 268), mutating from politically motivated and ideologically inspired "rational" violence into everyday terror and horizontal violence between individuals.

In contrast to vertical violence in the shape of repression, the guerrilla managed to create an entire new cultural script of violence. This revolutionary script of violence consisted of at least three subscripts. The first and most important subscript of violence was an "insurgent political culture" (Wood, 2003). With direct and indirect support of the Catholic Church inspired by liberation theology, the guerrillas were enabled to link own created leftist insurgent networks in rural as well as urban areas with religious networks built by the Catholic Church and particularly by catechists. The mobilization of peasants created the necessary links between both networks. Consequently, not only did guerrilla leaders convince peasants to join the revolutionary opposition to the government, but these peasants regained the "pleasure of agency" (Wood, 2003, p. 235) and the will to change the political and economic situation of El Salvador. The provision of security for civilians who faced or who feared to face victimization by ORDEN and other state institutions of repression finally complemented this insurgent script of violence. Seeking security and the means to defend themselves against ORDEN, peasants integrated into the guerrilla and exerted violence against state and para-state organizations (Pearce, 1986, pp. 177–182). Focusing on rural family vendettas in the beginning 1970s, Cabarrús (1983, pp. 185–197) furthermore shows that political arenas on a higher organizational scale were utilized to resolve local conflicts. By turning towards local actors, both primary organizations—the army and the guerrilla—were able to strengthen their mass basis, providing "security" for their rank-and-file. Once present in the countryside, both organizations opened personal windows of opportunity for violence, because long-lasting personal conflicts could now be interpreted through a political lens. Local conflicts, thefts, robberies, and long-standing family feuds were now violently resolved in the shadow of these superior organizations through the personal utilization of these "higher" organizations. Both, observers and rank-and-file members mention that "thirst for adventure" and "boldness" have been popular motivations to integrate themselves into the insurgency (Silber, 2011, pp. 41–69; Viterna, 2013, pp. 42–62). Once related to the guerrilla or the army, violence was reinterpreted and labelled as political or criminal, either by local actors to legitimate violence or by political actors to blame their rivals. The meaning of violence of this original horizontal type was thus manipulated without however altering violent practices themselves. Even though the revolutionary script of violence was dominant and its subscript of insurgent political culture was decisive in mobilizing violence, the guerrilla did not escape from co-opting ordinary horizontal violence.

The guerrilla was able to merge these three cultural subsets into a revolutionary cultural script of violence. Ideology and the insurgent political culture thus were, apart from mobilizing and organizing violence, most important in creating an entire organizational sphere through which the revolution could be launched. At the same time, ordinary horizontal violence seems to have continued, even in times of the civil war. On a strategic level, this revolutionary cultural script of violence enabled the different guerrilla organizations to launch guerrilla strikes. Later, in the mid-1980s, the FMLN then almost developed into an armed force, as it strengthened its organizational structure as well as territorial control (Wood, 2003, p. 131).

In Jamaica, the expanding role of the state-class became directly and indirectly linked with violence. Directly, yet established and already politicized youth gangs became integrated into the politico-ideological warfare between the two leading parties. The forced creation of party identity inside marginalized communities indirectly fostered the embeddedness of gangs in these same communities and led to partisan political conflicts inside and between conflicting communities. Garrison communities consolidated under these developments. Although first signs appeared that political parties were no longer able to control this situation, they were at least as powerful to co-opt the establishing informal structure inside communities. While at the onset of the Manley government, the economic situation was precarious enough to turn "already explosive social conflicts into a zero-sum game" (Huber & Stephens, 1986, p. 58), these conflicts became fueled by ideological controversies over Manley's development model.

During this time, the sporadic nature of previous violence began to change. Formerly, guns served as a fearful symbol of strength and gun related murders occurred only sporadically. At this time, the membership in gangs increased. Gangs of youths who were known to have little money and no resources "suddenly had vague 'jobs' getting $100 a week, motorscooters, and a gun" (Kitson, 1982, p. 173). As of then, guns were used to kill, and led to increasing levels of violence. These are first indicators for the sophistication of gun use. Initially, guns had been scarce in Jamaica, since arms contraband is difficult to obtain due to the geography of Jamaica as an island. During the 1970s, the supply of guns increased even though ammunition was still rare. While the use of guns strengthened the prestige of certain gang members and particularly of the leaders, shootings in which more than a couple of bullets were fired became a sign of economic success and power (Gray, 2003b; Sives, 2010). Another indicator is the increasing organization of violence. Due to the clientelist channeling of rents into garrison communities, partisan conflicts were now violently settled at a higher organizational scale but still remained on a horizontal level. Sometimes, these conflicts were even termed "party civil war" (Gray, 2003a, p. 81).

However, these violent conflicts not only followed a pure political nature, but provoked cycles of revenge between different communities. It turned out to be a "triangular war" (Basil, 1980, p. 315) between different youth gangs organized around both political parties and the Jamaica Constabulary Force (JCF). This trend increased even further towards the election of 1980.

During these elections, former youth gangs now appeared as "well-organized para-military-like groups, equipped with semi-automatic weapons" (Huber & Stephens, 1986, p. 236). At the same time and in the shadow of these mere political incidences, gun-driven property crimes and violent crime was on the rise (Senior, 1972, p. 31). In this regard, traditional modes of channeling violence increasingly lost their power and created new windows of opportunity for violence apart from traditional modes of organizing violence.

Different to Jamaica and El Salvador where violence was increasingly organized on higher stages, Belize in fact experienced a short peak of the level of violence in 1984. When Belize became independent and was still in the process of the creation of national institutions, it was challenged by an economic recession and SAPs of the IMF. Even before independence, crime rates increased and especially juvenile crime appeared to be a major urban problem. This led policy-makers and police officers to debate the "emergence of an increasing number of teenage offenders (…) particularly in the capital" (British Honduras Police Force, 1963, p. 4). By the early 1980s, this situation even worsened as it was claimed that "the main cause of concern was the incidence of robbery and stealing from persons, referred to loosely as 'mugging' in Belize City" (British Honduras Police Force, 1980). These are clear insights that the earlier established path of providing cultural scripts and underpinning these scripts by channeling rents towards the lower strata had ruptured.

Conclusion

With the end of the civil war in El Salvador in 1992, the dismantling of democratic socialism in Jamaica in 1980, and independence of Belize in 1981, the contemporary configuration of forms of violence becomes evident. These contemporary patterns of forms of violence developed out of legacies of rent-led development and emerging cultural scripts, which evolved over the *longue durée* in each case. Using both categories, the embeddedness of rents as well as the dynamics of cultural scripts of violence, it was possible to show distinct paths in which forms of violence emerged and changed over time.

In Jamaica, the weaknesses of an independent peasantry and the peculiarities of rent appropriation by a newly emerging state-class caused political leaders to be able to form political parties and to strengthen their power base by providing economic resources and party identities to the urban poor. By manipulating long-standing traditions of racial subordination and economic marginalization, these leaders and their parties became predominant mobilizers of violence, particularly in urban impoverished communities. These mobilizers co-opted subaltern groups into political parties. This was only possible, however, through the provision of economic resources in exchange for party loyalty. The analysis of cultural scripts of violence shows that earlier established cultural scripts persisted but were adjusted to new social contexts. Rent channeling was a prime facilitator of this process of adaptation. Therefore, new forms of violence arose and were integrated into the political system and the conflict between the two hegemonic parties. Youth gangs already existed and became quickly co-opted by the parties into this dyadic conflict. At the peak of this development, all forms of violence were related to this horizontal party conflict. With decreasing available resources, the integrational force of this path lost its validity.

The consequences of the dissolution of the Jamaican path will be discussed in detail in Chap. 5. It will demonstrate that violent actors formerly involved in political struggles gained increasing independence from their political roots. However, this is a still ongoing process. While politics became increasingly detached from violence and violent actors distanced themselves from the political competition between parties, forms of violence seems to have proliferated until today at first sight. This historical chapter, however, shows that violent actors and their corresponding forms of violence were already existent. As soon as the political conflict diminished, violent actors mutated towards a new raison d'être, such as organized gangs involved in the global drug economy, or simply remained in the scene (community violence and street gangs).

While in Jamaica, the politics co-opted violence and laid the framework in which forms of violence had to develop, El Salvador reveals a distinct dynamic. The strength of an independent peasantry compared to Jamaica, and the particular mode of rent appropriation, namely authoritarian oligarchic rule, impeded the direct co-optation of the subaltern class by the elite. Even though the peasantry became marginalized by the end of the nineteenth century, it struggled for cultural autonomy. Autochthonous cultural scripts such as honor as an organizational feature of violence remained and, as Chap. 4 will show, still remain relevant. While the oligarchy was unwilling or simply did not need to materially co-opt the lower strata, it used cultural scripts and their manipulation as a means to fragment and to decompose the peasantry. In contrast to Jamaica, where co-optation involved rent channeling, the oligarchy in El Salvador relied on the co-optation of cultural scripts of violence. However, the sharp bifurcation between the oligarchy and the marginalized and subordinated majority highlights the importance of vertical violence. Vertical violence furthermore escalated with the formation of the guerrilla and the beginning of the civil war. While the authoritarian oligarchic government co-opted cultural scripts of violence to strengthen their repressive capacity, the guerrilla fabricated an entire new cultural script of violence by creating an insurgent political culture, which allowed for revolutionary change.

In addition to vertical violence, violence between equally powerful rivals within the same social class has a long tradition and dates back to the early times of the rise of coffee cultivation. Although in El Salvador vertical violence was dominant, it did not completely replace horizontal violence. Horizontal violence even persisted during the civil war. Grievances, which initially emerged out of land conflicts in the nineteenth century, were steadily mobilized, manipulated, and even today fuel newly arising social conflicts.

During the civil war, the two major power blocks, the guerrilla as well as the authoritarian oligarchic government, were able to establish partial hegemony on the interpretation of meanings of violence. Once this political framework, in which different forms of violence were concentrated and tied together in a coherent system of ideology, slightly dissolved, new forms of violence seem to have emerged. These seemingly "new" forms, however, are based on earlier existent cultural scripts. What happened, indeed, was a deep transformation of the political economy of El Salvador. Chapter. 4 discusses these transformations and shows how they produced new enabling spaces of violence. At the same time, newly emerging mobilizers of violence are today able to draw on already established cultural scripts. The dissolution of El Salvador's historical path of dealing with violence gave rise to a complex situation in which different forms of violence overlay each other in terms of their historical roots, the cultural scripts they are drawing on, and the political economy in which they are embedded. While death squad violence punctually continues, repression spreads and gives rise to new forms of violence such as grassroots vigilantism and social cleansing. Ordinary horizontal violence between neighbors, family members, and whole families still continues. Finally, new actors arose during the civil war such as youth gangs and developed new forms of violence.

Finally, Belize's path of dealing with violence can be best described as a steady struggle to follow the Jamaican example. In contrast to Jamaica, however, direct access to rents through a dominant state-class were lacking. From the early beginnings, therefore, Belize was partially unable, from the Jamaican point of view, to co-opt violence and its forms into politics. From the Salvadorian point of view, in turn, Belize was unable to establish autochthonous forms of violence since the legacy of an independent peasantry historically lacked and the descendants of former slaves remained dependent on the urban forestocracy. Belize shares with both El Salvador and Jamaica that this intermediate path of dealing with violence was challenged in the early 1980s. And perhaps, Belize is the only case who virtually developed new forms of violence during this period. This will be discussed in Chap. 6.

Concerning the question of continuities and changes of violence, this chapter revealed a mixture of both for all three cases. As it was discussed in the introduction, a first group of authors exclusively draws on "new" causes of contemporary violence. A second group argues for linking today's violence to the ideologically fueled conflicts of the 1970s and 1980s. The analysis in this chapter in contrast shows that violence is deeply embedded in the history of all three societies. Today's forms of violence, at least in their cultural dimension, embark on longstanding cultural traditions which changed over time. Nevertheless, these cultural scripts already existed even before the escalation of apparent "political" conflicts during the "lost decade." In this same vein, this chapter shows that these political crises, that is the civil war in El Salvador and the party political conflict in Jamaica, are insufficient to explain contemporary forms of violence.

Co-optation and fabrication of cultural scripts of violence are the two concepts that are able to capture these dynamics. As it was argued, co-optation occurred in all three cases. In Jamaica, co-optation of violence involved channeling rents to urban poor communities in exchange for party loyalty. This enabled urban poor community members to exert violence in the name of politics. In El Salvador, in contrast, co-optation was restricted to cultural scripts and was mainly used to consolidate the repressive capacity of state and para-state organizations. In Belize, co-optation was incomplete as politics at the national level intended to create links to local-level politics. Because of lacking resources as well as cultural scripts that had not been strong enough, co-optation remained superficial. Finally, El Salvador as the only case under review shows the fabrication of an entirely new cultural script, namely, a revolutionary cultural script of violence.

Focusing on the *longue durée* of violence, this chapter exemplifies that the fundamental difference between Jamaica on the one hand, and El Salvador on the other, consists in the importance of either horizontal or vertical violence. The political economy of Jamaica and the legacies of British colonialism, slavery, and racial subordination not only impeded an independent peasantry to develop. On a much "deeper" level it impeded the organization of violence on the basis of autochthonous cultural scripts. When organization of violence took place during colonial rule, mobilizers of violence were forced to rely on existent but colonial cultural scripts of violence. When independence was promised after the Great Depression of the 1930s and the arising middle class gained access to "national" resources, it was easy to impose new cultural scripts linking violence to party identities. Only with this process, violence began to shift towards a horizontal level since it became integrated into partisan struggles. El Salvador, in contrast, proves the importance of both, continuing horizontal as well as erupting vertical violence in the *longue durée*. Even though Spanish colonialism and authoritarian oligarchic rule created a sharp class antagonism in El Salvador, which was outstanding compared to Latin American societies, an independent peasantry could develop. Even though this independent peasantry diminished significantly from the Liberal Reforms onwards, it did not dissolve immediately. The comparison of cultural scripts of violence accentuated the importance of honor in mobilizing violence. This suggests that in the *longue durée*, the peasantry at least preserved traditions of violence and therefore maintained a certain cultural autonomy. An interesting question, which cannot be answered in this study, is if this *relative* cultural autonomy of the Salvadoran peasantry (relative to Jamaica) is a structural precondition for the revolution, even though the peasantry apparently lost its economic autonomy. Thus, even though the immense social bifurcation in El Salvador (compared to other Latin American countries but not to the Caribbean) can explain the eruptions of vertical violence, the same fact does not account for horizontal violence.

NOTES

1. Indigo is a blue dye used for textiles in Europe and the Andes.
2. Logwood is a native dyewood used in European textile manufacturing.
3. The term ladino refers to formerly indigenous peasants who left their communities and became enculturated into Spanish Colonial culture. In the nineteenth century, the meaning of ladino changed. Before that, ladino referred to anyone not identified as either white or Indian.
4. Coffee cultivation is particularly prone to rent appropriation. Since between planting the tree (the initial investment) and the first harvest usually four to five years pass, the supply for coffee is inelastic. At the same time, the demand structure of coffee is equally inelastic. As an effect, prices are volatile and particularly subject to manipulations.
5. Great Britain integrated their colonies in two steps: initially, Barbados, Jamaica, and North America in the period between 1600 and 1650. In a subsequent step after 1750, other major colonies were acquired. Increasing military conflicts in the Caribbean forced Spain to retreat from Jamaica after the battle of Ocho Rios. With the Treaty of Madrid in 1670, Spain recognized British naval superiority.
6. The slave trade was abolished in 1807. Slavery was abolished in Jamaica in 1834. Slaves were however bound under the system of apprenticeship until 1838. The plantation was mainly owned by an absentee and managed by whites who lived in Jamaica. The bureaucratic apparatus managed the whole economic process. Work itself was done by slaves. For the economic rational of plantations vs. other types of production systems, see Wolf and Mintz (1977).
7. The racial nature of the oligarchy is evident. Until now, race is a common but complex category of interpreting social inequalities in Jamaica (Thomas, 2004). Inherent to this society was and still is that class and race overlap (Smith, 1965). Although it may sound unfamiliar to talk about "white," "brown," and "black" social groups, this is a longstanding social science tradition in Jamaica.
8. The colonial "state" in its initial phase therefore grew through control of labor and repression (Bulmer-Thomas, 2012). Coercion and denied access to land therefore was the initial idea behind state formation. In theory, both for the state as well as the planter elite, which in reality converged, increasing population should have provoked a switch in its behavior. While formerly labor was controlled though coercion and repression, an increasing labor surplus meant that the elite no longer needed to exclusively rely on repression. However, in the Jamaican case, this modest response of the elites is doubtful, since harsh punishments of even minor crimes continued (Paton, 2001, p. 284)

9. Mintz (1996, p. 96) distinguishes between proto-peasants, who "are slaves who later became peasant freedmen, either through emancipation (as in the case of Jamaica) or revolution (as in the case of Haiti)" and runaway peasants or maroons, "which were formed by escaping slavery rather than by submitting it." Indeed, larger maroon communities were founded instantly after the Spanish defeat. Two larger communities excel: the Leeward and the Windward communities. With the end of the First Maroon War in 1739/40, the British Navy came to recognize that it could not destroy maroon communities in Jamaica and searched for a peace agreement. The maroons in contrast had to accept that they have to continue to chase runaway slaves. The Second Maroon War in 1795/96 effectively proved this treaty (Price, 2003; Thompson, 2006; Wright, 1970).

10. Although the transition towards Crown Colony created several new central institutions, the Crown's authority fit into yet existing structures of power. The plantocracy still dominated large segments of the economy and even controlled the institutions newly created by the Crown (e.g. banana marketing agencies, local credit banks, local Justices of Peace). At the parish level, the power of the elite therefore remained intact (Post, 1969, p. 386).

11. Banana exports as a share of total exports increased considerably in the latter third of the nineteenth century. In 1870, banana production was virtually non-existent. In 1890, it made up19.1 percent of exports, in 1910 it made up 52 percent (Eisner, 1961, p. 238). Although banana production was dominated by metropolitan capital, a significant number of small peasants was engaged in banana production (Wiley, 2008, p. 75). However, in line with this trend, internal stratification among the peasantry developed with some peasants remaining in subsistence production and others buying additional land to get engaged in export. By 1890, peasants were producing almost 39 percent of cash crops, and 75 percent of total agricultural produce (Post, 1978, p. 37)

12. Belize's initial name was British Honduras. The name changed to Belize in 1973. Throughout this study, Belize will be used.

13. The question of land ownership in Belize is very complex. Since the British Empire did not claim sovereignty on the settlement until the official establishment of Crown Colony in 1862, the legal status of land was unclear. At least since the late eighteenth century, Great Britain did exercise de facto sovereignty (Bolland & Shoman, 1977).

14. More important than mahogany land initially was access to the rivers since the mahogany trees had to be cut on sight and then floated to the mouth of the rivers. Land tenure therefore developed with the claim on land nearby the rivers (Ashcraft, 1973, p. 29).

15. Among the most important ones was the rebellion in 1831 under the leadership of Samuel Sharp. The 1831 Rebellion, in which already more than

20,000 slaves may have been involved, provoked a mayor violent reaction of the oligarchy. More than 200 slaves were killed during the rebellion and another 300 were executed later on (Reckord, 1968, p. 122). Furthermore, in 1865 the Morant Bay rebellion broke out. Generally, civil unrest after Emancipation concerned concrete issues, such as personal freedom, access to land, and wages (Craton, 1996). Slave rebellions were frequent throughout the whole period of slavery.

16. See, e.g., Johnson and Lipsett-Rivera (1998) for a detailed discussion of honor violence in distance to superior authorities and for the different notions that honor violence had as soon as it got attached to a superior political level in colonial Latin America.

17. *Spanish Original: "Se ven por las calles multidud de niños vagos, sin oficio, sin concurrir á la escuela sin que se sepa á qué los dedican sus padres, y sin que nadie cuido de su conducta y educacion ... No hai quien no porte bajo la camisa puñales y otras armas prohibidas de dia y de noche, en la ciudad y en el campo."*

18. The police force in El Salvador from this time on was split in three different bodies. The Guardia Nacional, formed in 1912, was obliged to control the countryside; the Policía de Hacienda founded in the last decades of the nineteenth century initially with the aim of combatting smugglers and controlling the production and distribution of alcohol; and the Policía Nacional, which was created to particularly control urban areas.

19. Initially, the Jamaican Worker's Trade Union (JWTU) was founded in 1935. Bustamante, however, was expelled in 1937; in the same year he founded the Bustamante Industrial Trade Union (BITU), which led to the foundation of the Jamaica Labor Party (JLP) in 1943. In opposition, Norman Manley founded the People's National Party (PNP) in 1938 and, inspired by the Fabian labor movement, the Trade Union Congress (TUC) as the labor movement wing of the PNP in 1939 (Hart, 1999).

20. Citrus in the South of Belize (mainly in Stan Creek) is almost exclusively produced for export to the United States and the United Kingdom. Around 95 percent of the crop is destined for exportation. Producers of citrus include smallholders, independent medium- and large-scale producers, as well as corporate estates owned by international processing companies. Even though citrus production is concentrated on a small number of farms, less than 40 percent of citrus is grown on company estates (Moberg, 1991). Thus, production relies on the capacities of small-scale producers. The same applies to sugar, which is mainly planted in Orange Walk in the north. With the increasing significance of sugar, "medium sized cash crop producers" (Brockmann, 1985, p. 188) engaged in the production.

21. *Spanish Original: "(...) eran pequeñas riñas que terminaban al intervenir los agentes de la policía. Después ciertos estudiantes usaron hebillas gigantes*

en los cinchos, para golpear a los de la barra contraria; siguió el empleo de las piedras, ladrillos y garrotes como armas contundentes. El progreso de barbarie continuó (...). Y ahora, salen a relucir armas de fuego, se siguen lanzando piedras con la consiguiente destrucción y se golpea a sacerdotes."

22. These sources are derived from the critical analysis of newspapers from 1945 to 1980. The Estudios Centroamericanos presents as a valuable source as it published uncommented press overviews until the end of the 1970s.

23. *Spanish Original: "[e]l día primero del año – podriamos tomar cual quier otro día por vía de ejemplo – fue una fecha sangrienta para El Salvador (...) [con] (...) un saldo de 21 muertos y 21 heridos graves. Y no ha habido revolución, ni acontecimiento ninguno de carácter público (...) No ha sido más que brotes esporádicos de un mal popular que ca cundiendo como pedemos comprobarlo a diario en la prensa".*

24. *Spanish Original: "La delincuencia toma en El Salvador caracteres cada vez más graves y amenazantes (...). En los últimos días San Salvador vivió momentos de pánico cuando varios ladrones en pleno día y en el centro de la capital fueron sitiados durante varias horas por numerosos agentes policiales pesadamente armados, en el interior de estavlecemientos comerciales dondo pretendían robar, y unos y otros hicieron uso de armas de fuego habiendo resultado una persona muerta y dos lesionadas, actos reveladores de la gravedad de la situación."*

25. The first of these housing programs occurred in West Kingston in 1966 under JLP government. Black-o-Wall, a huge squatter settlement and one of the most deprived areas of Kingston, was destroyed by bulldozers and the Tivoli Gardens housing complex was created. The JLP boss in this area, Edward Seaga, who became prime minister in 1980, was one of the leading figures associated with the construction of Tivoli Gardens (Gray, 1991, p. 119). In the aftermath, living spaces were exclusively granted to JLP supporters. PNP supporters who formerly saw their houses destroyed by bulldozers, in contrast, were not allocated.

26. Increasingly, the *Phoenix City Gang* allied with the JLP and the *Vikings* with the PNP. Moreover, Edward Seaga, who became Minister of Development and Welfare in 1962, used his organizational resources to integrate West Kingston youth and particularly gang members into the Youth Development Agency (Gray, 2004, pp. 80–85). As an effect, Youth Development Agency "affiliation was soon regarded as tantamount to JLP affiliation."

27. Both Tom Tavares Finson (2012) and Paul Burke (2012) used this term in their interviews with the author to interpret party relations with the opposing party at this time.

28. Jamaica has long experienced outward as well as returning migration. A first phase can be dated immediately after Abolition; a second phase began in the early twentieth century when large numbers of workers migrated towards Panama to build the canal. That was followed by a third phase in the years before independence when many Jamaicans left the island to find proper work in the United Kingdom. Finally, a fourth phase began during the second term of Manley's government (Thomas-Hope, 1992).

29. The irony of Belizean SAPs was that many of these companies were bought by Lord Ashcroft, a British multimillionaire and the Tory's largest donor. While his Belize Bank accounted for almost 50 percent of banking in Belize, "it faced 80 separate charges of failing to comply with anti-money-laundering laws – charges the bank firmly denied – the case was withdrawn for fear that any damage to the bank would trigger the collapse of the Belizean economy" (The Guardian, 2009). He additionally owned the national telecommunication company, the shrimp register, the offshore business register, and a TV company, if not more.

30. The Truth Commission of 1993 found that state and para-state forces were responsible for 85 percent of violations against civilians (Naciones Unidas, 1993, p. 41).

REFERENCES

Acevedo, C. (1996). The Historical Background to the Conflict. In J. K. Boyce (Ed.), *Economic Policy for Building Peace. The Lessons of El Salvador* (pp. 19–30). Boulder, CO/London: Lynne Rienner.

Albiac, M. D. (2007). Los ricos más ricos de El Salvador. In R. Cardenal & L. A. González (Eds.), *El Salvador: la transición y sus problemas* (pp. 153–183). San Salvador, El Salvador: UCA Editores.

Alvarenga, A. (2006). *Cultura y ética de la violencia: El Salvador, 1880–1932*. San Salvador, El Salvador: CONCULTURA.

Alvarenga, P. (1998). Auxiliary Forces in the Shaping of the Repressive System. El Salvador, 1880–1930. In A. Chomsky & A. A. Lauria-Santiago (Eds.), *Identity and Struggle at the Margins of the Nation-State. The Laboring Peoples of Central America and the Hispanic Caribbean* (pp. 122–150). Durham, NC/London: Duke University Press.

Alvarez, Y. (1988). External Debt and Adjustment: The Case of Belize 1980–1986. *Social & Economic Studies, 37*(4), 39–56.

Anderson, P., & Witter, M. (1994). Crisis, Adjustment and Social Change: A Case Study of Jamaica. In E. Le Franc (Ed.), *Consequences of Structural Adjustment: A Review of the Jamaican Experience* (pp. 1–35). Kingston, Jamaica: Canoe Press.

Anderson, T. P. (1971). *Matanza: El Salvador's Communist Revolt of 1932.* Lincoln, UK: University of Nebraska Press.

Arnson, C. J. (2002). Window on the Past: A Declassified History of Death Squads in El Salvador. In B. B. Campbell & A. D. Brenner (Eds.), *Death Squads in Global Perspective. Murder with Deniability* (pp. 85–124). New York: Palgrave Macmillan.

Ashcraft, N. D. (1969). *Land Use and Trade: The Processes of Economic Change in British Honduras* (Ph.D. Dissertation). Waltham, MA/Boston, MA: Brandeis University.

Ashcraft, N. D. (1973). *Colonialism and Underdevelopment: Processes of Political Economic Change in British Honduras.* New York: Teachers College Press.

Ashdown, P. (1978). Antonio Soberanis and the Disturbances in Belize, 1934–1937. *Caribbean Quarterly, 24*(1/2), 61–74.

Ashdown, P. (1980). The Labourer's Riot of 1894 (Part II). *Belizean Studies, 8*(2), 22–28.

Ashdown, P. (1981). The Belize Elite and Its Power Base: Land Labour and Commerce Circa 1890. *Belizean Studies, 9*(5&6), 30–43.

Ashdown, P. (1982). The Belizean Elite. *Belizean Studies, 10*(1), 10–16.

Aubey, R. T. (1969). Entrepreneurial Formation in El Salvador. *Explorations in Entrepreneurial History, 6*(3), 268–285.

Babcock, E. C., & Conway, D. (2000). Why International Migration Has Important Consequences for the Development of Belize. *Yearbook. Conference of Latin Americanist Geographers, 26,* 71–86.

Bakan, A. B. (1990). *Ideology and Class Conflict in Jamaica: The Politics of Rebellion.* Montreal, QC: McGill-Queen's University Press.

Barnett, C. (1985). The Impact of the Mexican Peso Devaluation on Belize – 1982. *Belcast Journal of Belizean Affairs, 2*(1), 29–36.

Basil, W. (1980). *Surplus Labour and Political Violence in Jamaica: The Dialectics of Political Corruption, 1966–1976* (Ph.D. Dissertation). New York: City University of New York.

Bayly, C. A. (2004). *The Birth of the Modern World, 1780–1914: Global Connections and Comparisons.* Malden, MA/Oxford, UK/Melbourne, VIC: Blackwell.

Beckford, G., & Witter, M. (1980). *Small Garden… Bitter Weed: The Political Economy of Struggle and Change in Jamaica.* London: Zed Books.

Bolland, N. O. (1981). Systems of Domination After Slavery: The Control of Land and Labor in the British West Indies After 1838. *Comparative Studies in Society and History, 23*(4), 591–619.

Bolland, N. O. (2001). *The Politics of Labour in the British Caribbean: The Social Origins of Authoritarianism and Democracy in the Labour Movement.* Kingston, Jamaica: Ian Randle.

Bolland, N. O. (2003). *Colonialism and Resistance in Belize: Essays in Historical Sociology.* Benque Viejo del Carmen, Belize: Cubola.

Bolland, N. O., & Shoman, A. (1977). *Land in Belize: 1765–1871*. Kingston, Jamaica: University of the West Indies.

Bright, C., & Geyer, M. (2012). Benchmarks of Globalization: The Global Condition, 1850–2010. In D. Northrop (Ed.), *A Companion to World History* (pp. 285–300). New York: Wiley-Blackwell.

British Honduras Police Force. (1963). Annual Report of the British Honduras Police Force for the Year 1963, Belize Archives & Records Service Anr Box 23, #171.

British Honduras Police Force. (1965). Annual Report of the British Honduras Police Force for the Year 1965, Belize Archives & Records Service Anr Box 23, #171.

British Honduras Police Force. (1980). Annual Report of the British Honduras Police Force for the Year 1980, Belize Archives & Records Service Anr Box 23, #171.

Brockett, C. D. (2005). *Political Movements and Violence in Central America*. Cambridge, UK: Cambridge University Press.

Brockmann, T. C. (1985). Ethnic Participation in Orange Walk Economic Development. *Ethnic Groups, 6*(2/3), 187–207.

Bulmer-Thomas, B., & Bulmer-Thomas, V. (2012). *The Economic History of Belize: From the 17th Century to Post-Independence*. Benque Viejo del Carmen, Belize: Cubola.

Bulmer-Thomas, V. (1987). *The Political Economy of Central America Since 1920*. Cambridge, MA: Cambridge University Press.

Bulmer-Thomas, V. (2012). *The Economic History of the Caribbean Since the Napoleonic Wars*. Cambridge, UK: Cambridge University Press.

Burke, P. (2012, December 5). Interview by H. Warnecke. PNP Member, Former Leader of the People's National Party Youth Organization (PNPYO) Kingston, Jamaica.

Cabarrús, C. R. (1983). *Génesis de una revolución: Análisis del surgimiento y desarrollo de la organización campesina en El Salvador*. México: Ediciones de la casa chata.

Cardenal Izquierdo, A. S. (2002). *La democracia y la tierra: Cambio político en El Salvador*. Madrid, Spain: Centro de Investigaciones Sociológicas.

Chevannes, B. (1981). The Rastafari and the Urban Youth. In C. Stone & A. Brown (Eds.), *Perspectives on Jamaica in the Seventies* (pp. 392–423). Kingston, Jamaica: Jamaica Publishing House.

Ching, E. (2004). Patronage and Politics under General Maximiliano Martínez, 1931–1939: The Local Roots of Military Authoritarianism in El Salvador. In A. A. Lauria-Santiago & L. Binford (Eds.), *Landscapes of Struggle. Politics, Society, and Community in El Salvador* (pp. 50–70). Pittsburgh, PA: Pittsburgh University Press.

Ching, E. (2014). *Authoritarian El Salvador: Politics and the Origins of the Military Regimes, 18801940*. Notre Dame, IN: University of Notre Dame Press.

Clarke, C. (2006). *Decolonizing the Colonial City: Urbanization and Stratification in Kingston, Jamaica*. Oxford, UK/New York: Oxford University Press.

Clarke, C., & Howard, D. (2006). Contradictory Socio-Economic Consequences of Structural Adjustment in Kingston, Jamaica. *The Geographical Journal, 172*(2), 106–129.

Colindres, E. (1976). La tenencia de la tierra en El Salvador. *ECA: Estudios Centroamericanos, 31*(335/336), 463–472.

Colindres, E. (1977). *Fundamentos económicos de la burguesía salvadoreña*. San Salvador, El Salvador: UCA Editores.

Colonial Office. (1948). *Annual Report on British Honduras for the Year 1948*. London: Colonial Office.

Craton, M. (1996). Continuity Not Change: The Incidence of Unrest among Ex-slaves in the British West Indies, 1838–1876. In H. M. Beckles & V. Shepherd (Eds.), *Caribbean Freedom: Economy and Society from Emancipation to the Present* (pp. 192–206). Princeton, NJ: Wiener.

Craton, M. (1997). *Empire, Enslavement, and Freedom in the Caribbean*. Kingston, Jamaica: Ian Randle.

Curtin, P. D. (1969). *The Atlantic Slave Trade: A Census*. Madison, WI: University of Wisconsin Press.

Dalby, J. R. (2000). *Crime and Punishment in Jamaica: A Quantitative Analysis of the Assize Court Records, 1756–1856*. Mona, Jamaica: University of West Indies.

Davies, K. G. (1974). *The North Atlantic World in the Seventeenth Century*. Minneapolis, MN: University of Minnesota Press.

Davis, C. E. (1984). Evolution of Jamaica's Bauxite Taxation and Royalty Regimes: 1947–1984. *The JBI Journal, 3*(1), 79–108.

Davis, C. E. (1985). *The Jamaican Bauxite Industry: Present Situation and Prospects* (Department of Economics Occasional Paper Series: Vol. 4). Mona, Jamaica: University of the West Indies.

Diario Oficial. (1883, December 15). Estadística: Delitos. *Diario Oficial*, p. 1202.

Dickey, C. (1983). Behind the Death Squads: Who They Are, How They Work, and Why No One Can Stop Them. *New Republic, 189*(26), 16–21.

Downing, T. J. (1978). *Agricultural Modernisation in El Salvador, Central America* (Centre of Latin American Studies Working Papers: No. 32). Cambridge: University of Cambridge.

Dunkerley, J. (1982). *The Long War: Dictatorship and Revolution in El Salvador*. London/New York: Verso.

Dunn, R. S. (1972). *Sugar and Slaves: The Rise of the Planter Class in the English West Indies, 1624–1713*. New York: Norton.

Dur, P. F. (1998). US Diplomacy and the Salvadorean Revolution of 1931. *Journal of Latin American Studies, 30*(1), 95–119.

Edie, C. J. (1991). *Democracy by Default: Dependency and Clientelism in Jamaica.* Boulder, CO/London: Lynne Rienner.

Eisner, G. (1961). *Jamaica, 1830–1930: A Study in Economic Growth.* Manchester, UK: Manchester University Press.

Elsenhans, H. (2015). *Saving Capitalism from the Capitalists: World Capitalism and Global History.* New Delhi, India: Sage.

Eltis, D. (2000). *The Rise of African Slavery in the Americas.* Cambridge, UK: Cambridge University Press.

Eltis, D. (2003). Labour and Coercion in the English Atlantic World: From the Seventeenth to the Early Twentieth Century. In G. J. Heuman & J. Walvin (Eds.), *The Slavery Reader* (pp. 58–67). London: Routledge.

Estudios Centroamericanos (ECA). (1952). Crónica de El Salvador. *ECA: Estudios Centroamericanos, VII*(59), 65–70.

Estudios Centroamericanos (ECA). (1956). Crónica de El Salvador: Problema social que se agrava. *ECA: Estudios Centroamericanos, XI*(105), 304.

Euraque, D. (2000). On the Origins of Civil War in Nineteenth-Century Honduras. In R. Earle (Ed.), *Rumours of Wars: Civil Conflict in Nineteenth-Century Latin America* (pp. 87–102). London: University of London.

Everitt, J. C. (1986). The Growth and Development of Belize City. *Journal of Latin American Studies, 18*(1), 75–111.

Everitt, J. C., & Ramsey, D. (2008). Tourism as a Development Strategy in Belize. *Ara: Journal of Tourism Research, 1*(1), 1–14.

Figueroa, M., & Sives, A. (2002). Homogenous Voting, Electoral Manipulation and the 'Garrison' Process in Post-Independence Jamaica. *Commonwealth & Comparative Politics, 40*(1), 81–108.

Figueroa, M., & Sives, A. (2003). Garrison Politics and Criminality in Jamaica. In A. Harriott (Ed.), *Understanding Crime in Jamaica. New Challenges for Public Policy* (pp. 63–88). Kingston, Jamaica: University of the West Indies Press.

Funkhouser, E. (1992). Mass Emigration, Remittances, and Economic Adjustment: The Case of El Salvador in the 1980s. In G. J. Borjas & R. B. Freeman (Eds.), *Immigration and the Workforce: Economic Consequences for the United States and Source Areas* (pp. 135–176). Chicago, IL: University of Chicago Press.

Gaceta Del Salvador. (1847, March 28). Hay alcaldes en El Salvador? *Gaceta del Gobierno Supremo del Estado del Salvador en la República de Centro América,* p. 7.

Gaceta Del Salvador. (1848, March 24). Demostración de delitos. *Gaceta del Gobierno Supremo del Estado del Salvador en la República de Centro América,* p. 208.

Galloway, J. H. (1989). *The Sugar Cane Industry: An Historical Geography from Its Origins to 1914.* Cambridge, UK: Cambridge University Press.

Gannon, J. C. (1976). *The Origins and Development of Jamaica's Two-Party System, 1930–1975* (Ph.D. Dissertation). Saint Luis: Washington University.

Gould, J. L. (2010). On the Road to "El Porvenir": A Revolutionary and Counterrevolutionary Violence in El Salvador and Nicaragua. In G. Grandin & G. M. Joseph (Eds.), *A Century of Revolution: Insurgent and Counterinsurgent Violence during Latin America's Long Cold War* (pp. 88–120). Durham, NC/London: Duke University Press.

Gould, J. L., & Lauria-Santiago, A. A. (2008). *To Rise in Darkness: Revolution, Repression, and Memory in El Salvador, 1920–1932*. Durham, NC/London: Duke University Press.

Grant, C. H. (1976). *The Making of Modern Belize: Politics, Society and British Colonialism in Central America*. Cambridge, UK: Cambridge University Press.

Gray, O. (1991). *Radicalism and Social Change in Jamaica, 1960–1972*. Knoxville, TN: University of Tennessee Press.

Gray, O. (2003a). Predation Politics and the Political Impasse in Jamaica. *Small Axe, 7*(1), 72–94.

Gray, O. (2003b). Rough Culture or Avatar of Liberation: The Jamaican Lumpenproletariat. *Social & Economic Studies, 52*(1), 1–33.

Gray, O. (2004). *Demeaned but Empowered: The Social Power of the Urban Poor in Jamaica*. Kingston, Jamaica: University of the West Indies Press.

Guidos Véjar, R. (1980). *El ascenso del militarismo en El Salvador*. San Salvador, El Salvador: UCA Editores.

Hart, R. (1999). *Towards Decolonisation: Political, Labour and Economic Developments in Jamaica 1938–1945*. Kingston, Jamaica: Canoe Press.

Headley, B. D. (1988). War Ina "Babylon": Dynamics of the Jamaican Informal Drug Economy. *Social Justice, 15*(3/4 (33–34)), 61–86.

Headley, B. D. (1996). *The Jamaican Crime Scene: A Perspective*. Washington, DC: Howard University Press.

Herrera Mena, S. A. (2007). "No que muera, sino que se arrepienta el criminal y viva": El debate sobre el trabajo penitenciario en los impresos salvadoreños, 1880–1900. In A. M. Gómez & S. A. Herrera Mena (Eds.), *Los rostros de la violencia: Guatemala y El Salvador. Siglos XVIII y XIX* (pp. 189–223). San Salvador, El Salvador: UCA Editores.

Herrera Mena, S. A. (2011). Violencia legítima e ilegítima en El Salvador del siglo XIX: algunas reflexiones. In E. Rey Tristán & P. Cagiao Vila (Eds.), *Conflicto, memoria y pasados traumáticos: El Salvador contemporáneo* (pp. 137–152). Santiago de Compostela, Spain: Universidad de Santiago de Compostela.

Heuman, G. J. (1994). *The Killing Time: The Morant Bay Rebellion in Jamaica*. Knoxville, TN: University of Tennessee Press.

Heuman, G. J. (1995). Post-Emancipation Protest in Jamaica. In M. Turner (Ed.), *From Chattel Slaves to Wage Slaves: The Dynamics of Labour Bargaining in the Americas* (pp. 258–274). Kingston, Jamaica/Miami, FL: Ian Randle.

Heuman, G. J. (2003). The Free Coloreds in Jamaican Slave Society. In G. J. Heuman & J. Walvin (Eds.), *The Slavery Reader* (pp. 654–667). London: Routledge.

Higman, B. W. (2008). *Plantation Jamaica, 1750–1850: Capital and Control in a Colonial Economy*. Kingston, Jamaica: University of the West Indies Press.

Holt, T. C. (1992). *The Problem of Freedom: Race, Labor, and Politics in Jamaica and Britain, 1832–1938*. Baltimore/London: Johns Hopkins University Press.

Hoover Green, A. (2011). *Repertoires of Violence Against Noncombatants: The Role of Armed Group Institutions and Ideologies* (Ph.D. Dissertation). New Haven, CT: Yale University.

Huber, E., & Stephens, J. D. (1986). *Democratic Socialism in Jamaica: The Political Movement and Social Transformation in Dependent Capitalism*. Princeton, NJ: Princeton University Press.

Huber Stephens, E. (1987). Minerals Strategies and Development: International Political Economy, State, Class and the Role of the Bauxite/Aluminum and Copper Industries in Jamaica and Peru. *Studies in Comparative International Development, 22*(3), 60–102.

Inikori, J. E., & Engerman, S. L. (Eds.). (1998). *The Atlantic Slave Trade: Effects on Economies, Societies, and Peoples in Africa, the Americas, and Europe*. Durham, NC/London: Duke University Press.

James, H. (2001). *The End of Globalization: Lessons from the Great Depression*. Cambridge, MA: Harvard University Press.

Jefferson, O. (1972). *The Post-War Economic Development of Jamaica*. Kingston, Jamaica: Institute of Social and Economic Research, University of the West Indies.

Johnson, L. L., & Lipsett-Rivera, S. (Eds.). (1998). *The Faces of Honor: Sex, Shame, and Violence in Colonial Latin America*. Albuquerque, NM: University of New Mexico Press.

Kaufman, M. (1985). *Jamaica under Manley: Dilemmas of Socialism and Democracy*. London: Zed Books.

Kitson, D. (1982). Jamaica and the Electoral Coup of 1980. *Race & Class, 24*(2), 169–178.

Koselleck, R. (1972). Einleitung. In O. Brunner, W. Conze, & R. Koselleck (Eds.), *Geschichtliche Grundbegriffe* (pp. XIII–XXVII). Stuttgart, Germany: Ernst Klett Verlag.

La Prensa Gráfica. (1959, July 9). Las violencias deben terminar. *La Prensa Gráfica*, p. 18.

Lacey, T. (1977). *Violence and Politics in Jamaica 1960–70: Internal Security in a Developing Country*. Manchester, UK: Manchester University Press.

Lauria-Santiago, A. A. (1999). *An Agrarian Republic: Commercial Agriculture and the Politics of Peasant Communities in El Salvador, 1823–1914*. Pittsburgh, PA: University of Pittsburgh Press.

Lauria-Santiago, A. A. (2005). The Culture and Politics of State Terror and Repression in El Salvador. In C. Menjívar & N. Rodriguez (Eds.), *When States Kill: Latin America, the U.S., and Technologies of Terror* (pp. 85–114). Austin, TX: University of Texas Press.

Lauria-Santiago, A. A., & Gould, J. L. (2004). "They Call Us Thieves and Steal Our Wage": Toward a Reinterpretation of the Salvadoran Rural Mobilization, 1929–1931. *The Hispanic American Historical Review, 84*(2), 191–237.

Lewis, W. A. (1950). The Industrialisation of the British West Indies. *Caribbean Economic Review, 2*(1), 1–51.

Lindo-Fuentes, H. (1990). *Weak Foundations: The Economy of El Salvador in the Nineteenth Century 1821–1898*. Berkeley, CA/Los Angeles: University of California Press.

Lindo-Fuentes, H. (1995). The Economy of Central America: From Bourbon Reform to Liberal Reforms. In L. Gudmundson & H. Lindo-Fuentes (Eds.), *Central America, 1821–1871. Liberalism before Liberal Reform* (pp. 13–78). Tuscaloosa, AL/London: University of Alabama Press.

Lungo, M. (2000). *La Tierra Urbana*. San Salvador, El Salvador: UCA Editores.

MacLeod, M. J. (1973). *Spanish Central America: A Socioeconomic History 1520–1720*. Berkeley, CA/Los Angeles: University of California Press.

Mariscal, N. (1979). Regímenes políticos en El Salvador. *ECA: Estudios Centroamericanos, 34*(365), 139–152.

Marshall, W. K. (1968). Notes on Peasant Development in the West Indies Since 1838. *Social & Economic Studies, 17*(3), 252–263.

Mazzei, J. (2009). *Death Squads or Self-Defense Forces? How Paramilitary Groups Emerge and Challenge Democracy in Latin America*. Chapel Hill, NC/London: University of North Carolina Press.

McClintock, M. (1985). *The American Connection: Volume 1: State Terror and Popular Resistance in El Salvador*. London: Zed Books.

Meeks, B. (2000). *Narratives of Resistance: Jamaica, Trinidad, The Caribbean*. Kingston, Jamaica: University of the West Indies Press.

Mintz, S. W. (1987). *Die süße Macht: Kulturgeschichte des Zuckers*. Frankfurt a.M., Germany: Campus.

Mintz, S. W. (1996). The Origins of Reconstituted Peasantries. In H. M. Beckles & V. Shepherd (Eds.), *Caribbean Freedom: Economy and Society from Emancipation to the Present* (pp. 94–98). Princeton, NJ: Wiener.

Mintz, S. W. (2003). The Origins of the Jamaican Market System. In G. J. Heuman & J. Walvin (Eds.), *The Slavery Reader* (pp. 521–544). London: Routledge.

Moberg, M. (1991). Citrus and the State: Factions and Class Formation in Rural Belize. *American Ethnologist, 18*(2), 215–233.

Moberg, M. (1992a). Structural Adjustment and Rural Development: Inferences from a Belizean Village. *The Journal of Developing Areas, 27*(1), 1–20.

Moberg, M. (1992b). Continuity under Colonial Rule: The Alcalde System and the Garifuna in Belize, 1858–1969. *Ethnohistory, 39*(1), 1–19.

Moberg, M. (1996). Myths That Divide: Immigrant Labor and Class Segmentation in the Belizean Banana Industry. *American Ethnologist, 23*(2), 311–330.

Munroe, T. (1972). *The Politics of Constitutional Decolonization: Jamaica 1944–62.* Kingston, Jamaica: Institute of Social and Economic Research, University of the West Indies.

Naciones Unidas. (1993). *De la locura a la esperanza: La guerra de 12 años en El Salvador: Informe de la Comision de la Verdad para El Salvador.* San Salvador, El Salvador/New York: United Nations Publications.

Nairn, A. (1984). Behind the Death Squads. *The Progressive, 48*(5), 20–29.

North, L. (1982). *Bitter Grounds: Roots of Revolt in El Salvador.* Toronto, ON: Between the Lines.

Paige, J. M. (1997). *Coffee and Power: Revolution and the Rise of Democracy in Central America.* Cambridge, MA/London: Harvard University Press.

Paton, D. (2001). The Penalties of Freedom: Punishment in Postemancipation Jamaica. In R. D. Salvatore, C. Aguirre, & G. M. Joseph (Eds.), *Crime and Punishment in Latin America: Law and Society Since Late Colonial Times* (pp. 275–307). Durham, NC/London: Duke University Press.

Payne, A. J. (1994). *Politics in Jamaica.* New York: St. Martin's Press.

Pearce, J. (1986). *Promised Land: Peasant Rebellion in Chalatenango, El Salvador.* London: Latin America Bureau.

Pérez Brignoli, H. (1995). Indians, Communists, and Peasants: The 1932 Rebellion in El Salvador. In W. Roseberry, L. Gudmundson, & M. S. Kutschbach (Eds.), *Coffee, Society, and Power in Latin America* (pp. 232–261). Baltimore/London: John Hopkins University Press.

Phelps, O. W. (1960). Rise of the Labour Movement in Jamaica. *Social & Economic Studies, 9*(4), 417–468.

Piccato, P. (2001). *City of Suspects: Crime in Mexico City, 1900–1931.* Durham, NC/London: Duke University Press.

Porter, A. (1999). Introduction: Britain and the Empire in the Nineteenth Century. In A. Porter & W. R. Louis (Eds.), *The Oxford History of the British Empire: Vol. III: The Nineteenth Century* (pp. 1–28). Oxford, UK: Oxford University Press.

Post, K. (1969). The Politics of Protest in Jamaica, 1938: Some Problems of Analysis and Conceptualization. *Social & Economic Studies, 18*(4), 374–390.

Post, K. (1978). *Arise Ye Starvelings: The Jamaican Labour Rebellion of 1938 and Its Aftermath.* The Hague, Netherlands/Boston/London: Nijhoff.

Price, R. (2003). Maroons and Their Communities. In G. J. Heuman & J. Walvin (Eds.), *The Slavery Reader* (pp. 608–625). London: Routledge.

Reckord, M. (1968). The Jamaica Slave Rebellion of 1831. *Past & Present, 40*(1), 108–125.

Reed, N. A. (2001). *The Caste War of Yucatán* (Rev. ed.). Stanford, CA: Stanford University Press.
Restall, M. (2014). Crossing to Safety? Frontier Flight in Eighteenth-Century Belize and Yucatan. *Hispanic American Historical Review, 94*(3), 381–419.
Riekenberg, M. (2003). *Gewaltsegmente: Über einen Ausschnitt der Gewalt in Lateinamerika.* Leipzig, Germany: Leipziger Universitätsverlag.
Riekenberg, M. (2014). *Staatsferne Gewalt: Eine Geschichte Lateinamerikas (1500–1930).* Frankfurt a.M., Germany: Campus.
Savenije, W. (2009). *Maras y Barras: Pandillas y violencia juvenil en los barrios marginales de Centroamérica.* San Salvador, El Salvador: FLACSO.
Savenije, W., & Beltrán, M. A. (2005). *Compitiendo en bravuras: violencia estudiantil en el área metropolitana de San Salvador.* San Salvador, El Salvador: FLACSO.
Segovia, A. (1996). The War Economy of the 1980s. In J. K. Boyce (Ed.), *Economic Policy for Building Peace. The Lessons of El Salvador* (pp. 31–50). Boulder, CO/London: Lynne Rienner.
Senior, O. (1972). *The Message Is Change: A Perspective on the 1972 General Election.* Kingston, Jamaica: Kingston Publishing.
Sheller, M. (2001). *Democracy After Slavery: Black Publics and Peasant Radicalism in Haiti and Jamaica.* Gainesville, FL: University Press of Florida.
Shoman, A. (1990). Belize: An Authoritarian Democratic State in Central America. In Society for the Promotion of Education and Research (SPEAR) (Ed.), *2nd Annual Studies on Belize Conference: Selected Papers* (pp. 42–63). Belize City, Belize: SPEAR.
Shoman, A. (2010). *Belize's Independence and Decolonization in Latin America: Guatemala, Britain, and the UN.* New York: Palgrave Macmillan.
Shoman, A. (2011). *A History of Belize in 13 Chapters.* Belize City, Belize: Angelus Press.
Silber, I. C. (2011). *Everyday Revolutionaries: Gender, Violence, and Disillusionment in Postwar El Salvador.* New Brunswick, NJ: Rutgers University Press.
Sives, A. (2003). The Historical Roots of Violence in Jamaica. The Hearne Report 1949. In A. Harriott (Ed.), *Understanding Crime in Jamaica. New Challenges for Public Policy* (pp. 49–61). Kingston, Jamaica: University of the West Indies Press.
Sives, A. (2010). *Elections, Violence, and the Democratic Process in Jamaica, 1944–2007.* Kingston, Jamaica: Ian Randle.
Smith, M. G. (1965). *The Plural Society in the British West Indies.* Berkeley, CA/ Los Angeles: University of California Press.
St. Pierre, M. (1978). The 1938 Jamaican Disturbances: A Portrait of Mass Reaction Against Colonialism. *Social & Economic Studies, 27*(2), 171–196.
Stanley, W. (1996). *The Protection Racket State: Elite Politics, Military Extortion, and Civil War in El Salvador.* Philadelphia, PA: Temple University Press.

Stinchcombe, A. L. (1995). *Sugar Island Slavery in the Age of Enlightenment: The Political Economy of the Caribbean World*. Princeton, NJ: Princeton University Press.

Stone, C. (1980). *Democracy and Clientelism in Jamaica*. New Brunswick, NJ: Transaction Publishers.

Suter, J. (1996a). Matanza: Ethnozid als "Lösung" gesellschaftlicher Konflikte in Lateinamerika zur Zeit der Weltwirtschaftskrise. In S. Karlen & A. Wimmer (Eds.), *"Integration und Transformation": Ethnische Gemeinschaften, Staat und Weltwirtschaft in Lateinamerika seit ca. 1850* (pp. 397–425). Stuttgart, Germany: Heinz.

Suter, J. (1996b). *Prosperität und Krise in einer Kaffeerepublik: Modernisierung, sozialer Wandel und politischer Umbruch in El Salvador, 1910–1945*. Frankfurt a.M., Germany: Vervuert.

Sutherland, A. (1998). *The Making of Belize: Globalization in the Margins*. Westport, CN/London: Bergin & Garvey.

Tavares Finson, T. (2012, December 7). Interview by H. Warnecke. Member of the Senate of Jamaica (JLP). Electoral Commission of Jamaica. Kingston, Jamaica.

Taylor, W. B. (1979). *Drinking, Homicide, and Rebellion in Colonial Mexican Villages*. Stanford, CA: Stanford University Press.

The Guardian. (2009, November 1). 'Lord Ashcroft of Belize' Facing Eviction as Country Turns on Him. *The Guardian*.

Thomas, D. A. (2004). *Modern Blackness: Nationalism, Globalization, and the Politics of Culture in Jamaica*. Durham, NC/London: Duke University Press.

Thomas, M. (2012). *Violence and Colonial Order: Police, Workers and Protest in the European Colonial Empires, 1918–1940*. Cambridge: Cambridge University Press.

Thomas-Hope, E. (1992). *Caribbean Migration*. Kingston, Jamaica: University of the West Indies Press.

Thompson, A. O. (2006). *Flight to Freedom: African Runaways and Maroons in the Americas*. Kingston, Jamaica: University of the West Indies Press.

Tilley, V. Q. (2005). *Seeing Indians: A Study of Race, Nation, and Power in El Salvador*. Albuquerque, NM: University of New Mexico Press.

Viterna, J. (2013). *Women in War: The Micro-Processes of Mobilization in El Salvador*. Oxford, UK: Oxford University Press.

White, A. (1975). *Squatter Settlements, Politics and Class Conflict* (Occasional Papers: #18). Glasgow, Scotland: University of Glasgow.

Wiley, J. (2008). *Banana: Empires, Trade Wars, and Globalization*. Lincoln, NE: University of Nebraska Press.

Williams, P. J., & Walter, K. (1997). *Militarization and Demilitarization in El Salvador's Transition to Democracy*. Pittsburgh, PA: University of Pittsburgh Press.

Wilson, E. A. (2004). *La Crisis de la Integración Nacional en El Salvador, 1919–1935. Biblioteca de Historia Salvadoreña.* San Salvador, El Salvador: CONCULTURA.

Wolf, E. R. (2001). *Pathways of Power: Building an Anthropology of the Modern World.* Berkeley, CA/Los Angeles: University of California Press.

Wolf, E. R., & Mintz, S. W. (1977). Haciendas and Plantations. In R. G. Keith (Ed.), *Haciendas and Plantations in Latin American History* (pp. 36–62). New York/London: Holmes & Meier Publishers.

Wood, E. J. (2003). *Insurgent Collective Action and Civil War in El Salvador.* New York: Cambridge University Press.

Wright, P. (1970). War and Peace with the Maroons, 1730–1739. *Caribbean Quarterly, 16*(1), 5–27.

Wyatt, R. (1908). British Honduras Report on the Police Force, Belize Archives & Records Service Anr Box 23, #168.

Zamosc, L. (1989). Class Conflict in an Export Economy: The Social Roots of the Salvadorean Insurrection of 1932. In J. L. Flora & E. Torres-Rivas (Eds.), *Sociology of "Developing Countries". Central America* (pp. 56–75). London: Macmillan.

Zinecker, H. (2004). *El Salvador nach dem Bürgerkrieg: Ambivalenzen eines schwierigen Friedens.* Frankfurt a.M., Germany/New York: Campus.

Zinecker, H. (2007). *Kolumbien und El Salvador im longitudinalen Vergleich: Ein kritischer Beitrag zur Transitionsforschung.* Baden-Baden, Germany: Nomos.

CHAPTER 4

El Salvador: Transnationalization by Polarization and the Re-emergence of Violence

Not long ago, expectations regarding the development of El Salvador were optimistic when the processes of democratic transition spread throughout Latin America and finally "hit" Central America with the end of the internal violent conflicts. However, rule of law and non-violent conflict regulation have not yet been established. Violence strongly shapes the everyday life of ordinary citizens. Even though the Peace Accords in 1992 ended the civil war formally, violence has since been a persistent feature. Today, El Salvador is considered one of the most violent societies in the world.

The modernization of the oligarchy, which already began during the civil war, accelerated in the post-war period. Having controlled the production process in the period before the introduction of structural adjustment programs (SAPs), the oligarchy now focuses on controlling the effects of remittances. The deep division between the oligarchy on the one hand and subaltern groups on the other still exists and society polarized even further, and income inequality rose during the last decades.

The chapter shows that the political economy of remittances led to processes of social verticalization within subaltern groups resulting in the tendency to atomize the society. In El Salvador, remittances produce a vicious cycle of instability. The most visible consequence of this instability is the apparent dispersed and anomic organization of violence. This horizontal violence hinders a clear distinction between groups of offenders and groups of victims. The line between both becomes blurred and both

H. Warnecke-Berger, *Politics and Violence in Central America and the Caribbean*, https://doi.org/10.1007/978-3-319-89782-0_4

127

groups overlap. Firstly, traditional and yet established violent actors, death squads for instance, remained on the scene. Secondly, yet established but less brutal actors, such as localized youth gangs, transformed their forms of violence. Finally, newly arising violent actors as well as new forms of violence, such as community-oriented social cleansings, joined the violent game.

A further problem is the distinction between discourses and legitimizations of violence and "objective" violent facts. In a social situation characterized by this diffuse violence, a climate of fear is endemic. Violence in El Salvador cultivates fear and thus follows a longstanding tradition in absorbing horizontal violence. Sovereignty over meanings of violence emerges as an outstanding powerful tool. Many discursive free riders claim to mobilize violence without necessarily being able to do so. The exertion of violence appears to be disconnected from discourses on violence.

TRANSNATIONALIZATION BY POLARIZATION

During the last four decades, El Salvador developed from a predominantly rural society into an urban one and from a production economy into a service economy. The country also altered its role in the international division of labor from commodity production to the export of people. With this process, both the source of rent as well as the politics of appropriation completely changed.

With SAPs, El Salvador abandoned its traditional development path and discovered a new source of rent: migration and remittances. Today, El Salvador's largest economic pillar is the export of cheap labor and the resulting remittances (Gammage, 2006). Migration to the Global North accelerated with the civil war when many peasants living in the violence-ridden departments of Morazán and Chalatenango escaped and migrated to the larger cities in the United States. With the end of the civil war, this flow continued and even accelerated. However, post-war migration has been economically motivated.

The impact of remittances on El Salvador's society is tremendous. The World Bank's Development Indicators show that in 2014, the remittances flow of 4.23 billion dollars was equivalent to 16.7 percent of GDP, 66.1 percent of total exports, 892 percent of foreign direct investment, and 220 percent of the government's social spending. A fourth of El Salvador's population lives abroad and remittances are the single largest foreign income. The average remittances receiving household obtained more than

US $180 per month (Dirección General de Estadisticas y Censos [DIGESTYC], 2015). Remittances, *maquilas*, and tourism together accounted for around 90 percent of foreign exchange earnings in 2014. The constantly growing urban informal sector parallels this trend and absorbs almost 70 percent of the labor force.[1]

While traditional exports such as coffee, sugar, and cotton as a percentage of foreign reserves accounted for 81 percent in 1978, this percentage slumped to only 5 percent in 2004. At the same time, remittances grew from 8 percent in 1978 to 70 percent of foreign reserves in 2004 (Programa de las Naciones Unidas para el Desarrollo [PNUD], 2005, p. 7). Remittances thus are the single most important source of foreign exchange earnings. In absolute terms, the overall amount shortly peaked in 2009 with the onset of the world financial crisis, but soon dropped again and has been increasing since. In line with this increase, remittances additionally compensate for a continuously growing balance of payments deficit. The politics of rent appropriation fundamentally changed with a reorientation towards migration and remittances. The traditional oligarchy self-modernized and has increasingly focused on controlling consumption instead of production. At the same time, remittances are private income earnings accrued directly by subaltern groups. Inherent to this twofold process, however, is a vicious cycle of social instability.

Modernizing Oligarchic Rule

By withdrawing from productive sectors such as agrarian exports, the oligarchy successfully adapted to a changing economic environment. The oligarchy does not openly engage in major political processes. Consequently, it does not appear as an addressee for political claims expressed by subaltern groups. The oligarchy was able to escape from open violence.

The process of self-modernization took place in four steps (Paige, 1997, pp. 338–362; Zinecker, 2004). Firstly, the oligarchy experienced a rise of a modern sector as an additive wing of the oligarchy until the 1970s. Secondly, SAPs facilitated the oligarchy to engage in finance. By the mid-1980s, the modernizing wing had gained internal hegemony in the oligarchy's party Nationalist Republican Alliance (*Allianza Republicana Nacionalista*, ARENA). The Salvadoran Foundation for Economic and Social Development (FUSADES) and the support from the US government played a crucial role (Dijkstra, 1993, p. 65). The oligarchy was able to use SAPs to amplify its economic fundament from coffee production and exportation to banking and finance. Alfredo Cristiani, who became president in 1989, played a leading role in this process. During the wave of privatization initiated by SAPs, a group of members of leading families organized in FUSADES was able to purchase almost the entire banking sector of El Salvador and to monopolize finance. In addition, the oligarchy began to invest into new economic sectors, such as *maquila* and non-traditional agrarian exports. Thirdly, the oligarchy expanded on a regional scale by the end of the 1990s until 2007 (Segovia, 2006). This regionalization of oligarchic rule consisted primarily in the export of Salvadorian oligarchic capital in other Central American countries. Between 1997 and 2004, almost 85 percent of official intraregional investment in Central America came from El Salvador (Schneider, 2012, p. 118). Newly regionalized financial institutions coordinated the expansion into emerging sectors in Central America. The revival of political integration in the region, the dollarization of the Salvadorian economy in 2001, and the signing of the CAFTA-DR free trade agreement in 2004 highlighted these developments. Fourthly, the oligarchy was able to access the transnational remittances economy. At the end of 2007, all major banks controlled by the oligarchy were sold to multinational corporations (Bull, 2013). This juncture marks the end of the diversification strategy. When selling the vehicle of regionalization, the oligarchy already had arrived at its current realization of rent, namely the indirect appropriation of remittances. Today, the oligarchy almost entirely controls the tourism sector, major hotel franchise brands in the region, the official commercial sector with its largest shopping malls throughout Central America, the leisure sector with cinemas and theatres, the largest construction companies, computation, and primary products for non-traditional agrarian export producers. By focusing on these new and emerging economic sectors, the oligarchy finally accessed remittances indirectly by focusing on the demand structure of remittances receiving households.

Its primary task today is no longer monopolizing production, but controlling consumption. As an effect, the oligarchy enjoys larger autonomy vis-à-vis the subaltern class. Post-war economic restructuring and the rise of remittances therefore did not overcome the social verticalization that developed during the last centuries. Instead, remittances helped to reproduce this vertical relationship between the oligarchy and the subaltern class. While the oligarchy has benefitted greatly from these cash inflows from abroad, subaltern groups had to fall back on their own resources and are dependent on further migration to maintain their social wellbeing. This development has consequences for the analysis of the current situation of violence. Different to the troubled civil war period of the 1970s and 1980s, large-scale and state-led repression is no longer necessary in order to undermine subaltern political unrest. In a certain sense, the oligarchy achieved both depoliticizing social conflicts and transferring the reason for social unrest into the subaltern class itself.

Coping with Marginalization and Social Exclusion

This current political and economic situation based on the dominance of remittances has two crucial impacts. Firstly, it generates a vicious cycle of instability. Secondly, social conflicts shift to within the subaltern class. The inflow of migrant money reduces labor attendance of receiving households, but increases their consumption (Acosta, 2006). In contrast to the macro level where remittances prove to be stable, on the micro level enormous fluctuations are rather the rule than the exception. The frequency of remittances is highly volatile with a tendency to sending smaller amounts in shorter periods (Palacios & Hurtado de García, 2015). This means that remittances contribute to resource unpredictability at the micro level. Receiving households simply do not know when they will receive the next transaction. The vicious cycle of instability also affects non-receiving households as these households at least buy goods from the informal sector. Thus, fluctuations of remittances at the local level translate into price adjustments and most probably into increasing prices for non-tradable goods. Considering that the infra-subsistence informal subsector produces the largest share of non-tradable goods, the micro-volatility of remittances is further intensified by price pressures on non-tradables (Towers & Borzutzky, 2004, p. 32). Under contemporary economic conditions coupled with the modernization of oligarchic rule, remittances contribute to an enormous microeconomic instability as the volatility of the micro flow is reinforced.

Secondly, social conflicts are shifted to within the subaltern class. Remittances tend to atomize society since they are appropriated on an individual (or at least family) basis and therefore contribute to the atomization of society. Furthermore, remittances produce new inequalities at the local level among those households that receive remittances and those who do not. The capacity to consume because of remittances tends to stabilize these new inequalities. It is well documented that remittances in El Salvador lead to the "depoliticization of everyday life" (Baker-Cristales, 2004, p. 31) and to a "fragmented and diffuse" (Garni & Weyher, 2013, p. 74) class situation.

Enabling Spaces of Violence

Remittances do not produce violence directly, but they contribute to a social environment in which violence is rendered possible. By generating this vicious cycle of instability, remittances contribute to "a diffuse, amorphous fear, deeply unsettling in its lack of fixity" (Moodie, 2009, p. 81). These emotions of uncertainty, however, are accompanied by a very concrete setting: the fear of losing one's economic and social position (Lungo & Martel, 2003, p. 503). From the political economy perspective, the production of more durable social structures is difficult to achieve under these circumstances of lacking economic opportunities for subaltern groups, and remittances are the only available but highly volatile resource.

In this context, remittances produce an equilibrium between equal powerful actors and a group of actors inside the subaltern class. While verticalization between the oligarchy and the subaltern class was fueled during the twentieth century by structural inequalities and injustice—and in the light of oligarchic authoritarian rule the "enemy" was more than visible—today, remittances contribute to the fragmentation of collective action. Today's social cleavages are not only divide social classes but also families, neighbors, and communities. The vicious cycle of instability evoked by remittances substituted its political expression of sharp verticalization by a "troubling, isolating feeling of all against all" (Moodie, 2010, pp. 99–100). More than half of the Salvadoran population today lives in definite fear of violence (Instituto Universitario de Opinión Pública [IUDOP], 2009). Moreover, the diffuse character of violence intensifies feelings of fear and anxiety. Under these conditions, spaces that structurally enable violence are most likely to unfold among subaltern groups, even towards an individual level. Given the microeconomic instability of remittances in El Salvador and the modernized oligarchic rule, small changes in the amount of remittances are likely to open these spaces.

THE (RE)EMERGENCE OF FORMS OF VIOLENCE

Violence is essentially unpredictable and the daily talk of crime generates insecurities and feelings of "I could be the next." Coupled with social instability, the unpredictability of violence further intensifies widespread fears. The often-unknown actors of violence contribute to the unpredictability and opacity of violence. Impunity is the norm instead of the exception. Even in cases when perpetrators are known, people hesitate to report them in fear of retaliation. While some actors, such as death squads, remained on the scene even after the end of the civil war, other actors joined only recently. Furthermore, formerly peaceful actors have turned violent. At the same time, newspapers and politicians alike exploit and cultivate the discourse on violence and crime, thereby often create distorted meanings of violence. This fosters the unpredictability of brutal acts and the overall situation produces opportunities for free riders. The number of extortion cases is increasing and in some cases, extortion even became a "subsistence strategy" for entire families (Hume, 2009, p. 105; Wolf, 2012, p. 78). In a social situation in which violence becomes part of the everyday struggle of survival, the categories offender and victim are blurred and even rendered useless.

"Ordinary" Horizontal Violence

When participants of a focus group discussion were asked how residents perceived the work of the *alcaldía* and other state organizations to tackle the problem of violence, the skepticism of these communities regarding state institutions and the need to resolve conflicts on their own became obvious:

Carlos: *The community prefers to solve their problems among themselves. Well, there is a situation of serious mistrust…*

Silvia: *I think that this … Yes, this is my passage, and in my passage, they sell drugs, and I benefit because they protect me, right? So, in a certain way, even though I am not part of that (…) the police go and turns into my enemy. Why? Because they are going to see, and they are going to touch my interests. Then, all those who come and want to affect my interests, in a certain way, are becoming an enemy, then, when the police come and act, they become my enemy.*[2]

These quotes reveal two issues: first, community life often functions and develops in distance to the state. The mistrust of the police is omnipresent. In this light, communities prefer to or are even forced to solve their conflicts on their own, as Carlos explained. Second, it is interesting to note how quickly notions such as *"el enemigo"* and *"the enemy"* appear to describe a conflictive relationship between equals, between neighbors, between relatives, between *"todos que llegan y quieren afectar mis intereses,"* to *"all those who come and want to affect my interests"* as Silvia termed it.

As Chap. 3 showed, horizontal violence is deeply embedded in El Salvador's society. Only a superficial glance at the daily press provides an impression of the omnipresence of ordinary horizontal violence: a driver failed to give way and subsequently was shot dead; a man in one of the small cantinas refused to salute and his head was split with a machete (El Faro, 2014). While these events fill the newspapers and are accountable for the majority of homicides, they enjoy relatively minor attention in academic debates. The term horizontal violence hitherto referred to the violent relationship between more or less equal powerful actors. This subsection intends to further elaborate on the concept of horizontal violence.

A violent event that happened on an October morning in 2009 and that enjoyed attention for several weeks in the national newspaper further illustrates the relevance of horizontal violence. This event took place in a microbus of route no. 3, which runs from Soyapango, one of the agglomerations of San Salvador's 14 *municipios*, to the center of San Salvador. In the area where Boulevard del Ejército crosses Boulevard Venezuela, two men and a young woman joined the 20 passengers on their daily way to work. Soon thereafter, one of them forced the bus driver with a knife to close the doors and to drive on. The two others requested every single passenger to put their valuables, mobile phones, and wallets into a circulating plastic bag, threatening with knives. A 32-year-old *vigilante*, a private security guard who was working for one of the countless security companies that "secure" residential areas, shops, gas stations, and commercial malls, was among the assaulted crowd. Initially, he followed the order to pass his mobile phone. As the thieves figured that their plastic bag was still not full enough, they started a second round and came back to all the passengers, threatening them with their knives and ordering them to hand over more. The thieves also addressed a 19-year-old girl who was heavily pregnant. Against all advice, she began negotiating and quarrel arose. One of the thieves shouted at her, slapped and punched her, and finally stabbed her in her pregnant belly. Panic was on the rise, and the thieves immediately tried to escape with their stolen goods through the backdoors of the microbus. The vigilante drew his pistol, a 9mm, which he had managed to hide at the edge of his seat during the assault, and shot. The bullets hit two of the thieves, one of them with five shots, and an uninvolved passenger. In an interview given after the event, the vigilante stated, "I was outraged, that's why I got up and shot them" (La Prensa Gráfica, 2009).[3] The outrage, the disgust, and the blind rage at the assault led him to shoot, he told the journalists. Both injured thieves died shortly after in the hospital, and the pregnant girl, severely injured, recuperated. The vigilante finally was discharged when it was adjudged that he acted in legitimate self-defense. This particular violent event comprises a whole set of practices of violence that can be summarized as horizontal violence. The economic objective of the assault and its underlying emotional basis, envy, seem obvious. With the desire to make quick money, violence seems to follow an economic rational and the script of violence becomes pure calculation.

Statements expressed in a focus group discussion further exemplify this. When the author asked for the economic background of the community and if there are any differences between neighbors, the discussion directly exposed the link between envy and violence.

Silvia: *They are in the same miserable situation of poverty*
Raúl: *But ... these ... people ... Here, there are people who tend to think that this is a nice two-level house, and in all communities, there are people of this kind, right?*
Silvia: *It is not about big time changes, you see? In such a small house, twenty, fifteen little square meters, you won't see immediately what serves to give a proper style of life, to sustain your children, to continue and go ahead.*
Raúl: *And sometimes, they kill you for the house, for exactly this tiny difference*
Silvia   *Yes! Right. In this area here, this is normal*
Raúl: *You don't know, and perhaps, when you want to go out, they kill you*[4]

Furthermore, available statistics of the National Forensic Institute (*Instituto Medicina Legal,* IML) seem to confirm this envy violence. In 2003 ordinary crime was responsible for more than 57 percent of all homicides, while more than 28 percent was unknown. At a second view, however, envy violence is not the only sub-form of horizontal violence. The same statistics of the IML show that until 2010 the relation between economic and unknown motives almost turned: In 2010, slightly more than 14 percent of all homicides were attributed to ordinary crime and more than 73 percent were unknown (statistics were provided by Aguilar, 2014).

The violent incident in the microbus provides further insights into horizontal violence other than envy violence. The offender encountered a certain obstinacy of several passengers that were not willing to hand over their valuables. It is possible that the threat of violence by the offender was not convincing. In effect, however, the offender did not have the power to enforce his will. A whole sequence of violent practices was the result of this powerlessness. The depth of horizontal violence and the yet established cultural scripts of honor violence makes people know how to behave in these situations, how to react to this assault, and in the meantime, the script of honor violence delivers certain strategies of action.

Given the general level of fear in El Salvador (Hume, 2009, p. 93), obtaining, maintaining, and restoring equality in social interactions is a struggle for social recognition and honor violence becomes an appropriate means. Even ordinary and absurd conflicts without any discernible reason, such as controversies of drunkards, easily transform into personal revenge and quickly escalate into extremes to "resolve" these differences (Bejar, 1998, p. 99; Cruz, 2003, p. 1153). Honor and revenge frequently cause common and ordinary conflicts between normal citizens to erupt into violence. It can take the shape of family vendettas, cycles of revenge, wedding parties that turn into wild stabbings or even shootouts, bloody dramas of jealousy, and everyday frustrations that quickly lead to bloodshed (Savenije & Andrade-Eekhoff, 2003, p. 87). However, horizontal violence is not restricted to honor violence and revenge. The reaction of the vigilante illustrates a further issue. Shaken by the offender's attack of the pregnant girl and frustrated because of the thieves' brazenness to harass the passengers once again, the vigilante fell into impotent rage, which escalated into blind hatred. In other words, hatred and furious rage resulted from fear and the impotence to move in these situations. These practices of violence are different from practices of violence that follow sober calculations. Practices of violence induced by rage usually lack individual motivations. Rage therefore leads to arbitrary practices of violence and the offender even accepts the risk of self-mutilation (Neckel, 1999, p. 162).

The general concept of horizontal violence thus comprises at least three different sub-forms of horizontal violence. Each sub-form intends to produce equality in escalating social conflicts. Envy violence is used to regain equality on a material basis and practices of violence thus are focused on objects rather that subjects. Revenge, in contrast, seeks to regain equality by focusing on the very subjects. Finally, rage violence results from disrupted relationships between equals, but lacks definite objectives to regain equality. Rage violence is the escalation of revenge, but it is destructive in nature and therefore bears the risk to destroy the relationship.

Horizontal violence in these three different sub-forms is caused by general fear that is a result of the vicious cycle of instability induced and reinforced by enormous remittances inflows and the absence of political claims since the political addressees withdrew from society. Due to the lack of durable resources and the inability to structure the access to these resources, social actors are caught in a state of economic instability. Minor changes of resource endowments render violence possible because of this general fear. Revenge can be interpreted as a way to violently stabilize the state of instability to regain a certain sense of social order. Envy violence reinforces instability since the very trigger, the perceived change of resource endowments, is not able to structure social interactions in a durable sense. Rage violence develops in escalating horizontal violent interactions that do not follow visible and identifiable motives. Rage is only situationally able to overcome instability and only on an emotional level. It does not produce or maintain a social order. Particularly because of this latter form of violence, general fear as a fertile soil for violence is reinforced and reproduced.

To sum up, the vicious cycle of instability and the lack of available resources on an individual level triggers emotional processes, which easily erupt into violence. Today's emotional processes then complement the historical process described in Chap. 3 that generated and condensed the cultural script of honor violence. However, as these emotions are unable to structure the social actors' social environment in a durable manner, they intensify feelings of fear and reinforce the diffusivity of violence.

Mara *Violence*

Mara violence initially began as disperse and disconnected organizations of enduring horizontal violence. By strengthening their organizational capacity, *maras* became successful in mobilizing and structuring violence. Today, *maras* can be considered transnational youth gangs that are active in the local drug trade, appropriate massive amounts of money from extortions, and sometimes control entire communities (Cruz, 2010a). The following subsection describes the transformation of *mara* violence as a sequence of at least three forms of violence. The dynamics of *mara* violence expose that although still horizontal, practices of violence are now mobilized on a higher organizational scale involving more durable resources and more distinct cultural scripts.

A well-established gang system already has been existing in El Salvador for decades. Two critical junctures for the transformation of the *maras* are important. The first critical juncture occurred in the mid-1990s when the US government introduced a new immigration legislation (Thale & Falkenburger, 2006). The second critical juncture emerged with the anti-gang legislation and the politics of the tough hand in El Salvador in the early 2000s, which lead to a controversial discussion of whether *maras* morphed into groups of transnational organized crime or even violent political actors (Rodgers & Muggah, 2009; Shifter, 2012). The transformation of *maras* is part of a process in which youth gangs initially evolved as a product of larger historical developments, such as urbanization, segregation, and social exclusion. *Maras* were increasingly able to intervene in these processes and to create their own political economy of survival. In terms of culture, *maras* initially drew on available cultural scripts, such as honor violence. By organizing violence, however, they were able to manipulate these scripts and to inscribe their own meanings of violence. Initially, *maras'* strategic action loosely followed cultural scripts. Later, cultural scripts became condensed, embodied, and ultimately even prescribed clear sequences of violent practices.

The Fair Fight and la riña

In the early years, gangs developed independently in El Salvador and the United States. In El Salvador, urbanization, segregation, the lack of employment opportunities, and environmental reasons such as the earthquake in 1986, which devastated large parts of San Salvador, led to new socio-spatial exclusion. Refugees escaped the civil war and victims of the earthquake were forced to leave their homes. Some of those found shelter in the growing squatter settlements in and around San Salvador. Others migrated to the United States. According to gang theory, these factors facilitated the proliferation of local youth gangs. These youth gangs, as in the case of *barras estudantiles*, were founded around schools, colleges, or sport teams, or as in the case of *maras callejeras*, in local communities "on the streets" and on the famous street corners, to refer to Whyte (1943).

There may have been hundreds of single youth gangs, differing in the symbols they used and in the names they gave themselves. While some gangs took autochthonous names, such as *mara morazán* or *mara gallo*, others copied hard rock styles and called themselves for instance *mara ac/dc* (Argueta Rosales, Caminos Alemán, Mancía Peraza, & los Angeles

Salgado Pacheco, 1992). These gangs were deeply rooted in their local community and their territorially generated identity (Cruz, 2010a, pp. 384–385). The lack of socioeconomic opportunities to engage in the formal labor market and the perceived unavailability of future opportunities further catalyzed the overall politico-economic situation of instability at the micro level. Under these circumstances, the own community, the *barrio*, and the territory was the only available resource. Adolescents whom the formal social system in the form of the labor market and the education system failed to integrate or even rejected saw an immanent answer to social exclusion in the search for and the defense of a "proper territorial space" (González, 1997, p. 5). Establishing and defending the own territory against rival youth gangs inside the same *barrio* or against neighboring community gangs frequently escalated into violence (Savenije & Lodewijkx, 1998, p. 117). The typical form of violence under these circumstances was *la riña*, the street fight. Brawls and the reciprocal "fair fight"[5] in the streets generated their own dynamic. At the first view, these violent confrontations were completely unstructured and seemed like total contingency. However, practices of violence (as in stabbings, fistfights, etc.) reveal the availability of an already established cultural script. Firstly, the use of violence was essentially linked to the gangs' territory—to their *barrio* and their turf. Violence exclusively escalated at the edge of this turf. Outside this territory, meanings of violence were blurred and lost (Cruz, 2010a, p. 394). Secondly, brawls and street fights only rarely involved guns. The only weapons available were stones, sticks, and machetes. Thirdly, gang violence was rarely lethal. *Riñas* ended when one group escaped to their own turf or found shelter in protected spaces (Savenije & Lodewijkx, 1998, pp. 117–118). Finally, violence was used to generate prestige and honor inside the own peer group and to banish the rival group to "their" turf. The numerous wounds and scars were openly put on display in order to testify the fighters' courage and will to vouch and take responsibility for the own group. The brave fighter was able to attain prestige and honor and to build a reputation. Furthermore, he was able to produce fears and anxiety among the rivals. Practices of violence therefore were interwoven with meanings of honor (Smutt & Miranda, 1998, p. 31).

Violence generated security and power when gangs defended their turf and the position within the peer group. In the absence of durable resources, honor and prestige stabilized the lifeworld of turf-based gangs. Honor violence was essentially linked to the *barrio*. Violence against other youth gangs functioned like a mirror through which the own imagination of strength and identity could be created.

When resources are lacking, exerting violence structures the social world and overcomes the vicious cycle of instability at least temporally. Honor and prestige are unlikely to durably structure social interactions. Honor has to be constantly cultivated to be able to command respect and the recognition as a reputable group member. There are no available media in which honor can be stored or accumulated. Honor has to be continuously gained in violent interactions. The only "real" resource available is the own territory. Gangs marked their own turf with symbols such as graffiti and defended it against their rivals.

Under these circumstances, strategic action requires continuous provocations of rivals. Steady escalations were the consequence, however, without generating clear-cut hierarchies within or among gangs (Cruz & Carranza, 2005, p. 164). Gangs found themselves in the need of constantly producing and reproducing hierarchies within and among the gangs, which ultimately leads into an equilibrium based on the dominance in their own turf and the defense of this turf against rival intruders. Within gangs, leaders had to maintain honor and prestige to be accepted as a leader in the daily violent interactions with their rival gangs at the edge of their turf. *La riña*, the fair fight in the streets between rival gangs, the pivotal form of violence deployed by these localized youth gangs, was an outcome of the overall context of instability intensified by social exclusion and the need of youngsters to regain social recognition.

Hegemonial Gang Warfare

A second step in the development of *mara* violence occurred in the mid-1990s. At this time, new US immigration legislation ordered to deport foreigners with minor criminal offenses to their home countries. Subsequently, many Salvadorans living in the United States were forced to leave the country. Some of them were already integrated in US-based youth gangs; others did not have any gang affiliation. For many re-migrants, the deportation meant a cultural clash and a "painful rupture" (Zilberg, 2004, p. 762) once they arrived in El Salvador. However, some of them were able to transform this rupture into honor when gang members—and non-gang members—found their "home" in already existing local gangs introducing their own gang culture to El Salvador.

These newly arriving gang members were able to translate their experiences of forced migration into a reservoir of exposing their own honor, as one *marero* explained in an interview (cited in Smutt & Miranda, 1998, p. 37, my emphasis):

> *Another thing that they liked was that when I took off my shirt they could see the tattoos (...) it seemed like an honor to walk with that. That I spoke to them and that I was their friend, that was a privilege for them and they respected me, I invited them to a soda, beer, drugs (...).*[6]

Soon, local youth gangs adapted and appropriated the imported style of tattoos, graffiti, and clothes. These processes of cultural adaptation, appropriation, and mimesis transformed the homegrown gang landscape into two more or less hegemonial gangs—*MS-13* and *barrio 18*—which were able to enlarge their territorial scope of action (Savenije, 2007, p. 650). In a survey in 1996, already 85 percent of interviewed gang members belonged either to *MS-13* or to *Barrio 18*. Only 15 percent were affiliated with other gangs (Cruz & Portillo Peña, 1998, p. 199). The homegrown gang phenomenon thus continued in the framework of these two hegemonial gangs.

Since gangs initially developed inside communities and formed part of community life, the changing gang situation was fueled by the instrumentalization of yet existing conflicts inside and between communities. When the author of this book asked residents and community leaders during field research how the fragmented landscape of gang affiliation in the area had evolved, a common answer was that different gang affiliations were fed by long existing conflicts about land use between communities.[7] Therefore, the key issue of hegemonial *mara* evolution was not the result of "a vacuum in community political structures" (Barrios, 2009, p. 118) that was filled by the gangs. On the contrary, *maras* followed the traditional pathway of manipulation and co-optation of existent conflicts characterized in Chap. 3. The evolving hegemonial gangs identified these conflicts and used them for their own purposes. The effect was that formerly autonomously acting youth gangs now advanced to interlinked *clikas* of the same *mara*, sharing cultural symbols and gang identity. At the same time, *clikas* began to develop structures of hierarchy. Leaders were now called *palabreros* and the houses occupied to hold meetings were called *destroyer* (Carranza, 2005, pp. 32–33). The territory, important for identity formation of gang members in the previous phase, became an economic resource, since it provided opportunities to secure wellbeing and subsistence (Cruz, 2005, p. 1176). The evolution of two major *maras* transformed honor violence of formerly independent youth gangs.

At the first stage of *mara* development, honor was not only necessary for internal group cohesion and had to be steadily regained in regular violent interactions, it was also bound to the local gang turf. The relevance of honor was inserted into hegemonial gang identity, and violence became an integral part of this dyadic conflict. During this second stage, gang violence escalated and became increasingly lethal when firearms and guns arrived (Cruz, 2014, p. 137). However, guns did not necessarily transform the form of violence deployed by youth gangs. Instead, overall violence increasingly became a characteristic of gang warfare between the two large *maras*. Many *mareros* expressed this change by describing their violent interactions with the rival *mara* in terms of war and warfare. Violence was exerted in order to defend the own community, the territory, and the gang turf, and additionally, in order to defend the gang identity vis-à-vis the other gang as a gang member expressed in an interview cited in Santacruz Giralt and Cruz (2001, p. 65):

> *Regarding the question of why we kill (...) I did it in my life for a while, but I also did it to take care of myself, because I stained my body and I lived like in five different houses where an enemy neighborhood was, and to remove them from there, I had to kill one or two, so that they would leave, so that their morale would be lowered (...).*[8]

While honor violence persisted, the notion of honor slightly changed, as a gang member told:

> *Respect is earned by oneself, and one can earn it in different ways (...) by killing so many; he who kills has his respect because one already knows that he is a Starter. And if nobody wants to go with him, he is alone, he kills about three and, suddenly, he comes back like nothing happened. There, he gains more respect than the others because he took his own initiative.* (cited in Santacruz Giralt & Cruz, 2001, p. 66)[9]

Honor became almost exclusively related to what somebody did to the rival *mara*. Thereby the entire underlying cultural script of violence changed. The forming hegemonial gangs initially disturbed the longstanding violent equilibrium between different localized turf-based gangs. Quite often, gang members expressed their confusion about this new situation:

> *There, if you met a "vato" who is an enemy, from another gang with his family, his mother for example, you could not do anything to her; I could not do anything to them myself, even when I only had to shoot them. Today, it's different,* **they do not respect the rules:** *one can walk with all his family and his children, and right there, they'll take them out.* (cited in Cruz & Portillo Peña, 1998, p. 54, my emphasis)[10]

Gang members therefore claim that the rules of violence have changed. This is an indicator for the emergence of a new cultural script of violence. Whereas violence used to create respect and honor of individual gang members, honor violence is now related to gang warfare between *MS-13* and *Barrio 18*. This gang warfare not only co-opted localized youth gangs, but also instrumentalized their violence as a gang member explained:

> *Today, it is not like before. When you signaled to a rival gang member in the street, he assaulted you; today, he ignores the opponent's signal and passes unnoticed and inconspicuously, but then, he informs off the route that they will search and identify the other one.* (cited in Aguilar, 2007a, pp. 8–9)[11]

Practices of violence during this second stage ceased to be exerted within the concept of fair fights at the edge of gang turf. Instead, violence in the form of gang warfare served as a prime tool to create fear and anxiety among rivals and to portray the own strength and courage. Violence spread beyond the territory and practices of violence could easily be interpreted in the framework of the hegemonial gang warfare. The effect was a ubiquitous feeling of social impotence. As a result, every group sought to be the first to demonstrate strength, to pre-empt the rivals' violence, or to take revenge for yet suffered violence. The aspiration to "kill before being assassinated"[12] (Santacruz Giralt & Cruz, 2001, p. 66) became a driving force and huge cycles of revenge arose from this dynamic.

Staging brutalized practices of violence became a powerful tool for the gangs. By exhibiting their rivals' dead, humiliated, and sometimes even decapitated bodies in public spaces (Martel Trigueros, 2006, p. 396), the offending *mara* group was able to demonstrate its own force and its dominance over the rival. This generated a discourse and a new imaginary about the own strength and again created widespread fears among the enemies and the population. Gang violence thus became highly public and "omnipresent" (Cruz, 2010a, p. 395) and gangs cultivated their reputation of fear and force. In a focus group discussion, residents reflected this alteration by referring to their own fear:

Isabel: *This was a physical transformation [of the gangs, HWB]. Suddenly, they were terrible, with horrible tattoos. This shocked and intimidated me.*[13]

These practices of violence created a discourse that was not necessarily linked to the "objective" strength and force of certain *mara clikas* but to rumors. Without losing its previous relevance, the traditional script of honor violence turned into a structuring force on a higher organizational scale. The identity grown out of the "own" local turf was taken up in hegemonial *mara* identity. Social organization of violence thus differed considerably in this second stage compared to previous youth gang violence. With increasing availability of economic resources and cultural scripts adapted to gang warfare, honor, reputation, and prestige were translated into the internal rank and therefore acquired as symbolical capital.

Cultivated honor in gang warfare violence increasingly stabilized still informal internal hierarchies. Both *maras* became fraternal interest groups. An outstanding characteristic of both *maras* during this second stage was that the killing of one gang member was perceived as an injury to the entire *mara*. Within each *mara*, the honor of a member increased through assaults against rival gang members. The additional honor, which individual gang members were able to acquire in their violent interactions with rival gang members, corresponded with the status and prestige of the oppositional gang member during the confrontation. At the same time, acts of revenge for suffered violence were not exclusively directed against the initial offender, but threatened the entire gang peer group. During this second stage, *maras* were able to overcome the vicious cycle of instability imposed by the political economy of post-war development. They did so by monopolizing fear. However, the production of fear was essentially linked to inter-*mara* conflicts. *Maras* mutated into ad-hoc cartels of fear.

Beyond Horizontal Violence?
A third stage started with the implementation of gang suppression policies beginning in 2003, which are the second critical juncture in the development of *mara* violence. At this time, the Salvadoran government implemented zero-tolerance policies (*mano dura* and *super mano dura*). Although initially designed to combat crime, *mano dura* soon developed into a tool of "punitive populism" (Wood, 2014). Instead of combatting

EL SALVADOR: TRANSNATIONALIZATION BY POLARIZATION... 145

maras effectively, however, these policies caused *maras* to professionalize and to strengthen their internal cohesion.

These policies imposed a twofold strain on existing *maras*. *Mano dura* led to mass arrests of *mareros* who were easy to recognize through their symbols (i.e. tattoos, outfit style). Inside the prisons, *mareros* from different communities and geographic areas came together. This process was even intensified by the decision to detain *mareros* from the same *mara* in the same prisons. Consequently, formerly disconnected *clikas* sharing similar symbols and similar gang identity without being "physically" connected to each other established a network based on personal contacts in prisons. This reinforced internal hierarchies or established new ranks (Wolf, 2012, p. 80). Outside of prison, gang members also reacted on *mano dura* policies. To escape the hit-and-run with the police, *maras* were forced to abandon their visibility. More and more, *mareros* refrained from tattoos and their outfit style became more conventional. At the same time, *mareros* increased their mobility. To escape police raids, gang members abandoned their *clika* meetings and hangout areas in public spaces and increasingly resorted to vehicles as high-ranking police officers claimed in an interview (Ramírez Mejía, 2011).

Both processes required more resources. For the self-reproduction of *maras* as a social group, the provision of jailed gang members, the economic support of the gang members' families and communities, and the access to resources had to be expanded. The only available resources at that time came from the control over turf and communities. *Maras* therefore adjusted to the overall economic conditions of economic instability. By controlling their turf, *mareros* were able to generate revenues through extortion and the local drug trade. They were able to impose local taxes and control local markets.

Since they had already advanced to ad-hoc cartels of fear, *maras* easily expanded into civil society. During the second stage, fear was still produced by gang warfare and it was still reciprocally organized. In the third stage, however, the production of fear also affected ordinary people. These processes in turn led to changing practices of violence. Fear no longer dominated the context within which *mareros* had to live and to move. Instead, the production of fear became a powerful resource in the search for access to economic resources for gang members.

A first indicator is the weaponry used by *maras*. *Maras* frequently turned to the use of grenades and bombs in addition to the customary usage of firearms (ContraPunto, 2015; Santos Hérnandez, 2011). The already established dangerous reputation of *maras* enabled *mareros* to use this reputation to extract resources from their own community. While the *barrio* and the local community in which *mareros* grow up and live with their families still are an integral layer of *mara* identity, they now form part of a dispersed idea (Savenije, 2007, p. 637). By disconnecting from the *barrio*, the former code of providing for its own *barrio* lost validity.

In line with this changing script of violence, which formerly prevented violence against the own territory, the attractiveness to become a *marero* decreased considerably. *Maras* themselves raised the costs of integration by changing their initiation rites. Increasingly, they rely on recruitment by force. Practices of violence thus became detached from gang warfare, and increasingly served to acquire economic means. Practices of violence became more "rational."

Overall, this led to a rise in lethal *mara* violence (Aguilar, 2007b, p. 884). While violence inherent to gang warfare had almost exclusively targeted rival gang members, these recent changes of *mara* violence led to a shift or to the amplification of opposing groups and opportune victims.

By focusing on the extraction of resources, practices of violence had to fulfil an additional function: to create fears inside civil society as a whole and particularly fears that allowed for the control of local turfs to impose extortions. This is perhaps an overestimation of the economic rationale to wage violence. However, civil society came into the focus of *mara* violence, and at the same time, the level of violence inside *maras* increased (Aguilar, 2014). Consequently, the cultural script of violence inherent to gang warfare between the two *maras* produced or at least followed the internal organizational structure of *maras*.

Leadership, obedience, and the code of honor are essential mechanisms to maintain internal cohesion. With increasing availability of economic resources because of extortions and drugs, this cultural script of gang warfare proved to be partly incapable of channeling practices of violence. As a result, violence between different *mareros* of the same *mara* increased. A clear sign of this process is the division of *mara barrio 18* into two competing factions: *los revolucionarios* and *los sureños* in 2011.

Maras expanded their scope of action during this third stage. The increasing necessity to approach and to mobilize economic resources led *maras* to foster their dangerous reputation among the civil society. In the meantime, the inherent social substitutability of gang warfare as the primary principle of social organization of violence in the second stage was applied to entire communities controlled by *maras*.[14] By accessing more durable economic resources as an effect of *mano dura* policies, *maras* were increasingly able to mobilize practices of violence on a much higher scale of social organization.

Finally, they created entire cartels of fear that are based on the threat of being able to steadily recur to violence and that are able to control entire sectors of the civil society.[15] While the necessity to attain honor in everyday violent interactions was the primary mode of mobilization of violence in the first phase, the second phase provided opportunities to translate honor into symbolic capital and informal hierarchies such as ranks. In the third phase, *mano dura* facilitated the translation of honor into an economic factor. As an effect, not only did internal group cohesion alternate, but also *maras* experienced the rise of a new and perhaps emblematic social figure: the *sicario*, the lonesome hitman and contract killer.

This phenomenon reveals the ambivalence of this third phase. At the edge of *maras*, violence generates income through contract killing. In this reading, *mara* violence economized and disconnected from *mara* gang identity. The question, however, to what extent practices of violence disengaged from gang warfare and became economic ends is difficult to answer.

This perspective is challenged by the so-called gang truce between the leading *maras* (Zinecker, 2014, pp. 266–276). In January 2012, both *maras* entered into a dialogue facilitated by mediators that led to a truce in May 2012. The involvement of the state in the truce is still unclear.[16] In exchange for stopping gang-related violence (and only gang-related violence), *maras* were offered better prison conditions for some of their prison inmate gang members and the release of 30 high-ranking leaders from high-security prisons into "normal" penal institutions. While the role of the truce in the reduction of levels of violence is highly doubtful, it is interesting to take a closer look at the staging of the truce.

Following the narratives of the *mara* leaders surrounding the truce negotiations, the entire gang truce was staged as peace negotiations comparable to the signing of the Peace Accords in 1992. Gangs handed over their weapons, celebrated the signing of the truce, and in their self-image, they took political responsibility. Therefore, *maras* virtually entered a political arena. They did not directly challenge state authority, however. By using the output of violence as an asset in the negotiation, they were nevertheless able to translate their own capacity to produce fear and maintain their cartels of fear into political capital. Thereby, *maras* considerably gained political weight. Therefore, *mara* violence bears a vertical tendency.

Extortions and the practice to impose taxes already reveal this tendency. The increase in opportunities through the cartelization of fear provoked other attracted violent actors to vertical violence.

Repression and New Forms of Social Control

Among other things, vertical violence augmented historically by manipulating and absorbing horizontal violence. Although these vertical sub-forms of violence lost their apparent political function in the post-civil war period, they persist. Shortly after the end of the civil war, surveys on perceptions of crime and insecurity show that more than 16 percent of the population expressed their support for extrajudicial measures such as killing "*gente indeseable.*" undesirable people, and almost 46 percent would understand such acts (IUDOP, 1997). The number of those in favor of taking the law into their own hands even increased to more than 22 percent in 2009 (IUDOP, 2009, p. 5). Vigilantism is widely accepted in El Salvador. It even provoked political reactions of high-ranking politicians. In 2006, then President Antonio Saca warned the population to take justice into their own hands (cited in El Diario de Hoy, 2006). In 2012, then Minister of Justice and Public Security David Munguía Payés expressed his concern that organized groups and death squads may be operating in the country (cited in El Diario de Hoy, 2012b). In 2008, the human rights office of the Catholic Archdiocese of San Salvador, *Tutela Legal*, reported that more than 7 percent of the investigated cases of extrajudicial executions were related to social cleansings and not linked to the *Policía Nacional Civil* (PNC) or other state institutions (Tutela Legal del Arzobispado de San Salvador [TLA], 2008, p. 40).

A well-documented case of social cleansings took place on February 1, 2010 in Suchitoto where eight adolescents were killed (ContraPunto, 2010; El Diario de Hoy, 2010; La Prensa Gráfica, 2010). To date, Suchitoto is one of the main tourist sites of El Salvador. The small city never experienced high levels of violence and the presence of *maras* was almost unknown to inhabitants. Compared to the densely populated urban communities of San Salvador, Suchitoto is characterized by its calm atmosphere and community spirit based on the memory of civil war violence, which was particularly severe since Suchitoto was considered a left-wing city.

Widespread fears of *mareros* who allegedly wanted to establish a *clika* in the region of Suchitoto preceded the event in February 2010. People feared that several *mareros* wanted to recruit adolescents in the area. This alerted the community. The *junta directiva* organized a meeting to discuss how to react to the threat imposed by the presence of *maras*. The then director of the PNC stated in an interview "several adults warned them not to be fooled by gang members" (cited in El Diario de Hoy, 2010).[17] In the afternoon of the following day, a group of three people dressed in black searched for some of the teenagers and opened fire with semi-automatic weapons such as M-16 assault rifles and 9mm pistols. Eight teenagers were killed. The victims were virtually sprayed with bullets. The day after, these teenagers were found in a small river nearby their community. The identification of the victims was complicated by the brutal wounds. In some cases, even the heads were missing. In the newspaper coverage soon after the event, the families and relatives of these teenagers claimed that their children were never connected to *maras*. Finally, the mayor of Suchitoto offered financial support for the funerals of some of the teenagers killed in the occurrence. Events like this are commonplace in El Salvador even today.

The analysis of violent practices and the modus operandi suggests that this spontaneous violence to exercise control emerges as a compensation for instability and as a reaction to widespread fears. Firstly, practices of violence related to social cleansings are often expressive (Flores, 2011; Kowalewski, 1996). As the example of Suchitoto exemplifies, it is not simply about killing a suspected criminal, but about transmitting a message through violence.

These practices of violence aim at cleaning the own community and at threatening and warning future intruders. Social cleansings, as a subtype of vertical violence, follow processes of social closure at a local level. Secondly, perceptions of insecurity and the unavailability of legal resources enable practices of violence. Thirdly, the community collectively defends itself against threats. Often, these threats rely rather on perceptions than on hard facts since a large number of victims of social cleansings belong to "excluded social sectors or seen as 'dangerous' or 'undesirable'" (TLA, 2008, p. 40),[18] such as criminalized youths, homosexuals, and prostitutes. Social cleansings draw on a yet established community spirit that becomes easily mobilized in times of increasing fear. As the case of Suchitoto demonstrates, an abrupt intensification of the perception of insecurity is a necessary precondition. Finally, social cleansings frequently are enacted by community leaders and by groups of private interests (Campbell, 2002, p. 2).

Vigilantism as a localized form of vertical violence is thus closely related to the community context and to the possibility of strategic action in organizing spontaneous cultivations of fear. As soon as vigilantism becomes institutionalized, it bears the tendency to merge into an apparatus of repression. The contemporary situation in El Salvador has become even worse since this apparatus survived the Peace Accords, and because death squads are still operating in the country.

In late 1994, a group calling itself *Sombra Negra*, the black shadow, was formed in eastern El Salvador in the city of San Miguel (La Prensa Gráfica, 1996; Popkin, 2000, pp. 176–179). The *Sombra Negra* devoted itself to combat crime and to restore order. It specifically targeted alleged criminals, youth gang members, prostitutes, and homosexuals. *Sombra Negra* claimed that "the laws of the country were not working," that "the PNC did not have sufficient resources to combat crime," and that "too many crimes were committed in El Salvador daily" (*Sombra Negra* press releases cited in Amnesty International, 1996, pp. 3–4). Its victims were executed with multiple shots in the back or in the head, often using automatic weapons such as machine guns. Sixteen of its members were arrested in July 1995. Public prosecutors later on received death threats and their hotel was damaged by a spray of bullets.

Sombra Negra was by no means the only clandestine armed group. A report by the United Nations Observer Mission in El Salvador (ONUSAL) concluded that illegal armed groups and death squads, which had emerged during the civil war or even before, kept operating after the Peace Accords (Cruz, 2010b, pp. 158–160; Grupo Conjunto para la investigación de grupos armados ilegales con motivación política en El Salvador [Grupo Conjunto], 1994, p. 57). The report states that the clear political motivation of these groups

> *does not seem to build the only or essential engine of these structures, preferably dedicated to actions of 'common' crime, but with a high degree of organization and infrastructure (…) with strongly organized criminal structures, dedicated especially to the theft of banks, theft of vehicles and trafficking in arms and drugs.*[19]

These groups frequently form part of hidden powers, particularly in the confusing times shortly after the end of the civil war, in which local bosses and businessmen tried to maintain their economic and political influence and local power. In many cases, these armed groups were deeply interwoven with government and right-wing party structures. Some influenced voters during elections, and others intended to continue controlling social and political organizations. With increasing levels of violence and the state's inability to control violence and crime effectively, death squads reappeared. As in the case of social cleansings, the main group of victims are street children and youths who are alleged to support or to be member of *maras*, prostitutes, and homosexuals.

The modus operandi of death squads and *grupos de exterminio* often resembles those practices applied by death squads during the civil war. Many of the victims today are found in plastic bags nearby the larger highways or in refuse dumps with tied hands and clear signs of torture, and multiple headshots (Alegría, 2011). Frequently, death squads report about their actuation.[20]

In a communiqué that the author of this study found on the street during field research, a death squad advised that all *mareros* and common criminals should prepare. This group, who referred to itself as "*Brigada General Maximiliano Hernández Martínez*," a well-known death squad during the civil war, claimed to give to all those criminals the "medicine that they deserve" because of the ineffective security institutions that would them force to again go into action.

Interestingly, the communiqué is not only directed against *maras*, but also mentions ordinary criminals as their potential victims. Moreover, the communiqué resembles former communiqués of death squads during the civil war. Recently and against the background of increasing levels of violence, death squads seem to be on the rise. Clandestine mass graves are increasingly found, and the number of disappeared people rose to alarming levels, particularly during the gang truce (El Diario de Hoy, 2012a; La Página, 2009). The *Procuraduría para la Defensa de los Derechos Humanos* and various human rights organizations claim the involvement of off-duty police officers (Aguilar, 2007a, pp. 22–23; Arnson, 2002, p. 101). The PNC generally enjoys minimal support in the population. While information on police violence is hard to gather, the intensified conflict between *mara* violence in its third stage and the police force exemplifies the repressive character of police operations. Even the current president, Salvador Sánchez Cerén, recently stated that up to 30 percent of homicides have probably been committed by on-duty police officers (cited in El Faro, 2015). Moreover, the former director of the PNC, Mauricio Ramírez Landaverde, mandated that police officers are not only allowed to use their arms to defend themselves, but that the government will defend these police officers (cited in El Diario de Hoy, 2015). In the same interview, he acknowledged that the police officers should "shoot at the delinquents without fear." In a focus group discussion, these fears of police violence were steadily expressed:

Carlos   : *A situation that is very normal now in relation to the police …*
that people trust less in the police. So the community in general,
and that is not only here but also nationally, right? So this is gener-
alized … right? And this has even produced facts … facts of high
index that there is also violation of our rights, human rights that
we have, facts produced by the police, and it is clear that the PNC
is closer to the clika 18 than to the MS.[21]

The police remains a fundamentally repressive state institution. In theoretical terms, this is not surprising given that police officers themselves
need to move in a context of extreme instability and daily threats of being
victimized. Moreover, the Salvadoran police force has a longstanding
repressive tradition, which was not entirely dissolved through the creation
of the PNC following the Peace Accords in 1992 (Costa, 1999).

Given the mistrust of entire communities in the police force and the
resulting refusal to cooperate, police arrests often take the shape of brutal
raids. In fear of retaliation, the police is forced to enter communities during the night, masked and heavily armed. In an interview with the head of
the division of the PNC delegation in Mejicanos, Ortega (2011) mentioned that daily threats against police officers are commonplace.
Therefore, the police has to defend its authority in the area.

Usually, these police operations follow similar tactics: Initially, the police
closes down the small entry points to the communities and secures the exit.
Entering the communities, the police breaks into houses, using the element of surprise. In a focus group discussion, a resident exemplified:

Carlos: *You see? Those who thwart are beaten. The furniture is destroyed,*
right? Houses devastated. Once, a blindfold was taken on somebody
and they took him prisoner.[22]

After taking the suspect back to the police car and suspending the bar-
ricades, the police leaves the community with cocked rifles in convoy.

Practices such as breaking the doors and destroying parts of the interior
rather look like punitive raids than an arrest. Moreover, the police operations are mostly anonymous and faceless: police officers are masked, streets
are closed down, the mission is quickly executed, and soon after, the police
leaves. The police behavior resembles the practice of a gang since it does
not intend to maintain social order inside the community. Instead, it seems
that these practices are the result of the similar climate of fears in which the
population itself has to live. Moreover, it appears that police violence in

these cases is more the product of its own weakness. The weakness in creating and maintaining social stability thus is a trigger of violence in itself and places violence in "a ghostly space, a space that is hidden, where the law becomes its own transgression" (Zilberg, 2007, p. 47). The state's inability and weakness to overcome the political economy of instability facilitates its violence.

Conclusion

This chapter showed that the post-civil war period gave rise to a new development model characterized as transnationalization by polarization. The peculiarity of this development model lies in the parallel processes of the oligarchy's modernization and the increasing reliance of subaltern groups on remittances. Remittances, however, are ambivalent in the context of El Salvador. On a macroeconomic level, remittances introduce stability. On the microeconomic level, in contrast, and particularly due to the articulation of the informal sector, remittances lead to a vicious cycle of instability.

Both processes, the modernization of the oligarchy as well as the increasing weight of remittances, caused a shift from a predominantly vertical setting of violence during the civil war to the exertion of violence among equally powerful actors, particularly within the subaltern class. In line with this shift, already existent horizontal violence got amplified and reinforced. Due to remittances and their particular effects for subaltern groups, spaces that enable violence arose. However, durable resources that are a prerequisite for the permanent social organization of violence are lacking or difficult to access.

Consequently, the majority of the population is caught in an everyday struggle of survival, a struggle that becomes even more precarious in the face of the diffusivity of contemporary violence. This struggle does not only relate to the economic sphere. Everyday threats of victimization and everybody's fear of violence seem to create a violent stability in which the cultivation of fear arises as a powerful tool. It is a society on shaky foundations, in which minor changes may lead to far-reaching violent eruptions.

The discussion on horizontal violence showed that available resources fail to organize violence in a durable way. This also applies to youth gang violence. Youth gangs, however, managed to advance to *maras* by appropriating external cultural scripts, and in a relatively short period, local youth gangs became part of a broader and even hegemonial gang warfare.

The discussion furthermore showed that with the increasing capacity of *maras* to cultivate their own reputation, they were able to create their own political economy of survival. Again, the form of violence changed with this process. However, and particularly because of this plurality of forms of violence, violence today can hardly be controlled. Since the actors themselves do not dispose of the means to organize violence in a durable manner, they adopt cultural scripts of violence that require fewer resources to employ: they create contemporary preconditions and they orchestrate violence; thereby they cultivate fear. It becomes increasingly difficult to determine, as the discussion on death squads intended to show, if violent actors indeed employ certain forms of violence, or they are successful in creating that false perception by generating a discourse of fear.

As the discussion of *mara* violence showed, violence is a means to demonstrate power and to create a feeling of insecurity and fear among people who are caught in a struggle of survival within the social structures described earlier. The same dynamics could be demonstrated in the case of vigilantism although this latter form of violence was based on different cultural scripts.

NOTES

1. The informal sector, particularly in Salvadoran urban areas, consists of at least three subsectors. A first subsector comprises 1.7 percent of the labor force. It is widely described as a capitalist sector. A second subsector of almost 6 percent of the labor force consists of small enterprises that tend to invest on a regularly basis and range short above the subsistence level. The final and largest sector in which 91 percent of the informal labor force works is infra-subsistence, which means that less than the cost of survival is earned (see for this recent estimation, Andrade-Eekhoff & González, 2003, p. 26).

2. *Spanish Original: "Carlos: La comunidad prefiere entre la comunidad a como soluciona sus problemas Entonces, ahí hay una situación de desconfianza grave*

   Silvia: *Yo creo que este Sí esta es mi pasaje y en mi pasaje se venden drogas y yo me beneficio por que me protegen, ¿verdad? Entonces, en cierta manera, aunque yo no sea parte de eso, () cuando va a ir la policía y eso se convierte en mis enemigos ¿por qué? Por que van a ver y van a tocar mis intereses. Entonces, y todos los que llegan y quieren afectar mis intereses, en cierta manera, están convirtiendo en un enemigo, entonces, cuando la policía viene y actúa, se vuelve en mi enemigo*

3. *Spanish Original: "me indigné, por eso me levanté y les dispararé."*
4. *Spanish Original: "Silvia: Están en la misma situación de miseria de pobreza*

Raúl:	*Pero también este la gente ahí hay gente pues trae pensar esa es una buena casa de dos plantas en todas las comunidades hay esta gente, ¿verdad?*
Silvia:	*No son cambios animales, osea ¿ves?, en una casa tan pequeña, viente, quince metros cuadraditos, no se vea directamente por lo menos lo sirvió para dar un estilo de vida para sostener a sus hijos, para sacar adelante*
Raúl:	*Y a veces los matan por la casa, por esta diferencia*
Silvia:	*Aha, cabal, en esta zona es normal*
Raúl:	*No se sabe y tal vez cuando ya se vienen salir, los matan"*

5. The "fair fight" is a very typical form of violence attributed to localized youth gangs entangling social scripts of honor violence with the aim to gain and maintain identity, respect, and social recognition in a context of social marginalization (Vigil, 1988, p. 129).
6. *Spanish Original: "Otra cosa que les gustaba era que cuando yo me quitaba la camisa se veían los tatuajes () **parecía que era un honor andar con eso. Que yo les hablara y fuera amigo de ellos, era para ellos un privilegio y me respetaban,** yo los invitaba a una soda, cerveza, droga ()."*
7. The whole area where the author conducted participatory observations was built after the 1986 earthquake. Many communities evolved as illegal squatter settlements, and until today, many residents do not possess legal land titles. This situation was exacerbated by the immense internal migration flow from Morazán and Chalatenango to Mejicanos. Many of the residents of different communities suspected each other to have grabbed the land on which they claimed ownership.
8. *Spansh Original: "Con respecto a la pregunta de porqué matar () Yo en mi vida lo hice un tiempo, pero yo lo hacía también por cuidarme, porque yo ando manchado mi cuerpo y yo vivía como a cinco casas de donde estaba un barrio enemigo, y para quitarlos de ahí tenía que matar uno o dos para que se fueran ellos, se les bajara la moral a ellos ()"*
9. *Spansh Original: "El respeto se lo gana uno mismo, y uno se lo puede ganar de diferentes formas () matando tanto; el que mata tiene su respeto porque uno ya sabe que es de arranque. Y si nadie se quiere ir con él, él se solo, mata unos*

tres y, de volada, ya viene de regreso y como que nada pasó. Ahí, él gana más respeto que los demas porque tuvo iniciativa propia."

10. *Spansih Original: "Allá, si uno se encontraba con un «vato» que es enemigo, de otra pandilla con su familia, su mamá por ejemplo, uno no podía hacerle nada; yo mismo no pude hacerles nada cuando ya los tenía sólo para tirarles. Acá, es distinto, no te respetan las reglas: uno puede andar con toda su familia y sus hijos y ahí mismo le «ponen»"*

11. *Spansh Original: "Ahora no es como antes, que si uno le hacía señas a un pandillero rival en la calle, éste te agredía; ahora él ignora la señal del contrario para pasar desapercibido, pero después informa de la ruta que lleva para que lo busquen e identifiquen".*

12. *Spanish Original: "matar antes de ser asesinados"*

13. *Spanish Original: "Fue una transformación física [de las pandillas, HWB]. De repente estaban terribles, con tatuajes horribles. A mi me aterrorizaba."*

14. The burning of a bus of the route 47 in Mejicanos on Sunday June 20, 2010 might serve as an example when 17 passengers were burned to death. *Mareros* of the *barrio 18* murdered the bus driver and the fare collector, poured gasoline into the bus and on the passengers, set them on fire, and shot into the flames. The offending *mareros* claimed that this massive output of violence was supposed to take revenge for the murder of one of their leaders. Instead of killing rival gang members, however, the *mareros* decided to murder community members.

15. A showcase of this cartel of fear is the proclamation of a curfew by both *maras* in September 2010. Subsequently, almost 80 percent of public and private transport and 70 percent of business closed down. San Salvador seemed to be "paralyzed" during this event.

16. President Funes claimed that the state was not involved. However, (Mijango, 2014) mentioned that he had tight relations with the Minister of Justice and Public Security General Munguía Payés, and that the president himself might have been involved.

17. *Spanish Original: "varios adultos les advirtieron que no se dejaran engañar por los pandilleros"*

18. *Spanish Original: "sectores sociales excluidos o vistos como 'peligrosos' o 'indeseables'"*

19. *Spanish Original: "no parece construir el único o esencial motor de estas estructuras, preferentemente dedicadas a acciones de delincuencia 'común', pero con un alto grado de organización e infraestructura (...) con estructuras criminales fuertemente organizadas, dedicadas especialmente al robo de bancos, robo de vehículos y tráfico de armas y drogas".*

20. *Sombra Negra*, for instance, had its own newsletter (Mazzei, 2009, p. 198). Contemporary acting death squads even use Internet presence to communicate their daily death toll (see e.g. the following internet page: www.exterminiosnsv.gzpot.com, last access 25.11.2015) or social media (see e.g. www.facebook.com/SombraNegraElRegreso, last access 25.11.2015).

21. *Spanish Original: "Una situación que es muy normal ahorita en relación a la policía que la gente es a que menos confianza le tiene. Entonces la comunidad en general, y eso no solamente aquí sino a nivel nacional ¿verdad? Entonces esto si es generalizado ¿verdad? y esta ha dado hechos hechos de alto índice que hay también de violación de nuestros derechos, derechos humanos que tenemos, hechos de parte de la policía, y está claro que la PNC está más al lado de la clika 18 que a la MS"*

22. *Spanish Original: "¿Ves?, los que se interponen en el camino son golpeados. Los muebles llegan destruidos, ¿verdad?, casas devastadas Una vez se le pone una venda y se le lleva preso."*

REFERENCES

Acosta, P. (2006). *Labor Supply, School Attendance, and Remittances from International Migration: The Case of El Salvador. Policy Research Working Paper: Vol. 3903.* Washington, DC: World Bank.

Aguilar, J. (2007a). *Las maras o pandillas juveniles en el triángulo norte de Centroamérica: Mitos y realidades sobre las pandillas y sus vínculos con el crimen.* San Salvador, El Salvador: IUDOP.

Aguilar, J. (2007b). Los resultados contraproducentes de las políticas antipandillas. *ECA: Estudios Centroamericanos, 62*(708), 877–890.

Aguilar, J. (2014, May 16). Interview by H. Warnecke. Director of the Instituto Universitario de Opinión Pública (IUDOP), Universidad Centroamericana. San Salvador, El Salvador.

Alegría, G. (2011, August 24). Interview by H. Warnecke. Procurador Adjunto de Derechos Civiles e Individuales. San Salvador, El Salvador.

Amnesty International. (1996). *El Salvador: The Spectre of Death Squads.* London: Amnesty International.

Andrade-Eekhoff, K., & González, M. E. (2003). *Remesas, migración y vínculos con la micro y pequeña empresa en El Salvador.* San Salvador, El Salvador: FLACSO.

Argueta Rosales, S. G., Caminos Alemán, G. S., Mancía Peraza, M. R., & de los Angeles Salgado Pacheco, M. (1992). Diagnostico sobre los grupos llamados "maras" en San Salvador. Factores psicosociales que prevalecen en los jóvenes que los integran. *Revista de Psicología de El Salvador, 11*(43), 53–84.

Arnson, C. J. (2002). Window on the Past: A Declassified History of Death Squads in El Salvador. In B. B. Campbell & A. D. Brenner (Eds.), *Death Squads in Global Perspective. Murder with Deniability* (pp. 85–124). New York: Palgrave Macmillan.

Baker-Cristales, B. (2004). Salvadoran Transformations: Class Consciousness and Ethnic Identity in a Transnational Milieu. *Latin American Perspectives, 31*(5), 15–33.

Barrios, R. (2009). Malditos: Street Gang Subversions of National Body Politics in Central America. *Identities: Global Studies in Culture and Power, 16*(2), 179–201.

Bejar, R. G. (1998). El Salvador de posguerra: Formas de violencia en la transición. In Programa de las Naciones Unidas para el Desarrollo (PNUD) (Ed.), *Violencia en una sociedad en transición* (pp. 96–105). San Salvador, El Salvador: PNUD.

Bull, B. (2013). Diversified Business Groups and the Transnationalisation of the Salvadorean Economy. *Journal of Latin American Studies, 45*(2), 265–295.

Campbell, B. B. (2002). Death Squads: Definition, Problems, and Historical Context. In B. B. Campbell & A. D. Brenner (Eds.), *Death Squads in Global Perspective. Murder with Deniability* (pp. 1–26). New York: Palgrave Macmillan.

Carranza, M. (2005). *Detención o muerte: hacia donde van los "pandilleros" de El Salvador.* Rio de Janeiro, Brazil: COAV.

ContraPunto. (2010, February 3). A Suchitoto lo sacudió la muerte. *ContraPunto.*

ContraPunto. (2015, June 11). Nuevo ataque con granadas a puesto policial. *ContraPunto.*

Costa, G. (1999). *La Policía Nacional Civil de El Salvador (1990–1997).* San Salvador, El Salvador: UCA Editores.

Cruz, J. M. (2003). La construcción social de la violencia en El Salvador de la posguerra. *ECA: Estudios Centroamericanos, 58*(661/662), 1149–1171.

Cruz, J. M. (2005). Los factores asociados a las pandillas juveniles en Centroamérica. *ECA: Estudios Centroamericanos, 60*(685/686), 1155–1182.

Cruz, J. M. (2010a). Central American Maras: From Youth Street Gangs to Transnational Protection Rackets. *Global Crime, 11*(4), 379–398.

Cruz, J. M. (2010b). *Democratization under Assault. Criminal Violence in Post-Transition Central America.* Nashville, TN: Vanderbilt University.

Cruz, J. M. (2014). Maras and the Politics of Violence in El Salvador. In J. M. Hazen & D. Rodgers (Eds.), *Global Gangs: Street Violence across the World* (pp. 123–143). Minneapolis, MN: University of Minnesota Press.

Cruz, J. M., & Carranza, M. (2005). Pandillas y políticas públicas: El caso de El Salvador. In J. Moro (Ed.), *Juventudes, violencia y exclusión: desafíos para las políticas públicas* (pp. 133–176). Guatemala: MagnaTerra Editores.

Cruz, J. M., & Portillo Peña, N. (1998). *Solidaridad y violencia en las pandillas del gran San Salvador. Más allá de la vida loca.* San Salvador, El Salvador: UCA Editores.

Dijkstra, G. (1993). The Limits of Economic Policy in El Salvador. In W. Pelupessy & J. Weeks (Eds.), *Economic Maladjustement in Central America* (pp. 53–66). London: Macmillan.

Dirección General de Estadisticas y Censos (DIGESTYC). (2015). *Encuesta de Hogares de Propósitos Múltiples: 2014.* Ciudad Delgado, El Salvador: Ministerio de Economía.

El Diario de Hoy. (2006, August 22). Saca pide no tomar justicia por propia mano. *El Diario de Hoy.*

El Diario de Hoy. (2010, February 2). Ultiman a ocho pandilleros. *El Diario de Hoy.*

El Diario de Hoy. (2012a, January 7). Más de 2,007 desaparecidos en San Salvador. *El Diario de Hoy.*

El Diario de Hoy. (2012b, June 26). Munguía: grupos de exterminio operan en tres zonas del país. *El Diario de Hoy.*

El Diario de Hoy. (2015, January 20). Director de la PNC aconseja a policías "disparar sin miedo a delincuentes". *El Diario de Hoy.*

El Faro. (2014, April 10). No solo maras (I). *El Faro.*

El Faro. (2015, April 25). Presidente atribuye a Policía un 30% de los homicidios del mes más violento del siglo. *El Faro.*

Flores, N. (2011, August 12). Interview by H. Warnecke. Director del Departamento Seguridad Pública, FESPAD. San Salvador, El Salvador.

Gammage, S. (2006). Exporting People and Recruiting Remittances: A Development Strategy for El Salvador? *Latin American Perspectives, 33*(6), 75–100.

Garni, A., & Weyher, F. L. (2013). Dollars, "Free Trade," and Migration: The Combined Forces of Alienation in Postwar El Salvador. *Latin American Perspectives, 40*(5), 62–77.

González, L. A. (1997). Diagnóstico cultural, económico y social de El Salvador en los '90. In L. A. González & J. M. Cruz (Eds.), *Sociedad y violencia: El Salvador en la Post-guerra* (pp. 4–7). San Salvador, El Salvador: IUDOP.

Grupo Conjunto para la investigación de grupos armados ilegales con motivación política en El Salvador (Grupo Conjunto). (1994). *Informe del Grupo Conjunto para la investigación de grupos armados ilegales con motivación política en El Salvador.* San Salvador, El Salvador.

Hérnandez, S. (2011, August 26). Interview by H. Warnecke. Promotor Social, Fe y Alegría / Consejal de la Zona Zacamil, Alcaldía de Mejicanos, Mejicanos.

Hume, M. (2009). *The Politics of Violence: Gender, Conflict and Community in El Salvador.* Chichester, UK: Wiley-Blackwell.

Instituto Universitario de Opinión Pública (IUDOP). (1997). Estudio ACTIVA: la violencia en el Gran San Salvador. *Proceso, 18*(772), 10–12.

Instituto Universitario de Opinión Pública (IUDOP). (2009). *La victimización y la percepción de inseguridad en El Salvador en 2009. Boletín de prensa.* San Salvador, El Salvador: IUDOP.

Kowalewski, D. (1996). Countermovement Vigilantism and Human Rights. *Crime, Law and Social Change, 25*(1), 63–81.

La Página. (2009, September 20). Cementerios clandestinos, horror en El Salvador. *La Página.*

La Prensa Gráfica. (1996, May 26). Maras alerta por La Sombra Negra. *La Prensa Gráfica.*

La Prensa Gráfica. (2009, October 23). Me indigné, por eso me levanté y les dispararé. *La Prensa Gráfica.*

La Prensa Gráfica. (2010, February 3). Siete muertos y tres heridos tras tiroteo en Suchitoto. *La Prensa Gráfica.*

Lungo, M., & Martel, R. (2003). Ciudadanía social y violencia en las ciudades centroamericanas. *Realidad. Revista de Ciencias Sociales y Humanidades, 94,* 485–510.

Martel Trigueros, R. (2006). Las maras salvadoreñas: nuevas formas de espanto y control social. *ECA: Estudios Centroamericanos, 61*(696), 957–979.

Mazzei, J. (2009). *Death Squads or Self-Defense Forces? How Paramilitary Groups Emerge and Challenge Democracy in Latin America.* Chapel Hill, UK: University of North Carolina Press.

Mijango, R. (2014, May 15). Interview by H. Warnecke. Facilitator de la Tregua entre las Maras, Interpeace. San Salvador, El Salvador.

Moodie, E. (2009). Seventeen Years, Seventeen Murders: Biospectacularity and the Production of Post-Cold War Knowledge in El Salvador. *Social Text, 27*(2/99), 77–103.

Moodie, E. (2010). *El Salvador in the Aftermath of Peace.* Philadelphia, PA: University of Pennsylvania Press.

Neckel, S. (1999). Blanker Neid, blinde Wut? Sozialstruktur und kollektive Gefühle. *Leviathan, 27*(2), 145–165.

Ortega, C. A. (2011, August 30). Interview by H. Warnecke. Jefe de la Delegación de Zacamil, Mejicanos, Policía Nacional Civil, Mejicanos.

Paige, J. M. (1997). *Coffee and Power: Revolution and the Rise of Democracy in Central America.* Cambridge, UK: Harvard University Press.

Palacios, M. D., & Hurtado de García, X. (2015). *Perfil de los remitentes salvadoreños y caracterización de las remesas familiares desde Estados Unidos.* San Salvador, El Salvador: Banco Central de Reserva de El Salvador.

Popkin, M. (2000). *Peace without Justice: Obstacles to Building the Rule of Law in El Salvador.* University Park, PA: Pennsylvania State University Press.

Programa de las Naciones Unidas para el Desarrollo (PNUD). (2005). *Informe sobre Desarrollo Humano, El Salvador 2005. Una mirada al nuevo nosotros. El impacto de las migraciones.* San Salvador, El Salvador: PNUD.

Ramírez Mejía, H. A. (2011, August 9). Interview by H. Warnecke. Subdirector de Seguridad Pública, Policía Nacional Civil (PNC), San Salvador, El Salvador.

Rodgers, D., & Muggah, R. (2009). Gangs as Non-state Armed Groups: The Central American Case. *Contemporary Security Policy, 30*(2), 301–317.

Santacruz Giralt, M. L., & Cruz, J. M. (2001). Las maras en El Salvador. In ERIC, IDESO, IDIES, & Instituto Universitario de Opinión Pública (IUDOP) (Eds.), *Maras y pandillas en Centroamérica: Volumen I* (pp. 17–108). Managua, Nicaragua: UCA Editores.

Savenije, W. (2007). Las Pandillas Transnacionales o "Maras": Violencia Urbana en Centroamerica. *Foro Internacional, 189*(3), 637–659.

Savenije, W., & Andrade-Eekhoff, K. (2003). *Conviviendo en la Orilla: Exclusión social y violencia en el Area Metropolitana de San Salvador.* San Salvador, El Salvador: FLACSO.

Savenije, W., & Lodewijkx, H. F. M. (1998). Aspectos expresivos e instrumentales de la violencia entre las pandillas júveniles salvadorenas: una investigación de campo. In C. G. Ramos (Ed.), *América Central en los noventa: Problemas de Juventud* (pp. 113–150). San Salvador, El Salvador: FLACSO.

Schneider, A. (2012). *State-Building and Tax Regimes in Central America*. Cambridge, MA: Cambridge University Press.

Segovia, A. (2006). Integración real y grupos centroamericanos de poder económico. Implicaciones para la democracia y el desarrollo regional. *ECA: Estudios Centroamericanos, 61*(691), 517–582.

Shifter, M. (2012). *Countering Criminal Violence in Central America. Council Special Report: Vol. 64*. New York: Council on Foreign Relations.

Smutt, M., & Miranda, J. L. E. (1998). *El fenómeno de las pandillas en El Salvador*. San Salvador, El Salvador: UNICEF/FLACSO.

Thale, G., & Falkenburger, E. (2006). *Youth Gangs in Central America: Issues in Human Rights, Effective Policing, and Prevention*. Washington, DC: Washington Office on Latin America.

Towers, M., & Borzutzky, S. (2004). The Socioeconomic Implications of Dollarization in El Salvador. *Latin American Politics & Society, 46*(3), 29–54.

Tutela Legal del Arzobispado de San Salvador (TLA). (2008). *La violencia homicida y otros patrones de grave afectación a los derechos humanos en El Salvador. Informe Anual de Tutela Legal del Arzobispado de San Salvador*. San Salvador, El Salvador: Tutela Legal del Arzobispado de San Salvador.

Vigil, J. D. (1988). *Barrio Gangs: Street Life and Identity in Southern California*. Austin, TX: University of Texas Press.

Whyte, W. F. (1943). *Street Corner Society: The Social Structure of an Italian Slum*. Chicago, IL: University of Chicago Press.

Wolf, S. (2012). Mara Salvatrucha: The Most Dangerous Street Gang in the Americas? *Latin American Politics and Society, 54*(1), 65–99.

Wood, W. R. (2014). Punitive Populism. In J. M. Miller (Ed.), *The Encyclopedia of Theoretical Criminology* (pp. 678–682). Chichester, UK: Wiley.

Zilberg, E. (2004). Fools Banished from the Kingdom: Remapping Geographies of Gang Violence between the Americas (Los Angeles and San Salvador). *American Quarterly, 56*(3), 759–779.

Zilberg, E. (2007). Gangster in Guerilla Face: A Transnational Mirror of Production between the USA and El Salvador. *Anthropological Theory, 7*(1), 37–57.

Zinecker, H. (2004). *El Salvador nach dem Bürgerkrieg: Ambivalenzen eines schwierigen Friedens*. Frankfurt a.M., Germany/New York: Campus.

Zinecker, H. (2014). *Gewalt im Frieden: Formen und Ursachen der Gewaltkriminalität in Zentralamerika*. Baden-Baden, Germany: Nomos.

CHAPTER 5

Jamaica: Transnationalization by Force and the Transformation of Violence

In Jamaica, the main driver of violence has historically been the segmentation of the state-class. Parties, which evolved out of the 1938 labor rebellion, organized violence by incorporating social unrest and by overriding yet existent cultural scripts of violence with party identities. As an effect, the manipulation of these scripts and clientelist practices capitalizing on violence facilitated the stabilization of political parties.

Since the state-class became segmented into two competing factions organized around the two political parties, society was caught in a zero-sum game of violence. This horizontal violence was increasingly organized at higher scales, and led to several states of emergency. It even brought Jamaica close to a civil war in 1980. Moreover, this took place in a period in which party cleavages were underpinned by ideological stances and therefore integrated into a worldwide framework of interpretation of socialism against capitalism.

With the failure of Michael Manley's vision of democratic socialism and the forced opening of the Jamaican economy by international organizations and structural adjustment programs (SAPs), the state-class increasingly lost its ability to manipulate, organize, and control violence. From this time on, the state-class could neither maintain the monopoly on the provision of meanings of violence, nor could it promote these meanings with material incentives such as clientelism and rent-channeling.

Furthermore, emerging sources of rents, namely remittances and drug money, challenged the state-class. Both sources of rent differ in their mode

© The Author(s) 2019
H. Warnecke-Berger, *Politics and Violence in Central America and the Caribbean*, https://doi.org/10.1007/978-3-319-89782-0_5

of appropriation in comparison to the forms of rent appropriation inherent to state-class rule. Social groups partly in distance to state-class rule became beneficiaries of these rents since they had created alternative institutional settings to appropriate these rents. By both indirectly accepting this emerging political economic framework as well as even partly contributing to it, the state-class was perfidiously enabled to maintain its rule based on the institutional setting of the state and to increasingly relinquish clientelism. By doing so, however, the state-class shifted its network structure towards relationships with subaltern violent entrepreneurs who more and more enjoyed autonomy. Even though the state-class thus formally maintained its rule, it disconnected from local-level politics and entered a phase of its own demise.

SAPs functioned like an intersection in which the demise of the state-class parallels the rise of alternative forms of income. In the same instance, new social figures able to organize and manipulate violence became visible. Due to the new politico-economic framework, the internal cohesion of historically grown forms of violence became fragmented and newly arising violent actors concentrated on capitalizing on their own forms of violence. This process of specialization became particularly evident in the case of organized crime groups that emerged in Jamaica, professionalized in the United States, and subsequently reintegrated in Jamaica. At the same time, a local gang system well embedded in historically homogeneous communities evolved and secured its autonomy from the state-class. In this regard, local-level politics seemed to have flourished and, as the case of revenge and retaliation shows, developed into community violence.

The first part of this chapter describes the genesis of this new politico-economic framework by focusing on the demise of the state-class and evolving substitutes for subaltern groups. It then turns to the detailed analysis of forms of violence, which transformed during this period.

Transnationalization by Force

By the mid-1970s, the People's National Party (PNP) in power began to face a serious balance of payments crisis and was thus forced to engage in negotiations with the International Monetary Fund (IMF). Subsequently, severe economic cutbacks and austerity politics became the norm. After the bloodiest elections Jamaica ever saw up to then, Manley lost government power to the Jamaican Labor Party (JLP) and its leader, Edward Seaga, in 1980. Even though SAPs became the trigger of transnationalism by force, they did not alternate the overall economic structure. The traditional sources of foreign exchange remained. What indeed did change was the ranking of these sources. Tourism simply replaced bauxite as the prime development motor. This trend was accompanied by the immense growth of remittances.

Internally, however, SAPs provoked a threefold process of "adjustment." Firstly, they contributed to the dismantling and the subsequent demise of state-class rule with a deep impact on the power to mobilize and control violence. Second, SAPs caused the emigration of a substantial part of the population mainly to the United States in search for better economic opportunities and the subsequent rise of remittances as a main source of foreign exchange earnings. At the same time, and in line with this second trend, the informal economy began to flourish and expanded considerably. Consequently, SAPs allowed certain social groups to appropriate arising rents and to gain political independence. During this time, well-established and highly violent party militants turned towards the international drug trade, gained enormous sums of money, and therefore emancipated from political control and partisan patron-client relations.

The Demise of the Jamaican State-Class

From its very beginning, the state-class was fragmented into two segments, each of them led by a maximum leader able to organize political parties (Stone, 1980, p. 104). The two major parties, the JLP and the PNP with their roots in the labor movement, were able to organize this mass movement and to shape the path towards independence. The party in power gained access to resources and was able to appropriate these resources by holding state positions. With the emergence of bauxite mining, the state-class could increase state revenues and therefore enlarge its room of maneuver through fortified clientelist channels and the co-optation of the urban poor. While ideological divisions played a minor role in their initial phase, the period between 1972 and 1980, in which the PNP in power led by Manley turned towards democratic socialism, saw a deep ideological divide between PNP and JLP. From the very beginning, both segments of the state-class heavily drew on patronage politics and the co-optation of youth gangs as well as the creation of party militias to maintain their political positions (Edie, 1991). Clientelism of both segments as the social glue towards subaltern groups was highly territorialized but at the same time competitive (Gordon, Anderson, & Robotham, 1997,

p. 192). By the mid-1970s, however, the dominant mode of rent appropriation and channeling came into depression since bauxite revenues decreased.

The change towards an alternative development path did not materialize soon enough. Manley's third way between Socialist Cuba and open-market Puerto Rico therefore came to an abrupt end. With the end of democratic socialism, the demise of the state-class initiated. This demise went through at least three stages, which will receive further attention in the following.

The first stage of demising state-class rule began with the dissolution of democratic socialism and the PNP's turn towards SAPs in 1977. This initial period lasted until 1983. Politically, this first stage was characterized by the electoral turn from PNP to JLP. While the PNP government under Manley's democratic socialism focused mainly on changing the traditional development path and on improving the economic condition of subaltern groups through state control of the economy, the JLP government under Seaga came into power by focusing on free markets (Crichlow, 2003, p. 37). Economically, this stage was characterized by the turn towards stabilization imposed by the IMF to prevent a currency crisis.

SAPs did not only put an end to an alternative development path initiated by Manley, but also led to a lingering death of the state-class. When Seaga came to power in 1980 after the most violent elections Jamaica ever experienced, he found himself trapped between his ambitions to revoke democratic socialism and to pay off patronage expectations of his supporters (Edie, 1989, pp. 21–24). After some initial years of growth, Seaga finally had to accept several rounds of devaluation of the Jamaican dollar. Therefore, Seaga's government was forced to accept financial liberalization and in particular the opening of the exchange regime towards devaluation. External borrowing in times of declining economic output and exportation as well as heavy import dependency, particularly on basic food imports, had severe effects. First, import dependency caused rising costs of living. Second, external debt even increased from 1977 to 1993.

Although clientelism remained intact due to external borrowing, income distribution became more unequal, and rising investment and initial economic growth merely translated into increasing elite consumption (Anderson & Witter, 1994, p. 18). What became more and more evident during this first step was that the government was not able to consolidate its revenue level to maintain its clientelist practices.

By 1983 and with the acceptance of devaluation, Jamaica entered a second stage of the demise of the state-class. Seaga's government was still able to delay the complete introduction of SAPs until the end of his office term. However, Seaga intended to shift towards export promotion as it was envisaged by SAPs. Devaluation was a trigger, but it was accompanied by privatization of state ownership. A main effect was that the relationship between the state-class and capital interests shifted. Privatization of the tourism industry meant that foreign capital was dominating tourism. Moreover, the role of merchants and importers gained importance with the rising significance of tourism (Weis, 2005, p. 122). During these years, total government expenditure as a share of GDP fell from 35 percent in 1980 to 27 percent in 1987 as the World Bank's Development Indicators show. Until the end of 1989, before another electoral shift towards the PNP, the JLP in power was able to maintain this expenditure pattern fluctuating around 30 percent of GDP. In absolute terms, however, government expenditures decreased since GDP growth was negative until the end of the 1980s.

This had strong effects for the maintenance of state-class rule through clientelism. Since public expenditure stagnated and eventually even decreased, traditional ways of co-optation had to be abandoned (Payne, 1994, p. 98). The reduction of rent revenues available for clientelist co-optation of the urban poor did not end clientelism per se, but it changed the structure of patron-client relationships. Following Edie's (1991) analysis on clientelist relations during this same period, the center of the state-class, particularly the high-ranking leaders of the parties, lost the power to channel resources vis-à-vis the Members of Parliament (MPs). Clientelism therefore did not come to an abrupt end, but translocated to patrons other than the highest political leaders and gave a certain sense of autonomy to the lower ranking leaders of the constituencies.

When the PNP regained power in 1989, Jamaica entered a last phase of the demise of the state-class. The PNP with a new face under Manley and subsequently under P.J. Patterson further consolidated open-market policies and continued with their claim of no alternative (Payne, 1994, pp. 120–125). The PNP increased taxes and agreed to budget cuts, further discriminated domestic agriculture and removed subsidies for basic food production, and accelerated privatization (Huber & Stephens, 1992, p. 77). The economy, however, did not diversify. Internal debt rose to unexpected levels, unemployment remained at a continuously high level, and agricultural production stagnated (Weis, 2004a). What changed was the number of export earners, but the general structure of foreign exchange earnings remained untouched. Since then, tourism, non-traditional exports, migrant remittances, and bauxite exports have been dominating foreign trade. With the rise of tourism and remittances and the relative decline of bauxite, it became increasingly difficult for the state-class to access rent and to maintain its political status.

Following the SAP model well into the twenty-first century, the state-class was unable to maintain clientelism due to declining economic resources and the impossibility to access other sources of rent. The long-standing tradition of co-optation of subaltern groups via party politics, patronage, and clientelism gradually dissolved. The centers of each state-class segment thereby lost influence vis-à-vis an intermediary level formed by elected leaders of each constituency. At the same time, former political area leaders gained influence to maintain the electoral outcomes. Today, MPs are still important figures in the political game since they still control significant amounts of resources and offer work contracts to their clienteles. In contrast to former times, however, they do not dispose of resources to claim absolute dominance, at least at the local and community level.

In sum, the end of democratic socialism initiated the demise of the state-class. Members of the state-class feared to lose political control and elections. Without directly improving the economic situation of subaltern groups and particularly of the urban poor, the state-class accepted indirect improvements for subaltern groups (such as migration, remittances, and the booming informal sector) or even covered up illegal activities (such as the drug trade). Therefore, the opportunity to appropriate economic rents shifted away from the state towards the very subaltern groups.

Everyday Reactions to the Crisis: Household Strategies of Survival

The demise of the state-class had severe impacts on subaltern groups, and particularly on the urban poor. Given the long tradition of clientelism as a stabilizing component of state-class rule, financial cutbacks particularly in the area of social expenditures hit those segments of society that had to rely on distributional mechanisms and on patron-client relations to sustain their livelihood. Therefore, SAPs and their influence on the nature of state-class rule had the most severe impact on the most vulnerable groups of society.

Due to high levels of inflation as well as stagnating domestic agriculture, food prices increased considerably, leading to higher cost of living. Furthermore, the decline of the state-class imposed harsh restrictions on the labor market. On the one hand, public sector employment suffered sharp reductions (Anderson & Witter, 1994, pp. 29–30). On the other hand, agricultural employment decreased to such an extent that it made "much agricultural production in Jamaica obsolete" (Weis, 2004b, p. 68). With ceasing opportunities on the part of the state-class to further co-opt the lower strata, subaltern groups had to seek alternative sources of income. Particularly two emerging fields contributed to the persistence of precarious circumstances for the lower strata: first, the retreat from the formal labor market and the increased engagement in the informal sector, and second, migration and remittances. Both sources of income were and still are precarious and made subaltern groups prone to renewed clientelist practices from patrons that arose independently from the state.

A first option to escape the demise of economic opportunities lies in engaging in economic activities in the informal sector. The informal sector in Jamaica comprises 53 percent of the workforce and at least 40 percent of GDP (Inter-American Development Bank [IADB], 2006, p. 20). The informal sector grew considerably in line with the economic decline of the late 1970s and the 1980s (Witter, 2005). However, the Jamaican informal sector shows some peculiarities. Firstly, many middle-class workers who lost their jobs or seek better economic opportunities entered the informal economy. In terms of labor relations, 46 percent of the informal labor force is self-employed, 36 percent earns wages, and the remaining 18 percent are mainly intra-family unpaid workers. Wage earners who receive only little less than formal wage earners make up a significant part of the informal sector (IADB, 2006). Therefore, the capitalist part of the informal sector that relies on investment and profit seems to be very large. A second peculiarity lies in the goods produced and sold by the informal sector. Tradeable goods play a significant role, especially because entry barriers into the tradeable sector seem to be very low (Danielson, 2004, p. 83). Due to these peculiarities of the informal sector in Jamaica, economic changes are mitigated and do not lead to economic insecurity like in El Salvador.

A second option in securing livelihoods and escaping the economic misery arose out of migration. During the 1980s, migration particularly to the United States accelerated (Small, 2006; Thomas-Hope, 1992). As an outcome of migration, remittances today are among the most important sources of foreign exchange earnings for Jamaica (Ramocan, 2011). On the macro level, remittances remained stable until 1993 and then began to increase exponentially. With a short peak just before the world economic crisis in 2008, remittances recovered after the crisis and continued to grow. In 2014, remittances in Jamaica accounted for 16 percent of GDP and 39 percent of foreign exchange earnings. Around 30 percent of Jamaican households receive remittances, mainly from the United States where the largest stock of migrants lives (Kim, 2007, p. 8).

On the micro level, however, Jamaica exposes some peculiarities regarding remittances. While remittance receivers tend to consume their received money, particularly rural receivers appear under certain conditions to invest remittances in farming (Ishemo, 2009; Thomas-Hope, 2011, p. 221). Furthermore, remittances tend to be stable both on the micro level as well as on the macro level. The average remittance amount sent to Jamaica is US $310 per month. However, the amount sent per transaction increases with the frequency of the transaction. Recipients receiving remittances exclusively on special occasions, such as Christmas or family celebrations, get on average US $223 per year. Monthly recipients receive on average US $2676 annually. Recipients who receive remittances every two weeks collect US $5022 per year, and the highest amount flows to weekly recipients with US $11,453 per year. This latter category make up 17 percent of all recipients and their collected amount almost doubled GDP per capita in 2013 (Ramocan, 2011). The tendency of remittances to grow in line with the frequency of transactions well above a level at which remittances could still hold for an additional income supplementing other economic activities signals the stabilizing nature of remittances in Jamaica.

In sum, engagement in the informal sector as well as migration coupled with remittances help to mitigate the gradual demise of state-class rule and the resulting loss of income opportunities of large parts of the population. Both processes help to explain why the social implosion did not happen abruptly and immediately after SAPs were introduced. The possibly deepest reason for both the transformation of enabling spaces of violence and the rise of new violent actors lies in Jamaica's role in the international drug trade.

The Outlet Valve: Drugs and the Rise of the Dons

Since economic hardship worsened during times of structural adjustment, the production of *ganja* (marijuana) and the trafficking of cocaine were lucrative alternatives in Jamaica. The rise of drug production and trafficking as a comparative advantage of Jamaica had its roots in internal circumstances but was facilitated by external reasons. Internally, *ganja* production and consumption has deep cultural and religious roots in Jamaica (Campbell, 1987; Chevannes, 1994; Dreher, 1982). Externally, Jamaica became a leading exporter at the time when the Mexican marijuana corridor was closed by US anti-drug enforcement (Harrison, 1989, p. 124). Exportation of *ganja* in large quantities to the United States began in the late 1970s as a balloon effect of the increased eradication of Mexican marijuana. In this time, "marijuana plantations offered a profitable alternative against the background of such economic malaise" (Haughton, 2011, p. 219) and some 6000 Jamaican farmers are said to have been involved in *ganja* production (Griffith, 2002, p. 17).

When Jamaican drug traffickers began to export *ganja* they could rely on an already existing network of migrants in the United States. Once they controlled the street sales of *ganja* inside the United States, they were able to diversify into new drug branches. This process initiated at a time when immigration from Jamaica peaked. Many newcomers as well as second- and third-generation Jamaicans living in the United States joined the drug business. These groups used their migration networks and the opportunities given by the advent of crack, and became engaged in the street sales of crack cocaine during the mid-1980s (Hamid, 1991, pp. 826, 832). With increasing domestic marijuana production in the United States as well as the advent of cocaine, Jamaican traffickers increasingly engaged in the re-export of Colombian cocaine towards the United States besides street sales. Even though Jamaica still exports *ganja*, the trafficking of cocaine constitutes a much larger business (Platzer, Mirella, & Resa Nestares, 2004, p. 196). Cocaine trafficking in Jamaica lately came into depression because of a number of different reasons. By 2004, cocaine transshipment through the Caribbean route slumped with severe income effects for Jamaican traffickers (Harriott, 2011).

By 2000, at the height of cocaine trafficking, 435 metric tons of cocaine crossed the Caribbean route from Colombia via Jamaica and the Bahamas towards the United States. In this year, 47 percent of cocaine entering the United States was shipped through this route (Platzer et al., 2004, p. 192). In 2003, then Minister of National Security Peter Phillips stated that cocaine shipped through Jamaica made a street value between US $3 and $3.6 billion in the United States, representing between 40 percent and 50 percent of Jamaican GDP (Jamaica Observer, 2003). Both cocaine and *ganja* thus represent a large source of income in Jamaica, perhaps the largest single source of foreign exchange.

Theoretically, the appropriation of rent from drug production and trafficking depends on the ability to avoid competition at every single chain. Organizing the entire commodity chain in a single hand would thus secure the highest amount of rent. This, however, is a very unrealistic scenario since criminal organizations are caught in a dilemma between vertical integration and the length of command control (Kopp, 2004, p. 32). A network organization is thus more likely to evolve (Kenney, 2007, pp. 237–240). Actors in this network face restricted competition. These actors are unable to completely control the production price. The peculiarities of drugs therefore consist in the demand structure since price elasticity of demand for drugs and especially for cocaine tend to be low.[1] The largest part of rent emerges due to this tendency towards inelasticity; the global sum depends on the (high) price that consumers pay. The international drug trade is thus able to extract vast amounts of money because of the high real wage level in the Global North. The appropriation of these rents depends on two elements: the reduction of competition to maintain a certain price level and the possibility of every single actor to pass the product on to the next link in the chain with a substantial mark-up. In this framework, the power to guarantee the security of contracts and property rights is a central asset in maintaining its role in the drug economy.

On the national level, well-established political area leaders inside the garrisons and the MPs secured political support by redistributing state revenues to the inhabitants. These party militia leaders ensured internal political stability through the access to work contracts payed by the state and by controlling guns. With decreasing state resources and the decline of the state-class, the patrons of clientelism shifted from the party centers to the MPs (Buchanan, 1986, p. 41). Maintaining the stability of voting behavior inside the garrisons thus afforded access to alternative resources because the state-class was no longer able to produce the necessary levels of social and economic wellbeing. During the late 1970s, politicians found a valve in providing cover for the influx of guns and protecting economic activities outside direct state control, notably the drug trade (Clarke, 2006, p. 433). Due to arising opportunities posed by the drug trade, former party militia leaders increasingly engaged in non-political activities and thus reached economic autonomy from politics and the constituencies' MPs (Figueroa & Sives, 2003, p. 83). The line between politics and crime became blurred. Party militia leaders thus advanced to economic drug dons. This process did not change the internal structure of clientelism inside local communities, however, it signaled the alternative income structure of dons instead of state funds (Leslie, 2010, p. 27).

On the local level and in rural areas, restricted access to land and the collapse of agricultural programs such as Land Lease drove small peasants to search for alternative sources of income. Engaging in *ganja* cultivation appeared as a possible outlet to overcome market restrictions. During the late 1970s, *ganja* cultivation increased considerably, mostly on larger plots between 5 and 50 acres (Griffith, 1997, p. 34). With the new foreign policy under Seaga and his close relationship with the Reagan administration, Operation Buccaneer was initiated to fight marijuana production and exportation. Because of suppressing the *ganja* trade, it had an internal balloon effect. Increasingly, *ganja* traders engaged in cocaine trafficking. In contrast to these rural areas, in urban areas and particularly inside the garrisons, the dons' access to drug rents maintained the livelihoods of inhabitants as the nature of clientelism remained stable. Indeed, what happened was a change of the nature of the patron from political don to drug don.

In sum, drug money initially from *ganja* production and later on from cocaine trafficking stabilized the socioeconomic situation for many Jamaicans in times of economic deterioration and decline. While a formerly intermediary level of clientelist sub-patrons gained autonomy due to their access to drug money, the economic situation of clientelist subordination, particularly for the urban poor, remained. This is the root cause of rising levels of violence after 1980 as well as the emergence of a new dynamic of forms of violence as new opportunities for violence arose.

Enabling Spaces of Violence

In the Jamaican case, neither remittances nor the informal sector nor drugs produce violence directly. Contrary to conventional wisdom, the drug trade does not produce violence directly. Actors engaged in the drug trade are economic actors seeking to maintain or increase their economic benefits. Violence involves high transaction costs and only appears as *ultima ratio* when other compensatory mechanisms fail. The relevant link between drugs and violence is thus neither illegality nor the possibility to appropriate rents but the instability of transactions.[2]

Even though these different types of rent do not produce violence directly, they shape social contexts in which forms of violence are embedded. What has been described in Chap. 3 as the main historical driver of violence, namely partisan political identities as one layer of cultural scripts of violence and the mobilization of these identities through clientelism, now began to change with alternative economic opportunities through the inflow of new rents.

Clientelism functioned for a long time as an institutional setting and as social glue. It served as a force in the production of internal cohesion of urban poor communities as well as a main driving force of political gang violence. Clientelism thus generated stability, at least inside communities. The demise of the state-class as well as the rise of alternative resources led to alternations in traditional patron-client relations and therefore challenged clientelism as an institution to protect economic transactions. Depending on the depth of clientelism inside the community, different social spaces that enable violence evolved.

First, in communities in which party identity was contested and party militias struggled against each other in order to gain power and to mobilize votes, the demise of party support created a political vacuum. The demise of the state-class and the forced withdrawal of parties from local-level politics deprived community members and inhabitants of their stability. Given the nature of social closure and strong community bonds coupled with longstanding political party identities, the retreat of the state-class-generated opportunities for escalating horizontal violence between former party affiliates.

In communities or core garrisons, in which centralized control was established and party militias were able to impose their rule, the inflow of new economic rents not only generated autonomy of party militias from their party, but also led to enabling spaces of violence entangling forms of authority and domination with violence, hence to vertical violence. In these cases, clientelism remained stable even though state-class rule diminished. The alternation of patrons varying between political area leaders and economic drug dons maintained extreme social closure. Because the political cleavage between the two segments of the state-class fell apart or at least diminished, the political identity as the main cultural script of violence slightly dissolved. While the local identity of inner-city communities remained, arising drug dons were able to impose their own leadership style in the light of the increasing significance of drugs and to play on yet existing structures of clientelism and mobilization of violence.

As a subsequent effect, these new forms of social control clashed with yet existing claims of institutional forms of social control, namely the police. Given the long history of police repression in Jamaica as well as politicized policing against political rivals, the transformation of historically grown patterns of violence embedded in party conflicts created a social space in which violence easily erupted.

THE TRANSFORMATION OF FORMS OF VIOLENCE

With the beginning of the 1980s and on the background of SAPs as well as the demising state-class, violence in Jamaica transformed. These processes forcedly opened the historical path of the mobilization of violence through political parties and their affiliates in urban poor communities. While Jamaica was characterized since the birth of modern politics by horizontal violence on increasingly higher scales of social organization, the arising political economy contributed to separating different forms of violence that formerly were absorbed by politics. Against the background of demising state-class rule, the capacity of political parties to mobilize violence and to manipulate cultural scripts of violence diminished. At the same time, however, the homogeneous nature of garrisons remained. Even though the same actors of violence remained on the scene, their forms of violence transformed when cultural scripts of violence began to change and adapted to a newly arising social environment in which the state-class was unable to impose party identities.

In quantitative terms, violence increased after the election of 1980. Police statistics point to a change of violence with growing levels of drug-related murders and reprisals and decreasing homicides related to robberies (Harriott, 2000, pp. 12–16). At the same time, the quality of homicides began to change. Multiple murders and even mass killings became common (Harriott, 2003b, p. 97). Police violence and particularly police killings remained on a very high level fluctuating between 15 percent and 30 percent of all annual murders between 1978 and 2008 (Harriott, 2003a, p. 58).

On the level of strategic action, the two main clientelist pyramids and segments of the state-class increasingly lost power to organize violence and therefore to co-opt violent actors on the fringe. Even though the geographic distribution of violence remained stable with the majority of homicides occurring in urban impoverished communities, gangs and gang violence proliferated (Leslie, 2010, p. 9). The gang phenomenon in Jamaica, however, has to be treated carefully. At least two different types of gangs have to be distinguished: the local street gang, corner or defense crew on the one hand, and larger criminal gangs or organized crime groups on the other hand (Figueroa, Harriott, & Satchell, 2008, p. 112;

Levy, 2009, pp. 16–20). Both types are well embedded into community life. However, the violence of these types of gangs is highly different. The former, the defense crew, as the name indicates, defends the community from outside invasions, and enjoys respect and reputation inside the community. The latter, the criminal gang is highly engaged in transnational economic activities such as drug trafficking and money laundering, controls entire communities as states-within-states, and therefore exerts social control. While there might be some overlaps, the former type is a bottom-up gang rooted in the community; the latter is a top-down gang. Without clearly distinguishing between corner crews and criminal gangs, statistics emitted by the police suggest that there were 268 active gangs in Jamaica in the 2010s (Bailey, 2012; Ellington, 2012). Out of these, there might be approximately 12 organized crime groups, from which the *Spanglers* and the *Shower Posse* are the most notorious (Harriott, 2008).

The following subsections describe these transformations by focusing first on the nature of arising communal violence and local street gangs. Subsequently, the emergence of criminal gangs and groups of organized crime under the leadership of drug dons and their impact on forms of violence are taken under closer examination. Finally, the question whether police violence likewise changed will receive attention.

From Local Partisan Violence to Community Violence

With the demise of the state-class, the role of politicians in local-level politics changed and their potential to organize violence clearly diminished. The role of politics in identity formation, however, prevailed. Given the homogeneous pattern of social relations in garrisons marked by dense family relations, economic marginalization, and social exclusion, youth born into this "conflict box" (Levy, 2012a, p. 27) increasingly became disillusioned with party politics up to the point where partisanship was shed. While the organizational network of youths living in the same community remained, their cultural framework got privatized since party "political affiliations ceased to hold much water" (Levy, 2012b). Party political identity thus fragmented and reduced to the proximate community turf.

The lack of central political authority in loosely organized garrisons and the inability to effectively police further worsened this situation and generated widespread fears of retaliation and revenge for former violent acts (Harriott, 2000). At the same time, inter-community conflicts based on the political battles of the 1970s and beginning of the 1980s persisted, but were now interpreted in a new light. Frequently, the newly evolving violence was related to the older political battles and emerging conflicts became projected onto old political animosities (Levy & Chevannes, 2001, p. 14).

Due to the high level of violence in the 1980s and given the social closure of garrisons, almost every family has members who once became victims of violence or even were murdered. At the same time, violence still continues inside and at the edge of garrisons (Moncrieffe, 2008, p. 25). Since the partisan political identity remained as one layer of cultural scripts of violence but slightly diminished, and in the context of a living in distance to the state structures, defense against outside intruders became a necessary requirement for the entire community.

Without relying on partisan support, the only available actors to fulfil this need for security were street gangs and corner crews. These local street gangs formed in the context of marginality and social exclusion. Many of them were involved in petty crimes, but their primary aim was generating solidarity, creating a meaningful living, as well as defending the community (Mogensen, 2005). These local street gangs used the old lasting political cleavages to create social distinction vis-à-vis their rivals and therefore followed the history of their communities. Instead of fighting for political purposes, however, political cleavages were now interpreted as community differences and served for creating internal cohesion by stimulating external conflicts (Harriott, 2003b, p. 92). Therefore, petty conflicts and everyday quarrels over girls or over guns that were borrowed and not returned now were interpreted in the logic of community cleavages and not attributed to politics as it was the case in former times. "But having guns, and not fighting an external enemy, they began fighting each other" (Levy, 2012b).

Inherent to these street gang fights, which often turn into shootouts and frequently provoke homicides, is a horizontal relationship, expressed in the saying "*In gangsta world, dem kill fi wi; wi kill fi dem* [In gangster world, they kills ours and we should kill theirs]" (Moncrieffe, 2008, p. 33). Sequences of violent practices excreted by these defense crews thus reveal the importance of honor and were deployed to deliver notions of toughness, as a gang member explains (cited in Moncrieffe, 2008, p. 35):

Dem [They] *label wi* [us] *as gangsta but that's for now. We will show dem* [them]. *People both outside and inside di* [the] *community label wi* [us] *as gangsta* [gangsters]. *Nobody can be soft. If you look like idiot, man teck set* [men will terrorize you]. *Man use to come in, rape etc. Now di youth seh, you can't do this and it stop gwaan* [Now the youths say, you cannot do this and so it has stopped].

At the same time, however, honor does not simply serve as a regulatory force in the absence of more durable resources inside the street gangs. Due to the embeddedness of these street gangs in their communities, the notion of honor likewise extends beyond the gangs to the community and generates the acceptance of these gangs as defense crews. In this regard, the defense crew not only defends the community against outside rivals or enemies, but also generates internal community stability:

> *A man will have a problem, and him walk pass the police station, and go down a Jungle 12 because him get results. You report a matter that happened last night and within three hours, the matter is resolved.* (Charles, 2004, p. 65).

It is even acknowledged that defense crews carry out assassinations in order to maintain internal peace (Leslie, 2010, p. 30). A narration of a particular violent event given by Horace Levy (2012b) further exemplifies corner crew violence and a certain cultural script of violence. He remembered a particular instance back in the late 1990s when a conflict between an area in August Town called Jungle 12 and its neighboring community called Hermitage turned into a community war leading to several homicides (Jamaica Observer, 2002; The Jamaica Gleaner, 2011). Both warring communities still have opposite political affiliations; Jungle 12 is a PNP community and Hermitage, in contrast, is JLP affiliated. In the end, Jungle 12 brought itself to win the war, and Hermitage sent for help from Tivoli Gardens. Some Tivoli gunman, well trained in shootings, came up to support their affiliates. One day, there was a particular shootout. Usually these shootouts between corner crews or local street gangs happen quite in distance to each other or at a drive-by shooting if street gang members can afford to sustain a car. Moreover, corner crews do have guns, but they are not trained in shooting. Guns are more about the prestige and power delivered by the image of the gun than the practice of using it. Levy noted that "they have no practice really, skirmishes, and one or two might be dead but nothing more." But in this particular shootout, things happened differently. After the leader of the Jungle 12 corner crew was shot, a Hermitage man walked up to him and pumped bullets into his body.

"That is something the community never did," Levy states, "this is a criminal act, finishing him off, making sure that he is dead."

Firstly, the narrative points to the continuous existence of political relations between different neighborhoods. Even though partisan identity diminished, party identity was still a reliable cultural script of violence, which was easy to enact. Longstanding political conflicts and newly arising ones thus become difficult to distinguish since they are entangled in cycles of revenge of which the root cause is often unclear. Secondly, the brutal and expressive killing of the Jungle 12 leader attracts attention. In the perception of the community, this was an act of criminality; an act that did not follow the usual rules. The particular practices of violence exerted in this shootout brought an external meaning into this community conflict, namely the intended annihilation of the enemy. People were not concerned with the fact that the leader was killed, but with the modus operandi of his killing through which the logic of community conflict somehow got distorted.

Local defense crew violence follows a clear reciprocal relationship inherent to cycles of revenge (Charles, 2004, p. 41). Given the historically grown and sometimes forced homogeneity of communities, often based on kinship, street gang violence resembles community violence, and street gang members come close to the militant defense wing of the community.

Even though party identities prevail, the own community and its turf advances to a new cultural identity. Emerging cultural scripts of violence find their expressions in graffiti that are not related to party symbols. At the same time, community gangs turn towards their own "aesthetics of fear" (Jaffe, 2012a, p. 193) in gaining their own fearful reputation and respect by marking their turf and drawing boundaries as demarcations of influence.

Single conflicts or even acts of violence are interpreted in the framework of community cleavages based on longstanding political divisions between parties. Practices of violence exerted in these conflicts thus bear "notions of collective responsibility and punishment for display of solidarity (...) that is linked to the salience of primacy or group identity" (Harriott, 2003b, p. 96). Due to the perceived homogeneity, single acts of violence potentially escalate into even larger cycles of revenge and indiscriminate victimization of rivals.

In sum, the examples given show that community violence exerted by local street gangs are embedded in a horizontal relationship in which community conflicts are managed. The frequent form of community violence, the gang shootout, is often triggered by minor events or even appears arbitrary since these gangs easily draw on yet established hostilities between communities. Once enacted, however, cycles of revenge between communities erupt and escalate into larger violent outbreaks. In defending their own community, and without further support from political parties, these corner crews increasingly reestablish autochthonous cultural scripts of violence entangled in community defense apart from party identity. These community gangs evolved because of the need for security and defense, and to build identity. As a distinct characteristic of this community violence, the social substitutability of rival group members as potential victims can be observed. While in former times, social substitutability was bound to party affiliation, currently, it is based on community membership. Cycles of revenge and retaliation thus become interwoven with community identity and further lead to processes of communal social seclusion.

Transnational Gang Violence and New Forms of Social Control

In historically highly centralized garrison communities such as Tivoli Gardens (JLP) or Matthews Lane (PNP), "transnational circuits of violence" (Thomas, 2011, p. 34) developed and led to the emergence of larger and sometimes even transnational criminal gangs. They were initially funded by segments of the state-class and currently engage in drug trafficking, large-scale extortion, money laundering, and lottery scamming. The development into groups of organized crime and their professionalization can be described as a process of the export and subsequent re-import of gang members during which these members increasingly adapted to new social contexts. This process took place in at least four different phases.

A first phase until 1980 as already described in Chap. 3 saw the rise of party militias organized by charismatic leaders, such as George "Feathermop" Spence, Winston "Burry Boy" Blake, Anthony Welch, or Claude Massop with tight relationships to politicians and MPs in their constituencies. As area leaders and political dons of the garrisons, these social figures not only mediated between the urban poor and the top ranking official of the state class (Figueroa et al., 2008, p. 110). They also assumed state-like functions by providing security, mediating domestic conflicts, and economically supporting "their" inhabitants (Buchanan, 1986). Most importantly, these leaders were pivotal mobilizers and organizers of violence. By cultivating their fearful reputation of badness-honor they gained power inside the garrison (Gray, 2003, pp. 13–15). At the same time, they depended on MPs regarding the access to economic rents through state contracts and to guns.

The bloody election of 1980 initiated a second phase. Like many other Jamaicans, high ranking party militants such as Tony Welch (PNP), Jim Brown (JLP), and Delroy "Uzi" Edwards (JLP) migrated to the United States because of deteriorating economic conditions, fear of political persecution, and newly arising alternatives such as the developing *ganja* trade (Headley, 1988, pp. 70–71). After the 1980 election and the defeat of ideology, armed party militias were no longer needed and their members became freelancers (Meeks, 2011, p. 188). Trained in the use of partisan violence, they moved away from politics and applied their existing gang experience to new encounters, forming branches of their Jamaican gangs as *posses* in the United States and as yardies in the United Kingdom (Gay & Marquart, 1993; Gunst, 2003; Williams & Roth, 2011). The two largest and most notorious ones are the *Shower Posse*[3] and the *Spangler Posse*.[4] While these gangs were initially engaged in *ganja* street trade, by the mid-1980s they turned towards cocaine importation and street sales. From the very beginnings of US-based *posses*, they maintained close relationships with Jamaican home-based gangs inside their communities of origin. The success in the *ganja* and cocaine trade created new fortunes both for US-based *posses* and their Jamaican counterparts because "heads of the gangs returned to Jamaica flush with cash" (Meeks, 2011, p. 189). This cash inflow had an even larger impact since it came in times of economic decay and compensated for declining state-class rule. It became the new currency of dominance and control.

The gunmen in the United States and their *posses* further specialized in violence and quickly advanced to "the most ruthless and deadly of organized criminal groups" (Hazlehurst & Hazlehurst, 1998, p. 11). US authorities attributed more than 2900 drug-related murders to Jamaican US-based *posses* from 1985 to 1988. This number went further up in the 1990s to 4500 murders. The number of members mirrors the number of crimes. In the mid-1980s, authors estimate Jamaican *posses* to comprise more than 1000 members in the city of Miami alone, and almost 10,000 nationwide (Roth, 2010, p. 114). This figure increased to 22,000 members in the mid-1990s, divided into 40 different *posses* present in many cities and in 35 federal states (Williams & Roth, 2011, p. 301).

For US-based *posses*, violence became a "quintessential characteristic" (Gay & Marquart, 1993, p. 153). Practices of violence were staged to gain fearful reputation, which opened a spiral of brutalization (Gunst, 1989). Often, killing rivals implied torture and the staged annihilation of persons with dozens of gunshots from semi-automatic weapons.

This violent expertise of the *posses* likewise gained attention in Jamaica. Many of the gang members, particularly their leaders and notorious criminals, were deported to Jamaica (Barnes, 2009; Griffin, 2002). With their return, many of them either retired or re-integrated in criminal gangs with the support of their gang affiliates. During this time, criminal gangs seemed to have flourished by expanding their activities from the cocaine trade towards extortion of local business (Blake, 2013, p. 66). Precisely during this period, a new social figure and organizer of violence apart from the party militia gunman emerged in Jamaica, the "shotta don" (Bogues, 2006, p. 25). Particularly inside centralized garrisons, power shifted away from the MPs to these dons, and "many dons who command 'respect' are regarded as neighborhood protectors, despite their reliance on violence" (Clarke, 2006, p. 434). Although these dons do not engage in state-class driven rent appropriation, political affiliations still count and when election time approaches, these dons are held accountable for getting their inhabitants to vote for the traditionally supported party. However, successful shotta dons "draw on their own funds and their access to the means of violence, and the residents of their communities rely on them for the provision of 'public' services such as welfare, employment, and security" (Jaffe, 2013, p. 737).

Violent practices of similar brutality as *posse* practices of violence have been evolving in Jamaica. Increasingly, children and women have been intimidated, abducted, raped or even killed. Moreover, several victims have been burnt alive in their houses. "Bodies, usually male, bound and gagged are found in barrels, throats are slashed, victims are beheaded" (Levy, 2009, p. 35). Violence is thus exerted to express the territorial power of the dons, warning rivals and creating a reputation of being dangerous. Brutalized violence becomes functional for the establishment of internal order and the confirmation of hierarchy. Dons thus need to rely "on the credible threat of severe punishment (…), every don must 'sort out' those who 'dis the order', whether they are residents or outsiders" (Jaffe, 2012a, p. 190).

During this second stage, centralized garrisons developed into small fiefdoms where dons operated in more or less absolute impunity (Rapley,

2003, p. 28). Even a national committee, appointed by then Prime Minister P.J. Patterson to consider and recommend practical steps to reduce political tensions between the parties in the light of electoral violence, concluded that "the hard core garrison communities exhibit an element of autonomy in that they are a state within a state. The Jamaican State has no authority or power except in as far as its forces are able (sic!) to invade in the form of police and military raids" (National Committee on Political Tribalism, 1997, p. 6). Thus, even the "state" itself acknowledged that it is too powerless to directly impose control and its rule of law in these garrisons.

Operation Kingfish in 2004 and the subsequent successful attempt to crack down on the Caribbean drug trade route initiated a third phase of criminal gang development. When the drug trade began to decrease, criminal gangs, particularly the *Stone Crusher Gang* affiliated with the JLP as well as with the *Shower Posse*, found an economic substitute in lottery scam.[5] Even though the scam was executed by other people, these scammers were piggy-backing on their crimes. By extorting scammers, criminal gangs compensated for a loss in drug money. The geographic area in Jamaica where criminal gangs are active shifted towards the east of the island and eventually constructed a nationwide network of gang activity. Criminal gangs specialized in brutal violence and thus were able to enlarge their scope of reputation to impose a credible threat on scammers. At the same time, scammers employed these gangs to protect themselves against these threats. This new dynamic is responsible for more than 400 murders between 2006 and 2011 and more than 300 in the year 2014 alone (Bailey, 2012; Ellington, 2012).

A final phase began with the incursion into Tivoli Gardens and the extradition of Christopher "Dudus" Coke, the leader of the *Shower Posse*, in 2010.[6] The forced opening of Tivoli Gardens, the most centralized garrison community, as well as the resistance the security forces faced allow for a detailed view on micro violence inside this garrison and the role criminal gangs played. Furthermore, the incursion and the information that was made available because of the fall of the *Shower Posse* provide a detailed access to criminal gang violence and how this violence was entangled with everyday survival of the urban poor.

The information proved that criminal organizations obtain their income from transnational arms and drug trade, as well as from internal extortion and taxation of local business and the population living under their authority (Jaffe, 2012b, p. 221). While authority stems from the older partisan political conflicts of the 1970s and in particular from the community leaders' access to guns, a don today "cannot be someone who in the past has killed no one" (Levy & Chevannes, 2001, p. 7). Once established, their alternative governance structure inside these communities facilitated dons and their criminal gangs in maintaining "a level of security and order that was difficult or impossible for the police to achieve" (Jaffe, 2012a, p. 190). Apart from security, these criminal organizations even provide welfare and employment opportunities for their population. Even though the main pillar of the don's authority is the massive use of violence, many urban poor residents consider the don's rule rather legitimate.[7]

To a large extent, this acceptance is based on the provision of internal stability and security. There are even indications that the informal system of jungle justice became institutionalized with standardized punishments and a system of local courts (Jamaica Observer, 2010). In this sense, practices of violence exerted by dons or on behalf of dons primarily serve to control the local population living inside their respective spheres of influence. Contradictorily, violence thus justifies the need for even larger protection rackets and their criminal enterprises, but co-opts the local population as partisan identities did in former times.

These criminal gangs continued the historical tradition of co-opting urban poor residents. However, they have increasingly been emancipating from using party identities. By doing so, these gangs regularly come into conflict with the yet established "state." The incursion highlights this violent conflict between the state and criminal gangs. Even though the *Shower Posse* finally lost this war, it was temporally able to mobilize an entire counter-army of about 400 gunmen from all over the country to "defend" Tivoli Gardens. Eventually, the state accepted these rules of the don system, as leading state officials conceded de facto political power to dons. Then Prime Minister Bruce Golding (2010), for instance, justified the state of emergency in West Kingston with the criminal gangs' "calculated assault on the authority of the State." At least on a discursive level, he thus admits a certain horizontality to the state's relation to criminal gangs.

The Police and Enduring Forms of Social Control

It is well widely acknowledged that the Jamaica Constabulary Force (JCF) is a driver of lethal violence. Lethal violence executed by the JCF increased considerably during the late 1960s with the politicization of the entire JCF (Lacey, 1977, pp. 71–72). During this period, the JCF could not escape the co-optation by party politics. Political policing thus continued and even increased during the 1970s with the growing ideological cleavage between both segments of the state-class. During this period, the level of violence remained high, ranging from 30 percent of all homicides in 1978, to 42 percent in 1984, and oscillating around 20 percent since 1990 (Harriott, 2003a, p. 58).

Apart from these figures, two different levels of analysis related to policing have to be distinguished. First, on a structural level, the JCF is embedded in a historical system of social control that has its roots in the post-Emancipation period. This structural level, however, often crosses with the everyday practice of police officers frequently provoking violent events, which are related to the very situational dynamics of policing.

With regard to the first level, social control at least theoretically contradicts the segmented nature of state-class rule in Jamaica. Even though the JCF was born out of the desire to control the entire population in fear of revolution, this system changed with the beginning of modern Jamaican politics after 1938. Its primary role was to maintain the economic role of colonial authorities as well as of elites. Detailed descriptions of policing during the 1938 labor rebellion show that the police force was merely trained to leave the police station in case of demonstrations and riots. Apart from these "public crimes," the police force was weakly trained to enforce the rule of law in areas in distance to the state (Thomas, 2012, p. 206). There is a colonial legacy of policing in Jamaica (Harriott, 1997, 2000, pp. 72–74; United Nations Development Programme [UNDP], 2012, pp. 93–98). However, the need for policing changed after 1938.

The new idea behind policing after 1938 was also a form of social control of urban poor communities, since the state-class was not able to incorporate the entire society but exclusively factions in exchange for economic benefits. Post-independence policing emerged as a mode of getting subaltern groups in line. With the increasing ideological cleavages increased, both the level of violence exerted by the JCF and the need for political parties in power to rely on the police force to strengthen their political basis. The political legitimization of police violence therefore was and still is commonplace. For instance in 1967, then Prime Minister Hugh Shearer stated that "when it comes to handling crime, in this country I do not expect any policemen, when he handles a criminal, to recite any Beatitude to him" (Chevigny, 1995, p. 208). And some 30 years later in 1999, then Prime Minister P.J. Patterson acknowledged in an interview, that "while questionable killings and injury by members of the security forces will be thoroughly investigated (...) the Government would not allow the security forces to be fettered by that practice" (The Jamaica Gleaner, 1999).

In sum, the JCF has historically been involved in very high levels of violence, particularly in deadly police force, and fatal incidents are commonly legitimized as self-defense in shootouts with criminal elements. This brought about serious effects for internal police control. Corruption and the covering-up of certain events is widespread, and the relation with the communities is very poor. On the one hand, the JCF is often described as a "set of hooligans with guns and legal power" (Moser & Holland, 1997, p. 10). On the other hand, public surveys show an enormous support for police violence (Harriott, 2003a, p. 61).

Turning towards the practices of policing "in the streets" affords an alternative explanation. Highly armed, the police often enter and penetrate communities where criminals are suspected by night, and encounter enormous resistance. Due to the strength of criminal gangs, these police raids frequently take the form of a shootout. Several police officers hiding behind their police cars are caught in skirmishes with gunmen. This gives the "impression that the police are an army of occupation" (Figueroa et al., 2008, p. 102) rather than a police force maintaining public order and security.

A sequence of violent events enjoying primary attention in the newspapers at the end of April 2000 seems to be emblematic. It was reported that "the security forces had to impose a curfew on sections of east Kingston on Thursday night in the wake of extended violence there, which left one policeman dead, three others wounded and a suspected gunman shot and killed" (The Jamaica Gleaner, 2000d). The shootout with alleged criminals is a common practice for police officers, often resulting in several persons killed in the hail of bullets. Commonly, however, it remains unclear if the police stage the shootout to legitimize extra-judicial killings of on-duty police offers. An independent police advocacy commission found that only in 23 percent of 267 police shooting incidents, which produced 188 dead persons, the suspect's weapon could be found (Police Executive Research Forum [PERF], 2001, p. 42). This particular event in late April 2000, however, reveals a whole sequence of different violent events. During the shootout with the criminals, an area leader and well-known gunman was killed by the police. In retaliation for his death, criminals killed several police officers, and a whole cycle of revenge between the JCF as well as certain gunmen evolved (The Jamaica Gleaner, 2000a, 2000b, 2000c).

Even the JCF, at least in its everyday practice, does not escape the horizontal logic of violence. Even though the police force is designed to enforce rule of law and/or to exert social control, it faces serious challenges in approaching urban poor communities. The police as well as the gunman of criminal gangs are engaged in a violent relationship on a par with each other and mobilize situational fears as well as other emotions to navigate these particular events. By engaging in these cycles of revenge, the JCF implicitly accepts the equality of their counterparts and rivals, otherwise revenge and retaliation would not make sense. Both the cultivation of honor as well as the use of violence to maintain a "balance of terror" (The Jamaica Gleaner, 1986) are effects of this horizontal relationship that the police force has to accept because of its weakness and because of the strength of its adversaries.

Conclusion

This chapter showed that the new development model, shortly characterized as transnationalization by force, had to be introduced through SAPs. This development model had three major effects: firstly, the demise of the state-class and in line with this process the depletion of traditional channels of rent distribution through clientelism. Secondly, actors who were dependent on these channels increasingly searched for alternatives and found new opportunities in migration and remittances, the informal sector, and the drug trade. Finally, processes of extreme social seclusion in the garrisons continued with the rise of drug dons who developed into economic and political bosses independent from state-class rule.

In Jamaica, this new development model dissolved the traditional way of handling violence, namely the co-optation of different forms of violence into the political system. While the state-class was formerly able to manipulate cultural scripts of violence and to use violence for its own stability, this framework increasingly fragmented. In the past, almost every form of violence had been ascribed to the political conflict between the two leading parties; today, cultural scripts are reduced to the immediate social environment in which practices of violence occur. Thus, defense crews employ community violence against rival communities and their crews and members. This perpetuates longstanding cycles of revenge that date back to the times of party political conflict. At the same time, criminal gangs advanced from their political control and established entire fiefdoms that are based on the capacity to exert violence in and at the edge of garrisons.

As it was shown in El Salvador, fear and its cultivation played a decisive role in the organization of violence. However, fear in Jamaica is much more related to inter-group conflicts. A main driver of community violence exerted by defense crews as well as vertical violence to establish social order inside core garrisons is related to the production and the management of fear.

While the management of fear was formerly bound to the political conflict between the two major parties, the management of fear then appeared on different scales. Political parties were able, by providing partisan identity and by channeling economic resources, to co-opt forms of violence. Nowadays, forms of violence have lost their relation among each other and arising actors specialized in employing single forms of violence. In contrast to El Salvador, where forms of violence partly emerged with the new development model, Jamaica experienced the transformation of forms of violence with a tendency to emancipate from politics.

NOTES

1. The demand structure of drugs is heavily discussed in the literature. Earlier studies assumed a rigid price inelasticity for drugs (Eatherly, 1974; Koch & Grupp, 1973). Recent studies in contrast point to some price elasticity of demand (Caulkins & Reuter, 2010; Kopp, 2004, p. 57). However, this is not to say that drug demand is elastic, but it shows that consumers somehow react to prices and quantities.

2. Under certain and indeed very particular circumstances, however, the nature of the drug economy becomes prone to violence. Since rent appropriation in the drug economy depends on the opportunity to attain mark-up prices as well as to limit competition, criminal organizations will face a trade-off in times of fluctuating prices. In times of high prices, rent appropriation is straightforward. At the same time, high prices attract outsiders to engage in the drug economy. Established criminal organizations may react to increased competition by increasing vertical integration, at the same time, however, they might undermine internal cohesion by lengthening lines of command. In these cases, secure property rights and contracts are crucial. Both issues depend on the ability to deliver economic foreseeability and the credibility to be able to secure future economic outcomes. Excluding yet established institutions in general, and in times of fluctuating prices, thus creates windows of opportunity for violence. Integrating yet established institutions, however, will lead to different results. Since secure property rights and contracts in the drug economy depend on "institutions of protection," (Snyder

& Duran-Martinez, 2009, p. 270), which are able to deliver economic fore-seeability, the very changing nature of windows of opportunity for violence depend on a changing institutional setting.

3. The *Shower Posse* was the leading criminal gang and former party militia in Tivoli Gardens (JLP). In the United States, Vivian Blake arose as the leader of the *Shower Posse*. Based in Florida, Blake himself controlled the illegal arms and narcotic purchases of the posse. Regularly travelling between the United States and Jamaica, Lester "Jim Brown" Coke was the second leader at this time. Up to 1984, the *Shower Posse* was engaged in *ganja* trafficking and its retail sale in the United States. Within a couple of years, the *Shower Posse* established a transnational network between Jamaica and the United States. *Ganja* was brought from Jamaica to Miami and then distributed to other cities of the United States. In the mid-1980s, the *Shower Posse* used this network for cocaine trafficking and its retail sale (Gay & Marquart, 1993, p. 149).

4. The *Spangler Posse* is based in Matthews Lane (PNP) in downtown Kingston and evolved out of *Group 69*, a PNP party militia (Sives, 2003). Until 1992, it was led by Glenroy "Early Bird" Phipps. After his killing he was succeeded by his brother Donald "Zeeks" Phipps (Charles, 2009, pp. 57–60).

5. Lottery scam is an advance fee fraud in which an investor is asked to pay a fee before receiving his lottery win. Conservative estimates assume a criminal gain of approximately US $82 million in 2011 that had been scammed from American citizens (Caribbean Policy Research Institute [CAPRI], 2012, p. 6) (CAPRI, 2012, p. 6).

6. On August 25, 2009, the US government issued an extradition warrant for Christopher "Dudus" Coke, the leader of the *Shower Posse*. However, it took nine months that the Jamaican government followed the warrant. On May 23, 2010, Prime Minister Bruce Golding (JLP) imposed a state of emergency in Kingston, followed by massive attacks on the police by Dudus' supporters. Heavy battles involving guns and semi-automatic weapons took place in the next days while the security forces in a joint mission between the JCF and the JDF invaded Tivoli Gardens in order to arrest Dudus. Seventy-four people were killed during these events and 4148 people were detained. On June 22, 2010, Dudus was arrested on his way to the US embassy, detained, and brought to New York. See for a detailed analysis of this event, e.g. (Meeks, 2011; Sives, 2012).

7. In an interview with a local community area leader, however, expressions such as fear of being targeted still prevailed and the acceptance of the don's authority was not clear (Barnes, 2012) However, dons and their brutalized practices of violence are embedded in a whole cultural industry, reaching from dancehall music (Hope, 2006) to the iconography of dons in graffiti street art (Jaffe, 2012c).

REFERENCES

Anderson, P., & Witter, M. (1994). Crisis, Adjustment and Social Change: A Case Study of Jamaica. In E. Le Franc (Ed.), *Consequences of Structural Adjustment: A Review of the Jamaican Experience* (pp. 1–35). Kingston, Jamaica: Canoe Press.

Bailey, F. (2012, November 29). Interview by H. Warnecke. Director of the Organized Crime Investigation Devision, Jamaican Constabulary Force, Kingston, Jamaica.

Barnes, A. (2009). Displacing Danger: Managing Crime Through Deportation. *Journal of International Migration and Integration, 10*(4), 431–445.

Barnes, D. "Jahlava" (2012, November 27). Interview by H. Warnecke. Area Leader, Kingston, Jamaica.

Blake, D. K. (2013). Shadowing the State: Violent Control and the Social Power of Jamaican Garrison Dons. *Journal of Ethnographic & Qualitative Research, 8,* 56–75.

Bogues, A. (2006). Power, Violence and the Jamaican "Shotta Don". *NACLA Report on the Americas, 39*(6), 21–37.

Buchanan, P. L. (1986). *Community Development in the "Ranking" Economy: A Socio-Economic Study of the Jamaican Ghetto.* Kingston, Jamaica: College of Arts, Science and Technology.

Campbell, H. (1987). *Rasta and Resistance: From Marcus Garvey to Walter Rodney.* Trenton, NJ: Africa World Press.

Caribbean Policy Research Institute (CAPRI). (2012). *Background Brief: Jamaican Lottery Scam.* Kingston, Jamaica: University of the West Indies.

Caulkins, J. P., & Reuter, P. (2010). How Drug Enforcement Affects Drug Prices. *Crime and Justice, 39,* 213–271.

Charles, C. A. D. (2004). Political Identity and Criminal Violence in Jamaica: The Garrison Community of August Town and the 2002 Election. *Social & Economic Studies, 53*(2), 31–195.

Charles, C. A. D. (2009). Violence, Musical Identity, and the Celebrity of the Spanglers Crew in Jamaica. *Wadabagei, 12*(2), 52–79.

Chevannes, B. (1994). *Rastafari: Roots and Ideology. Utopianism and Communitarianism.* Syracuse, NY: Syracuse University Press.

Chevigny, P. (1995). *Edge of the Knife: Police Violence in the Americas.* New York: New Press.

Clarke, C. (2006). Politics, Violence and Drugs in Kingston, Jamaica. *Bulletin of Latin American Research, 25*(3), 420–440.

Crichlow, M. A. (2003). Revisiting Jamaica's 1980s: Maneuvers of an Embattled State Facilitating Neoliberalism. *Social & Economic Studies, 52*(2), 29–65.

Danielson, A. (2004). Poverty, Inequality and Growth in Jamaica, 1988–98, and Beyond. *Social & Economic Studies, 53*(1), 73–93.

Dreher, M. C. (1982). *Working Men and Ganja: Marihuana Use in Rural Jamaica*. Philadelphia: Institute for the Study of Human Issues.

Eatherly, B. J. (1974). Drug-Law Enforcement: Should We Arrest Pushers or Users? *Journal of Political Economy, 82*(1), 210–214.

Edie, C. J. (1989). From Manley to Seaga: The Persistence of Clientelist Politics in Jamaica. *Social & Economic Studies, 38*(1), 1–35.

Edie, C. J. (1991). *Democracy by Default: Dependency and Clientelism in Jamaica*. Boulder, CO/London: Lynne Rienner.

Ellington, O. (2012, December 13). Interview by H. Warnecke. Commissioner of Police, Jamaican Constabulary Force, Kingston, Jamaica.

Figueroa, M., Harriott, A., & Satchell, N. (2008). Political Economy of Jamaica's Inner-City Violence: A Special Case? In R. Jaffe (Ed.), *The Caribbean City* (pp. 94–122). Kingston, Jamaica/Miami, FL: Ian Randle.

Figueroa, M., & Sives, A. (2003). Garrison Politics and Criminality in Jamaica. In A. Harriott (Ed.), *Understanding Crime in Jamaica. New Challenges for Public Policy* (pp. 63–88). Kingston, Jamaica: University of the West Indies Press.

Gay, B. W., & Marquart, J. W. (1993). Jamaican Posses: A New Form of Organized Crime. *Journal of Crime and Justice, 16*(2), 139–170.

Golding, B. (2010). *Address to the Nation on the State of Emergency by PM Golding*, May 23. Retrieved from http://jis.gov.jm/address-to-the-nation-on-the-state-of-emergency-by-pm-golding-may-23-2010/. Last access 28 Jan 2018.

Gordon, D., Anderson, P., & Robotham, D. (1997). Jamaica: Urbanization During the Years of the Crisis. In A. Portes (Ed.), *The Urban Caribbean: Transition to the New Global Economy* (pp. 190–223). Baltimore/London: Johns Hopkins University Press.

Gray, O. (2003). Badness-Honour. In A. Harriott (Ed.), *Understanding Crime in Jamaica. New Challenges for Public Policy* (pp. 13–47). Kingston, Jamaica: University of the West Indies Press.

Griffin, C. E. (2002). Criminal Deportation: The Unintended Impact of U.S. Anti-Crime and Anti-Terrorism Policy Along Its Third Border. *Caribbean Studies, 30*(2), 39–76.

Griffith, I. L. (1997). *Drugs and Security in the Caribbean: Sovereignty Under Siege*. University Park, PA: Pennsylvania State University Press.

Griffith, I. L. (2002). Drugs and Political Economy in a Global Village. In I. L. Griffith (Ed.), *The Political Economy of Drugs in the Caribbean* (pp. 11–28). Basingstoke/Hampshire, UK: Palgrave Macmillan.

Gunst, L. (1989). Johnny-Too-Bad and the Sufferers. *The Nation, 249*(16), 549–569.

Gunst, L. (2003). *Born fi' Dead: A Journey Through the Yardie Underworld*. Edinburgh, UK: Canongate.

Hamid, A. (1991). Crack: New Directions in Drug Research: Part 1. Differences Between the Marijuana Economy and the Cocaine/Crack Economy. *International Journal of the Addictions, 26*(8), 825–836.

Harriott, A. (1997). Reforming the Jamaica Constabulary Force: From Political to Professional Policing? *Caribbean Quarterly, 43*(3), 1–12.

Harriott, A. (2000). *Police and Crime Control in Jamaica: Problems of Reforming Ex-Colonial Constabularies.* Kingston, Jamaica: University of the West Indies Press.

Harriott, A. (2003a). Policing and Citizenship: The Tolerance of Police Violence in Jamaica. *West Indian Law Journal, 28*(1), 51–73.

Harriott, A. (2003b). Social Identities and the Escalation of Homicidal Violence in Jamaica. In A. Harriott (Ed.), *Understanding Crime in Jamaica: New Challenges for Public Policy* (pp. 89–112). Kingston, Jamaica: University of the West Indies Press.

Harriott, A. (2008). *Organized Crime and Politics in Jamaica: Breaking the Nexus.* Kingston, Jamaica: Canoe Press.

Harriott, A. (2011). The Emergence and Evolution of Organized Crime in Jamaica: New Challenges to Law Enforcement and Society. *West Indian Law Journal, 36*(2), 3–28.

Harrison, F. V. (1989). Drug Trafficking in World Capitalism: A Perspective on Jamaican Posses in the U.S. *Social Justice, 16*(4), 115–131.

Haughton, S. A. (2011). *Drugged Out: Globalisation and Jamaica's Resilience to Drug Trafficking.* Lanham, MD: University Press of America.

Hazlehurst, C., & Hazlehurst, K. M. (1998). Gangs in Cross-Cultural Perspective. In K. M. Hazlehurst & C. Hazlehurst (Eds.), *Gangs and Youth Subcultures: International Explorations* (pp. 1–34). New Brunswick, NJ: Transaction Publishers.

Headley, B. D. (1988). War Ina "Babylon": Dynamics of the Jamaican Informal Drug Economy. *Social Justice, 15*(3/4 (33–34)), 61–86.

Hope, D. P. (2006). *Inna Di Dancehall: Popular Culture and the Politics of Identity in Jamaica.* Kingston, Jamaica: University of the West Indies Press.

Huber, E., & Stephens, J. (1992). Changing Development Models in Small Economies: The Case of Jamaica from the 1950s to the 1990s. *Studies in Comparative International Development, 27*(3), 57–92.

Inter-American Development Bank (IADB). (2006). *The Informal Sector in Jamaica.* Washington, DC: Inter-American Development Bank.

Ishemo, A. (2009). Migration and the Small Farming Experience: The Rio Grande Valley, Jamaica. In E. Thomas-Hope (Ed.), *Freedom and Constraint in Caribbean Migration and Diaspora* (pp. 280–301). Kingston, Jamaica: Ian Randle.

Jaffe, R. (2012a). Criminal Dons and Extralegal Security Privatization in Downtown Kingston, Jamaica. *Singapore Journal of Tropical Geography, 33*(2), 184–197.

Jaffe, R. (2012b). Crime and Insurgent Citizenship: Extra-State Rule and Belonging in Urban Jamaica. *Development, 55*(2), 219–223.

Jaffe, R. (2012c). The Popular Culture of Illegality: Crime and the Politics of Aesthetics in Urban Jamaica. *Anthropological Quarterly, 85*(1), 79–102.

Jaffe, R. (2013). The Hybrid State: Crime and Citizenship in Urban Jamaica. *American Ethnologist, 40*(4), 734–748.

Jamaica Observer. (2002, December 20). Gangs Stage Peace March. *Jamaica Observer.*

Jamaica Observer. (2003, March 30). Bill to Legalise Ganja for Private Use Soon, Says Nicholson. *Jamaica Observer.*

Jamaica Observer. (2010, June 4). Photographs: Shallow Graves, Torture Chamber Found in Tivoli. *Jamaica Observer.*

Kenney, M. (2007). The Architecture of Drug Trafficking: Network Forms of Organisation in the Colombian Cocaine Trade. *Global Crime, 8*(3), 233–259.

Kim, N. (2007). *The Impact of Remittances on Labor Supply: The Case of Jamaica. World Bank Policy Research Working Paper: Vol. 4120.* Washington, DC: World Bank.

Koch, J. V., & Grupp, S. E. (1973). Police and Illicit Drug Markets: Some Economic Considerations. *British Journal of Addiction to Alcohol and Other Drugs, 68*(4), 351–363.

Kopp, P. (2004). *Political Economy of Illegal Drugs.* London/New York: Routledge.

Lacey, T. (1977). *Violence and Politics in Jamaica 1960–70: Internal Security in a Developing Country.* Manchester, UK: Manchester University Press.

Leslie, G. (2010). *Confronting the Don: The Political Economy of Gang Violence in Jamaica.* Geneva, Switzerland: Small Arms Survey.

Levy, H. (2009). *Inner City Killing Streets: Community Revival.* Kingston, Jamaica: Arawak Publications.

Levy, H. (2012a). *Youth Violence and Organized Crime in Jamaica: Causes and Counter-Measures: An Examination of the Linkages and Disconnections.* Ottawa, ON: International Development Reseach Centre.

Levy, H. (2012b, November 14). Interview by H. Warnecke. Peace Management Initiative, Mona, Jamaica.

Levy, H., & Chevannes, B. (2001). *They Cry 'Respect'! Urban Violence and Poverty in Jamaica.* Kingston, Jamaica: University of the West Indies.

Meeks, B. (2011). The Dudus Events in Jamaica and the Future of Caribbean Politics. *Social and Economic Studies, 60*(3/4), 183–202.

Mogensen, M. (2005). Bandas corner y bandas area de las poblaciones marginales urbanas de Jamaica. In L. Downey (Ed.), *Ni guerra, ni paz: comparaciones internacionales de niños y jóvenes en violencia armada organizada* (pp. 206–219). Rio de Janeiro, Brazil: Viveiro de Castro Editora.

Moncrieffe, J. (2008). *Making and Unmaking the Young 'Shotta' [Shooter]: Boundaries and (Counter)- Actions in the 'Garrisons'. IDS Working Paper: Vol. 297.* Brighton, UK: Institute of Development Studies, University of Sussex.

Moser, C. O. N., & Holland, J. (1997). *Urban Poverty and Violence in Jamaica.* Washington, DC: World Bank.

National Committee on Political Tribalism. (1997). *Report of the National Committee on Political Tribalism.* Kingston, Jamaica: Government of Jamaica.

Payne, A. J. (1994). *Politics in Jamaica.* New York: St. Martin's Press.

Platzer, M., Mirella, F., & Resa Nestares, C. (2004). Illicit Drug Markets in the Caribbean: Analysis of Information on Drug Flows Through the Region. In A. Klein, A. Harriott, & M. Day (Eds.), *Caribbean Drugs: From Criminalization to Harm Reduction* (pp. 189–223). London/New York: Palgrave Macmillan.

Police Executive Research Forum (PERF). (2001). *Violent Crime and Murder Reduction in Kingston.* Washington, DC: Police Executive Research Forum.

Ramocan, E. G. (2011). *Remittances to Jamaica: Findings from a National Survey of Remittance Recipients.* Kingston, Jamaica: Bank of Jamaica.

Rapley, J. (2003). Jamaica: Negotiation Law and Order with the Dons. *NACLA Report on the Americas, 37*(2), 25–29.

Roth, M. P. (2010). *Global Organized Crime: A Reference Handbook.* Santa Barbara, CA: ABC-CLIO.

Sives, A. (2003). The Historical Roots of Violence in Jamaica: The Hearne Report 1949. In A. Harriott (Ed.), *Understanding Crime in Jamaica: New Challenges for Public Policy* (pp. 49–61). Kingston, Jamaica: University of the West Indies Press.

Sives, A. (2012). A Calculated Assault on the Authority of the State? Crime, Politics and Extradition in 21st Century Jamaica. *Crime, Law and Social Change, 58*(4), 415–435.

Small, J. (2006). Sequence of Emigration and Return: The Jamaican Experience. In D. Plaza & F. Henry (Eds.), *Returning to the Source: The Final Stage of the Caribbean Migration Circuit* (pp. 214–240). Kingston, Jamaica: University of the West Indies Press.

Snyder, R., & Duran-Martinez, A. (2009). Does Illegality Breed Violence? Drug Trafficking and State-Sponsored Protection Rackets. *Crime, Law and Social Change, 52*(3), 253–273.

Stone, C. (1980). *Democracy and Clientelism in Jamaica.* New Brunswick, NJ: Transaction Publishers.

The Jamaica Gleaner. (1986, October 15). Reassessing Americas Watch. *The Jamaica Gleaner*, p. 8.

The Jamaica Gleaner. (1999, July 12). PM: Counter-Attack Time: Promises Resources Wilt Be Found to Quell Crime/Murder Upsurge. *The Jamaica Gleaner*, p. 1.

The Jamaica Gleaner. (2000a, April 28). Policeman Shot Dead at Bar. *The Jamaica Gleaner*, p. 5.

The Jamaica Gleaner. (2000b, April 29). Another Policeman Killed. *The Jamaica Gleaner*, p. 1.

The Jamaica Gleaner. (2000c, April 29). Groups Sondemn Attacks on Police, Flare-Up of Violence. *The Jamaica Gleaner*, A3.

The Jamaica Gleaner. (2000d, April 30). Cop Slain, 3 Hurt. *The Jamaica Gleaner*, p. 1.

The Jamaica Gleaner. (2011, June 27). August Town Celebrates Three Years of Peace. *The Jamaica Gleaner*.

Thomas, D. A. (2011). *Exceptional Violence: Embodied Citizenship in Transnational Jamaica*. Durham, NC/London: Duke University Press.

Thomas, M. (2012). *Violence and Colonial Order: Police, Workers and Protest in the European Colonial Empires, 1918–1940*. Cambridge, UK: Cambridge University Press.

Thomas-Hope, E. (1992). *Caribbean Migration*. Kingston, Jamaica: University of the West Indies Press.

Thomas-Hope, E. (2011). Migration and the Role of Remittances in Food Security: The Case of Jamaica. *Border-Lines. Journal fo the Latino Research Center*, 5, 204–226.

United Nations Development Programme (UNDP). (2012). *Caribbean Human Development Report 2012: Human Development and the Shift to Better Citizen Security*. New York: United Nations Publications.

Weis, T. (2004a). Restructuring and Redundancy: The Impacts and Illogic of Neoliberal Agricultural Reforms in Jamaica. *Journal of Agrarian Change*, 4(4), 461–491.

Weis, T. (2004b). (Re-)Making the Case for Land Reform in Jamaica. *Social & Economic Studies*, 53(1), 35–72.

Weis, T. (2005). A Precarious Balance: Neoliberalism, Crisis Management, and the Social Implosion in Jamaica. *Capital & Class*, 29(1), 115–147.

Williams, C., & Roth, M. P. (2011). The Importation and Re-Exportation of Organized Crime: Explaining the Rise and Fall of the Jamaican Posses in the United States. *Trends in Organized Crime*, 14(4), 298–313.

Witter, M. (2005). The Informal Economy of Jamaica. In D. Pantin (Ed.), *The Caribbean Economy: A Reader* (pp. 434–463). Kingston, Jamaica: Ian Randle.

CHAPTER 6

Belize: Transnationalization by Coincidence and the Rise of Violence

Belize is a special case compared to many other Latin American and Caribbean societies. First, with little more than 300,000 inhabitants, the population of Belize is one of the smallest on the continent. The country remains rural with a strong focus on agriculture. For a long time, it has been known for its tranquility. In Central America, it is one of the few countries that never experienced major political turmoil or revolution, and it was never perceived as a hemispheric threat since political agitations did not occur. In comparison to most of the British Commonwealth, Belizean independence came late. Even though Belize gained self-government in 1964, it took almost 20 years more to reach de facto independence due to the territorial dispute with Guatemala. As the British "colonial dead end," it has historically been detached from the hot spots and global flows of commodities and ideas (Clegern, 1967).

This, however, changed in recent years. For the first time in history, Belize is among the most violent countries in the world in terms of its homicide rate. Violence is highly visible in Belize; newspapers and TV shows are filled with bloody stories on murders and assaults. As Chap. 3 has shown, Belize also has a history of violence characterized by the embeddedness of horizontal violence in everyday social interactions. The peculiarities of this history, however, exemplify that, on the one hand, horizontal violence was only partially integrated into politics as the population lacked direct access to rents that were centralized in the hands of elites. On the other hand, Belize did not sufficiently experience the evolu-

© The Author(s) 2019   197
H. Warnecke-Berger, *Politics and Violence in Central America and the Caribbean*, https://doi.org/10.1007/978-3-319-89782-0_6

tion of cultural scripts of violence for them to be powerful enough for the organization of single violent actors.

From the early beginnings, the Belizean political arena proved to be unable to absorb violence that originated outside of politics. However, the expanding party political conflict and the struggle for access to economic resources forced party political elites to approach local-level politics. Clientelist practices of rent channeling contributed to the development of party political identities, which, in turn, influenced cultural scripts of violence. Since independence, Belize experienced the expansion of political parties, until they eventually formed part of a segmented state-class. It is during this period that the level of violence increased. Violence, however, did develop irrespective of politics, even though the seeds of political manipulation of cultural scripts of violence had been historically planted. Indeed, Belize experienced the evolution of new forms of violence.

Today, violence is highly clustered in terms of geography, the social background in which it evolves, and in terms of the actors who resort to it. More than 59 percent of homicides take place in Belize City, and particularly in its southern constituencies commonly referred to as Southside. From more than 100 shootings per year, more than 90 percent occur in this area (Amandala, 2010b). Furthermore, this area is known for its high levels of social exclusion and the precarious living conditions residents face. Another reality in this area is that new forms of violence evolved over the last 30 years. Localized street gangs developed into a highly structured gang system spanning all over Southside Belize City, eventually reaching into the wealthier northern constituencies of the city and even beyond towards the rural districts. In addition, violence other than gang warfare can be observed, most visibly as police brutality. However, this is by no means the only context. Belize continues its historical path of horizontal violence, particularly in rural areas.

A lack of sources regarding violence, but an underrepresentation of the country in social science research more generally, present a challenge in this study. Conclusions drawn from this case, therefore and necessarily, have to be tentative in nature, as they are often based on suppositions rather than on "thick" evidence. Nevertheless, this makes research in and on Belize ambitious.

Transnationalization by Coincidence

At the onset of independence in 1981, Belize had already experienced a twofold economic and political shift. During the twentieth century, forestry exports as the main economic driver were replaced by agriculture, and in line with this process, the control of the economy had switched from Britain to the United States (Bolland, 1991, p. 88). The economy was still characterized by abundant available land, but labor, particularly skilled labor, and capital were scarce.

At the time of independence in 1981, Belize was dependent on sugar exports as the main foreign exchange earner followed by citrus fruits. Since sugar prices are highly volatile on the world market and local production is subject to weather conditions, Belize's primary aim was to diversify production and exports, but growth in Belize is highly volatile and dependent on external factors (Bulmer-Thomas & Bulmer-Thomas, 2012, p. 140). Taken together, economic diversification in Belize took two steps (Pisani, 2007, p. 69) and involved structural adjustment programs (SAPs), which were intended to support economic diversification by privatizing state-owned property and liberalizing foreign trade as well as the internal price regime.

Initially, at the time of the sugar crisis, Belize had to diversify its exports in order to stabilize its foreign trade. New export opportunities were non-traditional agrarian exports, such as banana, citrus, papaya, shrimp, and lobster. While sugar accounted for almost 60 percent of foreign exchange earnings in 1980, it decreased to 28 percent in 1990 and further to 7.8 percent in 2014. Both banana and citrus substituted this decrease with a peak in exchange earnings in the mid-1990s.[1] In a second step, tourism entered as a substitute. While the tourism industry was almost non-existent in the 1970s, it slowly grew to 7.7 percent of foreign exchange earnings in 1985. In 2014, tourism accounted for almost 50 percent of foreign exchange earnings. Overall, traditional and non-traditional agrarian exports (including marine products) together accounted for little more than 27 percent of foreign exchange earnings in 2014.

Political independence in 1981 thus initiated a process in which Belize should develop in less than 30 years from a rural and agrarian society into a service-oriented economy that is among the most open economies in Central America and the Caribbean. It is surprising that this fundamental societal transformation did not provoke major political turmoil. In terms of political economy, several compensating factors contributed to this stability.

A first compensating factor is migration. Outmigration accelerated with Hurricane Hattie in 1961, and in line with migration, remittances appeared (Ashcraft, 1973, p. 164). Since then, remittances have increased in absolute terms, particularly in the new millennium. In relative terms, however, they remained stable with around 10 percent of foreign exchange earnings and between 4 and 6 percent of GDP.

A second compensating factor is the drug trade. Production of marijuana started in the 1960s (British Honduras Police Force, 1971) but accelerated soon after Operation Condor successfully destroyed Mexican's leading position in marijuana exports to the United States (Andreas, 2009, p. 41). By the early 1980s, Belizean marijuana exports were estimated to account for 100 percent of total exports and more than 40 percent of GDP (Wiegand & Bennett, 1993, p. 206). At this time, Belize served as the fourth largest marijuana producer in the hemisphere (Bunck & Fowler, 2012, p. 85). Marijuana was cultivated mostly in the north of Belize in small plots of about one acre. With declining sugar prices, many small-scale sugar peasants engaged in marijuana production. After winning the general elections in 1984, the leader of the United Democratic Party (UDP) in government and Prime Minister Manuel Esquivel increased law enforcement against marijuana cultivation and allowed eradication measures to fight the drug trade. As a result, the marijuana harvest decreased considerably after 1986. With the end of marijuana exports, cocaine gained importance as a substitute and many former marijuana traffickers shifted to cocaine. Although international trafficking routes cross the country's territory, comparably less drug rents remain inside the Belizean economy than with the production of marijuana. Moreover, transshipment involves small speedboats or airstrips and small airplanes; the drug itself remains only temporally inside the country and does not create further backward linkages, which could be used for other economic purposes. The US government estimates that 37 percent of cocaine entering the United States is being trafficked through Belize (General Craddock, 2006, p. 14).

A third compensating factor is petroleum production. It began in 2005 and peaked in 2011. In this peak year, petroleum accounted for 21 percent of foreign exchange earnings. Although petroleum production largely contributes to government revenue, it provides an insignificant amount of jobs for the population. Its economic effects, apart from monetary inflows, are limited to enclaves.

In sum, Belize experienced the shift away from mahogany and sugar towards new export commodities and services. These trends laid the groundwork for the consolidation of a hybrid elite that consists of certain elements of state-class as well as oligarchic rule. While elitist rule remained intact and adapted to these new economic conditions, subaltern groups were negatively affected. The labor market did not expand sufficiently to integrate the growing labor force, and the stabilization of export earnings as well as state-class rule did not translate into economic wellbeing for the majority of society. Larger segments of the society are trapped in poverty and a growing subaltern group finds itself in a vulnerable scenario that oscillates between gaining economic stability and falling back into poverty (Government of Belize, 2004, 2010).

The new development in Belize is mainly focused on tourism, petroleum as well as non-traditional agrarian exports (including marine products). The latter product group is most vulnerable to external price shifts due to the high price volatility and at the same time most affected by economic ups and downs. Even though Belize as a notable exception did not experience accelerating urbanization after the 1980s, inner-city life in Belize and particularly in Southside Belize City became precarious. In line with ecotourism as the new development mantra, particularly rural Maya and Garifuna ethnic groups who live outside of Belize City in the northern and the southern coastal regions experienced a cultural revaluation. Creole inhabitants in urban Belize City, in contrast, are thus apart from economic, social, and geographic issues, furthermore excluded by ethnicity. Finally, these processes influenced the increasing urban gang system.

From Hybrid Elites to State-Class Rule

While some authors classify the Belizean elite as a "typical comprador bourgeoisie" (Bolland, 1991, p. 90), as a "new elite" (Petch, 1986, p. 1016), or even as "shadow players" (Duffy, 2000), this book argues that the contemporary elite in Belize consists of two factions. One resembles the "old" merchant oligarchy of the turn of the nineteenth century mahogany exporters. The other modern state-class faction is deeply entangled with the modern state. Lately, this latter faction became dominant without replacing the oligarchic faction. In terms of violence, this is an important issue since state-class rule, by definition, needs to organize its political base by co-optation instead of economically excluding subaltern groups.

During the post-independence period, Belize saw the consolidation of Belizean elites relying on the state in appropriating rents. Even though traditional segments of oligarchic rule continued to maintain its influence, high-level state positions became most important to access rents. The traditional source of political power in Belize, namely land ownership, lost political significance. The largest landholder, the Belize Estate and Produce Company (BEC), changed its owner several times. Some part of the land came under government control and another part was sold. By the 1960s when sugar production increased in the north of the country, small-scale producers eventually became landholders (Brockmann, 1985, p. 188). However, sugar production as a major engine of development experienced a severe crisis after Belize gained independence with decreasing world sugar prices. As an outlet, citrus, banana, and marine products served as alternative drivers of development. Almost 90 percent of the country's freehold land thus came under control of foreigners and transnational corporations (Lundgren, 1993, p. 365). With an impressive and likewise questionable land deal with Coca Cola, almost one eighth of the entire country was transferred to foreign capital in 1985 (Barham, 1992). The contemporary landholding elite is foreign with little interest in controlling politics inside Belize. The traditional merchant families with a history of legal and semi-legal business activities still are present in Belize and form part of a merchant segment of elite rule. This elite segment is exclusive since kinship relations and intra-elite marriages are still common (Judd, 1992).

The independence movement, which originated in labor unions throughout the 1930s, gained political importance by receiving key state positions. Soon after leaving labor unions, members of the middle class, educated at the catholic St. John's College, integrated into the state apparatus. After gaining self-government in 1964, the middle-class members' access to economic rents was facilitated by holding state positions. After independence in 1981, the state-class faction further consolidated its state-based economic role, first by using foreign trade as a resource, and second, by increasing public expenditure. The bulk of public revenues traditionally came from taxes on international trade, mainly through import and export licenses. Until 2005, the state extracted 41 percent of tax revenues from tariffs and trade licenses (Statistical Institute of Belize [SIB], 2013a, pp. 195–198). In 2005, the government introduced a goods and service tax to diversify its tax base. Lately, the government revenue structure changed because of petroleum production. Soon after the discovery of oil in Belize, the government introduced royalties as well as a 40 percent tax on oil. The result was an increase in total government revenue because of a higher amount of government income from taxation of oil. However, the details of government expenditure patterns are often obscure and non-transparent and "corruption is built into the system" (Sutherland, 1998, p. 63).

As elsewhere in the Caribbean, Belize thus entered an "independence pact" by which the basis of society—property rights and the class structure—will remain untouched in exchange for political freedom and choice (Girvan, 2015). As an effect, two political parties evolved as segments of state-class rule. Party identities coupled with clientelist practices served for a long time as a means to co-opt subaltern groups into politics: Political parties grew and strengthened their social influence by delivering a cultural framework as well as material benefits. As an effect, "there is little substantive difference between the respective policies of the two parties" (Medina, 1997, p. 152). The party in power, however, enjoys certain advantages in securing its voter base. It is able to provide jobs through state contracts (Moberg, 1991, p. 224) as well to control "the placing of schools, clinics, roads and community centres" (Bolland, 1991, p. 104). Thereby, the line between state positions and party positions got blurred and public expenditure is still used as election spoils and to co-opt subaltern groups by means of clientelism. Moreover, party campaigns during elections became more and more sophisticated in recent years. It is estimated that running a campaign in a single constituency at the time of independence cost about US $25,000. This sum increased to US $450,000 in 2005 (Ryan, 2005, p. 13). In effect, "politically motivated hand-outs are now a full-time phenomenon" (Shoman, 2011, p. 328). Culturally, however, this state-class faction behaves like traditional oligarchic elites in establishing kinship lines through intermarriage. Often, private business groups still have family members in state positions. Kinship thus is strongly interwoven with party affiliation.

Political parties today dominate almost all social and economic spheres, from school attendance, reference letters, and jobs to direct cash flows, state contracts, and import/export licenses. Usually, with changing parties in government, the contractor of import or export licenses loses his license, and both import and export privileges shift to his competitor. The state-class eventually gained dominance over the "older" merchant oligarchy. Moreover, it used ascending sources of rent to maintain and to enlarge its power base. Oil is the most recent example, but likewise the drug trade provides serval illustrations. While elite rule consolidated in the hand of a state-class segmented in two competing factions, each of them being organized in a political party, the livelihoods of subaltern groups became increasingly precarious.

Everyday Responses to Economic Volatility

Changing everyday strategies of survival reflect the deep transformation of the Belizean economy. Belize was and still is a predominantly rural country, and urbanization did not occur to the same extent as in many other Latin American and Caribbean societies. While the population grew almost 30 percent from 2000 to 2010, the share of urban population even decreased (SIB, 2013a). The economy is still unable to offset this increase by providing sufficient economic opportunities. Many rural inhabitants engage in subsistence production. Moreover, urban livelihoods became increasingly precarious due to the lack of proper employment and income opportunities. The fast social change Belize experienced since independence led to a large expectation gap. The economy entered a new stage of openness. It diversified from traditional agrarian exports via non-traditional agrarian exports to services. During the same time, people were forced to adapt to a new economic environment and a new cultural framework based on newly available knowledge on the American lifestyle delivered by TV and an emerging transnational network between migrants and Belizeans remaining in the country. This enormous change finally became geographically compressed in Belize City.

In the north and in the south of the country agricultural production expanded, first into sugar cultivation and after the sugar crisis of the 1980s, into the cultivation of citrus, banana, and into marine products. While small-scale producers initially benefitted from this expansion, the peasantry increasingly stratified. In the case of sugar, more than 4000 farmers grew cane on small plots by the early 1980s. In times of high sugar prices, many of those gave up subsistence production and expanded sugar cultivation (Brockmann, 1985). In the same vein, however, these farmers became dependent on international sugar prices and therefore faced immense annual price fluctuations. The crisis of the sugar economy by the early 1980s directly threatened the livelihoods of these peasants.

Since Belize accepted SAPs soon after independence, precarious conditions became a reality for ever-increasing segments of the population. SAPs forced Belize to abandon its internal agricultural price regime. As an effect of price liberalization, SAPs further intensified the beginning strati-fication inside the peasantry at the local level. A large part of the peasantry retreated from staple food production and engaged again in subsistence production while only a small share of the peasants intensified export ori-entation (Moberg, 1992, p. 2). Consequently, enormous tensions at the local level arose (Moberg, 1996, p. 322). Since parts of arable land are still not cultivated, these tensions are partly mitigated by the possibility of increasing subsistence production.

At the same time, however, under- and unemployment as well as pov-erty is on the rise, particularly since the 1980s. Given the increasing open-ness towards the world market, international fluctuations directly translate into internal economic hardship. As an effect, one third of the population was poor in 2002, despite the economic growth of the years before the study was undertaken. More than 10 percent were considered as living in extreme poverty (indigence). Both numbers even increased in the subse-quent years. A similar study conducted in 2009 found that poverty has risen to 41.3 percent and extreme poverty to 15.8 percent (Government of Belize, 2004, 2010). Labor mobility between economic sectors is very low (Devoto, 2006). On the one hand, the poorest part of the population does not benefit from economic growth, but rather those people living on the fringe of poverty. On the other hand, this second group is most vul-nerable since it regularly falls back into poverty in times of macroeconomic slowdown. This part of the population "on the fringe" is mainly based in urban areas, particularly in Belize City. Belize's urban areas thus are most affected by processes of economic change, both in good as well as in bad terms.

The economic situation suggested three outlet valves to encounter increasing economic hardship: emigration, tourism, and the engagement in the underground economy. However, all three valves only served on a micro level since their effects were soon counteracted on the macro level by increasing immigration, ethnic polarization, and a new cultural framework.

Emigrants went mostly to the United States. Belize has a large history of migration with many Belizeans working at the Panama Canal and during World War II in the United States (Babcock & Conway, 2000). Emigration peaked after Hurricane Hattie but remained on a very high level thereafter. In the 1980s, a second wave of migration started (Straughan, 2004, pp. 153–155). By the mid-1980s, an estimated fourth of the entire Belizean population lived in the United States. In the post-independence decade, more than 40,000 people and in the following decade during the 1990s, between 20,000 and 25,000 Belizeans left their country (Straughan, 2007). Migration thus seems to have slowed down. During both periods, the majority of migrants were women, as labor market expectations in destination countries were higher among this group. In terms of ethnicity, the vast majority of emigrants are either Creoles or Garifuna, both stemming from urban settings in Belize. By the mid-1990s, in effect, a transnational network of mainly urban Belizeans had evolved with "absentee parents" living and working in the United States, many of those in Chicago and Los Angeles (Matthei & Smith, 2007, p. 280). The reliance on remittances of many family members, children and grandparents left behind, was and is a subsequent outcome.

Simultaneously, immigration accelerated, particularly with increasing inflows of refugees escaping the Central American civil wars in the 1970s and 1980s. Between 1977 and 1992, more than 30,000 immigrants are said to have entered the country in search of a permanent residence, many of those coming from war-torn El Salvador (Cornebise, 2005). This inflow had serious effects on the distribution of ethnic groups in Belize and gave rise to a highly politicized discourse on fears of "latinization" (Woods, Perry, & Steagall, 1997, p. 82). While the majority of emigrants stem from Creole or Garifuna groups, Spanish Central American immigrants strengthened the "Spanish" group in Belize. In contrast to Creole and Garifuna, who mainly live in the cities, Central American immigrants have long experienced a struggle for land and subsistence. Therefore, many of them engage in subsistence production and even land grabbing to sustain their livelihoods, which frequently raises reservations, doubts, and even ethnic tensions. Particularly in the perception of Creoles and Garifuna, the traditional balance of ethnicity became increasingly threatened (Bolland, 2003, p. 208; Stone, 1994).

The ascending tourism industry provided a second outlet valve. Officially, 28 percent of total employment is in tourism (SIB, 2013b, p. 309). However, many of the jobs are badly paid, precarious, and volatile due to the fluctuating nature of tourism depending on weather conditions and yearly changing touristic preferences (Key, 2002). In addition, there is an increasing grey zone of informal employment, including sex workers (McClaurin, 1996). Apart from precarious employment gains, thus, tourism is benefitting enclaves. Tourism, however, does have a large impact on the ethno-cultural framework in Belize. While research in the mid-1990s pointed to the "emergence of a public national culture" (Wilk,

1995, p. 113) that might have functioned as a post-colonial unifying "national" framework, the opposite happened with the advent of tourism. Since ecotourism is the mantra of the new state-led development, certain ethno-cultural groups are particularly successful in inventing "their" culture based on tourists' expectations and therefore contribute to reshaping ethnic identities (Holmes, 2010). Mayan as well as Garifuna are both perceived as more interesting by tourists as they are able to perform their own attractive cultural productions. Tourism thus is likely to contribute to socio-cultural closure since some ethnic identities are revalued and proved to be more successful in the commodification of ethnicity. Others, in contrast, and in particular the urban-based Creole population, which already resents the Latinization of Belize, further experience cultural devaluation.

Finally, a third outlet valve came into being with the drug and contraband trade. When many small-scale sugar producers in the north of the country experienced deteriorating economic conditions in the early 1980s, a substantial part of them shifted to marijuana production. In these areas, a new wealth due to the drug trade evolved. The Belizean homegrown cannabis plant quickly emerged as a market brand in the United States and "Belizean Breeze" gained popularity. When eradication measures started to combat marijuana production in the mid-1980s, the cocaine trade was a suitable substitute. In contrast to marijuana production, however, the cocaine trade continued the elitist path of contraband trade, which offered little economic opportunities for peasants and urban dwellers (Bunck & Fowler, 2012, pp. 102–105).

In sum, even though the economy diversified in the post-independence period from agriculture into services, conditions on the labor market worsened. While the largest part of the population living in poverty remains dependent on subsistence production, socioeconomic as well as ethnic exclusion is a social reality for many in Belize City and has led to very volatile livelihoods.

At the time when people were challenged to adjust to a sharply changing economic environment, an additional factor came into play: the appropriation of a new cultural framework. In 1981, TV was introduced in Belize. Indeed, TV has had a serious impact on a predominantly rural and agricultural society in which only 60 percent of Belize's households enjoyed electricity. In 1980, only a little more than 2500 TV sets were registered in Belize (Bolland, 1987, p. 67). This number expanded to 15,000 in 1985, which was a considerable number of total households

(Petch, 1987). It was a cultural invasion that heavily shook the traditional cultural "order" of Belize (Wilk, 1994, p. 95). It provided a new landscape of cultural meaning. TV created a new sense of transnationalism since it generated desires to migrate and likewise created new obligations on migrants to return successfully (Snyder, Roser, & Chaffee, 1991). It led to a new consumerism since new consumer styles were imported and new wants were created. Coupled with the increasing visibility of tourist money, the experience of this TV-led consumerism and changes in import patterns brought the entire cultural framework to shake up.

However, subaltern groups were not only passive consumers. This cultural shift had an immense influence on the power relations in Belize. At least, TV opened the opportunity to forms of cultural production to which politics did not have direct access (Lent, 1989). Everyone was soon able to watch TV, and the elite lost its monopoly on cultural production since the elite is "no longer the only thing to emulate or envy, for it is no longer the source of new things, the local agent and representative of the metropole. They no longer sit ahead of everyone else on the time line" (Wilk, 1994, p. 98). Fashion and cultural style was no longer channeled directly through the elite but could be checked, verified, and screened by subaltern groups.

Enabling Spaces of Violence

The embeddedness of rents in the socioeconomic system contributes to a social environment that renders violence possible. However, neither do rents appropriated from international trade produce violence directly. The new economic opportunities after Belize gained independence mitigated poverty, under- and unemployment, and released pressure from politics. Even though the indicators of poverty and unemployment increased, Belize exited the mono-agricultural export model, which possibly would have been even more prone to international economic cycles. However, it did so imperfectly. In economic terms, diversification further opened the economy, and international business cycles still translate directly into economic hardship for the population. Thus, the political economy today is characterized by enormous instabilities.

Furthermore, the lack of economic stability easily leads to fears of losing the social positions already gained. Widespread social fears are to be expected in this context. Moreover, these fears are multiplied by the desire of cultural self-production and the inability to underpin this desire with economic means. While in the Belizean case quick cultural enhancement due to the introduction of TV created new desires and needs, the economic situation, particularly in this vulnerable social group, did not equally deliver the material background to fulfil these needs. Social fears thus are reinforced by the desire to maintain a cultural style.

The overall structure of rent in Belize generated a situation of instability, particularly for the most vulnerable urban group, which regularly has to fear falling back into poverty in times of economic decline. In contrast to former times, however, the susceptibility to economic volatility and instability is "reduced" to particular social groups, and due to processes of socioeconomic and ethnic segregation to particular geographic areas. Southside Belize City is the geographic area where this is most visible. The majority of Creole population lives in this area. Households of often broken and disrupted families are ridden by the consequences of migration and receive mostly small amounts of remittances. Overcrowding as well as an unclear structure of land ownership are common, and unemployment rates are as high as up to 50 percent. Compared to the national level, Southside Belize City residents are not among the poorest, but particularly among the most vulnerable group to economic instability (Government of Belize, 2010, p. 214).

EMERGENCE OF NEW FORMS OF VIOLENCE

Belize experienced in its post-independence period a sharp rise of violence in terms of homicides. In relative terms, however, this rise is questionable since at the onset of the 1970s, the level of violence already oscillated around 20 homicides per 100,000 inhabitants. Nonetheless, in the period after 1981 and in line with the above-mentioned fast social transformation, violence urbanized. Currently, more than 50 percent of total homicides occur in the Belize district, and almost 40 percent of total homicides take place in Southside Belize City where only 10 percent of the total population live.[2] Even in Southside Belize City, however, homicides occur in some specific geographical areas.

While in rural areas violence is predominantly exerted with knives and machetes, in these urban encounters, violence mainly involves the use of firearms (Gayle & Mortis, 2010, p. 283). Available data and newspaper coverage suggest that rural horizontal violence remained stable, while the increase of the level of violence is mainly an increase in urban violence.

Indeed, rural violence still and often takes the form of family quarrels and cycles of revenge (Warnecke-Berger, 2017). Unfortunately, however, detailed data on these forms of violence is currently not available.

Gang Violence

Violent youth gangs are primary violent actors in Belize today. Even though there is much speculation on the presence of *maras*, there is no evidence to this suspicion. Belizean gangs are held accountable for 80 percent of homicides by government officials and police officers (Haylock, 2012; Vidal, 2012). Historically, gangs evolved in the 1980s after independence in times of economic crisis and in the context of increasing precarious urban livelihoods. A second stage was initiated by the appropriation of new cultural scripts and the simultaneously emerging opportunity to appropriate new resources from the drug trade. By this time, the gang culture became vitalized by embarking on the dyadic conflict between *Crips* and *Bloods*. The reason for the evolution of *Crips* and *Bloods* in Belize, however, is still unclear. Both, gang migration from the United States due to the deportation of criminal youth and the cultural appropriation of gang cultural scripts facilitated by the advent of TV may explain the evolution of *Crips* and *Bloods* in Belize. Soon after this dyadic conflict emerged in the mid-1990s, a complex gang system evolved in Belize City with more than 24 different youth gangs, each loosely affiliated to *Bloods* or *Crips* and each forming alliances against and among each other. These 24 gangs today comprise around 500 gang members nationwide (Vidal, 2012). A final and third step then started with contingent shifts inherent to this gang system. Consequently, cultural scripts appropriated in the previous stage diminished and the *Bloods* and *Crips* lost significance. Because of these systemic shifts, however, the level of violence increased.

"Bases" and Street Gang Violence

As an effect of socioeconomic and ethnic marginalization, particularly in Belize City with its precarious living conditions in Southside, many young adolescents formed street gangs. They called themselves "bases" and organized around localized urban spaces such as the street in which they lived or the local public space on the corner between two blocks. In contrast to media perceptions at that time, these localized youth gangs were not "necessarily dens of vice and iniquity" (Rutheiser, 1993, p. 116), but groups of solidarity of otherwise excluded young people without social and economic opportunities. Street gang membership had a strong socio-economic as well as cultural and ethnic correlation. Research in the 1980s revealed that these bases had a "ubiquitous presence in the city" (Rutheiser, 1993, p. 115) since they were found in virtually all commercial and residential areas, the wealthiest neighborhoods in Northside Belize City being a notable exception. At this time, almost 15 percent of male Creole secondary school students in Belize City reported that "they frequented bases on at least a weekly basis" (Rutheiser, 1991, p. 37). While the private appropriation of public spaces is quite common in Belize, bases were "'Creole thangs' exclusive to Belize City" (Rutheiser, 1993, p. 115). Usually, these base members were either unemployed or working in precarious short-term jobs. Many of them were hustling. "Beginning in mid-morning, base crews passed their time listening to rap and reggae, smoking *ganja* and (more recently) crack, engaging in petty crime, and alternatively hassling passers-by or being hassled by the police, whom they referred to as 'Babylon boops'" (Rutheiser, 1993).

The only available study on bases described these street gangs as "isolated and localized networks of association" (Rutheiser, 1993, p. 116) in which street-corner identity formation prevailed. Petty crimes and minor harassments were essential parts of everyday interactions. Even though there are no detailed studies on violence at this time and interview partners as well as historical accounts in newspapers neglected the fact of street gang presence, it is very unlikely that gang violence during this stage took a lethal form (Amandala, 2007). This, however, changed with the second stage of gang violence in Belize.

The Arrival of Bloods *and* Crips

The second stage of gang violence was the effect of three interrelated processes occurring in the first half of the 1990s. The first of these processes was the change in drug trafficking with massive ganja eradication measures undertaken by the newly elected UDP government in 1983. By the end of the 1980s, marijuana production for export almost entirely came to an end (Bunck & Fowler, 2012, p. 85). The loss of income from marijuana was compensated by an increase in cocaine trafficking. At the same time, a local market for cocaine developed and drug consumption partly shifted from *ganja* to crack (Broaster, 2012).

The second process was the deportation of criminal adolescents from the United States to Belize. During 1992 and 2002, 1122 deportees reached Belize, 688 of them being deported because of major crimes (Griffin, 2002, p. 61). These deportees came in their majority from South Central Los Angeles, an area where Latin as well as Afro-American gangs developed in the 1970s, and to where many Belizean Creoles and Garifuna had been migrating since the 1960s (Matthei & Smith, 2007). Increasing numbers of deportees thus arrived in Belize at a time in which the public discourse was highly focused on fears of Latinization and in which a connection was seen between immigration of Central American refugees and increasing levels of crime in Belize. When deportation started, the same fear linked deportation to increasing violence. For instance, then Minister of Home Affairs Elito Urbina stated that "small but persistently growing cadre of displaced youths (…) are responsible for most of the criminal activity which has terrorized the nation and attacked the social psyche" (Belize Today, 1994).

Finally, the advent of TV in Belize in the early 1980s provoked a shift in consumption patterns. The American cultural industry and particularly movies on violence and gangs became accessible for Belizeans. Newspapers commented on the rising significance of American television by expressing that it "has become a cancer for our children who are not in school, because they are not sophisticated enough to filter out the filth and enjoy that which is entertaining. With American television and its emphasis on sex and violence replacing the sports programs in Belize City, the outlet for the excess energies of our delinquent young has become involvement in what sex and violence they can find or create hence the young gangs roaming the streets" (cited in 1993, p. 236). Even police officers and social workers noted that TV provoked violence and led to changing expressions of violence.

> In 1986, a movie was shown in Belize called "Colors." After that movie was shown, there was a lot of fighting, right after that movie between them people. (Broaster, 2012)

This particular movie on the enduring gang warfare between *Bloods* and *Crips* in Los Angeles was often named as an initial trigger in Belize.

These three processes did have an influence on yet existing bases and their members. By the early 1990s, bases discursively appeared as affiliates to American gangs, particularly to *Crips* and *Bloods* (Covey, 2015; Washington Post, 1989). At the same time, bases now identified themselves as members of either *Bloods* or *Crips*, and each of them claimed detailed geographical turfs. The definition of these turfs was an expression of yet established socioeconomic processes of segregation within Belize City: the *Crips* claimed Northside Belize City, and the *Bloods* Southside (Rutheiser, 1993, p. 116). In the meantime, gang graffiti of either *Bloods* or *Crips* appeared in the city to mark their own turf, something that did not exist in prior times (Matthei & Smith, 1998, p. 285).

While bases appropriated the US gang style and the dyadic conflict between *Crips* and *Bloods*, they did so imperfectly. American-based *Crips* and *Bloods* make extensive use of signs to exemplify their differences, for example, hand signals and language (Covey, 2015). Apart from differences in clothing, however, these signs were never entirely adapted in Belize (Broaster, 2012). Even though Belizeans are claimed to have committed gang crimes in the United States (New York Times, 1997), and even though researchers have pointed to gang migration as a possible explanation for the evolution of *Bloods* and *Crips* in Belize, empirical evidence is not available and it is still unclear if leading gang members in Belize had a live history in American gangs.

Nevertheless, *Bloods* and *Crips* gang symbols are still important in Belize and form part of a distinct identity layer. Colors and clothing style do have a heavy weight on each gang identity (Gayle & Mortis, 2010, p. 232).[3] Bases soon developed a dyadic gang identity by way of cultural appropriation. Indeed, the rise of different bases loosely identified with either *Bloods* or *Crips* soon developed into serious gang warfare. Belizean gangs began to develop the same code of the street revolving around the cultivation of honor and prestige to stabilize internal hierarchies by picking up external fights. Violence led to a fearful reputation and thus created respect.

> Everybody wants to be known as the "big man" out on the streets. We do not want to be seen as weak; we want everyone to think we are "bad" enough, and that we are willing to do anything. Even going to prison is power; the image and reputation of being a "killer, murderer, or a prisoner" is seen as big and something to be valued and respected. (cited in Sistema de Integración de Centroamérica, Secretaria de la Integración Social [SISCA], United Nations Population Fund [UNFPA], & Interpeace, 2012, p. 31)

Instructed by appropriated cultural scripts of violence from TV, movies, and general discourses on American gang culture, gang members began to desire guns to increase their reputation and eventually to overcome their rivals. With drug trafficking involvement, finally, the gangs were able to acquire economic resources and to increase their reputation of fear against rival gangs by investing in weapons.

> Money controls Belize. Vanity is everything; money is power; it determines your self-value and respect in Belize. So, you need to pick up a gun to get what you want because no one will provide you with it or with the opportunities to get it, so you just have to go get what you need. Guns equal to power on the streets. Without guns how will a youth survive? (cited in SISCA et al., 2012, p. 27)

The most visible initial event revealing this warfare was the killing of the alleged leader of *Majestic Alley Crips*, Derek "Itza" Brown, in 1992, and several weeks later the retaliatory killing of Lyndon "Tunan" Arnold in New York City, the then leader of the *George Street Bloods* (Amandala, 2005, 2007). Both killings were said to be about drug turf, since both major gangs increased drug trafficking activities (Cassanova, 2012). After this event, horizontal violence between gangs became more and more entrenched and the level of violence increased. This gang warfare points to a new cultural script of violence. With the emergence of new cultural meanings of gangs, practices of violence changed with increasing shootouts and murders. Shootouts, retaliation, and reprisal killings enacted an enduring cycle of violent events. Interestingly, violent practices since then hardly changed, and gangs did not escape the horizontal relationship inherent to gang warfare.

The stability of practices of violence is highlighted by an event in 2013 when four alleged members of the *George Street Gang* were brutally killed by cutting the throats of the victims. When the victims were discovered by residents of the neighborhood, a short-lived riot developed because some of the residents suspected the Gang Suppression Unit (GSU) of the police department to have killed the gang members. Being asked for the reason of this suspicion, residents, gang members, and bystanders stated that "the murders have been the work of the GSU (…) because traditionally, gang warfare is conducted with the thunder of bullets, not stealthy, cutthroat murder in the early morning, heard by no one" (Amandala, 2013a).

These statements articulate the underlying cultural script of gang warfare: Gang violence has to be public. The offender as well as the victim have to show up in respect for each other, and the bystanders and witnesses have to recognize this respect demanded by the unwritten rules of this type of horizontal violence. According to this practice, the clandestine murder in the morning "heard by no one" thus could not have had anything to do with gang warfare. Furthermore, honor and respect, on which the gang member and his internal position inside the gang relies, depends on the responsibility the offender takes for the killing he commits (Hyde, 2012). This responsibility is the underlying form of generating respect and honor and therefore needs witnesses. This logic of gang warfare eventually leads to highly public practices of violence, the shootout in the street. Gangs are caught in a zero-sum violent game, which has led to escalating levels of gang violence without alternating the dominant form of violence exerted by gangs.

The Localized Gang System and Its Dynamics

Crips and *Bloods* gang identity never became hegemonic in the sense of co-opting existing base identities and forming two larger gang blocks. Instead, gangs have remained localized and still draw their identity from the protection and the claim of their corner or street. Consequently, a mosaic of different gangs, loosely affiliated with each other based on shared identities of belonging to *Bloods* or to *Crips*, emerged in Belize City. Figure 6.1 shows this mosaic.

Out of these 24 different gangs, the *George Street Gang* is the most powerful in terms of membership. This gang comprises up to 150 gang members and well developed internal informal hierarchies. The leaders are called "Generals," their-high ranking followers "Lieutenants," and the rank and file "Soldiers." Its main rivals are the *Southside Gang* and the *Pregnant Alley Gang*, that both rank second in terms of organizational capacities. Most of the other gangs are based on ad hoc structures of between 10 and 30 members without clear leadership roles or internal ranks (Vidal, 2012).

Given the less institutionalized nature of the vast majority of gangs in Belize City, gangs form alliances among each other in order to safeguard their own survival, particularly against the *George Street Gang*. However, due to the lack of durable resources of each gang, these alliances are short-lived and outcomes of situational contexts depend on the capacity to mobilize violence on a daily basis. As an effect, single violent incidents can disturb the overall equilibrium, and a minor violent event might even threaten the entire system. Gangs are thus forced to react immediately on signs or the threat of retaliation to regain equality vis-à-vis rivals. Violence

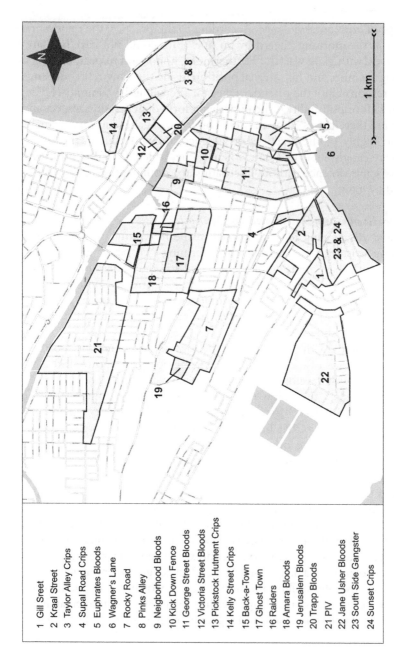

1 Gill Sreet
2 Kraal Street
3 Taylor Alley Crips
4 Supal Road Crips
5 Euphrates Bloods
6 Wagner's Lane
7 Rocky Road
8 Pinks Alley
9 Neigborhood Bloods
10 Kick Down Fence
11 George Street Bloods
12 Victoria Street Bloods
13 Pickstock Hutment Crips
14 Kelly Street Crips
15 Back-a-Town
16 Raiders
17 Ghost Town
18 Amara Bloods
19 Jerusalem Bloods
20 Trapp Bloods
21 PIV
22 Jane Usher Bloods
23 South Side Gangster
24 Sunset Crips

Fig. 6.1   The mosaic of gangs in Belize City. (Source: own elaboration based on information provided in interviews with Broaster (2012), Vidal (2012), and Hyde (2012) and OpenStreetMap under ODbL)

in this context develops into "an epidemic-like process of social contagion" (Papachristos, 2009, p. 76) as rival gangs compete for dominance. Individual disputes and single violent events in this context are able to impact relations between different gangs, thereby shaping the character of the entire gang system.

The reason of single violent events then becomes unimportant. In the perception of single gangs, violence creates "noise" on which the gang members have to react given the imperfect information on the stability and resilience of their alliances. In fact, violence then erupts in time-dependent clusters in which a single event is immediately followed by several shootouts and even killings for revenge (Amandala, 2010b; Channel5Belize, 2014).

The lack of geographic mobility of gang members further cements the violent equilibrium between these gangs because of their reliance on local turf and the subsequent tight relationship with the community in which they live. Given the high levels of social exclusion in Southside Belize City, gangs filled a multi-layered sociocultural vacuum inside marginalized communities. Gangs that emerged inside these communities delivered status and respect not only for the gangs themselves but also for the entire community. Material resources the gang redistributed to the community further underpin this respect.

> It's not always girls and money. Sometimes not even salt. Most of us do anything to get by. Sometimes people think that we all have lots of money. I remember the first time we rob a place it's because we had no money coming from anywhere else. No gang do just one thing, we do several things. You have to keep the youth them with a least a mouthful. For many of the youth they parents forsake them, government don't care. They only have us. We cannot fail them as everybody else already do that so if the drug thing fail we ketch and kill. We just fill the gap 'til things turn again. Remember no one give us anything. Wi men. Everybody ready to take though, fuck! So like Nike we just do it! (cited in Gayle & Mortis, 2010, p. 311)

Redistribution towards the community led to the acceptance of gangs inside the community. However, redistribution "is not about economic status. Some of the residents survive because of the gang" (Hyde, 2012). Gangs even guarantee community welfare in providing money to send children to school or to support families in times of economic hardship (Gayle & Mortis, 2010, p. 310). Thus, the community is forced to adopt the gangs' code of the street (Gayle & Mortis, 2010, p. 234). At the same time, the community provides shelter for gang members in times of police raids. Inside communities, there is a "culture of silence" (Vasquez, 2012) and one police officer claims about the problem that:

> When the police come into these communities to address the leader of the gang, is that the community turn on the police (…). The community feels like those leaders and those gangs itself is what helps them (…). (Hyde, 2012)

Thus, gangs are dependent on the support of the community in exchange for material resources as well as respect and moral support. The entire gang system becomes further stabilized since the lack of gang mobility renders conflict avoidance impossible.

Two factors explain why the entire system remained stable although the level of violence increased. First, the gangs became increasingly embedded into their communities. Today, gang membership and family ties are often interwoven. When sons or brothers gain respect or even leading ranks by inheritance, the lines between gangs and families even become blurred. When the rules of social substitutability of revenge killings change, the logics of violence are likely to change in order to apply to the entire community.

A second factor finally is the forced escalation through the use of weaponry in this gang warfare. With increasing economic resources, grenades were used beginning in 2008 (Amandala, 2008a, 2008b). A resident commented on the escalating nature of gang violence in Belize:

> (…) 12 o'clock on the dot, you could hear the amount of guns ring out, and in each neighbourhood … along with the fireworks. One neighborhood, if you fire probably one with a 9 millimeter [gun]; somebody else will fire about 5 or 10 [shots]. Another block will fire with a machine gun. That's how it goes. It's just who has the bigger gun. (cited in Amandala, 2011a)

Gun ownership inside gangs has been democratized; therefore, the reputation of the gun owner was inflated. Since Belize does not produce guns and gun importation is restricted, the availability of weapons is reduced to handguns. This constitutes an objective barrier for the escalation of weaponry used in gang warfare. However, gang members circumvented this barrier by stealing grenades from the Belizean Defence Force as well as the remaining British Army Training Support Unit Belize (Amandala, 2012c). The grenade attack on Mayflower Street in 2008 showed that gangs seek to continuously increase their strength vis-à-vis their rivals. However, as soon as one single gang experiences an innovation, other gangs copy and learn by imitating this innovation and regain equality in order to maintain the equilibrium. Soon after the Mayflower grenade attack, other grenade attacks occurred from different gangs, however, all of them using the same stolen grenades (Amandala, 2008b).

This violent equilibrium eventually became threatened by the rising strength of the *George Street Gang*, supposedly due to its involvement in the drug trade (Cayetano, 2012). The *George Street Gang* managed to kill its main rivals in 2010. Andre "Dre" Trapp, the alleged leader of the *Southside Gang*, was gunned down in front of Belize City's central courthouse, followed by the killings of Giovanni "Nose" Lauriano, a high-ranking member of the *Brick City Gang*, and Ervin "Beans" James from the *Ghost Town Gang* (Amandala, 2010a; Channel5Belize, 2010a, 2010b).

The increase of the level of violence, the frequency of lethal practices of violence, as well as the escalation of the weaponry used by gang members led the government to initiate a truce in September 2011. Initially, it began as negotiations between eight gangs. After some months, the most powerful joined the truce. At the end, 13 leaders of different gangs accomplished truce negotiations to end gang warfare in exchange for economic opportunities to abandon gang life (Amandala, 2012b). A truce had already been achieved in 1995 with mixed results. This time, the head of the government, Prime Minister Dean Barrow himself joined the negotiations. The government provided a work program for 15 gang members of each gang involved in the truce, spending more than US $440,000 annually channeled through the Ministry of Works, essentially paying gang members to stop shooting each other. However, the truce came under serious attack because of two different reasons.

Internally, the gangs had not been able to maintain peace between each other. The killing of *George Street Gang* leader Shelton "Pinky" Tillett in 2012 not only disturbed the truce, but resulted in top-level revenge killings between several gangs (Amandala, 2012a). After a couple of days, the alleged killer of Shelton "Pinky" Tillet, Arthur Young (the leader of the *Taylor's Alley Gang*), died in police custody,[4] followed by the murder of the *Southside Gang* leader Jermaine 'Horse" Garnett. Particularly the murder of the leader of the strongest gang, the *George Street Gang*, led to immense internal fighting and the subsequent split into two competing factions (Channel5Belize, 2012, 2013). As an effect, the violent equilibrium between the 24 gangs was regained, even though the truce officially endured. However, this equilibrium emerged on a higher level of violence with murder occurring not only between gang members but also between community members as retaliation for gang violence and therefore undermined the essential precondition of a gang truce.

Externally, the government announced in December 2012 that for maintaining international debt payments, it had stopped the truce since money ran out to further sustain the works program (The Belize Times, 2012). Initially, the truce led to decreasing number of homicides, but with the intensified inter- and intra-gang conflict, it began to increase again. Apart from changing patterns of gang violence, however, the truce opened a political arena in which the gang leaders themselves enjoyed a political auditorium. High-ranking politicians, such as the prime minister, joined the truce negotiations and therewith politically recognized the strength of gangs. When taking the larger history of violence in Belize into account, it becomes clear that the political engagement of high-ranking officials in gang negotiations remains a challenge as party politics have always been drivers of violence in providing cultural scripts of violence for actors in conflict to settle their disputes.

In conclusion, gangs in Belize developed because of the reasons put forward by gang theory, namely social exclusion in times of extreme economic instability and multiple marginality (Vigil, 2003). While there is no evidence that bases in their initial phase of development were violent or even developed a clear-cut cultural script of violence, this eventually changed with the cultural appropriation of American gang scripts, particularly with *Bloods* and *Crips* identities. Since then, the fight for honor and respect involved the use of handguns and led to gang warfare between the different gangs. However, these cultural scripts never gained hegemony in the sense that they were able to co-opt yet existing cultural scripts and subordinate these scripts to the dyadic gang conflict between *Crips* and *Bloods*. In contrast, autochthonous cultural scripts weight heavy. By way of (partial) cultural appropriation by exiting bases, however, a gang system of 24 different gangs evolved and led to an equilibrium of violence between these gangs. Since then, gangs have been caught in a zero-sum game, which makes multiple short-lived alliances between different gangs possible. The reason of this trend is the diminishing role of *Bloods* and *Crips* gang identity. Observers acknowledge that today, these identities are less important in gang conflicts than they have been in former times. Without changing the cultural script of violence, the level of violence and the frequency of shootings increased, which is perhaps due to the strength of the entire gang system. As long as the entire gang system remains stable, however, single gangs are forced to maintain equality in strength among each other in order to survive.

In the Shadow of Gangs: Everyday Violence

While gangs today are responsible for the majority of homicides in Belize, they do not commit all homicides. This observation alone is an important fact. However, very little is known about violence outside of gang fights. Gang violence is mainly gun violence: shootouts between different gang members and reprisals as well as revenge killings. According to police statistics, between 2002 and 2009 Belize saw 703 murders. The vast majority of these murders were committed with firearms. However, 23 percent of homicides involved the use of knives (Segura, 2012). In the countryside, and particularly in Cayo, stabbings occur more frequently.

In 2011, then Minister of Police and Public Safety Douglas Singh stated that apart from gang related homicides, "other types of murders, such as those arising from fights and family disputes, have increased" (Singh, 2012). According to Singh, these violent conflicts often originate in "bad passions." Police officials stated that cycles of revenge on land issues as well as family quarrels are the main driver of violence in rural areas (Segura, 2012).

Taking the larger history of violence in Belize into account, this observation does not surprise. However, the public debate in newspapers as well as official statements of politicians and police officers almost entirely neglect rural violence. Gang violence thus covers other forms of violence. Notwithstanding this exclusive focus on urban gang violence, at least some tentative comments explain the importance of horizontal violence in the shadow of gang warfare.

Firstly, in urban areas where gangs are active, community conflicts are managed by gangs. When those incidents of violence are categorized as gang-related incidents, official statistics hinder the proper assessment of these acts. However, even the community police unit is aware of community conflicts, quarrels between neighbors or intra-family conflicts that are "resolved" by gang members on behalf of relatives or friends (Hyde, 2012). Even though the root cause of violence itself may not be related to gang warfare, the conflict then becomes deeply interwoven with gang life. Given the precarious livelihoods in urban Southside Belize City and the general absence of the state, gang warfare transcends the boundaries of gangs and co-opts entire communities. The logic of cultivating honor through the reputation of fear then becomes a logic of its own. Individuals adapt to an environment in which the cultivation of a reputation of fear advances to a dominant mode of social action. However, it remains unclear if the possession of a gun is sufficient to increase its own fearful reputation, or if the use of the gun signals the steady need to rely on violence. Sources are too sparse to get a more detailed picture of ordinary horizontal violence.

Secondly, in rural areas where gangs as well as state institutions are absent, horizontal violence has occurred over the entire period of analysis. Although sources are more than scarce on rural horizontal violence, taken the historical level of violence, it would not surprise that everyday horizontal violence simply continued at the same level since living conditions improved even less in rural areas. A background factor of horizontal violence might be Central American immigration and the subsequently increased ethnic resentments and fears of Latinization. Many immigrants built subsistence squatter settlements in order to maintain their livelihoods; others worked on citrus and banana plantations, which at that time served as the prime engines of development employers often used immigrants who were willing to work for lower payment to segment the labor force on the plantations by emphasizing ethnicity. In this process, workers themselves internalized ethnic differences. Regularly, this led to "conflicts between ethnic groups which originated in many instances from displacement of high-paid Belizean workers by immigrants has increasingly assumed a phenotypic, cultural and linguistic dimension" (Moberg, 1997, xxx). Even a report prepared for the United Nations High Commissioner for Refugees (UNHCR) on the situation of refugees in Belize stated that

> there are, unfortunately, numerous stories of refugees in Belize City who have been the objects of racial harassment, assault by Creole youths, or mistreatment at the hands of police. (Montgomery, 1991, p. 15)

Ethnicity became a problematic issue when workers themselves began to interpret economic differences along ethnic lines. These conflicts occasionally led to "lethal conflicts that erupt[ed] in the banana fields and adjacent communities. After each payday, a small but predictable stream of farm workers [would] visit the doctor's clinic in Mango Creek to have their machete cuts dressed, broken bones splinted, or gunshots wound treated" (Moberg, 1997, p. 127). Because of the lack of data, however, it remains unclear if the social environment in rural Belize had already been prone to violence and newly emerging cultural scripts of ethnicity served as triggers for longstanding violent conflicts, or if those conflicts newly emerged due to immigration and economic changes.

Police Violence, Vigilantism, and Social Control

The death of Arthur Young, the leader of the *Taylors Alley Gang*, in police custody, shed light on police brutality and the use of excessive force by this institution. The annual reports of the Office of the Ombudsman of Belize show elevated numbers of complaints made against the police. The police enjoys a very violent reputation, and people live in constant fear of excessive police force (Gayle & Mortis, 2010, p. 242). In the present context, in which the police proves to be unable to cope with increasing levels of violence, police brutality seems to have become an everyday practice. This includes the beating of children in the streets, torture of suspects in custody as well as police killings. Urban Creole youth are particularly exposed to police violence, but police brutality is not restricted to this group (Moore, 2012). Even the US State Department (2014, p. 2) in its human rights report referenced "police used excessive force and other allegations of abuse," listing at least three cases of death in police custody.

The Belizean Police Department (BPD) was created to maintain social peace in the face of labor uprisings. From the very beginning, its raison d'être was social control and the police thus evolved as a paramilitary institution (Bolland, 2003, p. 177). Indeed, a consultant report on the state of policing in Belize in 2008 by Harold Crooks (2008, p. 76) concluded that police officers still have to pass a police training of "highly militarized nature" and internal discipline still "depends upon military drill to instil obedience." However, the same report acknowledges that the BPD is characterized by an "unrecognized crisis of indiscipline among Constables and Corporals." The BPD is underfunded, poorly equipped, and the "standard of policing is still from the 1950s" (Wade, 2012).

When it comes to violence exerted by police officers, three different contexts have to be distinguished. A first context is the lack of authority and the forced recourse to violence in situations in which the police faces equally powerful violent actors. In these cases, the horizontal nature of the conflict setting explains the police's susceptibility to violence. As a gang member in an interview stated:

> We don't respect dem; dem tief jus like we, dem rape jus like we, dem work
> for de big Spanish man just like we. It is easier I look up to a Boss than look
> up to a police who dah suffer jus like we. (cited in Gayle & Mortis, 2010,
> p. 137)

Thus, even though the police enjoy a reputation of fear, at least gangs discursively maintain equality to the BPD. In the face of equally powerful rivals, the police are forced to engage in conflicts, which easily become violent.

A second context are situations in which police officers are in clear-cut spaces of absolute dominance. The cell in the police station is one of these spaces. A person in custody is likely to be victimized when self-defense against brutalities of police officers in charge is impossible. Practices of violence in these settings are pure torture. In Belize, it is not unusual to be held in custody facing police brutality. Even killings are documented (Amandala, 2015a, 2015b, 2015c).

Finally, a third context is quasi-institutionalized form of police violence. Since murder rates have been increasing in recent years and in reaction to urban gang warfare, the government formed the Gang Suppression Unit (GSU) as a special unit of the BPD in 2010. Since then, the GSU attracted attention in numerous notorious incidents, after which victims reported having been beaten with baseball sticks and clubs (Amandala, 2013b). For instance, in 2011, the GSU approached the *George Street Gang* during a funeral. A resident later on reported to a newspaper that the GSU

> trailed them all the way from the funeral site, until they arrived on George
> Street at around 5 p.m. The police have made it a (habit/procedure) of sorts
> to follow the residents of George Street all the way home after a funeral of
> one of their associates. (Amandala, 2011b)

When the GSU could not find the gang members they intended to arrest, they damaged the vehicle of a neighbor. The residents told a newspaper that

> the police kicked over the liquor and food that they were preparing for the
> repast of Charles Woodeye, and the police wielded a wooden bat at his head
> and his arm. Both these men had to receive stitches. (...) after they hit him
> several times with a baton, and he was bleeding, he asked for medical atten-
> tion, and another officer kicked him in the face and told him to shut up. (...)
> He tried to explain to the arresting GSU officer that he was only in the area

delivering liquor, but the man ignored him and brought a wooden baseball bat down in the direction of his head. (...) he blocked the hit with his right arm, and it was broken by the blow. (Amandala, 2011b)

Similar violent sequences happened some months later when the GSU invaded a home on Dean Street and "brutalized the residents, beating them with bats and clubs" (7NewsBelize, 2013). Even though the GSU was founded to get control of the gang situation, practices of violence deployed by this police unit seem to be characterized by the overall institutional weaknesses inherent to policing in Belize. Driven by these weaknesses, policing leads to punitive raids. Armed with guns, tear gas, baseball sticks, and bats, the GSU invades the rival territory in the search for gang members. Brute force becomes an everyday strategy of policing. A resident commented on this behavior that

Sometimes police act like gangs too cause they shoot all over the place and hurt people. (cited in Gayle & Mortis, 2010, p. 242)

Thus, the police itself is not only perceived as a gang, its modus operandi resembles gang violence. As they fear to be victimized themselves, the police are forced to produce fear. The GSU confirms the horizontal relationship with gangs by relying on the cultivation of fear through the massive staging of practices of violence.

CONCLUSION

This chapter shows that Belize's development path, termed as transnationalization by coincidence, lacks a coherent strategy. Instead, it can be described as a muddling through, and eventually state-class rule gained dominance. Despite this dominance over competing factions, state-class rule is still too weak to co-opt larger sectors of the population. This development path opened new economic opportunities for Belize, but the distribution of these opportunities remains unequal. Certain subaltern groups are trapped in precarious conditions, particularly in socioeconomic and ethnically marginalized urban encounters.

In these areas, gang violence proliferated. However, the discussion on gang violence shows that contrary to El Salvador, forced migration and the deportation of criminal youth from the United States is not sufficient to account for the emergence and the dynamics of gang violence;

autochthonous factors play a role as well. The discussion furthermore reveals that the availability of cultural scripts does not necessarily lead to their application. The external cultural scripts provided by TV are only followed if they are merged with already established cultural scripts. This explains why gang violence in Belize never took the same hegemonial shape as it was shown to occur in El Salvador.

Furthermore, the discussion on gang violence exemplified the processes that organize horizontal violence on a higher social scale, and ultimately entire communities. Historical processes are crucial to understand the dynamics of gang violence. Contrary to both El Salvador and Jamaica, gang violence in Belize created an ultra-stable system in which gangs are in a constant power struggle and form alliances among each other to prevent the rival's hegemony. As it was further shown, gang violence, similar to El Salvador, follows the cultivation of fear. Fear easily transcends the gang system and even influences police violence. In contrast to El Salvador, however, fear never became omnipresent, particularly because gang violence remained a closed system, and, as the discussion on the rules of revenge showed, never transcended to the entire society.

NOTES

1. This and the following data used to describe the foreign exchange pattern are figures provided by the Central Bank of Belize, World Bank Development Indicators, UN ComTrade Database and compiled and processed by the author.
2. Data was provided by the Belize Police Department (BPD) and by (Broaster, 2012; Segura, 2012). There are no reliable data on the detailed spatial and social distribution of violence. Police data suggest that urban violence located in Belize City, and particularly in Southside Belize City, increased. The districts of Orange Walk as well as Cayo range second with some further 22.5 percent respectively. The southern districts of Stann Creek and Toledo rarely experience homicides.
3. Red and blue are at the same time the colors of both leading parties. The six constituencies of Belize City Southside (Queen's Square, Albert, Collet, Lake Independence, Port Loyola, and Mesopotamia) are strongholds of the UDP (red) and at the same time historically led by *Bloods* (red). Belize City Northside constituencies (Freetown, Fort George, Caribbean Shores, and Pickstock) have been dominated for long time by PUP (blue) representatives as well as dominated by *Crips*. Even though there is no evidence on the

gang-politics link, many Belizeans speculate about possible relations between party representatives in the constituencies and local gangs.

4. Arthur Young was a flamboyant personality. He could never be convicted of this and several other murders. The subsequent police custody challenged the GSU and gave rise to immense speculation on his mysterious death in police custody.

REFERENCES

7NewsBelize. (2013, February 13). PM Barrow Says He Suspects that GSU Was Involved in GSG Beatdown. *7NewsBelize.*

Amandala. (2005, July 20). From the Publisher. *Amandala.*

Amandala. (2007, July 30). From The Publisher. *Amandala.*

Amandala. (2008a, May 20). Grenade Carnage on Mayflower! *Amandala.*

Amandala. (2008b, November 18). The City's Third Grenade Goes Off! *Amandala.*

Amandala. (2010a, June 11). Dre Trapp, Southside Boss, Shot Dead Mid-Morning on Regent Street. *Amandala.*

Amandala. (2010b, July 13). Over 100 Shootings in Belize City. *Amandala.*

Amandala. (2011a, January 4). Belize's Crime Crisis – The Stories Behind the Stories. *Amandala.*

Amandala. (2011b, August 30). GSU Goes Berserk on George Street! *Amandala.*

Amandala. (2012a, April 24). City's 2 Top Dons Shot Dead in 48 Hours. *Amandala.*

Amandala. (2012b, June 1). $880,000 for Gang Truce and CYDP Since August 2011. *Amandala.*

Amandala. (2012c, September 12). Offensive Carnival Day Grenade Came from BATSUB. *Amandala.*

Amandala. (2013a, January 11). 4 Throats Cut; City Shuts Down in Panic. *Amandala.*

Amandala. (2013b, December 13). GSU Brutality Costs Taxpayers $205,000. *Amandala.*

Amandala. (2015a, June 9). Boy, 17, Dies After Halfhour in Police Custody. *Amandala.*

Amandala. (2015b, June 12). 2 Caye Caulker Cops Charged with Murder. *Amandala.*

Amandala. (2015c, June 12). They Beat Him to Death! *Amandala.*

Andreas, P. (2009). *Border Games: Policing the U.S.-Mexico Divide.* Ithaca, NY: Cornell University Press.

Ashcraft, N. D. (1973). *Colonialism and Underdevelopment: Processes of Political Economic Change in British Honduras.* New York: Teachers College Press.

Babcock, E. C., & Conway, D. (2000). Why International Migration Has Important Consequences for the Development of Belize. *Yearbook. Conference of Latin Americanist Geographers, 26*, 71–86.

Barham, B. L. (1992). Foreign Direct Investment in a Strategically Competitive Environment: Coca-Cola, Belize, and the International Citrus Industry. *World Development, 20*(6), 841–857.

Belize Today. (1994, August 5). Ministry of Home Affairs Launches Crime Fight Foundation. *Belize Today*, p. 7.

Bolland, N. O. (1987). United States Cultural Influences on Belize: Television and Education as "Vehicles of Import". *Caribbean Quarterly, 33*(3), 60.

Bolland, N. O. (1991). Society and Politics in Belize. In C. Clarke (Ed.), *Society and Politics in the Caribbean* (pp. 78–109). New York: Palgrave Macmillan.

Bolland, N. O. (2003). *Colonialism and Resistance in Belize: Essays in Historical Sociology*. Benque Viejo del Carmen, Belize: Cubola.

British Honduras Police Force. (1971). Annual Report of the British Honduras Police Force for the Year 1971, Belize Archives & Records Service Anr Box 23, #171.

Broaster, E. (2012, October 17). Interview by H. Warnecke. Director of Conscious Youth Development Program, Belize City, Belize.

Brockmann, T. C. (1985). Ethnic Participation in Orange Walk Economic Development. *Ethnic Groups, 6*(2/3), 187–207.

Bulmer-Thomas, B., & Bulmer-Thomas, V. (2012). *The Economic History of Belize: From the 17th Century to Post-Independence*. Benque Viejo del Carmen, Belize: Cubola.

Bunck, J. M., & Fowler, M. R. (2012). *Bribes, Bullets, and Intimidation: Drug Trafficking and the Law in Central America*. University Park, PA: Pennsylvania State University Press.

Cassanova, P. (2012, October 21). Interview by H. Warnecke. Conscious Youth Development Program; Belize Truce Committee, Belmopan, Belize.

Cayetano, L. (2012, October 30). Interview by H. Warnecke. RESTORE Belize, Belize City, Belize.

Channel5Belize. (2010a, April 9). Ervin James Killed While Socializing with Friends. *Channel5Belize*.

Channel5Belize. (2010b, July 19). Two Sunday Night Murders; "Nose" Lauriano Gunned Down on Highway. *Channel5Belize*.

Channel5Belize. (2012, April 24). Gang Truce Dying with Leaders; South Side Gangster Shot in Chest. *Channel5Belize*.

Channel5Belize. (2013, January 14). 2nd in Command of the George Street Gang Laid to Rest. *Channel5Belize*.

Channel5Belize. (2014, September 28). 2 Dead, 6 Injured in Retaliatory Shootings, Belize City on Lockdown. *Channel5Belize*.

Clegern, W. M. (1967). *British Honduras: Colonial Dead End, 1859–1900*. Baton Rouge, LA: Louisiana State University Press.

Cornebise, M. (2005). Belizean Population and Migration Trends. *Bulletin of the Illinois Geographical Society, 47*(1), 1–17.

Covey, H. (2015). *Crips and Bloods: A Guide to an American Subculture*. Santa Barbara, CA: ABC-CLIO.

Crooks, H. (2008). *A Review of the Belize Police Department*. Belmopan, Belize: Belize Ministry of National Security.

Devoto, F. (2006). *Belize: Poverty and Economic Sector Performance*. Washington, DC: Inter-American Development Bank.

Duffy, R. (2000). Shadow Players: Ecotourism Development, Corruption and State Politics in Belize. *Third World Quarterly, 21*(3), 549–565.

Gayle, H., & Mortis, N. (2010). *Male Social Participation and Violence in Urban Belize: An Examination of Their Experience with Goals, Guns, Gangs, Gender, God, and Governance*. Belize City, Belize: RESTORE Belize.

General Craddock, B. J. (2006). *Posture Statement of General Brantz J. Craddock, United States Army Commander, United States Southern Command Before the 109th Congress House armed Service Committee, 16 March 2006*. Washington, DC: U.S. Government Printing Office.

Girvan, N. (2015). Assessing Westminster in the Caribbean: Then and Now. *Commonwealth & Comparative Politics, 53*(1), 95–107.

Government of Belize. (2004). *2002 Country Poverty Assessment*. Belmopan, Belize: Government Printers.

Government of Belize. (2010). *Country Poverty Assessment 2009*. Belmopan, Belize: Government Printers.

Griffin, C. E. (2002). Criminal Deportation: The Unintended Impact of U.S. Anti-Crime and Anti-Terrorism Policy Along Its Third Border. *Caribbean Studies, 30*(2), 39–76.

Haylock, N. (2012, October 18). Interview by H. Warnecke. Ministry of National Security, Belmopan, Belize.

Holmes, T. J. (2010). Tourism and the Making of Ethnic Citizenship in Belize. In D. V. L. Macleod & J. G. Carrier (Eds.), *Tourism, Power, and Culture: Anthropological Insights* (pp. 153–173). Bristol, UK: Channel View Publications.

Hyde, D. (2012, October 23). Interview by H. Warnecke. Director of Comunity Policing Unit, Belize Police Department, Belize City, Belize.

Judd, K. H. (1992). *Elite Reproduction and Ethnic Identity in Belize* (Ph.D. Dissertation). City University of New York, New York.

Key, C. J. (2002). The Political Economy of the Transition from Fishing to Tourism in Placencia, Belize. *International Review of Modern Sociology, 30*(1/2), 1–18.

Lent, J. (1989). Country of No Return: Belize Since Television. *Belizean Studies, 17*(1), 14–36.

Lundgren, N. (1993). Women, Work, and "Development" in Belize. *Dialectical Anthropology, 18*(3/4), 363–378.

Matthei, L. M., & Smith, D. A. (1998). Belizean "Boyz 'n the 'Hood"? Garifuna Labor Migration and Transnational Identity. In M. P. Smith & L. E. Guarnizo (Eds.), *Transnationalism from Below* (pp. 270–290). New Brunswick, NJ: Transaction Publishers.

Matthei, L. M., & Smith, D. A. (2007). Globalization, Migration and the Shaping of Masculinity in Belize. In R. E. Reddock (Ed.), *Interrogating Caribbean Masculinities: Theoretical and Empirical Analyses* (pp. 267–285). Mona, Jamaica: University of the West Indies Press.

McClaurin, I. (1996). *Women of Belize: Gender and Change in Central America.* New Brunswick, NJ: Rutgers University Press.

Medina, L. K. (1997). Development Policies and Identity Politics: Class and Collectivity in Belize. *American Ethnologist, 24*(1), 148–169.

Moberg, M. (1991). Citrus and the State: Factions and Class Formation in Rural Belize. *American Ethnologist, 18*(2), 215–233.

Moberg, M. (1992). Structural Adjustment and Rural Development: Inferences from a Belizean Village. *The Journal of Developing Areas, 27*(1), 1–20.

Moberg, M. (1996). Myths That Divide: Immigrant Labor and Class Segmentation in the Belizean Banana Industry. *American Ethnologist, 23*(2), 311–330.

Moberg, M. (1997). *Myths of Ethnicity and Nation: Immigration, Work, and Identity in the Belize Banana Industry.* Knoxville, TN: University of Tennessee Press.

Montgomery, T. S. (1991). *Refugees in Belize, 1991: A Report to the United Nations High Commissioner for Refugees.* Belmopan, Belize: Government Printers.

Moore, A. (2012, November 8). Interview by H. Warnecke. Attorney at Law; National Committee for Human Rights, Dangriga, Belize.

New York Times. (1997, October 30). 24 Members of *Crips* Gang Are Arrested in a Sweep by Police. *New York Times.*

Papachristos, A. V. (2009). Murder by Structure: Dominance Relations and the Social Structure of Gang Homicide. *American Journal of Sociology, 115*(1), 74–128.

Petch, T. (1986). Dependency, Land and Oranges in Belize. *Third World Quarterly, 8*(3), 1002–1019.

Petch, T. (1987). Television and Video Ownership in Belize. *Belizean Studies, 15*(1), 12–14.

Pisani, M. J. (2007). Belize's Foreign Trade Performance Since Independence: Neo-Dependent Challenges and Opportunities. In B. S. Balboni & J. Palacio

(Eds.), *Taking Stock: Belize at 25 years of Independence* (pp. 46–75). Benque Viejo del Carmen, Belize: Cubola.

Rutheiser, C. (1991). *Culture, Schooling, and Neocolonialism in Belize* (Ph.D. Dissertation). John Hopkins University, Baltimore.

Rutheiser, C. (1993). Mapping Contested Terrains: Schoolrooms and Streetcorners in Urban Belize. In R. L. Rotenberg & G. W. McDonogh (Eds.), *The Cultural Meaning of Urban Space* (pp. 103–120). Westport, CT: Bergin & Garvey.

Ryan, S. (2005). Disclosure and Enforcement of Political Party and Campaign Financing in the CARICOM States. In S. Griner & D. Zovatto (Eds.), *From Grassroots to the Airwaves: Paying for Political Parties and Campaigns in the Caribbean*. Washington, DC: Organization of American States.

Segura, M. (2012, October 29). Interview by H. Warnecke. Assistant Commissioner of Police; Head of National Crimes Investigation Branch, Belize Police Department, Belmopan, Belize.

Shoman, A. (2011). *A History of Belize in 13 Chapters*. Belize City, Belize: Angelus Press.

Singh, D. (2012, October 24). Interview by H. Warnecke. Attorney at Law; Former Minister of National Security (UDP), Belize City, Belize.

Sistema de Integración de Centroamérica, Secretaria de la Integración Social (SISCA), United Nations Population Fund (UNFPA), & Interpeace. (2012). *National Public Policy Proposal: Prevention of Youth-Involved Violence in Belize 2012–2022*. Belize City, Belize.

Snyder, L., Roser, C., & Chaffee, S. (1991). Of Cultural Import Foreign Media and the Desire to Emigrate from Belize. *Journal of Communication, 41*(1), 117–132.

Statistical Institute of Belize (SIB). (2013a). *Abstract of Statistics: 2012*. Belmopan, Belize: Government Printers.

Statistical Institute of Belize (SIB). (2013b). *Belize Labour Force Survey 2013: Preliminary Findings*. Belmopan, Belize: Government Printers.

Stone, M. C. (1994). *Caribbean Nation, Central American State: Ethnicity, Race, and National Formation in Belize, 1798–1900* (Ph.D. Dissertation). University of Texas, Austin.

Straughan, J. F. (2004). *Belizean Immigrants in Los Angeles* (Ph.D. Dissertation). University of Southern California, Los Angeles.

Straughan, J. F. (2007). Emigration from Belize Since 1981. In B. S. Balboni & J. Palacio (Eds.), *Taking Stock: Belize at 25 Years of Independence* (pp. 254–282). Benque Viejo del Carmen, Belize: Cubola.

Sutherland, A. (1998). *The Making of Belize: Globalization in the Margins*. Westport, CN/London: Bergin & Garvey.

The Belize Times. (2012, December 15). Gang Truce Dead. *The Belize Times*.

United States Department of State. (2014). *Belize 2013 Human Rights Report: Country Reports on Human Rights Practices for 2013*. Washington, DC: United States Department of State, Bureau of Democracy, Human Rights and Labor.

Vasquez, J. (2012, October 19). Interview by H. Warnecke. Principal of Hummingsbird Elementary School, Belize City, Belize City, Belize.

Vidal, M. (2012, November 5). Interview by H. Warnecke. Assistant Superintendent; Chief of Gang Supression Unit, Belize Police Department, Belize City, Belize.

Vigil, J. D. (2003). Urban Violence and Street Gangs. *Annual Review of Anthropology, 32*(1), 225–242.

Wade, L. (2012, November 5). Interview by H. Warnecke. Journalist, PlusTV, Belmopan, Belize.

Warnecke-Berger, H. (2017). Forms of Violence in Past and Present: El Salvador and Belize in Comparative Perspective. In S. Huhn & H. Warnecke-Berger (Eds.), *Politics and History of Violence and Crime in Central America* (pp. 241–279). New York: Palgrave Macmillan.

Washington Post. (1989, September 16). Crack, L.A.-Style Gangs Trouble Torpid Belize. *Washington Post*, pp. A26.

Wiegand, B., & Bennett, R. (1993). The Will to Win: Determinants of Public Support for the Drug War in Belize. *Crime, Law and Social Change, 19*(2), 203–220.

Wilk, R. R. (1994). Colonial Time and TV Time: Television and Temporality in Belize. *Visual Anthropology Review, 10*(1), 94–102.

Wilk, R. R. (1995). Learning to Be Local in Belize: Global Systems of Common Difference. In D. Miller (Ed.), *Worlds Apart: Modernity Through the Prism of the Local* (pp. 110–133). London, UK/New York: Routledge.

Woods, L. A., Perry, J. M., & Steagall, J. W. (1997). The Composition and Distribution of Ethnic Groups in Belize: Immigration and Emigration Patterns, 1980–1991. *Latin American Research Review, 32*(3), 63–88.

CHAPTER 7

Forms of Violence in Comparative Perspective

This study seeks to answer why the selected cases exhibit similar forms of violence even though they are most different regarding political economy and cultural articulation. The historical chapter on the development of contemporary patterns of violence exemplified these differences through a detailed description of each case. Subsequently, forms of violence currently observable in each country were examined, detailing the processes in which forms of violence evolve and change.

By diachronically comparing inside cases, the chapter on the development of contemporary violence revealed the emergence of cultural scripts of violence on the one hand. On the other hand, it described the respective appropriation and distribution of rents, and it provoked tentative comparative conclusions on how violence was historically framed. The chapters on the case studies chapters focused on predominant forms of violence in each case.

This comparative section will reflect on forms of violence in a cross-case perspective. The chapter completes the empirical part and leads to the general conclusions of this study. In a first step, the comparison of similar forms of violence across cases highlights similar mechanisms that produce the forms of violence. In a second step, this chapter scrutinizes the conditions enabling these mechanisms.

© The Author(s) 2019   233
H. Warnecke-Berger, *Politics and Violence in Central America and the Caribbean*, https://doi.org/10.1007/978-3-319-89782-0_7

Similar Forms of Violence Across Cases

Even though the cases are different regarding their political economy, their respective cultural articulation, they show similar forms of violence. The most important similarity is the presence of both horizontal and vertical violence in all three cases. Horizontal and vertical violence, however, are rather general distinctions between levels at which violence is organized and used. While the historical chapter shows that horizontal violence is embedded in each society under review to differing extents, the case studies further accentuate the processes through which horizontal violence emerges and changes. Horizontal violence will therefore receive further attention. This is followed by the discussion of vertical violence. The final subsection summarizes the mechanisms of each form of violence.

Horizontal Violence

In all three cases, social conflicts shifted to within the subaltern class, creating spaces in which horizontal violence is rendered possible but not necessary. Even though this process was partly disrupted in El Salvador due to the failed revolution and the subsequent civil war, it continued after 1992. In El Salvador, horizontal violence inside the subaltern class intensified with the Liberal Reforms of 1881/1882, and since then has formed part of a depth structure of violence. As opposed to the other two cases, horizontal violence in El Salvador became embedded at the deepest level. In Jamaica, horizontal violence increased after the Great Depression of the 1930s. It only rarely occurred as individual acts, but instead in the form of collective action. Furthermore, El Salvador shows the entanglement of horizontal violence with honor and the impossibility to transfer these cultural scripts to larger arenas, such as politics. In Jamaica, in contrast, horizontal violence was fueled by party identities. After the 1930s, horizontal violence was mainly linked to a political arena, namely the dyadic party conflict between the People's National Party (PNP) and the Jamaica Labor Party (JLP). In contrast to El Salvador, where the need of individuals to defend their honor and to (re)gain social recognition through the exertion of violence historically remained a script of violence mobilized at the individual level, horizontal violence in Jamaica was densely interwoven with party identities and therefore easily transcended the individual level to the collective defense of honor and respect along party identitarian cleavages.

Belize, again, presents as an intermediate case. Similar to Jamaica, party identities have been used to organize horizontal violence, by providing a political arena. At the same time, however, horizontal violence partly remained autonomous of party political identities and thus followed the individual defense of honor and respect in remote areas in distance to political parties similar to El Salvador. In other words, the scale of social organization of horizontal violence differs and two sub-forms of horizontal violence can be distinguished: Ordinary horizontal violence on a low level of social organization will be reviewed in a first step, followed by the analysis of gang violence.

Ordinary Horizontal Violence

This study defines horizontal violence as violence between equals without involvement of superior agents. The study highlights the reciprocity of violent practices. However, although horizontal violence has been detected in each case, there are significant variances between different sub-forms of horizontal violence.

The variances of horizontal violence are based on the scale of social organization and the degree of reciprocity as will be shown in the following. First, ordinary horizontal violence, which takes place predominantly on a relatively low scale of social organization, is the most dominant form of violence in El Salvador. Ordinary horizontal violence occurs between individuals. In Jamaica, horizontal violence happens on a higher scale of social organization as entire communities are in conflict with each other, and often involving defense crews as predominant actors of horizontal violence. In Belize, horizontal violence is both located on an individual level and incorporated into gang violence.

In El Salvador, the complexity lies in the diffuse appearance of horizontal violence; the complexity of the Jamaican case consists in the relevance of horizontal violence in inter-group dynamics; Belize again is an intermediate case since signs of both poles are discernible. In Jamaica, the pivotal role of revenge in the conflicts between different communities illustrates that equality among these communities can be maintained by violence. In El Salvador, in contrast, violent actors fail to maintain equality, leading to the diffusivity of violence.

This difference in the articulation of ordinary horizontal violence becomes particularly evident when comparing cycles of revenge within each case. In El Salvador, revenge erupts in reaction to violence that was previously experienced by individuals. In these contexts, revenge becomes an expression of individual feelings of tarnished honor and newly provokes reactions to restore honor. Given the larger history and the importance of honor as a cultural script of violence in El Salvador, emotions such as envy and rage easily merge with honor. In Jamaica, revenge is an essential group dynamic, cycles of revenge endure for years, and victims seek revenge for offenses suffered long ago. Revenge between different conflicting communities thus perpetuates the equality among groups.

At the same time, the levels of social substitutability are different. The concept of social substitutability describes how one group member becomes substitutable for another in violent interactions (Kelly, 2000, p. 5). In El Salvador, social substitutability is an individual matter; sometimes it concerns feuding families, but never involves entire communities. In Jamaica, in contrast, cycles of revenge between communities, historically fueled by party identities and only recently disconnecting from political parties, endure up to 12 years, as Chap. 5 argues. While in El Salvador single violent offenses are most likely to be followed by similar individual acts of retaliation, violent situations in Jamaica are detached from each other. In this latter case, the single act of violence is embedded in a whole series of violent practices, which are logically related but situationally and temporally disconnected.

While in El Salvador, honor as a regulating force within conflicts in distance to state authority is individually cultivated and thus leads to individual expressions of horizontal violence, violence in Jamaica follows a group logic and is based on the social substitutability of community members. Although in both cases horizontal violence is present, this book shows in the case of revenge that horizontal violence is socially organized on different scales. The comparison of the different scales of social organization between El Salvador on the one hand and Jamaica on the other hand uncovers another process inherent to the social organization of violence.

In order to explain the mechanisms of horizontal violence, it is necessary to answer the following questions: Firstly, why does horizontal violence in El Salvador remain on an individual scale of social organization and even diverge into several sub-forms?; secondly, why is horizontal violence in Jamaica organized on a group scale in contrast to El Salvador, thereby integrating singular violent events in a larger history of group differences, which eventually lead to endless cycles of revenge?

To answer these questions, the detailed analysis of reciprocity of violence as one of the definitional criteria of horizontal violence is important. In Jamaica, the importance of revenge in inter-community conflicts indicates the reciprocal nature of violent relationships. In El Salvador, the reciprocity of horizontal violence seems to be incomplete, as it usually leads to the diffuse appearance of violence.

Reciprocity evolves out of and requires the equality of actors involved in a violent relationship. This equality can be a subjective perception or it can exist factually. For all three cases, the analysis of horizontal violence reveals that perpetrators resort to violence either to claim equality between rivals or to regain equality. The claim in itself, even though it might never lead to the successful (re)establishment of equality, illustrates the deep roots of horizontal violence: actors feel and expect the equality between themselves and their rivals. These partly objective and partly subjective dimensions of horizontal violence become particularly evident in sequences of retaliation and revenge.

Revenge is only opportune between equals (Boehm, 1984). Revenge does not intend to annihilate the rival, but to re-establish a certain kind of balance and equality between individuals and groups (Paul, 2005, p. 247). It only appears if yet established rights and obligations are violated. Violence is consequently used to regain equality (Elwert, 1991, p. 169). Sequences of violent practices in cycles of revenge often follow rigid and ritualized cultural scripts to maintain equality (Schlee and Turner, 2008). Thus, revenge is in a sense an ideal type of horizontal violence as it intends to produce or to maintain a mutual relationship of recognition. As violence is exerted to reproduce equality in this relationship, revenge is the purest form of reciprocity.

At least for the case of El Salvador, however, two different sub-forms of horizontal violence have been highlighted, in which this pure form of reciprocity is deficient. Most evidently, rage exposes this disruption of reciprocity. Furious practices of violence induced by rage and hatred have no specific objective. The typical social figure who exerts this furious violence in blind rage is the berserk.[1] Berserk violence involves the idea of "payback time" (Palermo, 1997, p. 3) and is related to the idea of revenge. The difference between revenge violence and rage violence, however, lies in the degree of reciprocity. Berserk violence induced by rage renders reciprocity arbitrary or even dissolves mutual rights and obligations, which are fundamental characteristics of reciprocity. Rage thus does not form a bond between rivals in conflict, but disrupts this bond. Rage and furious violence simply express strong hostilities (Neckel, 1999, p. 163). During the violent incident on the Salvadoran public bus described in Chap. 4, the vigilante was beside himself with rage. In a certain sense, he lost his capacity to navigate in a social world. Practices of violence then become arbitrary, and the wild shooting of the vigilante lacked the selection of victims that the logic of shootings in the case of retaliation would prescribe. Thus, revenge represents reciprocity, rage violence, however, disrupts reciprocity. Although revenge and rage violence both originate in a horizontal relationship between rivals, revenge is able to (re)establish equality whereas rage violence only claims equality and then jeopardizes or even destroys this relationship.

Envy violence occupies a middle position in terms of the degree of reciprocity (Simmel, 1992/[1908], p. 312). Envy violence is based on the perception of relative deprivation compared to equals. The envy can either concern the object possessed by others or another subject because this person is in the position to possess a certain object (Rawls, 1971, pp. 534–540). According to this logic, relative deprivation also implies a horizontal relationship. While retribution and revenge are defensive forms of violence to regain reciprocity and to re-establish the equality among different opponents, violence induced by envy is an offensive form of violence. It relies on the perception that the envied is both the creator of one's own unfulfilled desire and the adversary who should not live in better conditions than oneself. Thus, strategic action in the social organization of violence is based on a different mechanism. In the case of revenge, different violent events that already happened in the past are synchronized. Revenge is about the extension of time. Revenge enlarges the scope of time into the past. Today's violence reacts to violent in the past. In the case of envy, in contrast, synchronization additionally affects the future, since it is supposed to hinder the rival prospectively to "escape" from equality. Thus, even though envy requires the wish for a state of equality, reciprocity in the face of relative deprivation gets incomplete.

While revenge can be seen as a violent compensation for failed reciprocity, envy violence originates in the comparison with adversaries whose smallest material advantage receives undivided attention (Neckel, 1999, p. 150). The frustration resulting from comparisons, even in the case of small amounts of money or prestige, turns into violence. While revenge signifies reciprocity between subjects, violence because of envy refers to the resource endowments of social actors. Envy violence thus develops under circumstances of restricted reciprocity as a minimal requirement of equality between social actors. Often, however, the initial cause of violence is difficult to detect and therefore acts of revenge and acts of envy violence become blurred.

Coming back to the differences of horizontal violence between El Salvador and Jamaica, apparently, this variance is not only restricted to the degree of reciprocity but also to the scale of social organization. In contrast to Jamaica, where the community scale of violence and the strong scripts of revenge tend to regulate violent interactions between feuding communities, in El Salvador, the low level of social organization and much weaker cultural scripts of violence are unable to durably manage social relationships and to maintain a certain level of reciprocity in the exertion of violence.

Due to the low level of social organization, weak cultural scripts, and lacking resources, the situational logic of violence seems to be crucial for the emergence of ordinary horizontal violence in El Salvador. In Jamaica, however, the possibilities to maintain cycles of revenge between entire communities over a long period seem to be decisive. Particularly due to the low level of social organization, horizontal violence in the case of El Salvador almost entirely follows a situational logic in which emotions are crucial. Minor movements in horizontal relationships are able to intensify the fear of victimization situationally and then lead into violent escalations.

Time is constricted in these situations. The political economic climate forces the constriction of time. What counts is the immediate "now," and this "now" is so instable, volatile, and unforeseeable that the structuration of violence beyond the single event is difficult to achieve. Strategic action in this environment is purely emotionally driven, since durable resources are lacking and cultural scripts of violence are too weak to prescribe linking different practices of violence. Once these situational spaces evolve, strategic action materializes in reaction to the possibility of being victimized and turns into unstructured panic. The underlying mechanism for ordinary horizontal violence in El Salvador thus is best described as forward panic (Collins, 2008, pp. 83–92).

In Jamaica, the contrary is the case. Singular incidents are linked to longstanding antagonisms between communities in the perception of group members. A single violent event, thus, is interpreted as part of a larger history of animosities. While in El Salvador, the very situational context causes forward panic to lead to violence, in Jamaica, strategic action detaches violent events from their particular context and integrates them into a yet existing antagonism.[2] Instead of constricting time, the opposite is the case in Jamaica. Strategic action is less emotionally driven but builds on the extension of time, since different violent practices occurring at different points of time as well as possibly in different spaces are brought into a logical sequence of revenge. The mechanism for horizontal violence in Jamaica, thus, is backward synchronization, since different practices of violence are linked in retrospect.

The Organization of Horizontal Violence: Gang Violence

Gang violence emerged as a sub-category of horizontal violence in all three cases. Since the empirical information on gang violence gathered for each case study is the densest among all forms of violence, detailed and specific conclusions can be drawn. Although it appeared in each case, it did so with large differences. This sub-section will address these differences and subsequently analyze similarities in order to uncover the mechanisms for gang violence and its dynamics.

In El Salvador, today's *mara* violence developed in three steps. Initially, local street gangs emerged that were largely embedded in their communities. These street gangs existed long before *maras* even became visible. Street gang violence started to change in a second step with increasing deportation of criminal youth from the United States. In many cases, these deportees had already been members of street gangs in the United States and brought their gang experiences back to El Salvador. Within a few years, a hegemonial gang warfare between *mara salvatrucha* and *barrio 18* evolved. In a third step, *mano dura* policies changed gang violence. From then on, gang violence became independent from hegemonial gang warfare and spread to communities or was even directed against the state.

Similar to El Salvador, gang violence in Jamaica appeared in the context of street gangs inside and on the edge of urban marginalized communities. In a second step, however, the party political conflicts co-opted gang violence. Party identity thus fueled street gang violence. In a third step, together with the demise of the state-class, gang violence split up into two different forms of violence. On the one hand, gang violence continued in the form of community violence within fragmented political communities. On the other hand, gang violence was exported to the United States, professionalized there, and then returned to Jamaica as criminal gang violence or organized crime.

The beginnings of gang violence in Belize resembled those of Jamaica and El Salvador. Excluded youth formed street gangs and committed minor crimes and acts of violence to generate solidarity and to strengthen internal cohesion. In the second step, gang violence in Belize experienced a similar inflow of criminal deportees from the United States as in El Salvador. At the same time, the case of gang violence in Belize illustrated processes of cultural appropriation of gang culture through TV. Even though the conditions seemed to be comparable to El Salvador, hegemonial gang warfare between *Crips* and *Bloods* did not evolve in Belize and gang violence remained culturally embedded within communities. Consequently, a complex gang system emerged involving 24 active gangs. By adopting practices of violence from rivals, the gangs systematically escalated violence and since then have been caught in a violent zero-sum game.

In all three cases, gang violence initially evolved as street gang violence, and cultural scripts as well as the political economy of violence exhibit strong similarities. This conclusion confirms theoretical findings of street gang theory (see e.g. Hagedorn, 2008; Klein & Maxson, 2006).

Cultivation of honor serves as a means to (re)gain social recognition in contexts in which the perceived lack of future opportunities particularly for adolescents is prevalent, and the politico-economic is instable and fails to deliver durable resources. Current instabilities, however, differ considerably depending on the politico-economic peculiarities of each case. In El Salvador, instability became a defining feature with the increasing weight of remittances. In Jamaica as well as in Belize, instability is restricted to particular urban encounters. Despite these differences, the analysis of street gang violence revealed that the cultivation of honor in everyday confrontations is a powerful tool in (re)gaining social recognition in all cases.

Honor and its (re)production depends on very concrete experiences of violence. Exerting violence against perceived rivals creates honor and the own body as the only available resource is presented with the honor-generating scars and wounds. Moreover, honor translates into internal group cohesion. Street gang violence with its rituals (e.g. the fair fight) serves this purpose. In organizing violence, street gang members circumvent and overcome the lack of resources by producing symbolical capital (honor). Honor becomes an important resource and, at the same time, a point of reference for rules of violence. Street gang violence remains horizontal since it depends on the provocation of conflicts against equal rivals. In these conflicts, reciprocal claims among street gangs establish an equilibrium between internal cohesion of the gangs and external threatening.

The question arises why street gang violence changed in a second step and why it developed differently in each case. In El Salvador, street gang violence merged into a dyadic hegemonial gang warfare between two *maras*, which were initially founded in the United States. Instead, gang violence in Belize largely remains at the community level. In Jamaica, political parties co-opted street gang violence and integrated gangs into a larger political arena in which the conflict between the two political parties as segments of the state-class predominated.

The comparison between El Salvador and Belize is important since in both cases, gang violence was influenced by external gang culture. In El Salvador, a newly arising cultural script of gang warfare absorbed yet established cultural scripts of honor violence that are inherent to street gang violence. Existing studies hitherto focused on forced migration and deportation to explain this change. Since the overall politico-economic context for gangs remained almost stable, gang migration is one important explanation for the change of gang violence in both cases. However, forced migration and deportation cannot explain, at least not in detail, how the sheer presence of deportees changed a street gang system that had been developing for decades.

What indeed changed, however, was the cultural script of violence while the political economy remained stable. Street gang identity became integrated into the cultural script of hegemonic gang warfare. Two different mechanisms of this change are plausible. First, once arrived in El Salvador, deportees who formerly established a stronger cultural script of gang warfare in the United States convinced or even forced local street gang members to adopt this new cultural script. Second, street gang members socialized in El Salvador culturally appropriated the newly available cultural script either because it was perceived as helpful in fulfilling street gangs' claims, or simply because it seemed "cool" or even superior. The case of Belize suggests that the second mechanism was at work. External cultural scripts of gang violence in Belize were mainly made accessible with the introduction of TV and the subsequent opening to an entirely new cultural framework. Moreover, this new cultural framework served as a powerful tool in Belize as it was able to undermine the cultural superiority of elites. In Belize, compared to El Salvador, however, the dyadic gang identity was not fully appropriated. In El Salvador, the newly emerging dyadic gang conflict among *mara salvatrucha* and *barrio 18* was powerful enough to absorb existing street gang identities. In Belize, local identities remained strongly related to the local community in which gang members lived. In this latter case, the perceived difference between *Crips* and *Bloods* only partially served to fuel former scripts of street gang violence. Finally, the case of Jamaica seems to have experienced the opposite extreme. In Jamaica, political parties co-opted and overwrote cultural scripts of gang violence with party identities. Even though processes of deportation and cultural contact similar to Belize and El Salvador took place in Jamaica, the change of cultural scripts of gang violence was minor.

Why then did El Salvador experience the entire appropriation of gang warfare, Belize the incomplete appropriation, and Jamaica almost no appropriation? Of most explanatory value is the case of Belize. This case illustrated the importance of cultural appropriation. At the same time, Belize shows that cultural appropriation alone does not explain the entire appropriation of cultural scripts. This leads back to the political economy.

In Belize, social closure led by rent channeling and further accelerated by ethnic exclusion already created a strong sense of community belonging. In El Salvador, in contrast, the generalized volatility and instability caused by the peculiarities of inflowing remittances coupled with modernized oligarchic rule destroy community solidarity and cohesion. The overall instability in El Salvador might explain the "success" of the newly emerging cultural script of gang violence, since it enabled a bottom-up process of stabilization. This stability, however, was only successful inasmuch as practices of violence against the rival group continued. Gang warfare in El Salvador thus entered a "cultural loop" (Whitehead, 2004, p. 13) to maintain stability. Violence thus required further violence to overcome instability, which eventually created a hegemonial gang warfare between the two *maras*. In Belize, social closure of communities was strong enough to co-opt external cultural scripts. In the Jamaican case, rent channeling and the extreme social closure of communities even prevents the appropriation of external cultural scripts of violence, since existing scripts have been rigid enough to remain dominant.

Apparently, the connections between political economy and cultural scripts depend on the specific prevalence of rents and the availability as well as rigidity of cultural scripts. Moreover, these constellations are established on different scales of social organization. Rules of violence exertion render these scales visible. While at the beginning of the development of gangs in all three cases, retaliation concerned the initial offender, this direct relationship between offender and victim began to dissolve. As soon as the gangs' internal cohesion grew stronger, the social substitutability of legitimate victims increased. In line with this change, violence became lethal: Initially, injuring the rival served to portray the offenders' strength; later the rival had to be killed. Reciprocity in these conflicts extended beyond the initial offender to anyone from his group. It became an inter-group logic of conflict.

In El Salvador, the second stage of gang violence provoked a shift in the social substitutability of legitimate victims from single offenders to entire group members. While formerly, the single offender had to "pay" for his offenses, in the second stage, any member of the rival group was a target of revenge for preceding acts of violence. At this stage, however, the community did not play a major role in El Salvador. Although practices of violence were geographically omnipresent, the rules of social substitut-ability only pertained to members of the rival *mara*. Appropriation of cul-tural scripts was followed or accompanied by backward synchronization of gang violence because appropriation was so successful. In Belize and par-ticularly in Jamaica, due to the embeddedness of gang violence in com-munities and, respectively, in the party political conflict, social substitutability transcended single street gang members and involved members of the political (in Jamaica) or social (in Belize) community. Partial (Belize) or denied (Jamaica) appropriation was accompanied or fol-lowed by backward synchronization of violence even beyond gangs.

In El Salvador, the appropriation of gang warfare enabled street gangs to establish internal hierarchies and, subsequently, to produce their own political economy to temporally overcome instability. Obtaining access to and appropriating external cultural scripts of gang warfare strategically facilitated the further production of internal stability of gangs. They became increasingly independent from contextual factors such as the com-munity turf of former street gangs. At the same time, however, violence became omnipresent in this second stage and two hegemonial *maras* evolved. While in El Salvador gang violence was thus organized by an independent actor, namely by *maras*, in Belize, gang violence has been far more integrated in community life. In Jamaica, finally, gang violence became almost indistinguishable from politically fueled community vio-lence. In this latter case, and contrary to El Salvador, a superior actor, political parties, succeeded in co-opting youth gangs, thereby lifting gang violence to a higher organizational scale.

In sum, the comparison of this second step of gang violence develop-ment showed that the determining factors of the evolution from street gang violence to gang warfare are the degree of politico-economic insta-bility and the strength of yet established cultural scripts. In contexts in which the overall political economy tends to be instable and cultural scripts are weak, violent actors can gain importance by appropriating external cultural scripts. In contrast, in cases where politico-economic instability is mitigated or limited by social closure and cultural scripts are rigid, the appropriation of external cultural scripts is less likely. The comparison of this second step of gang violence development thus has explanatory value for the much broader question how societies are shaped by the impact of culturally distant societies: The comparison exemplifies that this impact is not simply a diffusion from the center to the periphery or the adaptation to a flat world, but a complex appropriation of external scripts depending on earlier established autochthonous realities.

The comparison furthermore shows that through this process of appropriation, power relations were shaped. This last issue is related to the question of why gang violence developed further in a third step and why this development also differs in all three cases. Why was gang violence in El Salvador not absorbed by a hegemonial dyadic gang warfare, but transcended to entire communities and eventually turned into vertical violence? Why did Jamaica see the division between community violence and vertical violence exerted by groups of organized crime? Why did gang violence in Belize remain in a systemic equilibrium as a mixture of community and gang violence?

In El Salvador and Jamaica, this third step of gang violence was triggered by a shift in the political economy, and gangs were forced to adapt to this shift. In El Salvador, *mano dura* policies intensified the need of *maras* to search for alternative sources of income. In Jamaica, clientelist channels of rent distribution dried out with the demise of the state-class and facilitated a shift to the drug economy. In Belize, in contrast, gang violence remained almost entirely unchallenged, fragmented, and interwoven with community life. Criminal gang violence in Jamaica as well as *mara* violence in El Salvador in this third stage share an important similarity. While formerly, fear used to be the trigger of violence, it has become the purpose. *Maras* in El Salvador as well as criminal gangs in Jamaica essentially grew by managing fear and by controlling the production of fear through violence. As an effect, both violent actors advanced to cartels of fear and their particular forms of violence eventually escaped the logic of horizontal violence. In Belize, in contrast, the violent equilibrium between several gangs prevented single gangs from moving in the same direction. Even though Jamaica and El Salvador share this similarity, there is still a huge difference. Although gang violence in its last steps in both cases tends towards vertical violence, their scale of organization remains different. In Jamaica, criminal gang violence is almost entirely embedded in core garrison communities, and community membership is not to distinguish from gang membership. The don is the business leader of the gang as well as the political leader of the community. In El Salvador, the community-gang relationship is much more characterized by predation. These variances in similar forms of violence are mirrored in the general political economic path of development. As Chap. 3 illustrates, authority in the case of El Salvador, long-lasting authoritarian-oligarchic rule has always been dependent on the exclusion of subaltern groups. In Jamaica, in contrast, state-class rule has always been dependent on the co-optation of subaltern groups.

In El Salvador, *maras* emerged out of politico-economic instability and competed, perhaps unintentionally, in overcoming instability through violence. This provided them with a certain economic as well as cultural independence both from superior authorities as well as from communities from which they personally stem. Possibly, this independence in the social organization of their violence made the hegemonial gang warfare endemic and *maras* so powerful. In Jamaica, gang violence was co-opted by the state-class. The extreme social closure in garrison communities as well as the rigidity of party identities still determine the embeddedness of gang violence in communities. Gangs in Jamaica simply continued co-opting and thereby followed state-class rule.

Vertical Violence

Different to horizontal violence, which this book defined as a violent relationship between people with equal positions in the societal hierarchy, the defining characteristic of vertical violence is the violent relationship between unequal actors. Vertical violence reveals power differentials of competing violent actors. In all three empirical cases, repression and other forms of vertical violence have a history that dates back to colonial times. The case of Jamaica renders this point particularly evident. The Jamaica Constabulary Force (JCF) was founded immediately after the Morant Bay rebellion to guarantee "peace" and to suppress rebelling social movements. As in El Salvador and Belize, the roots of policing are deeply interwoven with political authority and domination, such as the enforcement of labor relations and regulations or the prohibition of vagrancy. In Jamaica and Belize, vertical violence is almost entirely restricted to state institutions such as the police force. In El Salvador, vertical violence is more fragmented since in addition to police violence, it encompasses at least grassroots vigilantism and death squad violence. The following section asks why, despite all differences, vertical violence is present in all three cases, and why El Salvador again is the outlier with fragmented vertical violence.

Police Violence

With the rise of "modern" politics in the aftermath of the Great Depression of the 1930s, policing fulfilled different political functions and the role of repression began to change.

In El Salvador, authoritarian-oligarchic rule, almost per definition, relied heavily on repression, and the threefold official security apparatus developed an institutional division of labor for the purpose of repression. However, since repression could not prevent the formation of the revolutionary left and potential uprisings, the elite created parastatal institutions of repression such as the Organización Democrática Nacionalista (National Democratic Organization; ORDEN). Repression increased by co-optation, particularly through ordinary horizontal violence. This process not only provoked the escalation of the level of violence to the skyrocketing peak of homicides in 1979, but it also exemplifies the power of superior authorities to manipulate local-level politics. After the end of the civil war, the newly founded National Civil Police (PNC) was unable to redeem the promises of the Peace Accords, and violent repression remained an everyday practice. However, the PNC lost its potency to co-opt different subforms of vertical violence. Parastatal repression in the shape of death squads and vigilantism from within communities therefore continued in addition to police violence.

In Jamaica, the rise of the state class after the labor rebellion of 1938 enabled political co-optation of the police force that followed the segmentation of the state-class along party lines. Thereby, the ruling segment of the state-class used the police forces to undermine political support for the rival party. Thus, police violence continued the colonial path of suppressing social unrest among subaltern groups. With very little changes, this has persisted until today, even though state-class rule fragmented.

In Belize, the historical nature of police violence is almost unknown due to the lack of historical sources. Since independence at the beginning of the 1980s, it became evident that violence is difficult to prove, simply because of the low level of institutionalization of the police force. With the formation of the Gang Suppression Unit (GSU), however, institutional-ization increased, and for the first time, vertical violence inscribed in an institutional logic became visible.

While police violence is present in all three cases, although with some variance, only in El Salvador can different forms of vertical violence can be detected. The comparison of police violence provides further insights. In all three cases, the police lack the institutional capacity to maintain internal social order or even peace. In the light of rising levels of violence and, of the increasing scale of social organization of gang violence as it was argued previously, the police forces are confronted with the challenges of policing in a quasi-permanent state of emergency "in the streets." Since police offi-cers themselves are exposed to victimization and death threats in their daily work, the recourse to violence is an essential means of survival. To distinguish between the lone wolf police officer using excessive force on duty and institutionalized police violence is crucial, even though it is often difficult in practice (Huggins, Haritos-Fatouros, & Zimbardo, 2002, p. 120). In the latter case, practices of violence follow certain rules of engagement and rigid cultural scripts; the case of the lone wolf police offi-cer, however, depends on individual factors and resembles the amorphous nature of ordinary horizontal violence discussed earlier.

The analysis of policing, and particularly of the precise sequences of violent practices during police raids, not only reveals the steady recourse to violence, but also the precise mechanisms with which this recourse hap-pens. The case study chapters exemplified that police raids show astonish-ing similarities with important differences. In all three cases, these raids in suspicious communities follow a certain script that is incongruent with "official" already institutionalized rules of engagement. During these raids, the police block the entries to the communities and cordons and even lock down the communal area. The police is forced to proceed this way because it lacks the capacity to maintain security due to the strength of "rival" violent actors and because of its own fear of being victimized. These closed spaces then enable brute force.

The difference of policing across the cases lies in how "large" the space is that the police are able to lock down. In El Salvador, the spaces in which police violence evolves are limited to certain *pasajes* within communities and sometimes to entire communities that are raided. In Belize, where police violence often occurs in police custody, this space is even limited to the police cell. Extreme practices of violence, torture or even killings, are possible inside the cell. Outside this space, the police lack the capacity to structure violence. In the case of Jamaica, at the other extreme, the analysis of the incursion of Tivoli Gardens in Chap. 5 points to the usage of almost the same rules. However, the police force locked down an entire part of Kingston, and as the term incursion already signals, invades this space.

In all three cases, the cultural scripts of violence resemble each other since the police rely on strategies of encapsulation of violence.[3] Encapsulation describes the process by which the execution of practices of violence is enabled and at the same time limited to a specific spatial order. It is particularly notable that the case of El Salvador—the case with the longest history of state-led repression—reveals that the police are less capable to structure space than in Jamaica, where repression was incorporated into segmentary state-class rule.

For the case of Belize, where policing is barely institutionalized, encapsulation was visibly restricted to the immediate environment of the police. However, this eventually changed with the formation of the GSU. Even though the GSU is capable of encapsulating violence in a much larger space than traditional police units, the cultural scripts still contradict sober, institutionalized logic. Although the GSU embodies increasing institutionalization due to resources made available for policing, the cultural script of violence still remains weak and is related to situational factors. In Jamaica, in contrast, cultural scripts of police violence are even rigid. However, the police force is challenged with equally powerful rivals, at least in the case of criminal gangs. The comparative analysis of police violence thus shows that the social organization of violence—exemplified by the "size" of spaces of encapsulation—is not restricted to its own potency in merging cultural scripts and resources on a certain scale, but also on the scale of social organization of rival violence. Even though police violence as the long arm of the state is per definition vertical, the police are forced to accept a horizontal relationship with almost equally powerful rivals. In some cases, even cycles of revenge emerge between the police force and criminal gangs. The last decades thus saw a trend in decreasing differentials of power of the police force vis-à-vis other violent actors.

In summary, the historical legacy of repression, the lack of resources of which the police force dispose, and the relative strength of violent actors in distance to state authority are common factors and forced the police to rely on strategies of encapsulation. Particularly the public deniability of state-led repressive violence, however, makes empirical research on vertical violence so challenging (Wolpin, 1991). In all three cases, the distinction between the lone wolf police officer recurring to violence to defend himself and a more institutional use of violence become blurred.

Vigilantism

El Salvador turns out to be the most complex case regarding vertical violence, since it is not restricted to police violence. Different to Belize and Jamaica, police violence in El Salvador is compensated by vigilantism from within communities and by death squad violence. The question why vertical violence in El Salvador split into three sub-forms thus remains unanswered.

A first reason lies in the availability of stronger cultural scripts of repressive violence in El Salvador. Given the long history of state-led repression, it is not surprising that death squad violence as well as vigilantism survived for a long time. Both forms of violence share an apparent similarity: Victims are killed selectively. For analytical purposes, however, vigilantism can be distinguished from death squad violence based on the rigidity of the cultural script of violence. Vigilant violence reaches from a very fluid, informal and diffuse pole to a highly formal, organized, and even institutionalized pole (Huggins, 1991). Hence, it is possible to distinguish spontaneous forms of vigilant violence from more organized forms. This continuum can be translated into the concept of vertical violence. Vigilantism arises either from within civil society to compensate for a lack of public social control and to locally execute sanctions in order to defend social order, or it arises as an extended arm of the state to control civil society in order to defend a certain image of society. The former refers to grassroots vigilantism and social cleansings and the latter case to death squads. In both cases, vigilantism reflects the perceived loss of state control because the state hands over the monopoly of violence to private justice groups. The state's ability to monopolize violence is fragmented both in Belize and in Jamaica. But at the same time, vigilantism in these cases is less endemic.

The question arises why this variety of vertical violence is only present in El Salvador, and not in Jamaica or Belize, even though in all three cases horizontal violence signals the lack of state control over means of violence. Why does community violence in El Salvador take the form of vigilantism while community violence in Jamaica remains horizontal? This firstly depends on the strength of possible rival violent actors. Secondly, the precise mechanisms of social organization differ. In Jamaica, backward synchronization determines communal violence. This synchronization of meaning in Jamaica only functions in retrospective. Violent actors strategically assign meaning to past sequences of violent practices regarding their role in the retaliation process: once this community did something to us; now, we have to strike back. The mobilization of the counterstrike in the now requires the link to a past event, and this link has to be created. Almost the same process takes place in El Salvador in the case of both subforms of vigilantism, grassroots vigilantism and death squad violence. However, there is an important difference. In El Salvador, the same mechanism, the synchronization of meaning, is prospective. It is not about retaliating past violence, but to pre-empt future violence. Contrary to community violence in Jamaica, which is caused by backward synchronization, thus, vigilantism follows forward synchronization. This mechanism makes vigilantism particularly prone to co-optation, since the formation of vigilantism is based on the definition of present actors that are suspicious in producing future crisis. Vigilantism thus depends on the perception of an insecure future, while community violence in Jamaica is much more oriented towards violent events that have already happened in the past and that need to be retaliated. Thus, while vigilantism is much more concerned with re(gaining) power disparities, community violence in contrast is related to the establishment of equality.

Mechanisms of Forms of Violence

The preceding subsections highlighted similarities and differences in forms of violence across the three cases. The comparison revealed mechanisms determining the evolution of forms of violence. Violent actors produce forms of violence strategically. Strategic action links the use of resources and the activation of cultural scripts of violence through the social organization of violence.

These mechanisms include backward synchronization, forward synchronization, as well as forward panic. Backward synchronization enables the exertion of violence due to the extension of time through which violent events of the past are linked to the need to react in order to restore equality. Forward synchronization, in contrast, enables violence by projecting the exertion of violence to an imaginary future disruptive act. Both mechanisms produce imagined sequences of violent practices by synchronizing meanings, and both fulfil the purpose of maintaining and/or (re) establishing a certain (yet existent) social order. Both mechanisms are based on the extension of time in order to synchronize sequences of violence. Finally, forward panic enables violence through emotions and stress. Forward panic is based on the constriction of time and demands immediate reactions.

The following forms of violence extracted from the comparison of the three cases can be related to specific mechanisms.

- **Ordinary horizontal violence** is caused by the mechanism of forward panic. Under the conditions of weak cultural scripts, lacking resources, and a low scale of social organization, forward panic leads to ordinary horizontal violence. However, ordinary horizontal violence remains amorphous and practices of violence are arbitrary.
- **Street gang violence** is a first step towards the social organization of horizontal violence. The mechanism of backward synchronization causes street gang violence, provided symbolic capital and stronger cultural scripts of violence are available. As an effect, practices of violence result in cycles of revenge and sequences of retaliation.
- **Gang warfare** likewise is caused by backward synchronization. However, gang warfare expresses the organization of horizontal violence on a higher scale than street gang violence, involving higher amounts of resources and stronger cultural scripts of violence.
- **Community violence** is most comparable to gang warfare. Similarly, it is organized on a higher scale; it involves the use of resources as well as stronger or even rigid cultural scripts. As in the case of gang warfare, the mechanism that enables cycles of revenge is backward synchronization. The difference, however, lies in the question of which particular violent events are synchronized with the help of strategic action. In the case of community violence, every kind of violence against the community is taken into account, while in the case of gang warfare, exclusively gang violence is integrated into imagined synchronized sequences of violent practices.
- In the case of **grassroots vigilantism**, **police violence**, and **death squad** violence, forward synchronization prevails. These forms of vigilantism can be distinguished according to the scale of social organization. While grassroots vigilantism is organized on a lower scale of social organization, death squad and police violence involve the use of both higher amounts of resources and stronger cultural scripts.

Explaining Forms of Violence

Having clarified the mechanisms that determine particular forms of violence, the question remains when and under what conditions these mechanisms are activated. Since all three cases under research expose similar forms of violence with similar underlying mechanisms but diverge in their politico-economic as well as cultural configuration, a final comparative step needs to uncover similar processes in all cases that provoke these mechanisms to generate forms of violence.

The Embeddedness of Rents

The previous empirical chapters exemplified the very uneven articulation of each case's development model and the differences in the politico-economic preconditions. Structural adjustment programs (SAPs) were implemented in all three countries at the end of the 1970s and during the 1980s and became major critical junctures. The resemblance of the programs and their relative simultaneity suggest that these policies have provoked similar outcomes, namely the rearrangement towards an export-led growth model. The adaptation of SAPs, however, affected each case differently. SAPs reshaped power relations and class configurations based on historical preconditions and existing social structures. The particular adaptation to and arrangement of SAPs therefore produced different outcomes in each case.

El Salvador's current development model, shortly described as transnationalization by polarization, is characterized by a twofold process. On the one hand, oligarchic rule self-modernized as the oligarchy adapted to a new transnational economic environment. By capitalizing on the remittance economy, the oligarchy has been able to mostly withdraw from society. On the other hand, subaltern groups are caught in a vicious cycle of instability due to the particularities of the remittance flow, in which the microeconomic volatility is reinforced and multiplied. In Jamaica, transnationalization was forced by SAPs. Since then, state-class rule has been fragmenting, however, it did not entirely dissolve. The state-class increasingly lost its potential to co-opt subaltern groups. State-class rule initially was fostered in political strongholds, the so-called garrison communities. The demise of the state-class provoked the need for social groups to seek for new economic alternatives and led to a shift in garrison life. Those groups adapted to this new economic environment by renewing fragmented clientelist ties with emerging patrons or by adapting to the precarious conditions. Belize's development model, termed transnationalization by coincidence, is a strategy of muddling through, and state-class rule eventually became dominant. However, state-class rule is still too weak to co-opt larger social sectors. Even though this development model opened new economic opportunities for Belize, certain subaltern groups are caught in a state of living on the fringe, particularly in socioeconomic and ethnically marginalized urban encounters.

Even though the sources of rent are similar, the comparison of these rents suggests huge differences. In El Salvador, the volatile nature of remittances on the micro level calls for attention. While remittances also contribute heavily to foreign exchange earnings in Jamaica, their effect on the overall economic structure is completely different. In El Salvador, the remittances are highly volatile with a tendency to lower amounts in shorter periods. While remittances in El Salvador appear as a stable resource on the macro level, they contribute to a vicious cycle of instability on the micro level. The precarious nature of the informal sector further reinforces this instability. In Jamaica, remittances are almost equally important in absolute as well as in relative terms measured as a share of GDP. However, they do not produce a comparable state of instability. The amount sent per transaction increases with the frequency of transactions, which ultimately leads to stability on the micro and on the macro level. Furthermore, the informal economy, into which much of migrant money flows, does not multiply and reinforce instability, on the one hand, because the micro effects of remittances in Jamaica are stable, and on the other, because the informal sector itself is smaller and less precarious than in El Salvador.

Apart from all politico-economic differences, however, a shared feature of the political economy of each case leading to violence is the intensification of conflicts among smaller groups within social classes that struggle over the access to economic surplus. Even though the sources of rent as well as their appropriation in all three cases were and are different regarding settings, scales of appropriation, and historical experiences, they share a similar outcome: the volatility and social and economic instability of livelihoods. While in El Salvador, the dominance of remittances and its contagious tendency through the particular articulation in the informal sector produced a vicious cycle of instability that has eventually affected the entire subaltern class, in Jamaica, the breaking away of traditional rents and the rise of even more instable substitutes induced economic instability. In Belize, finally, the newly possible rent extraction in sectors such as tourism likewise produce instability. Therefore, three highly different develop-ment models that emerged in different politico-economic conditions with different histories and legacies currently share a similar outcome.

It is thus not the specific source of rent that produces enabling spaces in which mechanism of forms of violence unfold, but the social and eco-nomic context of rents. Apart from all politico-economic differences, the societal context of rents shares a pivotal similarity. In all three cases, the emergence of forms of violence is triggered by the volatility, instability, and unpredictability of economic resources. Thus, neither resource abun-dance nor resource scarcity lead to violence. Instead, the very instability of the appropriation of economic rent leads to violence.

Volatility, instability, and unpredictability can be mitigated by existing structure(s), such as established social closure, clientelism, or partly through migration. In Jamaica, state-class rule used to prefer clientelism to co-opt subaltern groups and therewith prevented instability. In Belize, albeit to a much lesser extent, the hybrid elite and later on the dominant state-class likewise relied on clientelism. In El Salvador, instability and volatility have long been precarious, at least since the Liberal Reforms in the nineteenth century, after which authoritarian-oligarchic rule rarely employed mitigating factors such as clientelism.

Although rent leads to instability, volatility, and unpredictability in all three cases, it does so to different extents, depending on the respective historical experience in appropriating and channeling rents. This, how-ever, does not only hold true for the differences across cases, but likewise for the differences inside each case. In other words, instability, volatility, and unpredictability occur unevenly. Precisely the different scales where instability occurs enable strategic action to rely on different sets and amounts of resources.

While instability is a trigger for violence, the particular distribution of resources determines the ability of social action to use violence and the precise mechanism "behind" this engagement. The peculiarities of the contagious articulation of remittances in El Salvador are able to explain the diffuse nature of violence. The already existing and continuous social clo-sure induced by centralized rents such as bauxite and drug rents in the case of Jamaica and partly in the case of Belize explains the condensed nature of violence. That is to say, as soon as volatility and instability in El Salvador became a general feature eventually affecting the entire subaltern class, it impeded the social organization of violence beyond the individual level. In contrast to El Salvador, communities in Jamaica that are dependent on clientelist ties are caught in a zero-sum game among each other. However, in this latter case, group membership remains important in order to maintain access to resources and facilitates the social organization of violence on a group scale.

The political economy approach provided here is thus able to identify the trigger for forms of violence and to reveal the circumstances in which strategic action employs certain mechanisms for the formation of forms of violence. On which particular cultural script of violence strategic action draws in the execution of violence, however, remains unanswered.

The Dynamics of Cultural Scripts

Having described mechanisms through which practices of violence are formed as well as politico-economic circumstances under which mechanisms are employed, a final question of how and why forms of violence change still requires answering. The analysis of the role of cultural scripts in the production of forms of violence will provide details on the dynamics of forms of violence.

In contrast to rents and their effects for (de)stabilizing social relationships, the cultural scripts of violence are more difficult to analyze. In the case of El Salvador, the historically underlying cultural script of honor violence serves as a fertile soil, particularly for ordinary horizontal violence. Due to the lack of resources and the resulting low scale of social organization, cultural scripts of horizontal violence remain fluid. Practices of violence only follow loose and sporadic rules. This becomes most evident in the case of berserk violence. Overall, the weak character of cultural scripts loosely related to historically rooted scripts of honor violence is an expression of the current diffusivity of violence in El Salvador. In Jamaica, in contrast, the rules of horizontal violence are stronger. In this case, different practices of violence that appear temporally independent from each other (in the extreme with a 12-year difference) are linked to each other through strong scripts that in some cases even prescribe retaliation. Linking different practices of violence takes each practice out of the specific context in which it was exerted eventually bears the potential to escalate. Finally, in Belize, cultural scripts of horizontal violence are easily co-opted by gangs. In this latter case, ordinary horizontal violence is difficult to distinguish from gang violence.

Where cultural scripts had been linked to the access to resources via clientelism and where rents had produced social closure as in the case of

Jamaican garrison communities, the logic of revenge and the importance of group honor are easily interlinked and merge into yet existing cultural scripts (e.g. party identities). When cultural scripts remain weak, they are loosely linked to individual emotions. Paradoxically, it seems to be easier to manipulate strong yet established cultural scripts than to produce strong cultural scripts out of weaker ones.

That is to say that cultural scripts of violence not only follow the internal logic of linking different practices of violence as the mechanisms of forward synchronization, backward synchronization, and forward panic indicate, but are exposed to external influences other than the very violent act. Strategic action then not only follows the rules of violence, but also manipulates these rules. These processes of manipulation therefore are most important to understand and explain the dynamics of forms of violence.

The comparison revealed three different processes of manipulation that lead to changes in the forms of violence: fabrication, co-optation, and appropriation. First, the case of the formation of revolutionary violence in El Salvador in Chap. 3 highlights fabrication. The fabrication of cultural scripts depends on conviction, and on ideology. Fabrication is unique to El Salvador. Co-optation, in contrast, is a common process of all three cases. Co-optation is most evident in Jamaica, where the state-class succeeded in co-opting subaltern forms of violence over a long period. In Belize, the state-class struggled to co-opt subaltern groups, and eventually, it proved to be too weak to follow the Jamaican path. In El Salvador, co-optation only took place in the case of repressive vertical violence. Additionally, evidence points to a certain role of co-optation in the case of the revolutionary violence in El Salvador. While fabrication signals at least the potential to produce a new form of violence, co-optation, in contrast, describes the integration and incorporation of already existent cultural scripts of violence. Since forward synchronization is dependent on the perception of a threat, forms of violence provoked by this mechanism are particularly prone to co-optation. In this case, co-optation does not need to incorporate the entire form of violence, but it may suffice to either focus on the vertical synchronization of threat-perceptions, thus on the cultural scripts, or to manipulate violence by providing resources.

The last process highlighted in this chapter is cultural appropriation.[4] Appropriation describes the integration of external cultural influences into a cultural framework. Appropriation ranges between fabrication and co-optation, since it describes the subversive use and the manipulation of something existent. Street gang violence is most susceptible for appropriation. Under the condition of cultural exchange and the strategic use of external cultural influences, cultural appropriation increases the social organization of gang violence. Neither fabrication nor co-optation can fully explain the change of street gang violence.

Notes

1. The term berserk originated from Old Norse language and describes a furious warrior who went into battle naked and without armour in god-like rage or as if obsessed by gods (Shay, 1998, p. 119). The "*berserkergang*," the furious violence of the berserk, is well documented in studies on war related violence, particularly during the Vietnam War (see e.g. Greiner, 2003). Shay (1998, p. 124) shows that the most important trigger of berserk violence is the painful loss. Berserk violence is characterized by an intense irritation, the loss of the capacity to distinguish, light-heartedness, the feeling of being invulnerable, the loss of sensations of pain.

2. Theory on ethnic violence acknowledges that these processes are driving forces of polarization and dichotomization. Tambiah (1990, p. 750), for instance, refers to "transvaluation" and "focalization" in describing processes by which "the climactic acts of violence by groups and mobs become in a short time self-fulfilling manifestations, incarnations and re-incarnations, of allegedly irresolvable communal splits."

3. In explaining the massive violence during Nazi Germany, Swaan (2001, p. 269) argues that elites have "mobilized barbarism for their own purposes and carefully encapsulated it into special compartments of local decivilization, where even wild destructiveness has been made instrumental."

4. See for the concept of appropriation, e.g., Certeau (1988). Appropriation comes close the German concept of "Eigen-Sinn." According to Lüdtke and Templer (1995, p. 313), "Eigen-Sinn" denotes "wilfulness, spontaneous self-will, a kind of self-affirmation, an act of (re)appropriating alienated social relations on and off the shop floor by self-assertive prankishness, demarcating a space of one's own. There is a disjunction between formalized politics and the prankish, stylized, misanthropic distancing from all constraints or incentives present in the everyday politics of *Eigen-Sinn*. In standard parlance, the word has pejorative overtones, referring to 'obstreperous, obstinate' behavior, usually of children. The 'discompounding' of writing it as *Eigen-Sinn* stresses its root signification of 'one's own sense, own meaning'. It is semantically linked to *aneignen* (appropriate, reappropriate, reclaim)."

REFERENCES

Boehm, C. (1984). *Blood Revenge: The Anthropology of Feuding in Montenegro and Other Tribal Societies*. Philadelphia: University of Pennsylvania Press.

Certeau, M. d. (1988). *The Practice of Everyday Life*. Berkeley, CA/Los Angeles: University of California Press.

Collins, R. (2008). *Violence: A Micro-Sociological Theory*. Princeton, NJ: Princeton University Press.

Elwert, G. (1991). Gabe, Reziprozität und Warentausch: Überlegungen zu einigen Ausdrücken und Begriffen. In E. Berg & L. G. Löffler (Eds.), *Ethnologie im Widerstreit: Kontroversen über Macht, Geschäft, Geschlecht in fremden Kulturen* (pp. 159–177). München, Germany: Trickster.

Greiner, B. (2003). First to Go, Last to Know. *Geschichte und Gesellschaft, 29*, 239–261.

Hagedorn, J. (2008). *A World of Gangs: Armed Young Men and Gangsta Culture*. Minneapolis, MN: University of Minnesota Press.

Huggins, M. K. (1991). Introduction: Vigilantism and the State – A Look South and North. In M. K. Huggins (Ed.), *Vigilantism and the State in Modern Latin America. Essays on extralegal Violence* (pp. 1–18). New York: Praeger.

Huggins, M. K., Haritos-Fatouros, M., & Zimbardo, P. G. (2002). *Violence Workers: Police Torturers and Murderers Reconstruct Brazilian Atrocities*. Berkeley, CA/Los Angeles: University of California Press.

Kelly, R. C. (2000). *Warless Societies and the Origin of War*. Ann Arbor, MI: University of Michigan Press.

Klein, M. W., & Maxson, C. L. (2006). *Street Gang Patterns and Policies*. Oxford/New York: Oxford University Press.

Lüdtke, A., & Templer, W. (Eds.). (1995). *The History of Everyday Life: Reconstructing Historical Experiences and Ways of Life*. Princeton, NJ: Princeton University Press.

Neckel, S. (1999). Blanker Neid, blinde Wut? Sozialstruktur und kollektive Gefühle. *Leviathan, 27*(2), 145–165.

Palermo, G. B. (1997). The Berserk Syndrom: A Review of Mass Murder. *Aggression and Violent Behavior, 2*(1), 1–8.

Paul, A. T. (2005). Die Rache und das Rätsel der Gabe. *Leviathan, 33*(2), 240–256.

Rawls, J. (1971). *A Theory of Justice*. Cambridge, London: Belknap Press.

Schlee, G., & Turner, B. (2008). Wirkungskontexte des Vergeltungsprinzips in der Konfliktregulierung. In B. Turner & G. Schlee (Eds.), *Vergeltung. Eine interdisziplinäre Betrachtung der Rechtfertigung und Regulation von Gewalt* (pp. 7–47). Frankfurt a.M., Germany/New York: Campus.

Shay, J. (1998). *Achill in Vietnam: Kampftrauma und Persönlichkeitsverlust*. Hamburg, Germany: Hamburger Edition.

Simmel, G. (1992/[1908]). Untersuchungen über die Formen der Vergesellschaftung. In *Soziologie. Gesamtausgabe* (Vol. 11). Frankfurt a.M.: Suhrkamp.

Swaan, A. d. (2001). Dyscivilization, Mass Extermination and the State. *Theory, Culture & Society, 18*(2–3), 265–276.

Tambiah, S. J. (1990). Presidential Address: Reflections on Communal Violence in South Asia. *The Journal of Asian Studies, 49*(4), 741–760.

Whitehead, N. L. (2004). Introduction: Cultures, Conflicts, and the Poetics of Violent Practice. In N. L. Whitehead (Ed.), *Violence* (pp. 3–24). Santa Fe, NM: School of American Research Press.

Wolpin, M. D. (1991). State Terrorism and Death Squads in the New World Order. *Peace Research Review, 12*(3), 1–78.

CHAPTER 8

The Cultural Political Economy of Violence: A Conclusion

This book shows empirically that violence is a historical phenomenon in El Salvador, Jamaica, and Belize, and it is path dependent. In all three societies, oligarchies came to power through monopolizing landed property. These oligarchies blocked the subalterns' access to economic surplus. This created particular opportunities for vertical violence. The book furthermore shows in the case of El Salvador that although vertical violence erupted in the 1930s and the 1970s and 1980s, horizontal violence is found on an even deeper level. Forms of violence developed in El Salvador through activating cultural scripts of honor, which are rooted in the cultural and economic independence of peasant communities. The case of Jamaica, in contrast, shows that slavery impeded the development of autonomous scripts of violence. Instead, slaves appropriated colonial scripts of violence. Belize reveals hybridity in this regard, as it exposes similarities to both other cases.

The Great Depression of the 1930s ruptured these three different paths. In El Salvador, the forming state co-opted yet existing horizontal violence and integrated it into its capacity of repression. In the 1970s and 1980s, the forming guerrilla was able to fabricate a completely new cultural script of violence. The case of El Salvador thus highlights the impact of cultural scripts. Jamaica highlights that rent channeling led to new forms of violence. These forms of violence then became linked to cultural scripts, especially to party identities. The case of Jamaica thus reveals the pivotal role of economic resources. Again, Belize is a hybrid in this regard.

© The Author(s) 2019
H. Warnecke-Berger, *Politics and Violence in Central America and the Caribbean*, https://doi.org/10.1007/978-3-319-89782-0_8

Here, both the co-optation of horizontal violence as well as rent channeling and party identities play a crucial role in forming violence.

Despite these historical differences and although the three societies developed in different economic directions during the last four decades, it turned out that they have been marked by similar forms of violence, at least since the mid-1980s. In all three cases, horizontal violence exists on different scales of social organization. The study points to the continuity in El Salvador: horizontal violence endured throughout the entire twentieth century and even beyond. The peace agreements of 1992 disrupted the ideological framework, in which vertical violence was organized. However, horizontal violence has been remaining. It even dominates today. The volatile and instable microeconomic distribution of rents blocks the durable and supra-individual organization of violence. Today, forms of violence are situated on an individual scale of social organization in El Salvador. The study shows that social actors engage in a logic of reciprocity through exerting their respective forms of violence. They try to maintain equality among them by recurring to violence, but they ultimately fail to reach this goal. In Jamaica, depoliticized but still extreme social closure in urban marginal communities leads to replacing former party identitarian violence by continuous cycles of revenge between different marginal communities. Again, horizontal violence outlives political conflicts. In Jamaica, horizontal violence is organized on a higher organizational scale than in El Salvador, and the logics of reciprocity are maintained. This, however, blurs the distinction between revenge violence and first instances of ethnic violence. In contrast to both cases, Belize is again a hybrid. In Belize, horizontal violence is rooted in rural communities. Horizontal violence occasionally leads to revenge between larger families. However, it rarely ends lethally. At the same time, first instances of reciprocal cycles of revenge between different urban marginal communities appear. This form of violence, however, is strongly correlated with gang violence in Belize.

In all three cases, gang violence is tremendous. The study demonstrates that gang violence develops in two different directions. In El Salvador, contemporary *maras* unite three different forms of violence, which this study describes as fair fight, hegemonial gang warfare, and first instances of vertical violence. In Belize, gang violence only comprises the first two forms of violence, however, with strong variations. In Jamaica, finally, different violent actors each use exclusively one of these forms of violence.

Even though all those factors that the gang literature attributes to contemporary extreme gang violence (e.g. social exclusion, migration, deportation of gang members from the United States) are present in each case, this book demonstrates that the potency of cultural scripts of violence explains the evolution of gang violence. Within a short period, a hegemonial gang warfare between the two rival *maras* develop in El Salvador out of the primordial form of violence of youth gangs, the fair fight. In Belize, in turn, the same conditions like in El Salvador are prevalent, but gang warfare between *Bloods* and *Crips* is only partially appropriated from the United States. In Belize, this gang warfare leads to an ultra-stable gang system with 24 warring gangs that remain in a zero-sum game and that today only loosely refer to the cultural symbols of *Bloods* and *Crips*. In Jamaica, autochthonous forms of violence even prevail, and Jamaican gangs are exported to the United States. While in El Salvador cultural appropriation is particular powerful and ultimately enables gangs to establish their own political economy of survival, in Belize, historical processes of social closure lead to partial cultural appropriation, but at the same time afford to adjust cultural scripts to local contexts. In Jamaica, these same processes of extreme social closure lead to the professionalization of yet existing violent actors.

All three cases share that gang violence follows specific logics of revenge. This book documents that the differences of gang violence are related to the social substitutability of victims of revenge violence. In El Salvador, the evolution and the unification of three forms of violence by a single violent actor (*maras*) succeeds by enlarging the social substitutability. Today, not only the rival gang members themselves but also the entire population of those communities where the rival gang members live are held substitutable for past violent events. In Belize, this substitutability remains within youth gangs. In Jamaica, in turn, even different violent actors are getting active depending on the type of victim.

Finally, the book demonstrates that vertical violence and especially violence that is employed by (para)state actors is present in each case. While in El Salvador repression is linked to death squads and communal groups of social cleansings (grassroots vigilantism) as well as the police, in Belize and in Jamaica, the police is the sole perpetrator of vertical violence. The study shows in the case of El Salvador that death squad violence as well as grassroots vigilantism draw on historical cultural scripts of repression, which are now again activated in new economic situations. Police violence in contrast depends on the situational encapsulation of violence. However, encapsulation is different in each case. In Jamaica, the police is able to escalate violence in the entire communities. In El Salvador, the encapsulation of violence is restricted to certain areas of communities. Finally, the encapsulation of violence in Belize is restricted to individual police stations in which extreme escalations of violence against prisoners becomes possible.

The results of this book highlight that three mechanisms cause the development of forms of violence: forward panic, forward synchronization, and backward synchronization. In contexts of resource instability in which social actors are thrown back on the immediate now, and in which historical available scripts of violence cannot be activated, those actors are caught in a microsocial zero-sum game between each other. Minimal shifts and changes in these situations lead to forward panic and enact violence. Through recurring to violence, these weak actors seek to maintain or to regain equality between them and their rivals. At the same time and linked to the low level of social organization of violence, this type of horizontal violence is unable to restore reciprocity. Forms of violence, which forward panic causes, remain diffuse. Backward synchronization relies on withdrawing singular practices of violence from their original social context and integrating these practices in new social contexts. Backward synchronization causes revenge. Finally, forward synchronization relies on linking imagined and future practices of violence with today's actions. Forward synchronization causes preventive violence, which eventually leads to vigilantism.

In methodological regard, this study intended to grasp violence itself. Following recent and particularly anthropological approaches to violence, this study sought to understand violence from within, to understand violence by focusing on the very act. In methodical regards, it looked closely at practices of violence, descriptions and narratives of how, when, and where violence happened, and the doing of violence. Concurrently, however, this study is not only concerned with understanding violence in all its facets by zooming in, but goes beyond that by zooming out again to an abstract level. This essentially interdisciplinary effort faces a contradiction; a contradiction that runs like a thread through the entire study. This contradiction is inherent to the epistemological position, to the analytical vocabulary, and to the relationship between micro and macro level of analysis. Finally yet importantly, it played a role for the methodology.

The analytical tool kit assembled and elaborated in this book finally provided an initial starting point. "Initial" is important, since the empirical part of this study exposed that this tool kit is still too inept and provisional. In the best case, it is a starting point. However, the empirical results of the study now allow readjusting this tool kit. The study answered the first research question, namely, what forms of violence are, by developing a definition and therefore concretizing the entire concept of forms of violence. A form of violence is as a specific subset of violent practices that a social actor routinely uses to make claims on other social actors. Forms of violence consist of violent practices. Strategic action links different practices of violence by drawing on cultural scripts and material resources. As a result, a set of different or even similar practices of violence evolves. This definition led away from the direct focus on violent actors towards the analysis of practices of violence.

Therefore, it is not important to follow swinging from one extreme to another, from the lack to the abundance of resources, or from "one unreality to another" (Cramer, 2006, p. 287), but to study historical experiences in detail. An initial step to carry out this analysis is to expand the conceptual framework to capture the embeddedness of rents. By distinguishing the sources of rent and their (political) appropriation, the book outlined the particular social embeddedness of rents, highlighting the tendency of rents to promote social verticalization as well as social closure, which eventually lead to resource instability, volatility, and unpredictability. Strategies of rent appropriation, however, do not evolve in a vacuum; they depend on historical experiences and on the power of actors to follow these strategies. Thus, not only do politics matter, but so do history, economics, and culture.

In situations of instability and unpredictability of resources, the above-mentioned mechanisms take effect. At the same time, this is related to the general causes of violence per se, which have not been at the center of analysis in this study. Linking back the findings of this study to the question of what causes violence finally allows not only for a reflection on future theoretical and methodical questions, but also for the development of a last building block of the entire bridge. This building block, however, remains tentative and hypothetical and needs to be taken under closer examination by future research.

THE PRODUCTION OF FEAR

Not the presence of rents per se, but their effects in shaping social relations is crucial for explaining violence. Rents are ambivalent, and only specific effects are important in the explanation of forms of violence. The most pivotal characteristic of rents that this study empirically exposed is their capacity to produce instability, volatility, unpredictability, and particularly the unpredictability of future social situations because of changes regarding both social closure and social verticalization. While anthropological literature already accentuated the unpredictability of future situations as a trigger for violence (Armit, 2011, p. 505; Ember & Ember, 1992), this study links those situations to the effects of rents and therefore sheds light on the interrelations between dynamics of socioeconomic development and their impact on producing and shaping violence.

While the study initially set in when and where violence already happened and thus excluded the causes of violence per se, the results of the book allow for concretizing even beyond the causes of forms of violence towards a general explanation of violence. A possible link is the concept of fear. Fear is a powerful stimulus of violence in all three cases. Commonly, instable social situations coupled with the unpredictability of resources and of future outcomes produce strong feelings of fear.[1] It is fear, a powerful, disruptive, and destructive individual feeling (Reguillo, 2002) that easily transcends the individual level, penetrates entire societies, and renders these societies "frightened."[2]

As the concept of rent, fear has two dimensions. Fear comprises, on the one hand, an objective component. On the other hand, it is a subjective and individual feeling. Objectively, fear arises under precarious economic conditions. Small changes in the economic situation, particularly against the backdrop of an expected precarious future, and the awareness of the risk to face poverty in the context of developing societies, leads to fear (Flam, 2006, p. 23). Subjectively, fear arises out of feelings of powerlessness or social impotence,[3] out of the perceived inability to actively shape the social environment (Kemper, 1978; Tuan, 2013). Fear prevents people from acting; however, it forces people to react.

Fear is related to violence. On a very definite level, fear is a trigger for the exertion of violence (Riekenberg, 2014; Taussig, 1984). Fear undermines the trust in the peaceful mode of action of fellow citizens (Putz-Osterloh, 2000, p. 8). In fearful situations, action is restricted to very basic modes of social action, and perhaps it is restricted to *re*action. Fear may drive people to escape, to flee the situation (Alber, 2004). It may force people to remain in a state of rigidity induced by shock. Finally, fear drives people to attack, and to exert violence. In this sense, "fear that the other may be about to strike in the mistaken belief that we are about to strike gives us a motive for striking, and so justifies the other's motive." Fear therefore functions as a "multiplier effect (…) as a result of this compounding of each person's fear of what the other fears" and supports the escalation into violence (Schelling, 1960, p. 206; 209).

Following the findings of this book, fearful situations tend to produce a zero-sum game between rivalling actors, finally leading into a security dilemma. In addition, as anthropological approaches to violence highlight, the unpredictability of future outcomes promotes perceptions among conflicting rivals that the continuation of peaceful interactions becomes too risky (Helbling, 2006). In other words, rivals morph into enemies, and fearful situations escalate into violence.

The theory of rent contributes to this issue by providing a framework to analyze economic dynamics that lead to social contexts that are characterized by instability and resource unpredictability. As the present book shows, the sources of rent do not encourage violence, that is to say, oil, drugs, and diamonds do not lead to violence. The particular social embeddedness of rents determines the potency of rents in promoting instability and unpredictability. However, rents produce these effects on distinct scales. While members of an oligarchy are not necessarily affected, subaltern groups in contrast may be. Therefore, the analysis of the particular embeddedness of rent has to uncover at what precise social scale unpredictability, instability, and volatility occurs and if and/or how it affects other social groups apart from those who directly appropriate these rents. Only this question allows understanding how and for whom fear is produced.

The concept of fear thus functions as a last building block to finish the bridge between politico-economic and culturalist arguments. The concept of fear would even rise to an own category linking both riversides, if it became possible to distill these situations of fear through politico-economic approaches, referring to the embeddedness of rents and then zooming into these situations by focusing on cultural scripts and practices of violence. The concept of fear could then replace the approach to spaces that structurally enable violence, which are still too vague to account for the detailed processes in which violence and its forms evolve.

THE MANAGEMENT OF FEAR

What social actors make of situations in which fear becomes predominant, however, is another question and calls for a detailed analysis in a second step. By managing fear, social actors strategically structure their environment and contribute to overcome instability. Surely, in many situations strategic action does not have to rely on violence to overcome instability but on negotiation or cooperation. All three cases analyzed in this study share that strategic action made use of violence to overcome instability. However, mechanisms count. Strategic action does not necessarily rely on violence to end fearful situations, but it makes use of these situations and therefore reinforces fear.

All three mechanisms uncovered in this study, forward panic, backward synchronization, and forward synchronization, are mechanisms that link different practices of violence, subsequently leading to forms of violence. Related to the concept of fear, these mechanisms determine strategies to handle and to manage violence in fearful situations. Interestingly, however, these mechanisms rely on different perceptions of time. In the case of forward panic, strategic action is forced to constrict time. Forms of violence enacted by forward panic are reactions to generalized fear. However, in these situations actors lack the resources and the scripts to structure the environment beyond the immediate "now." Backward as well as forward synchronization, in contrast, follow the extension of time, although in different temporal directions. While backward synchronization draws on experiences made in the past, linking the past with the present, forward synchronization projects the present in the dark future, linking the present with future crises. These mechanisms encourage social actors to strategically make something out of fear; they manage fear. Forms of violence then arise out of strategies to manage fear.

By managing fear, violence is formed. Managing fear, however, relies on previous experiences, on already condensed cultural scripts, and on the learned, usual, or even habitual appropriation of resources. Therefore, managing fear depends on historical experiences and on the particular articulation of the situative fear. This study shows under which conditions of politico-economic resource endowments as well as available cultural experiences practices of violence are exerted and *at the same time* condensed into forms. These mechanisms are the smallest struts in the theoretical bridge developed in Chap. 2. They allow to link different practices of violence by referring to larger struts, to cultural scripts as well as resources.

The causes for forms of violence are thus rooted in the management of fear. The present study furthermore exemplifies that the emergence of forms of violence does not necessarily depend on the violent actor but on strategic action. There is a huge difference between both concepts. Similar mechanisms enable different violent actors to deploy similar forms of violence. Since these mechanisms involve the strategic use of cultural scripts and therefore of meaning systems of violence, the manager of fear does not necessarily have to be part of the violent event. Again, this creates the possibility that two completely different violent actors exert the same form of violence.

Thus, understanding the management of fear is crucial for understanding and explaining violence. However, managing fear is not simply restricted to certain isolated situations or events. Once produced, violence—as the analysis of the hegemonial gang warfare between two *maras* shows—follows a cultural loop. Following this idea, it is most plausible that equilibria of violence evolve because social actors intend to overcome fear by using violence in a temporal sequence, thereby creating further animosities and finally reinforcing fear. In this regard, it is not violence that is self-reinforcing, but it is fear.

THE MONOPOLIZATION OF FEAR

The present book finally highlights how different forms of violence change over time. It uncovers the dynamics of forms of violence. Referring to the processes of cultural appropriation, fabrication, and co-optation allowed describing the manipulation of forms of violence and the struggle to make use of these forms of violence.

Actors can succeed in manipulating cultural scripts and therefore alternate meaning systems of violence by cultivating fear. The detailed and comparative perspective on gang violence, for instance, exemplified that as soon as actors, who think they need to overpower an opposing rival, recognize that they are able to manage fear, they will use their capacity to impose a state of fear as a resource for their own reproduction. In the case study on El Salvador, this study even uncovered the processes under which *maras* developed into cartels of fear by expanding their fearful reputation towards entire communities and eventually towards civil society. Thus, violent actors create their own political economy of fear, purposefully intervene in the management of fear, and finally are able to cultivate or even monopolize fear.

The processes behind the change of forms of violence—fabrication, co-optation, and cultural appropriation—that this study discovered precisely describe how fear is increasingly cultivated or even monopolized. The concept of cultivation of fear was originally introduced by Elias (Elias, 1982, p. 47) who states that the "cultivation of human fears is one of the most fundamental sources of power and domination of humans over humans. On its basis systems of domination developed in abundance." All three processes have a common purpose, namely that it is not about the cultivation or even the monopolization of *violence* but about the cultivation of *cultural scripts of violence* in fearful situations; the cultivation of meanings instead of the cultivation of material artefacts.

This is not to be mistaken with the monopolization of violence as it is, for instance, brought into discussion by theories of state-formation, above all by Weber (1968) in his definition of statehood. The monopolization of violence would equal the encapsulation of violence in an institutional setting and therefore the objectivation of violence (Gerstenberger, 1990). Again, it is about fear with the purpose to produce, control, synchronize, and thereby to strategically change meanings of violence. This of course may to lead to the monopolization of violence, but only under certain particular circumstances. With a much higher probability, however, actors will focus on a minor part of violence to claim or maintain claims of power. Thereby, they either co-opt meaning systems of violence or oppose meanings of violence by fabricating meaning systems.

This perspective on violence then allows reconsidering the relation of state-formation and violence and reaches towards the very heart of political science. Contrary to theories of "elimination struggles" (e.g. Elias, 1997; Tilly, 1985) that analyze violence in a zero-sum scenario, which eventually leads to processes of state formation, the analysis of cultivations of fear suggests that this zero-sum situation is less the outcome, but the change of forms of violence. In these situations, staging of violence and the creation of a reputation of fear become essential means. In a certain sense, and although these situations tend to be characterized by a lack of resources, violent actors are enabled to create their own resources by producing an image of strength. In this sense, how violent actors present and portray themselves through the exertion of violence is not necessarily indicative of their "real" strength but rather creates discourse.

By monopolizing fear, actors thus do not necessarily gain the "the power and the capacity to dictate who may live and who must die" (Mbembe, 2003, p. 11), but they are enabled to cultivate a certain image and a fearful reputation that cause people to trust in the capacity of violent actors. In this fine distinction lies the essence of necropolitics.

Final Reflections

The theoretical bridge between political economy and culturalist theory elaborated in this study seeks to overcome the current theoretical cleavage between "rationalists" and "constructivists," between approaches analyzing factors of social existence and approaches focusing on factors of consciousness. The theoretical bridge advises to get close enough to the very act of violence as well as to stay detached enough to catch the entire historical flow of violence. Methodologically, this poses certain problems. The very act of violence can rarely or even never be observed directly, and the researcher needs to draw on secondary sources to reconstruct this act or the sequence of different acts. Initially, the study relied on participatory observation, focus group discussions, as well as expert interviews getting close enough to violent acts. However, all three methodical tools proved to be too unspecific to achieve this goal. Since fear, as it was outlined earlier, is a steady companion of violence and eventually drives people to silence or even to suppress their experiences and memories of violence, the research needs to rely on "ascriptions of violence" (Bonacker, 2002, p. 31) rather than on the detailed observation of violence. Therefore, the reliability of data on violence is a critical issue.

Research on Violence and Social Science Disciplines

The present study made its interdisciplinary approach explicit and followed it from the very beginning: It used political economy, particularly in its variant of theories of development, and culturalist theories, primarily theories of social practice.

A first contribution of the study is to research on violence. The study of violence itself is not a stand-alone discipline, but research is conducted by different disciplines. Each single discipline has its own theoretical access to violence, last but not least to its respective "form of violence." A truly interdisciplinary approach to violence then hardly emerges since even at the fundamental level of conceptual development, every discipline takes different directions. A primary task to which this study thus points is to rethink concepts and to engage in a discussion on what the concepts of violence and forms of violence seek to express. Without a priori accepting theory development as a major task of research on violence, the discussion could reengage in talking about what research on violence is about, and finally, perhaps, to understand theory development as sense-making of violence. This study shows that the combination of different approaches is possible, benefitting from both dominant research paradigms.

This study has developed a relational concept of violence and distinguishes between horizontal and vertical violence, which shows that research on violence could sharpen its understanding of violence by focusing on relationships in which practices of violence are embedded and out of which these practices emerge. Both terms encourage rethinking more fundamental concepts to which violence is commonly related, such as politics or crime.

A second contribution is to theories of development, and more generally to area studies. Since the end of the 1980s, developmentalist thinking became increasingly focused on the question if its terminology, (under) development, still is accurate enough to account for all the diversity that researchers encompassed in the Global South.[4] With the advent of the critique on orientalism (Said, 1979), the idea flourished that the Third World or the Global South do not exist, but that these concepts are discursive claims of power of the Global North and expressions of eurocentrism. A strategy to exit this claimed theoretical impasse of theories of development could be to concentrate on contemporary and historical empirical phenomena, such as violence, and to use the advances in order to understand the particular context in which these phenomena occur. Following the initial observation that the contemporary world system might be at a crossroad and violence seems to return in both the Global North and the Global South, theories of development could (re)gain explanatory power by enlarging their focus towards neighboring phenomena, finally understanding and explaining violence.

A final contribution is to the contemporary cleavage between two larger traditions of thought, between approaches concentrating on social existence and approaches focusing on social consciousness. This study intended to show that a middle position between these two positions is possible. However, this position only becomes opportune if the focus shifts from the continuous repetition of the assertion that one tradition would be better equipped to understand reality to particular phenomena, notably on violence, thereby gaining from both poles and thus enlarging the own explanatory power. Instead of claiming their superiority of discourse or of the economy over the respective "rival," the disciplines would be better advised to focus on precise empirical situations in which the one or the other research tradition can be "tested." The discussion then would even advance towards the "empirization" of the cleavage.

Reconsidering the Comparative Method

These three contributions find their current expression in the methodological tool kit through which empirical results were produced. This study thus raises an issue that even transgresses the disciplinary border of social sciences, including research on violence, and calls for general methodological reflections.

This study followed a comparative approach. Since the study is partially based on theories of development and focuses on current empirical cases in the Global South, it touches on discussions of area study research and its mistrust of comparisons.[5] Increasingly, area studies reject comparisons as a feasible method. The opponents' argumentation asserts, first, that there is nothing to compare; the entities to be compared would be too different and, ultimately, there are no similar phenomena. Second, the comparative method is the expression of a Eurocentric perspective. The criticism claims that Europe's history is considered normality and against that background, deflections and abnormalities are detected and asserted. Theoretical models once elaborated by means of those comparisons are therefore understood as a general neo-colonial practice. Third, it is impossible to speak of independent variables, hence variables that point to certain causalities. The opponents instead focus on the reciprocal interaction and interference as well as the cultural transfer. Since comparisons lost ground, ideographic perspectives have been more and more replacing nomothetic perspectives.

Thus, social sciences, and particularly research on development and research on violence focusing on specific areas, face a dilemma. In order not to be reproached for "blurred genres" (Geertz, 1983, p. 21), these groups of researchers have to develop their own disciplinary identity. With the end of the Cold War, researchers with a focus on particular areas of geopolitical relevance brought themselves into disrepute of being too close to politics. However, these researchers confronted and still confront the challenge not to lose their research object—the particular area—due to globalization and its influence on global diffusion. The implications for the comparative method are far reaching. Because of globalization, independent variables dissolve, which are, however, important and necessary for the exposure of causal mechanisms. Consequently, area studies already concentrate more and more on processes of transfer and cultural exchange, thus on processes of diffusion (Middell, 2013).

In line with the solution of researching diffusion, authors today prefer comparative designs and case selections that focus on immediately converging and historically deeply entangled societies. In this light, the identity of area studies is more and more shaped by the focus on allegedly homogenous areas. Comparisons inside these areas, however, reproduce the homogeneity of the same areas. The concentration on processes of diffusion, cultural exchange, and transfers of ideas is thus a real solution. The analysis of processes of diffusion is not able to uncover the precise social mechanisms that produce social phenomena. Concentrating on cultural exchange and transfer then suggests interpreting history as a voluntarist and conflict-free process.

This study points to a twofold solution. First, the modified most different systems design allows for the control of processes of diffusion in comparative designs and for research processes of transfer of cultural scripts. In the case of gang violence, this study shows that cultural exchange does not necessarily lead to the cultural appropriation of the same ideas. Instead, cultural exchange is the effect of a field of power in which yet established historical experiences and "hard" politico-economic structures count. At the same time and contrary to theories of diffusion, this study shows that even though the three cases under research are particularly prone to global diffusion and in a subordinate position in the contemporary world system, they still shape the imposition from the Global North. The discussion on SAP policies, for instance, showed that each case under review adapted within a particular field of power and following particular historical legacies. This is not to neglect the bitter outcome of these processes, however, the discussion showed that these countries are more than simple agents that blindly follow a certain principal.

Second, it is important to not only focus on inter-area comparisons and the enlargement of the comparative design, but also to considering the dynamics of capitalism itself. This would raise the question of how the capitalist world system produced waves of incomplete penetration of the periphery. Only due to this penetration, unequal developments arose and still arise, which finally renders it necessary to talk about areas in the sense of different regional patterns of development and integration into the world system. Lastly, it would become possible to respond to the current articulation of the world system and the potential global return of diffuse violence with a detailed study of how these waves of incomplete penetration of the periphery finally produce resonances in the center of capitalism, possibly dissolving historically grown class antagonisms as the underlying driving forces of capitalism itself.

NOTES

1. For social scientists, talking about fear is perhaps still unfamiliar since it is a concept from psychology and the related discussion on the internal life of the human mind. However, if it is possible to translate the concept of fear into an appropriate social science language, it will finally allow linking the research of social existence with the research of social consciousness. Furthermore, if fear is a trigger for violence, to which the cases already point, the search for the causes of violence has to consider the production of fear. Particularly psychological approaches acknowledge the relationship between instability and fear "because all situations to which no expectations apply, which therefore are maximally indeterminate, result in fear" (Putz-Osterloh, 2000, p. 5).

2. The term originally stems from (Stanfield, 1998, p. 61) and describes the inability of weak social actors, who are far too limited in their resource endowments, to organize a durable and steady control of their social environment. In these contexts, violence is exerted simply because of the fear of being victimized by other actors.

3. By referring to impotence, I want to express something Fromm (1993, p. 135) termed "*Ohnmachtsgefühl.*" The term *Ohnmacht* as used by Fromm "describe(s) a basic condition of the subject's constitution; a revolution of the vegetative system brought about by somatic rather than sensorial and emotional factors and producing finally a retroactive effect on the contents of consciousness" (Brachfeld, 1951, p. 27). Fromm uses the term to describe a social impotence characterized by powerlessness.

4. In political science, area studies became integrated with theories of development (Schäbler, 2007, p. 27). With the end of the Cold War, however, theories of development were confronted with the reproach that the most fundamental term, development, remains unclear. This led to a debate on the question if the Third World is too heterogeneous to be captured by a single term and therefore cannot be understood and explained by a single grand theoretical narrative. The dominant view today asserts that the Third World as a unifying category and the underlying empirical similarity that would enable to classify certain societies as an area do not exist (e.g. Schuurman, 2000).

5. For some time, authors have been arguing that different areas are either too heterogeneous or similarities among different areas too superfluous. In terms of comparative methodology, the *tertium comparationis* lacks (Espagne, 1994). Another group of authors argue, as it was already mentioned regarding the critics of development theory, that areas are the exclusive product of discourses and expressions of Western colonialism. In both approaches, it does not make sense to use comparative methodology. In

contrast, the best methodological access to areas consequently brought into discussion by these approaches is the ideographic reconstruction of single cases and the thick description of particular events (Gibson-Graham, 2004). At the same time, the argument arose in social sciences that it is not worth using comparisons. In particular, it is argued that comparisons only produce artefacts; comparisons simplify; reduce the complex world to certain variables; and recently, that comparisons only deflect hegemonic entities in discursive elements. Particularly this is the main critique of *histoire croisée*, transfer studies, and entangled history on nomothetic comparisons (e.g. Werner & Zimmermann, 2006).

REFERENCES

Alber, E. (2004). Meidung als Modus des Umgangs mit Konflikten. In J. M. Eckert (Ed.), *Anthropologie der Konflikte: Georg Elwerts konflikttheoretische Thesen in der Diskussion* (pp. 169–185). Bielefeld, Germany: Transcript.

Armit, I. (2011). Violence and Society in the Deep Human Past. *British Journal of Criminology, 51*(3), 499–517.

Bonacker, T. (2002). Zuschreibungen der Gewalt: Zur Sinnförmigkeit interaktiver, organisierter und gesellschaftlicher Gewalt. *Soziale Welt, 53,* 31–48.

Brachfeld, O. F. (1951). *Inferiority Feelings in the Individual and the Group.* London: Routledge.

Cramer, C. (2006). *Civil War Is Not a Stupid Thing: Accounting for Violence in Developing Countries.* London: Hurst.

Elias, N. (1982). *Über die Einsamkeit der Sterbenden in unseren Tagen.* Frankfurt a.M., Germany: Suhrkamp.

Elias, N. (1997). *Über den Prozess der Zivilisation: Soziogenetische und psychogenetische Untersuchungen.* Frankfurt a.M., Germany: Suhrkamp.

Ember, C. R., & Ember, M. (1992). Resource Unpredictability, Mistrust, and War: A Cross-Cultural Study. *The Journal of Conflict Resolution, 36*(2), 242–262.

Espagne, M. (1994). Sur les limites du comparatisme en histoire culturelle. *Genèses, 17,* 112–121.

Flam, H. (2006). Emotions' Map: A Research Aagenda. In H. Flam & D. King (Eds.), *Emotions and Social Movements* (pp. 19–40). London: Routledge.

Fromm, E. (1993). Zum Gefühl der Ohnmacht. In E. Fromm (Ed.), *Die Gesellschaft als Gegenstand der Psychoanalyse. Frühe Schriften zur Analytischen Sozialpsychologie* (pp. 134–158). Frankfurt a.M., Germany: Suhrkamp.

Geertz, C. (1983). *Local Knowledge: Further Essays in Interpretive Anthropology.* New York: Basic Books.

Gerstenberger, H. (1990). *Die subjektlose Gewalt: Theorie der Entstehung bürgerlicher Staatsgewalt.* Münster, Germany: Westfälisches Dampfboot.

Gibson-Graham, J. K. (2004). Area Studies After Poststructuralism. *Environment and Planning A, 36*(3), 405–419.

Helbling, J. (2006). *Tribale Kriege: Konflikte in Gesellschaften ohne Zentralgewalt.* Frankfurt a.M., Germany: Campus.

Kemper, T. D. (1978). Toward a Sociology of Emotions: Some Problems and Some Solutions. *The American Sociologist, 13*(1), 30–41.

Mbembe, A. (2003). Necropolitics. *Public Culture, 15*(1), 11–40.

Middell, M. (Ed.). (2013). *Self-Reflexive Area Studies.* Leipzig, Germany: Leipziger Universitätsverlag.

Putz-Osterloh, W. (2000). Angst und Handeln aus psychologischer Sicht. In F. Bosbach (Ed.), *Angst und Politik in der europäischen Geschichte* (pp. 1–11). Dettelbach, Germany: Röll.

Reguillo, R. (2002). The Social Construction of Fear. Urban Narratives and Practices. In S. Rotker (Ed.), *Citizens of Fear. Urban Violence in Latin America* (pp. 187–206). New Brunswick, NJ/London: Rutgers University Press.

Riekenberg, M. (2014). *Staatsferne Gewalt: Eine Geschichte Lateinamerikas (1500–1930).* Frankfurt a.M., Germany: Campus.

Said, E. W. (1979). *Orientalism.* New York: Vintage Books.

Schäbler, B. (2007). Einleitung: Das Studium der Weltregionen (Area Studies) zwischen Fachdisziplin und der Öffnung zum Globalen: Eine wissenschaftsgeschichtliche Annäherung. In B. Schäbler (Ed.), *Area Studies und die Welt: Weltregionen und neue Globalgeschichte* (pp. 11–44). Wien, Austria: Mandelbaum.

Schelling, T. C. (1960). *The Strategy of Conflict.* Cambridge/London: Harvard University Press.

Schuurman, F. J. (2000). Paradigms Lost, Paradigms Regained? Development Studies in the Twenty-First Century. *Third World Quarterly, 21*(1), 7–20.

Stanfield, M. E. (1998). *Red Rubber, Bleeding Trees: Violence, Slavery, and Empire in Northwest Amazonia, 1850–1933.* Albuquerque, NM: University of New Mexico Press.

Taussig, M. (1984). Culture of Terror – Space of Death: Roger Casement's Putumayo Report and the Explanation of Torture. *Comparative Studies in Society and History, 26*(3), 467–497.

Tilly, C. (1985). War Making and State Making as Organized Crime. In P. B. Evans, D. Ruschemeyer, & T. Skocpol (Eds.), *Bringing the State Back In* (pp. 169–191). Cambridge: Cambridge University Press.

Tuan, Y.-F. (2013). *Landscapes of Fear.* Minneapolis, MN: University of Minnesota Press.

Weber, M. (1968). *Economy and Society: An Outline of Interpretive Sociology* (G. Roth & C. Wittich, Ed.). Berkeley/Los Angeles: University of California Press.

Werner, M., & Zimmermann, B. (2006). Beyond Comparison: Histoire Croisée and the Challenge of Reflexifity. *History and Theory, 45*(1), 30–50.

Index[1]

---

[1] Note: Page numbers followed by 'n' refer to notes.

© The Author(s) 2019
H. Warnecke-Berger, *Politics and Violence in Central America and
the Caribbean*, https://doi.org/10.1007/978-3-319-89782-0

in El Salvador, 151, 152, 247, 248,
250, 263
in Jamaica, 175, 176, 185, 186,
247, 249
Posses, *see* Youth gangs, in Jamaica

R
Rebellion, *see* Labor rebellion
Rent
mode of appropriation, 85, 163
sources of, 67, 163, 168, 203, 254,
265, 267
Revolution, 2, 16, 29, 32, 79, 92, 93,
99, 103, 104, 110, 112n9, 185,
197, 234, 275n3

S
Seaga, Edward, 114n25, 114n26,
164, 166, 167, 173
Slavery
in Belize, 61, 65–68
in Jamaica, 61, 63, 65, 68, 69, 110,
111n6, 261
State-class
Belizean, 85, 198, 225, 246, 257
Jamaican, 85, 90, 93, 98, 105, 107,
109, 165–168, 185, 242,
245–247, 249, 255, 257
Structural adjustment programs
(SAPs), 98–102, 106, 115n29,
127–130, 163–168, 170, 175,
187, 199, 204, 205, 253, 274

U
United Democratic Party (UDP),
96, 200, 211, 226n3

V
Vigilantism
death squad, 31, 48n6, 247,
250–252
grassroots vigilantism, 31, 109,
247, 250–252, 263
Violence
horizontal, 3, 12, 29–32, 46, 47n4,
48n5, 69, 71–73, 75, 79, 80,
84, 91, 93, 97, 103–105,
108–110, 127, 128, 133–137,
144–148, 153, 163, 174, 175,
197, 198, 209, 214, 215, 221,
222, 226, 234–248, 250, 252,
256, 261, 262, 264, 272
typology of, 9, 31
vertical, 2, 12, 29–32, 46, 69,
71–73, 75, 79, 103, 108,
110, 147–150, 153, 174,
188, 234, 245–250, 257,
261–263, 272

Y
Youth gangs
in Belize, 210, 263
in El Salvador, 7, 128, 137–144,
150, 153, 155n5, 244, 263
in Jamaica, 92, 165

CPI Antony Rowe
Eastbourne, UK
March 04, 2019